NAT TURNER,

BLACK PROPHET

NAT TURNER,
••••• BLACK PROPHET •••••

A Visionary History

ANTHONY E. KAYE
WITH GREGORY P. DOWNS

Farrar, Straus and Giroux

NEW YORK

Farrar, Straus and Giroux
120 Broadway, New York 10271

Map adapted from David F. Allmendinger Jr., *Nat Turner and the Rising in Southampton County* (Baltimore: Johns Hopkins University Press, 2014).

Library of Congress Cataloging-in-Publication Data
Names: Kaye, Anthony E., author. | Downs, Gregory P.
Title: Nat Turner, black prophet : a visionary history / Anthony E. Kaye,
    with Gregory P. Downs.
Description: First edition. | New York : Farrar, Straus and Giroux, 2024. |
    Includes bibliographical references and index.
Identifiers: LCCN 2024006647 | ISBN 9780809024377 (hardcover)
Subjects: LCSH: Turner, Nat, 1800?–1831. | Turner, Nat, 1800?–1831—Influence. |
    Turner, Nat, 1800?–1831—Religion. | Southampton Insurrection, 1831. |
    Slave rebellions—Virginia—Southampton County—History—19th century. |
    Enslaved persons—Virginia—Southampton County—Biography.
Classification: LCC F232.S7 K39 2024 | DDC 975.5/55203092 [B]—dc23/
    eng/20240209
LC record available at https://lccn.loc.gov/2024006647

Our books may be purchased in bulk for promotional, educational, or business use. Please contact your local bookseller or the Macmillan Corporate and Premium Sales Department at 1-800-221-7945, extension 5442, or by email at MacmillanSpecialMarkets@macmillan.com.

www.fsgbooks.com
Follow us on social media at @fsgbooks

10 9 8 7 6 5 4 3 2 1

To the people whom Tony loved and who loved him,

especially Melissa, Vivian, Theo, Ellen, and Chip

Contents

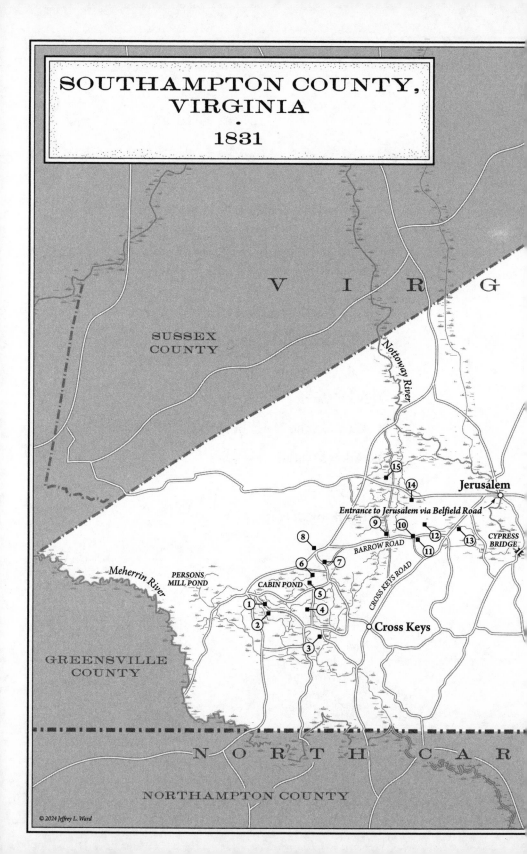

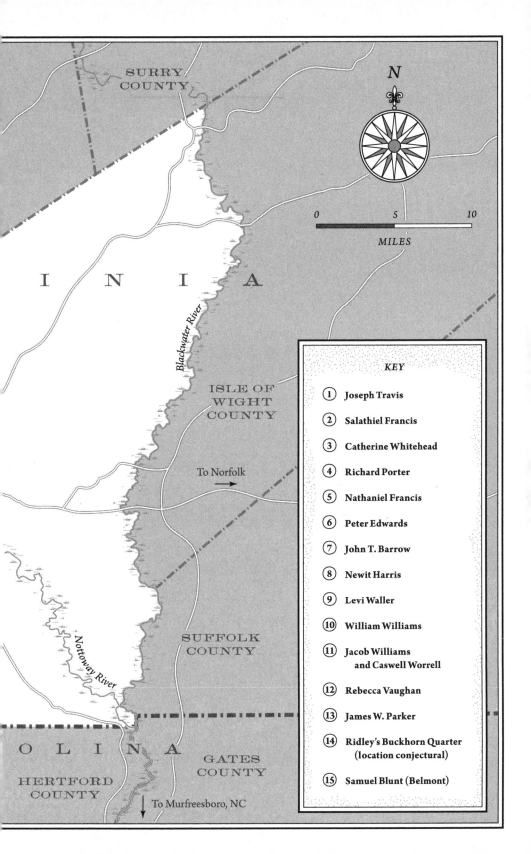

SURRY
COUNTY

N

0   5   10

MILES

Blackwater River

I N I A

ISLE OF
WIGHT
COUNTY

To Norfolk →

SUFFOLK
COUNTY

Nottoway River

O L I N A

HERTFORD
COUNTY

GATES
COUNTY

↓ To Murfreesboro, NC

KEY

① Joseph Travis

② Salathiel Francis

③ Catherine Whitehead

④ Richard Porter

⑤ Nathaniel Francis

⑥ Peter Edwards

⑦ John T. Barrow

⑧ Newit Harris

⑨ Levi Waller

⑩ William Williams

⑪ Jacob Williams
   and Caswell Worrell

⑫ Rebecca Vaughan

⑬ James W. Parker

⑭ Ridley's Buckhorn Quarter
   (location conjectural)

⑮ Samuel Blunt (Belmont)

Introduction

On August 22, 1831, a mysterious enslaved man named Nat led a company of Black people in attacks upon whites in the rural neighborhood of Cross Keys, Virginia, on the southern edge of Southampton County, bordering the North Carolina state line. Over the course of two days, Nat and the band killed approximately fifty-five white people with guns, axes, and fence posts as they headed toward the county seat of Jerusalem on the Nottoway River. They killed men in battle, but they also killed men and women in their homes and in their beds—especially enslavers and prominent landowners. They killed children, even infants, and left one baby's body in a fireplace. It was one of the largest slave rebellions in U.S. history, matched only by an 1811 rebellion near New Orleans and exceeded only by the ranks of people who claimed their freedom in joining the British armies in the Revolution and the War of 1812, and the U.S. Army in the Civil War, efforts scholars have been slow to classify as slave rebellions despite their similarities to events we call rebellions in other countries.

After a hard-fought battle near the end of the day on August 22, Nat's company camped at a nearby plantation, then attacked early the following morning. When that attack was repelled, white Virginians— beginning with people from Jerusalem, later joined by men from as far away as Richmond and Norfolk and North Carolina—launched a counterassault to terrorize enslaved people into submission, killing dozens of local Black people in retribution. To reassert the authority of the law, white elites quickly organized trials that condemned eighteen men to be hanged, others to be sold out of state. But as these trials ground on, Nat, the leader of the company, could not be found. He hid close to home for two months as rumors spread of his whereabouts.

Finally, on October 30, 1831, Nat surrendered to a white man in the woods near the pond where the rebellion began. Over the next eleven days, Nat spoke repeatedly about the rebellion to white people in the neighborhood, to lawyers in Jerusalem, to passersby, and to Thomas Gray, a white lawyer who wrote down what were purported to be Nat's words and published them as Nat's *Confessions*, a book that sold staggering numbers of copies in its time and that continues to be read and puzzled over today.

Although there are many narratives written by enslaved people or their interlocutors, the *Confessions* is startling because it records not just Nat's actions but his descriptions of a series of visions sent by "the Spirit," visions that directed Nat to carry out his glorious and terrible task. The Spirit spoke to Nat, revealing "knowledge of the elements, the operation of tides, and changes of seasons." The Spirit showed Nat "white spirits and black spirits engaged in battle" as "blood flowed in streams"; then it revealed "drops of blood on the corn," "hieroglyphic characters and numbers," and images of men on the "leaves in the woods." The Spirit unveiled the true meaning of the constellations in the sky: "They were the lights of the Saviour's hands, stretched forth from east to west, even as they were extended on the cross on Calvary." The Spirit told Nat that "the time was fast approaching" when he should take up the yoke that "Christ had laid down" and "fight against the Serpent." We can never know for certain when Gray was accurately recording Nat's words and when he wasn't, but we know Gray did not wholly invent these stories. Many other people heard Nat speak of similar visions, both before and after his capture.[1]

Over the nearly two centuries since the revolt, Nat has remained a uniquely troublesome historical figure, too dangerous for some, too strange for others. Local white elites made Nat into a "fanatic" motivated by personal delusions, not by the widespread misery of enslaved people. Virginia's legislature, however, took the lessons of Nat's rebellion more seriously, considering it a portent of more uprisings to come, debating the future of slavery, and considering plans for the gradual emancipation and the expulsion of Black people. Black and white abolitionists for their part turned Nat into an icon of armed resistance, a warning to white people about the consequences of slavery. Local Black people made of Nat a folk hero and a harbinger of the rebellion of enslaved people in the Civil War thirty years later. White-led but biracial churches in Virginia and beyond struggled with Nat's reading of Christianity; some congregations expelled Black members; some barred Black preachers from giving sermons without white oversight; some white pastors delivered sermons on the biblical justifications for slavery. In the twentieth century, Nat's revolt inspired a blockbuster novel that prompted searching, trenchant critiques.[2] In the twenty-first century, a feature film about Nat became knotted in crimes alleged against one of the filmmakers. In 2021, Richmond, Virginia, unveiled the Emancipation and Freedom Monument that includes Nat's name among Virginians who contributed to the struggle; only Nat's name provoked significant debate.[3]

Nat's story resonates because he lived at the crossroads of the most powerful forces in early national American life: slavery and evangelicalism, race and revolution. Scholars have long recognized the richness of this story and over the past century have uncovered troves of information about the revolt and its context from oral histories, censuses, religious records, and other sources. They have detailed both what happened in 1831 and how those events were shaped by contexts both cosmological and decidedly concrete: the religious revivals of the early nineteenth century and the spread of slavery by white settlers to the areas around Southampton County.

This so-called Southside of Virginia was nestled between two contrasting regions of the commonwealth—the plantation economy along the James River and the Tidewater, and the much-smaller-scale farming in the mountainous western counties. Although precise lines vary, Southside essentially covers the region south of the James River, west of the Tidewater, and east of the Blue Ridge Mountains. Southampton and its surroundings were a direct offshoot of the plantation regions but not fully part of them, and Nat's life would be shaped by the swampish land, its relatively small clusters of farms, and the form of slavery that developed there as handfuls or dozens of enslaved people worked orchards and fields of food crops for and alongside white landowners.

Still, for all the valuable new scholarship on the area and on slave rebellions more generally, it remains difficult to see three central aspects of Nat's story: his life as a Methodist, as a prophet, and as a man his followers called General. One section of the *Confessions* describes a childhood in the Methodist faith, a second details Nat's extraordinary visions, a third narrates his command of a military company. The latter two roles—prophet and general—emerged from the first: a Black enslaved Methodist child studying the world around him, a world of warfare and revival.

Nat was called a prophet repeatedly in his lifetime, and any reckoning with him requires taking the claim seriously. In the weeks between the attacks and Nat's surrender, a Southampton County man—probably Thomas Gray himself—wrote to a Richmond newspaper that Nat "had acquired the character of a prophet" in "his immediate neighborhood," based on his "conversations with the Holy Spirit."[4] When Gray interviewed Nat in the Jerusalem jail cell, shortly before Nat's trial, the atheistic Gray interrupted Nat's tale of words and visions from "the Spirit" to ask, "What do you mean by the Spirit?"

"The Spirit that spoke to the prophets in former days," Nat answered.[5]

EVERY INTERPRETER OF Nat's rebellion has wondered at these lines. What does it mean that Nat compared himself to the prophets of "former days"? And what does it mean that some of his neighbors believed Nat to be a prophet? For some local white southerners, the reference proved that Nat was disturbed. Gray wrote that Nat was a "gloomy fanatic . . . revolving in the recesses of his own dark, bewildered, and overwrought mind." Possibly a judge echoed this assessment in sentencing Nat to die, suggesting that Nat might have been "led away by fanaticism." In December the state's governor similarly dismissed the rebels as "deluded fanatics." If a fanatic sparked the rebellion, then the rebellion was no indictment of slavery or even of the specific enslavers in the Cross Keys neighborhood; the rebellion was solely the product of an insane mind.[6]

Sympathetic writers and historians tend to underplay the role of prophecy in Nat's story. Fearful that Nat's unusual religious beliefs undermine his role as a rebel, they sometimes domesticate Nat's faith into a contributing motivation, explaining it in dry theological or literary terms, rejecting the stories of his revelations as a white-led propaganda effort to obscure the real basis of the rebellion, or overlooking his religiosity in confusion or embarrassment. In sympathetic interpretations, we see Nat primarily as an Atlantic revolutionary, Black nationalist, or generic enslaved rebel, roles that crowd out his self-description as a prophet.

This book emphasizes the claim that Nat saw himself not just as a prophet but as a particular kind of prophet, in the specific way early nineteenth-century evangelical Christians understood the Hebrew Bible prophets. This is a much more sweeping claim than it may at first sound. Inspiring Black political leaders, especially Martin Luther King Jr., are almost always compared to prophets. A major biography of Frederick Douglass termed him the "prophet of freedom."[7] Absent a close connection to the term's religious roots, "prophet" becomes an amplifying compliment for an inspiring, forward-looking person. No wonder scholars and authors mention Nat as a prophet without dwelling on it; there seems to be little of significance to say.

To Nat and his contemporaries, prophecy was not merely inspirational leadership. Prophecy had a specific meaning: a prophet literally heard the voice of God and acted upon it. This form of direct communication from God was common enough that Puritans and early national evangelical leaders distinguished between *normal prophecy*— believers' experience of a voice repeating important biblical verses— and *dangerous prophecy*: the communication of messages from God or the Spirit that contained words or images not found in the Bible. Normal prophecy was just that, normal, a commonplace experience of a voice speaking received truths. But a dangerous prophet heard God or the Spirit say something that was not in the Bible. Sometimes a prophet also saw visions. Such immediate, direct revelation was commonly described in the Hebrew Bible and in parts of the Christian Testament, especially the book of Revelation. And periods of religious revival have often been accompanied by prophets claiming immediate, direct revelation of new truths; many Christian theologians tried to curb those revivals by closing the book on open, direct revelation in the contemporary world.

Open, direct revelation was simply too threatening for many Christian sects to countenance. Direct revelation undercut the power of the pastor and of the established church; if anyone could claim divine direction, then it would be impossible for the church to exercise authority. This fear was no abstraction: there were often people claiming to have received messages from God, especially in times of political upheaval.

Direct revelation posed a further problem that directly relates to Nat: it often threatened mass bloodshed. The prophets of the Hebrew Bible frequently heard God or the Spirit tell them to go slaughter unbelievers or enemies. So, too, does Revelation tell a gruesome story of Christ returning to draw rivers of blood from the Serpent, destroy the world, and inaugurate the kingdom of God.

These dangers were not confined to biblical times. Direct revelation raised fears of slaughter and disruption in periods of crisis in the early modern world. As the Protestant rebellion disrupted Christianity in sixteenth-century Europe, the Protestant visionary Thomas Müntzer raised a peasant army of eight thousand under the promise that God would directly intervene in the battle and "inaugurate the kingdom that 'shall stand forever,'" in the words of Daniel. Ten years later, radical Anabaptists under the influence of the prophets Melchior Hoffman and Jan Matthys seized control of the city of Münster, executing or expelling people who were not

Anabaptists, communalizing property, proclaiming the kingdom of David, anointing Münster the "New Jerusalem," and raising expectations that Christ would soon return in front of an avenging army. In the seventeenth-century English Civil War, many prophets—including women—claimed divine revelation, prompting worry among establishment Protestants that these prophets meant to turn the civil war into a holy massacre.[8] Puritans carried this fear of immediate revelation with them to the colonies that became the United States, warning followers "not to look for any *revelation* out of the Word." When Anne Hutchinson confessed that the "mouth of the Lord hath spoken" to her, promising to deliver her "sede" from captivity and "utterly destroy all the nations," Puritan judges banished her.[9]

The Puritan leader John Winthrop used the word "enthusiasm" to denounce Hutchinson as a purveyor of dangerous immediate revelation, and the word would play a role in shaping Nat's own religious education. During his childhood in the early nineteenth century, the Methodism he was raised within was frequently accused of enthusiasm. This enthusiasm might take the form of mass singing or large revivals. But it also could refer to the "method," the training that Methodists undertook to prepare themselves to receive direct experience of God. John Wesley, the guiding light of early Methodism, accepted his followers' visions, and many Methodists went beyond Wesley, claiming to have received direct revelations.[10]

This Methodist surge was part of the disruptions in the colonies in the late eighteenth century that created openings for prophets claiming direct revelation from God. Responding to the political transformations of the colonial Revolution against Britain and the religious upheavals of the subsequent Second Great Awakening, Baptists, Methodists, and other sects grew too dramatically to be forced into any sort of sanctioned form. Many white and Black prophets claimed to have received commands from God, some couched in the common evangelical language of warfare. Many prophets were, like Nat, Methodists, a denomination with a particularly strong fixation on the imagery of religious warfare. In this era, unaffiliated prophets like Joseph Smith and Robert Matthews, both influenced by Methodism, claimed to found entirely new branches of Christianity, while the former Baptist William Miller became convinced he had discovered the precise date of Christ's Second Coming and thus of the apocalyptic warfare to follow.

Nat did not found a new branch of Christianity, but he seemed to offer himself as a biblical prophet and warrior. Nat's words suggest he was not simply treating biblical prophets as models in the way all Christians try to follow scriptural guides. What Nat might have suggested was that he thought of himself as reenacting a biblical type. This is a much more significant claim, though not inherently a problematic one for evangelicals. The Bible provided types that would be repeated in later generations, with each repetition expanding the meaning and helping bring about the fulfillment of God's kingdom. To treat Joshua as a model, one simply emulated his virtues. But if God called one to fulfill the type of Joshua, one might carry out religious warfare that went even beyond Joshua's in order to change history, to expand its boundaries. God creates types; one does not choose to follow them, nor know to what ends God is utilizing them. Many Hebrew Bible types were fulfilled by the Christian Testament, as Jesus expanded and fulfilled the type established by Jonah in his nights in the fish's belly.

Although typology itself is commonplace in Christian writings, when applied to the present and the future, types—like prophecies—become much more disruptive and threaten the destruction of enemies or even the end of the world. Anne Hutchinson suggested that she might fit the type of Abraham, Daniel, or Jesus, though of course without implying that she was the Messiah. "You see the scripture fulfilled this day," Hutchinson told her inquisitors, according to one account. Typing remained common in the decades before Nat's birth; white ministers routinely compared the United States to the biblical Israel, with some explicitly "typing" the new nation as an expanded fulfillment of God's promises to his chosen people. By the time Nat was a child, Methodists—like other Christians—frequently turned to typology to piece together the relationship of the Hebrew Bible to its fulfillment in the Christian Testament and its future fulfillment in the kingdom of God. Perhaps—although no one can say with certainty—Nat expressed this same notion of cosmological fulfillment in his response to Thomas Gray's reminder that his rebellion had been defeated: "Was not Christ crucified?"[11]

For Black evangelicals, types could raise powerful, destabilizing questions about God's chosen people in a slaveholding society. Who today was the Pharaoh of the Hebrew Bible, who the Moses, who the new Israelites? While enslaved people always questioned the morality of slavery, these critiques took new form in the late eighteenth and early nineteenth centuries. Black early national evangelicals stood at the confluence of two powerful historical currents: the expansion of slavery and the mass conversion of enslaved people. The nation was simultaneously becoming more committed both to slavery and to evangelical Christianity. In the nineteenth century, white slaveholders expanded their reach into the southern interior—in part through the cotton gin, and in part through political claims and military strikes on land inhabited by Native peoples—and a million enslaved people were transported from the Atlantic coast to the Mississippi River valley in a Second Middle Passage. Meanwhile, evangelical Christianity spread rapidly through free and enslaved Black worlds, sparked by the same revivals that inspired white conversions. In the nation's densely settled plantation belts, enslaved people might fashion their own churches—with or without the enslaver's sanction. In northern cities and in a few southern cities, too, Black Protestants began to create their own independent denominations, including the African Methodist Episcopal Church. In areas with smaller plantations and holdings of enslaved people like Southampton County, however, biracial churches, like the meeting that Nat's family attended, were common. In every setting, Black evangelicals studied types for the overthrow of slavery, pondering the relationship of race to God's promises.[12]

Most Black evangelicals aimed to convert white people—as Nat at times did—but many also wondered whether slaveholders represented the recurrence of the biblical tyrants, and thus if God might punish them as he punished Pharaoh. In an address "to those who keep slaves, and approve the practice," the Black Methodist Richard Allen reminded slave owners that God "destroyed" "Pharoah [sic] and his princes" for "their oppression of the poor slaves." Allen led Black Philadelphia Methodists out of their segregated congregation and into the independent AME church, and there he compared slave owners repeatedly to Pharaoh and reminded them of "the dread insurrections" even as he also urged Black Methodists to be forgiving. Allen's collaborator, the Black Methodist Daniel Coker, wrote a dialogue in which an "African Minister" called on Black people to "take your weapon to destroy this mighty Goliath," although the weapon he favored was scripture. Coker also cited Isaiah's "vision" of a "sinful nation, a people laden with iniquity" that provoked the Lord to "anger," and a pledge from Isaiah that the Lord "cometh out of his place, to punish the inhabitants of the earth for their iniquity: the earth also shall disclose her blood."[13]

In Nat's childhood, there seemed to be a possibility that white evangelicals could deliver themselves, the nation, and the enslaved population from destruction by emancipating individual people and undermining slavery. Many Baptists and Methodists—and even more non-evangelical Quakers—considered it a Christian duty to manumit individual enslaved people in the late eighteenth and very early nineteenth centuries. In Southampton many evangelicals did just this. Some were members of the extended white Turner family that migrated into what was then a frontier and became prominent Methodists and enslavers in the area. Among the siblings and cousins of Nat's first enslavers were Turners who emancipated individual people or even large families; these free Black Turners lived among them, embodied signs of the potential for evangelical Christianity to triumph over slavery.

Clearly Nat's parents wished this destiny for their son. But manumission would not resolve the problem of American racial slavery, nor of Nat's struggle for self-definition. As slavery became more profitable in these new southeastern lands, a new generation of enslavers fought back against Christian critique, wresting control of southern churches, and increasingly sermonizing on the biblical sanction for slavery. Fewer evangelicals spoke against slavery; fewer freed their own people. While some other Turners did free people, the Turners who owned Nat and his family followed the other trajectory, expanding their holdings in land and enslaved people in backcountry Virginia, becoming more evangelical *and* more committed to slavery. In the process people like them turned Methodist and Baptist faiths away from their manumitting pasts and into bulwarks of slavery.

In the bleak 1820s during Nat's adulthood, many Black evangelicals and some Black prophets began to ask more directly whether the type for the Egyptians might be found in the enslavers, the type for the Israelites in the enslaved people of the country. If white people would not end slavery, the fulfillment of God's kingdom might require drastic action. Perhaps no Black American stated this more starkly than Nat's contemporary Methodist David Walker, who argued in his *Appeal* that American slaveholders were the modern-day Egyptians, crueler than Pharaoh, with their "hardened" hearts. "When God almighty commences his battle on the continent of America, for the oppression of his people, tyrants will wish they never were born," Walker wrote. Nat, disappointed in the Turner family's failure to manumit him, likewise shifted from converting white people to making war on them.[14]

Nat was only one among many Black and white prophets making startling claims in the early national period; what made Nat more unusual was another identity he embraced: warrior. In his neighborhood of Cross Keys, some enslaved people called him a prophet, but some called him General Nat. These need not be two different identities; the prophetic books of the Hebrew Bible are full of warfare and generalship, and the book of Revelation is both prophecy and war story. But Nat's embrace of the role of commander likely reflects his knowledge of another important historical event: the enlistment of many local Black soldiers in the British forces in the Revolution and the War of

1812. This knowledge about the area's Black warriors likely helped him and others make sense of the enslaved rebels in nineteenth-century evangelically inspired uprisings in Richmond, Charleston, Demerara, and Sierra Leone. The Haitian Revolution, born of different faiths and hopes, likely inspired him, too. Nat obliquely referred to this knowledge when he told his collaborators to avoid the errors of other rebellions by keeping their plans secret and their leadership compact, as other rebels had not. He did not seek to emulate those rebellions; he sought to improve upon them.

In treating Nat as a warrior and a general, this work treats rebellion not as a crime but as an act of war. In some ways, this is a small change of perspective, and one anticipated by other scholars, but its implications are important. If we define rebellions as crimes, we look for motives. Crucially, this is true even when we examine crimes to which we are sympathetic. But this search for motives can quickly become a distraction. The general motives of the people in Nat's band are obvious: they hated slavery. What requires more historical analysis are Nat's strategies, tactics, and timing—all things that military historians study and that historians of slavery have increasingly sought to analyze in their accounts of rebellions. Once we move past the *why*, we can more clearly examine the *how*. This is one way of prying open Nat's story.[15] Virginia's governor, John Floyd, who had served in the War of 1812, echoed this military interpretation in 1831, describing Nat's rebellion and the white counterattack as "such a warfare."[16]

It may be less of a surprise, then, that the same Nat who learned Methodism with and from white neighbors and enslavers also ordered his followers to kill them. As a soldier and as a prophet, what else would he think that armies did? The Hebrew Bible was full of examples of slaughter by the Israelites seeking to fulfill God's prophecies and create a new kingdom. It was killing that overthrew tyrants, and the book of Revelation suggested that it was killing that would inaugurate God's kingdom.

This, then, is the story of the rebellion Nat led, the reasons he urged his company to kill, and the new world he hoped to bring into being.

A NOTE ON AUTHORSHIP

This is, however, a story with its own complicated history. In June 2016, Tony Kaye asked me to prepare to take on a task he aimed not to leave to me: the authorship of this book on Nat and his rebellion. Confronting his diagnosis of esophageal cancer, Tony was both sustaining his hope that he might survive its ravages and preparing for the possibility that he might not. Over the next ten months, we exchanged emails and phone calls about the book and met once at his home in North Carolina and again in New York City. In 2017, as he declined, he, through his wife, Melissa, sent me a large cache of computer files that included drafts of several chapters and notes for others. After he died on May 14, 2017, Melissa mailed me two boxes of documents he had photocopied. His giant stacks of books, with their amazing and sometimes disputatious notations, were left to friends at the National Humanities Center and elsewhere.

The book that follows remains Tony's work, even though I have written or rewritten almost every word of it. The form of authorship on the title page reflects our understanding that this book would consist of his arguments and research but my words. To free me from asking whether I agreed with all his interpretations, we decided to forgo stating that it was written by Kaye "and" Downs. (In the postscript I will step out of my co-author role briefly to expand on my view of Tony's relationship to scholarship on Nat.) To acknowledge that the work involved a significant amount of reframing, writing, rewriting, and reimagining, we rejected the convention of saying it was by Kaye and "edited by" Downs. Thus, we settled on this as a book by Kaye with Downs. It is my interpretation of the product of his intelligence and creativity as he struggled with his own illness and also with the question that sustained him: How, in the face of evidence to the contrary, do people sustain their hope that the world can be made anew?

NAT TURNER,
BLACK PROPHET

····· **1** ·····

Holy Warriors Against the New Egypt

Fifty-six years before Nat launched his attack and more than two de-cades before his birth, enslaved Black men in and around Southampton County took up arms against slaveholders. They fought for the British against the Patriots in the colonial rebellion Americans call the Rev-olutionary War, struggling for their freedom and, they hoped, for the freedom of their families and neighbors. Some of them compared their campaign to Exodus, their enslavers to the biblical Egyptians. Thirty-seven years later, when Nat was twelve, more Southside enslaved people took up arms for the British against the American slaveholders, once again under the British promise of freedom. In between the Revolution-ary War and Nat's rebellion, enslaved and free Black people in Virginia and the seaboard states also prepared smaller strikes against slavery without the immediate prospect of foreign intervention. While there were many differences between global wars and those smaller-scale neighborhood rebellions, many of the participants shared a common source of references and inspirations: the Hebrew Bible.

Nat was unique, but the rebellion he led was not, at least not when we count Black service for the British in the Revolutionary War and War of 1812 as Black rebellions. Nat was born into a region marked by Black people's violent military campaigns against their enslavers, campaigns that taught local people lessons about warfare and rebel-lion. Most tantalizing of all for our understanding of Nat's rebellion, many of those Black soldiers were, in the parlance of the day, awakened by the evangelical religious revivals that marked Nat's Black and white world in Southampton County. Some were Methodists, following the faith that shaped Nat's childhood and the worlds of his family and of the white people who claimed ownership of him. Some of these Southside enslaved Virginians were themselves prophetic warriors who cast themselves as types of the Hebrew Bible prophets, their people as types of the Jews, enslavers as types of Egypt.

For all his distinctive qualities, Nat was in some ways typical, and our effort to understand him requires us first to step away from his compelling individual story and to look at his context. Nat responded to broad transformations in the experience of Black people in Southside Virginia over the late eighteenth and early nineteenth centuries. Wars between European empires created space for both white and Black Virginians to rebel and redefine power relationships. The newly formed United States expelled Native people and protected the expansion of slavery into the backcountry, entrenching slaveholder power in state and national governments. And transatlantic religious movements and revivals spread Methodism, Baptism, and other faiths that fashioned newly intimate relationships between believers and their God. For some, religion and international warfare taught caution. But others, presumably the ones Nat looked to as models, found in this confluence of the diplomatic and the divine the inspiration to strike.

Nat likely heard about the doings of near neighbors in the War of 1812, when he was a boy, and perhaps of their ancestors in the Revolutionary War. We know for certain that other Black people in the county knew this history. During Nat's rebellion, other Black Southampton residents spoke about the fact that the British twice had offered freedom for anyone who would fight against the local slaveholders, and they used this information in their efforts to comprehend the events of 1831. A white woman named Nancy Parsons heard an enslaved man explain Nat's rebellion in this way: the "British were in the county" and "if they came by he would join them & assist in killing all the white people—that if they succeeded he would have as much money as his master."[1] Just before the 1831 rebellion, an enslaved man named Ned said that the British were coming and "he expected to be free before long."[2] Other rumors turned the Revolutionary analogy on its head, making Nat akin to George Washington; by some accounts Nat said he intended to conquer Southampton "as the white people did in the revolution," a claim reinforced by Nat's original plan to launch his attack on July 4.[3] Not everyone attributed Nat's rising to the British, but many people knew what events Ned and Nancy Parsons referred to. Perhaps Nat and his neighbors also heard about other examples of the Black military tradition, Black soldiers in Florida or Haiti or Cuba. Perhaps he heard of rebellions launched across the Atlantic by the very Southside Methodists who fought for the British in the Revolution.

Still, Ned and Nancy Parsons were not quite right. Nat was not simply reenacting those rebellions; he was trying something different. In the British wars, Black soldiers looked to the power of the British Crown, but Nat appealed to a different sovereignty, that of an interventionist God. This shift from rebels for the king to rebels for the King was itself a product of transformations in the political, diplomatic, and religious climate. By 1831, there was little hope for a distant earthly monarch to free them; American independence had been established, for better or worse. And there seemed to be little hope for an American political body to intervene, not with the power that slaveholders asserted in Richmond and Washington. While there was little hope for an antislavery political sovereignty, broad claims of God's sovereignty were ever more visible because of Methodist and Baptist revivals. But if Nat's appeal to the heavens was an innovation, his attention to time-honored tactics and strategies showed that he was still looking to the prior rebellions as models.

NAT'S PLACE WAS Southside Virginia on the fringes of the Chesapeake Bay region. It had taken white Virginians almost a century to settle this area after they established a toehold on the James River in the early seventeenth century. First moving in to present-day Norfolk, white settlers slowly began to press deeper into the Tidewater. Beyond the reaches of the Tidewater lay what became known as Southside, the band of low-lying, piedmont counties that were neither part of the mountains nor in easy contact with the Chesapeake

Bay, not as accessible to merchants as the Tidewater, not as isolated as the hill country. Everywhere white people moved, they brought enslaved people with them. Southampton County, where Nat lived, lay beyond Virginia's original limits of colonization, established at the Blackwater River by a 1634 act meant to sustain peace with Indigenous peoples. Some white settlers nonetheless moved into the area in violation of the law over the next decades, but the colonial House of Burgesses did not lift the ban on settlement in what became Southampton until 1705.[4]

Even after settlement was legalized, the area that became Southampton County was at the fringe of this movement of peoples. Southampton was not easily reached by navigable rivers until the port at Old South Quay grew in the eighteenth century. But as the soils along the James and the Tidewater were depleted by years of planting and crowded by population growth, white settlement and slavery pushed deeper into the piedmont and the fertile area along the North Carolina border. Still, this region was isolated; settlers from west of the Blackwater River lived five days' travel from the courthouse in Isle of Wight County; to reach those newer settlers, in 1749 Southampton County was created from the area west of the Blackwater. By 1755 about four thousand white people and two thousand enslaved Black people lived there, almost all working on farms, growing fruit, corn, and other crops.[5] The shallow and brush-choked Nottoway River bisected the county north to south, and the small county seat of Jerusalem sat on its northeast bank, connected to the outside world by roads. The best land for farming lay in the southern edge of the county near North Carolina, and settlers soon filled that region, known as Cross Keys.[6]

One of the white settlers who moved down from the James River area was William Turner Sr., grandfather to the white man who claimed Nat's ownership at the time of Nat's birth. In 1714, William Turner Sr. obtained his first land in the area, then more in 1728. By 1749, William Turner Sr. had settled there permanently, living about six miles north of the neighborhood Nat would eventually grow up in, and he claimed twenty-one enslaved people as his property. Planters like Turner carefully allocated the rights to enslaved people in their wills, leaving records of the swelling population of Black people in the region. After William's death in 1766, his son Benjamin Turner Sr. rapidly expanded the family holdings, buying nearly 1,400 acres in the southern tier of the county, where the Norfolk fine sandy loam was more conducive to large-scale agriculture than the clay soils of the upper county.[7]

These Turners were part of a much larger tide of white settlers driving enslaved people into Southside and the Chesapeake. By the first U.S. census of 1790, there were almost six thousand enslaved people in Southampton County and slightly more white people than that, and there were similar numbers of enslaved people in nearby Sussex and Norfolk. Even more enslaved people were held to the north in Tidewater Virginia's Caroline, Hanover, and Gloucester Counties.[8] As these white settlers moved south and west, they disrupted their own familial networks and even more so the familial networks of the enslaved people they brought with them.

In these new grounds, many white people shrugged off their ancestral ties to the Anglican Church that dominated the Tidewater and James River areas, and a number joined the fast-spreading Methodist and Baptist churches that spurred the Second Great Awakening. Many came to Methodism through the class meetings that defined the sect, the small gatherings of laypeople to pray and learn. Baptists, an older but rapidly growing sect, also sought to expand their numbers by recruiting Black members in this period. Baptists tended to form independent or semi-independent Black congregations, while many Methodist churches in young settlements included both Black and white members, participating together—if never equally—in the practices that formed early nineteenth-century Methodism.[9]

In the 1770s, the colonial rebellion that Americans called the Revolutionary War threatened planters' power in backcountry Virginia as in the rest of the colony. When Virginia planters and New England merchants moved toward rebellion against the British, enslaved people noted the weakened position of the enslavers, and British troops at times actively enlisted Black soldiers against them. Although the main battles took place north of Southampton, the lines of escape and enlistment in the British army reached down into the areas that Nat would later call home. Black people in Nat's region considered the effect the war could have on their lives and many ran toward the British. Some of those enslaved people from the Southside counties were, like Nat, part of that ongoing, unruly, sometimes uproarious Methodist revival.

During the spring and summer of 1775, enslaved people in Virginia talked of rising up, and reports of conspiracies spread up and down the James River as planters and enslaved people gossiped about the tense relations between imperial officers and colonists.[10] A Virginia convention lamented white people's unreadiness to defend the colony "in Case of Invasion or Insurrection." As the situation teetered on the brink, white and Black Virginians pondered the history of slave uprisings.[11]

British policy opened a window to turn talk into action. On April 21, 1775, two days after the battles at Lexington and Concord, Massachusetts, Lord Dunmore, the royal governor of Virginia, ordered his soldiers to seize the colony's stores of gunpowder. Almost immediately, armed and angry white colonists gathered outside the Governor's Palace demanding the gunpowder so they could use it to respond to "various reports" from "different parts of the country" that "some wicked and designing persons have instilled the most diabolical notions into the minds of our slaves." The next day, when the mayor and speaker of the legislature met with Dunmore, the royal governor turned fears of slave insurrection against the Patriots, stating he would help put down any insurrection if—and only if—the colonists acceded to the power of the royal government. Seeking to scare white planters into submission, Dunmore informed the politicians of a report from Surry County—just north of Southampton—about an insurrection scare, "which at first seem'd too well founded." Instead of buckling before Dunmore's threats, planters and small farmers formed new militia companies to protect their lives and property.[12]

Fearing the militia would march on the capital, Dunmore threatened to arm the enslaved people and order them to spread "Devastation wherever I can reach."[13] Soon hundreds of enslaved people from counties around Nat's Southampton entered on the British side, fighting against local white leaders and against slavery. Finally, on November 7, 1775, Lord Dunmore issued a proclamation formally promising freedom to men held by rebellious colonials if they enlisted to fight with a royal regiment.[14] While the proclamation extended only to men and only to those held by rebels, most of the enslaved people who made it to his lines arrived in family groups.[15]

Within days of Dunmore's proclamation, Black Southsiders began to run for the British lines. A man named Moses Wilkinson fled Nansemond County with a number of other enslaved people from the same plantation. Wilkinson was one of the early rush of two hundred to three hundred enslaved people who made it to a British ship moored in the James River. Soon a "great many" from neighboring Isle of Wight and Nansemond joined the Ethiopian Regiment.[16]

FOR THOSE LOOKING for precedents for Nat, few figures are as compelling as Moses Wilkinson, an enslaved Methodist preacher in Nansemond County, just east of Nat's Southampton. A powerful speaker who repeatedly drove his followers into frenzies, Wilkinson was one among a number of enslaved Virginians who became fired with the evangelical spirit of Methodists and Baptists in the years after the Evangelical Revival, or First Great Awakening. In the year leading up to the colonial crisis, Wilkinson presided over clandestine religious meetings in the outer reaches of the Great Dismal Swamp. There, he preached on the analogies between the enslaved Virginians and the Israelites in the book of Exodus. Just as Moses the Hebrew had guided the enslaved Israelites out of bondage in Egypt, Wilkinson the African promised his enslaved congregation that God would bring them to the promised land. Many Christians of that era, including theologically distinct New England Calvinists, saw in these moments repetitions of biblical times, and it is impossible to know how literally his congregation took these sermons. At minimum sermons such as these helped persuade people to see themselves as worthy of God's favor. Some listeners might well have been convinced they were God's chosen people, selected to relive the Israelites' exodus, freedom, and conquest. A careful scholar of runaway enslaved people in the Revolutionary War noted that "it is very possible" that Wilkinson "was following the precedent of his biblical namesake and leading his followers across the water to freedom."[17]

Along with the heavens, enslaved people looked to the Crown. Many enslaved rebels in the late eighteenth to early nineteenth centuries believed they were rising in obedience to the orders of a distant king who was on their side. Scholars have traced this faith in distant kings to West African understandings of kingly power and obligation, to a politics of hope sometimes called naive monarchism, to the imperial rivalries that shaped the era, and to enslaved people's reinterpretation of planters' resentment of monarchical meddling in local affairs. The British dissemination of Dunmore's orders surely played a key role; people like Wilkinson had good reason to believe that the king was on their side and that planters were arrayed against them. Their faith likely gave them the hope to believe their actions could work through earthly powers to bring God's plan into being.[18]

Wilkinson and his compatriots were merely the first wave of rebellious enslaved Virginians. By the war's end, about 3,400 enslaved people from the greater Chesapeake area had reached British lines. Hundreds were from Southside counties, including an Isle of Wight man named Caesar, an "Excellent pilot" who aided the British ships.[19] In early 1776 an enslaved woman named Mary fled from Norfolk County, inspired in part by the networks and beliefs she had developed in weekly late-night Methodist praise meetings where she sang of salvation and deliverance. So, too, did her fellow Norfolk County Methodist Nathaniel Snowball flee with his wife, Violet, and son Nathaniel, enslaved in Princess Anne County.[20] When British troops sacked Portsmouth and Suffolk, east of Southampton, in May 1779, between 500 and 1,500 enslaved people followed them.[21] Later in the war, in January 1781, the British commander Benedict Arnold raided the James River area, and perhaps 300 enslaved people from neighboring plantations followed him to Portsmouth.[22]

Initially, the most impressive spectacle for enslaved people was likely Wilkinson's Ethiopian Regiment as they did hard service for the British in their time in the Chesapeake Bay. On December 9, 1775, the regiment—until then used in training and fortification building—clashed with Virginia militia who killed or captured more than a hundred Loyalist soldiers, including many of the Black troops. A Patriot officer dismissed the Ethiopian Regiment as a "ragged crew."[23]

But this was not the end of the story. Moses Wilkinson survived that battle and retreated with several hundred other Loyalist troops to the British fleet for protection. In dismal camps at Tucker's Point, the Loyalists suffered as smallpox tore through their "shattered remains." There were almost three hundred graves at Tucker's Point when the British and the surviving Loyalists fled the site for Gwynn's Island.[24] There, depleted Black Loyalists lay prostrate in huts as disease consumed them. In early August 1776, the remaining Black Loyalists departed with Dunmore and his ships. When white Virginia militia arrived at the island, they "were struck with horrour at the number of dead bodies, in a state of putrefaction, strewed . . . about two miles . . . without a shovelful of earth upon them."[25] Observers reckoned that as many as eight hundred people died at the two British camps, including two-thirds of the Ethiopian Regiment.[26]

Moses Wilkinson was among those who suffered from smallpox. Although he did not die, the virus left him blind and lame for the rest of his life. But the smallpox did not sap his spirit. With Dunmore's fleet, Wilkinson and the remaining Ethiopian Regiment fled to New York, in British hands since the successful November 1776 campaign against George Washington's troops. There, Wilkinson and his neighbors joined two thousand African Americans seeking their liberty behind British lines amid the fifty-five thousand British soldiers and seamen concentrated around the city.[27]

Led by Wilkinson, these Southside Black Loyalists began to build a community of inspired Methodists in a city at war. By then Wilkinson was known to other Black Methodists as Daddy Wilkinson and had become the most influential Black preacher in New York City. Another prominent preacher was his fellow Southside man Luke Jordan, Wilkinson's closest collaborator. Nearly all the five hundred Afro-Virginians in New York were Methodists, and many were part of extended families and kin groups. Among the dozen refugees from the Wilkinson plantation, for instance, were Jordan's wife and son and Mary Perth and her three daughters.[28] Black Loyalists settled together, creating safe havens such as "the Virginia Negro houses."[29] The scholar Cassandra Pybus wrote, "Of all the stories told and retold within the community of runaways, perhaps the most pivotal was that of Moses leading the Israelites out of enslavement in Egypt. A significant narrator of this potent story of deliverance from bondage was the prophetically named Black preacher who had led his flock from Virginia in 1776." Wilkinson blended Wesleyan oral communication and "spontaneous religious response to create a form of religious expression that could coexist with older African infusions such as conjuring, divination, and sorcery." Like other inspired Methodists, he was accused of "enthusiasm" for appealing "to visions to reveal the will of God and divine the sure road to eternal salvation."[30]

As New York became the British army headquarters, the Southside migrants worked as wharf hands, carpenters, cartmen, and wagoners. They drummed for Hessian troops and served in an all-Black carpenters' corps and the Virginia Company of Blacks. Wilkinson and others labored for the Royal Artillery Department and bedded down in four row houses converted into barracks. All the while they struggled with the common problems of occupied New York: disease, housing shortages, price inflation, and thieving British soldiers. While their lot was not easy, Black Loyalists were relatively well paid for their army work. In 1780 the British increased the standard wage for military laborers to ten shillings, five times the going rate before the war.[31]

Back in Nat's Southampton County, the war cut enticingly close to home for enslaved people and uncomfortably so for white residents. Many of the white males over sixteen served on the Patriot side, and they were called more than half a dozen times to defend the ports at Hampton Roads, where the James, Elizabeth, and Nansemond Rivers empty into Chesapeake Bay. In the nearby Dismal Swamp, pro-British guerrillas launched small excursions to disrupt Patriot forces and erode local morale. Still, before 1781, the war seemed at a distance, if not a safe one. But then, Lord Cornwallis led the British forces up from North Carolina to the James River, creating what one local historian calls "pandemonium throughout central and southeastern Virginia." British cavalry raided Southampton County's most important port on the Blackwater River at Old South Quay and destroyed warehouses and ferries along the upper Chowan River just across the border in North Carolina.[32]

Although the war came home to Southampton County in 1781, it soon came to an end with Cornwallis's October surrender. While white Patriots celebrated, Wilkinson and other Black Southside migrants feared for their freedom. No longer could they hope to return to the Chesapeake Bay region as honored and protected subjects of the British; their homelands and family members were under the control of the victorious planter rebels. And they faced immediate danger. As the British prepared to evacuate New York, enslavers rushed into the city to hunt for the people they claimed as their human property. Black Loyalists feared, one refugee recalled, "our old masters coming from Virginia, North Carolina, and other parts, and seizing upon their slaves in the streets of New York, or even dragging them from their beds."[33] The son of Mary Perth's enslaver, John Willoughby Jr., indignantly complained to the British commander in chief, Sir Guy Carleton, that he and his neighbors would be financially ruined if their slaves left New York with the Loyalist convoy. But Willoughby received no help from Carleton and never found Mary Perth and her children.[34]

As the Southside migrants evaded their pursuers, they also tracked global politics. The 1783 Treaty of Paris that ended the Revolutionary War set off disturbing rumors that the British would leave behind slave refugees when they evacuated North America. Indeed, article 7 of the treaty plainly prohibited the British from "carrying away any Negroes."[35] But Carleton told General George Washington that under his understanding of the laws of war, the refugees were no longer property but free men and women. To deliver them up to their owners "would be a dishonorable Violation of the public Faith pledged to the negroes in the Proclamations."[36] Thus, in the summer of 1783 the Southside Methodists were among three thousand Loyalists who departed New York for Nova Scotia.

These Southside soldiers had hoped to be emancipated into a free Virginia, but having fled their homes and the slaveholders, they came to believe they must find a new Promised Land. Once again, the man named Moses, Daddy Wilkinson, led them through his preaching and his force of will. If his given name, Moses, suggested a man born to lead a chosen people out of bondage, his patronymic, Daddy, at once patriarchal, intimate, and affectionate, spoke to the bonds of kinship, hierarchy, authority, and feeling that tied his congregation together. By the time they reached Birchtown, Nova Scotia, the smallpox-plagued Wilkinson could neither stand nor walk, and the brethren often carried him on their shoulders to the meetinghouse.[37] Still, the frail Wilkinson preached with such power and "his feelings were so exquisite and he worked himself up to such a pitch" that it seemed more than his body could bear.[38] Wilkinson's preaching knocked one unconverted woman off her feet, literally as well as figuratively, and she cried for mercy for two solid hours. Her writhing over the next six days left her husband astonished at her spiritual "agony."[39] Within months a visiting white minister found that Wilkinson had been the "principal instrument" for converting sixty settlers in the area.[40] A scholar of Black Loyalists in the region wrote that the Black Loyalists noticed that "God did not seem to speak to those older [segregated white] churches in quite the same way he did to them, the blacks. Inevitably, this produced a feeling of being closer to God, of being, in fact, a chosen people, an elite group of Christians whom God regularly visited and whose role it was to preserve the truth of the moment of salvation."[41]

Wilkinson had no monopoly on the role of Methodist prophet in this Nova Scotia community. A missionary from a dissident Methodist sect warred against Wilkinson for religious supremacy. This missionary was John Marrant, a free Black preacher who had grown up in New York, Florida, and South Carolina. Converted by the legendary George Whitefield, Marrant lived among Native peoples in the Carolina backcountry, then served in the Royal Navy during the colonial struggle. After making his way to London, he joined a Methodist sect called the Countess of Huntingdon's Connexion. When his brother informed him of the need for ministers in the Loyalist settlements in Canada, Marrant departed England to bring light to the masses in Nova Scotia. There, he found a vibrant Methodist sect led by Wilkinson, white itinerant Freeborn Garrettson, and others. The two sides viewed each other with suspicion and contempt; Garrettson was sure Marrant was sent by the devil, while Marrant suggested Wilkinson was the devil's instrument.[42]

Wilkinson and Marrant struggled over their competing claims to God's mantle. Because both styled themselves prophets, neither could stand to share the primacy of God's favor with the other. When Wilkinson permitted Marrant to preach at the Wesleyans' meeting-house before "a very large congregation," Marrant proceeded to try to spirit away the congregation right under Wilkinson's nose.[43] On a Sunday in December 1785, Marrant revealed himself to be a prophet sent to save the Loyalists. In his sermon he told the congregation, "For Moses truly said unto the fathers, a prophet shall the Lord your God raise up unto you of your brethren, like unto me; him shall ye hear in all things whatsoever he may say unto you." Marrant reckoned the Methodists' response with evident satisfaction. "Ten were pricked to the heart, and cried out, 'Men and brethren what can we do to be saved.'" Styling himself as Moses's heir, Marrant meant to use his authority to undermine Wilkinson. When "old man" Wilkinson struck up a hymn, Marrant slipped in unbeknownst to Wilkinson and "gave out the hymn over his head." By Marrant's account, "the house rang with the praises of God" as Wilkinson slinked away. But Wilkinson would not be so easily dislodged; he continued to direct meetings and services from his desk at the meetinghouse, and Marrant found himself excluded.[44]

Wilkinson sustained the loyalty of his congregation by offering his own vision of the Exodus story he had been telling and retelling since his time in Nansemond County. The Southside Methodists had not yet reached the promised land in Nova Scotia, he told them; they needed to embark upon a new exodus in search of a new home. There were good reasons not to think of Nova Scotia as the promised land. For one thing, there was not enough land. In Nova Scotia, Black Loyalists struggled to gain an economic foothold or a position of equality in a fierce and inhospitable environment. Therefore many scrambled to make a living. But even those who did accumulate land looked elsewhere for escape. White Loyalists would never accept them as respectable British subjects, much less as equals. The promised land was not just land; it was a place where Black people could be powerful. It is impossible to disentangle the practical and spiritual calls that drove Black Loyalists. For Wilkinson, the two blended together. Finding a better situation in Africa was both practical and spiritual.[45]

Wilkinson therefore looked to a new promised land across the Atlantic. He supported the plan of the abolitionist John Clarkson and the Halifax Quaker Lawrence Hartshorne offering a grant of twenty acres, plus ten for a wife and another five for each child, to every man in Nova Scotia who migrated to a "Free Settlement on the Coast of Africa." The Sierra Leone Company also offered the Black Loyalists what they could not find in Nova Scotia: equality. "The civil, military, personal and commercial rights and duties of Blacks and Whites shall be the same and secured in the same manner" in Sierra Leone.[46] Wilkinson convened an assembly of 300 to 400 settlers on a rainy October night to hear Clarkson's pitch for the colony in Sierra Leone.[47] Several times the crowd interrupted Wilkinson with applause. Three days later Wilkinson's congregation—families comprising 514 men, women, and children in all—decided to make the exodus as a body.[48] Wilkinson's fervor and his faith had prevailed over his rival. By the time the Methodists left Nova Scotia for Sierra Leone, they had members enough to conduct fourteen classes, and Marrant was left behind with a congregation of but forty souls.[49]

BY 1800, THE YEAR of Nat's birth, Wilkinson's Methodist congregation accounted for more than half the settlers in Sierra Leone and the lion's share of the company's struggles for control, struggles that culminated with a Methodist rebellion in Sierra Leone.[50] Soon after their arrival in Sierra Leone, these Methodist Black migrants demanded their promised land. But their champion John Clarkson did not remain governor long, and his successors, especially Zachary Macaulay, bitterly disappointed the Methodist Southsiders.[51]

While Clarkson had ruled by persuasion and cajolery, Macaulay turned to severity and decree.[52] "Strong language and a decided peremptory tone are absolutely necessary," Macaulay judged.[53] Unyielding, brutally self-confident, and self-righteous, Macaulay combined an abolitionist's zeal with a plantation overseer's expectation of deference. In July 1794, the youthful governor dressed down the venerable Wilkinson for his congregation's purported faults: "the notoriously irreligious lives of some of their members," their failure to follow Methodist discipline or the laws of the colony, and "the encouragement given to discontent and rebellion."[54] Macaulay derisively referred to "our mad Methodists" under the sway of Wilkinson and Luke Jordan.[55]

Even as other evangelical migrants like the Southside Baptist preacher David George tried to accommodate the company, the Methodists fought back.[56] Isaac Anderson, an elder in Wilkinson's church, carried a petition of complaint to the directors in London. "We are just at the mercy of the People you send here to give us what Wages they Please & charge us what they like for their Goods," they argued.[57] Clarkson's replacement "seems to wish to rule us," the emissaries charged, "as if we were all Slaves."[58] When Macaulay revoked Black preachers' power to oversee marriage, Wilkinson's congregation and other followers signed a letter proclaiming their loyalty not to Macaulay but to the "Governor of the universe . . . [W]e consider ourselves a perfect church, having no need of the assistance of any worldly power to appoint or perform religious ceremonies for us." Their spirit, Macaulay said, "was that of rebellion itself." He called them exemplars of the ignorance of "those who extol *vox populi* as *vox Dei.*"[59] Company leaders grumbled that the waterfront street where Wilkinson's assistant Luke Jordan lived with other members of their church should be called "Discontented Row."[60] Methodists bragged, "We are the people of the Mathodist connection that are calld people of a ranglesome nature."[61]

These "ranglesome" Southside Methodists dove deeper into their shared religious faith during Wilkinson's 1796 revivals. In his preaching Wilkinson "outstretches his voice at times to terror and frightfulness," a later Methodist missionary wrote, and he inspired startling transformations among the congregation.[62] At one service the sisters and brethren, children especially, "were struck down to the ground by 'the power of his preaching,'" crying out in anguished conviction of their own sin, one step in the Wesleyan path to conversion.[63] Their personalistic faith, resistance to authority, and emphasis upon grace worried the Anglican Macaulay, who denounced "the enthusiastic hair brained unmeaning rhapsodies of our mad Wesleans"[64] and wished a senior Methodist from abroad would teach them obedience, "for at present their government is a pure democracy."[65] Macaulay's invocations of the dreaded charge of enthusiasm likely signaled Wilkinson's claims to hear God's voice. "When Daddy Moses preached about the delivery out of oppression and over the mighty waters into the land of Canaan, his congregation had a very firm idea of what this meant in their own lives," Cassandra Pybus wrote.[66]

The Methodists found a great deal to critique in Macaulay's leadership. In 1794, Macaulay capitulated to a French gunboat attack after refusing to arm the Southside settlers.[67] In 1796, a slave ship captain threatened to carry Black dockworkers to enslavement in the West Indies. When the men fought back, the company arrested them.[68] Methodists then helped lead an uprising against the company; over three days of rioting, bands of Methodist protesters confronted Baptist Loyalists at the gates of the governor's house. All eight arrested ringleaders were members of Wilkinson's congregation, that "firm body of malcontents."[69] In July 1797, Methodists resisted Macaulay's order to attend Anglican services twice a day and forswear Methodist-run Sunday school.[70] Methodists boycotted Anglican services for years even as Baptists conformed to the company's order.[71] In the Methodists' resistance to Macaulay's edicts, the exasperated governor observed, they had acted as "a kind of Jacobin club" under the aegis of a "Junto of preachers."[72] Wilkinson and his lieutenants wrote sadly to the departed Clarkson, "We wance did call it Free Town, but since your absence we have a reason to call it a town of slavery."[73]

Some Black Virginia Methodists led a battle for self-governance that would culminate in a rebellion against the company. In late 1796 two Wilkinson-affiliated Methodists, Nathaniel Snowball from Norfolk and Luke Jordan from Nansemond, began to organize an exodus four miles west to Pirate Bay to escape their "bondage from this tyrannous crew." At first Wilkinson and his ally Anderson decided not to join them, and only thirty families departed. But over time the colony grew, and Anderson became a leader there.[74]

Over the next three years, residents of this new settlement at Pirate Bay claimed their independence one office at a time, petitioning unsuccessfully to appoint a judge and two justices of the peace in 1799.[75] After Macaulay left Sierra Leone in 1799, the settlers on their own chose the Methodist Isaac Anderson as a justice of the peace and the Methodist preacher Mingo Jordan as judge. They turned their constabulary of elected hundredors and tithingmen into a legislature complete with an upper and lower house, and their representatives proceeded to adopt laws governing everyday matters in Freetown.[76]

In 1800, as Nat was born, Virginia Methodists in Sierra Leone led an armed rebellion to defend their claims of independence. When the new governor refused to recognize the Black judge, settlers asserted their right. On September 3, 1800, the heads of households convened to write a frame of government—"a paper of laws"—covering matters from trade to farming and livestock keeping. Crowds assembled three weeks later to peruse the new code in town and in the hinterland. In turn, the governor deputized loyal Black settlers to arrest several men on charges of treason. Isaac Anderson and two others escaped the dragnet and formed a camp outside town with forty men.[77]

To suppress them, the company turned to Maroon veterans from the Trelawny War in Jamaica. These Maroons were the descendants of African enslaved people who had fled into the Jamaican interior and established communities the British could not defeat and so had made treaties with. Some Maroons had already fought with the British against enslaved people and captured runaways. So it was not surprising that they continued to ally themselves with British imperial officers when they were transported to Sierra Leone. On October 2, the Maroons launched a surprise assault on rebels that killed two and took thirty prisoners. Over the next week, Maroons captured the rest or drove them into hiding. Some rebels were banished for life, others sent to a company plantation.[78] On December 22, 1800, the governor's court sentenced Anderson to be hanged.[79]

The Methodist rebellion in Sierra Leone had been broken. Still, the rebellion helps us see the religious fervor and military tactics that influenced people who had been enslaved in Southside Virginia and the Chesapeake region in the decades before Nat's birth. We cannot say specifically how much Nat or even his family knew of the exploits of Wilkinson and the other rebellious and warlike Methodists from Southside Virginia, nor can we say how literally these Virginia Methodists took their talk of exodus and biblical typology. But the flight to British lines and the efforts of the Ethiopian Regiment were signal events in the area around Norfolk and were discussed, fearfully, by white Virginians for years and likely remembered and reinterpreted by enslaved people, perhaps as emblems of Black military service, perhaps as warnings of the disappearance of those Black soldiers. Whether or not Nat knew directly of the experiences of Southside Methodists in Sierra Leone, the religiously inspired and organized rebellion there suggests how evangelical faith could help Black Virginians see themselves not only as worthy of God's love but also as God's chosen people.

Meanwhile, in the decades after the colonists' rebellion, slavery spread rapidly into the interior of the southeastern states. The number of enslaved people in the nation rose from 697,624 in the 1790 census to 893,602 in the 1800 census, an increase of 28 percent. The growth was decidedly in the Southeast, which was the only region with an increasing population of enslaved people; in New England, the enslaved population fell to fewer than 1,400 people, and the number in the "middle states" from New York to Delaware also declined, if slightly, and that number would drop in each subsequent census. In Virginia, powered by the spread of tobacco and food crop planting, the number of enslaved people grew from 292,627 to 346,968. Throughout the Atlantic Seaboard, farmers pushed slavery deeper into the central, up-country regions, moving into the piedmont south and west of Southampton, especially eastern Georgia and central North and South Carolina. In Georgia and South Carolina the spread of slavery between 1790 and 1800 was tied closely to the spread of up-country cotton cultivation following the 1793 invention of the cotton gin. Cotton production grew from 1.5 million pounds in 1790 to 35 million pounds in 1800. Even more ominously, new slave states had been carved out in Kentucky and Tennessee. Soon after Nat's birth, the United States' acquisition of the vast Louisiana Territory would create the potential for even more slave states and even more cotton cultivation, as would the dispossession of Cherokee, Muscogee, Choctaw, Seminole, Chickasaw, and other Native people from their lands. In the years before Nat's birth, the institution of slavery was growing larger and more powerful.[80]

So, too, was the image of Black men in arms. In the 1790s, stories of the Haitian Revolution led by Black soldiers spread throughout the United States. Like all revolutions, the war in Haiti had complex origins: enslaved people's armed rebellion, white colonists' resistance to French laws, free Black uprisings in support of the French Revolution and Republic, and rival European empires' interventions. In 1793 enslaved people, having been promised that slavery would be abolished, joined French Republican officials in war against both foreign powers and recalcitrant white colonists. The formerly enslaved soldier Toussaint Louverture joined the French Republic's forces in 1794, the year the French government decreed an end to slavery, becoming their military leader and an international icon of Black generalship. In 1802, after a counterrevolution in France, Napoleon launched a massive attack on Haiti, forcing Toussaint to surrender and accept transport to France, where he died. But in 1804, Haitian forces defeated the French army and declared the country free and independent; the second successful American revolution resulted in the creation of the first self-governing Black republic in the New World. Soon, stories of Haiti spread across the sea to the United States. Many whites told fearful tales of massacres, making Haiti a negative example they wished to avoid. Free Black communities everywhere celebrated Haitian independence. It is clear that some enslaved people—and likely those around Nat—either heard independently about Haiti or inverted the fearful stories of enslavers, making heroes of the people the masters called villains. Decades later Nat began the rebellion on a key anniversary of the Haitian uprising, though we cannot say for certain that he intended that reference.[81]

In September 1800, a month before Nat's birth, stories of an enslaved rebellion in Virginia's capital raised the prospect of an evangelical Virginia counterpoint to Haiti. A man named Gabriel was charged with planning a rebellion of enslaved people in Richmond. The planning had begun with a gathering of enslaved people at a spring near a local Baptist church. When one of the rebels, having second thoughts, warned that they hadn't seen the biblical portents that urged on the Israelites, Gabriel's brother Martin answered from Leviticus: "I read in my Bible where God says, if we will worship him, we should have peace in all our Lands, five of you shall conquer an hundred and a hundred, a thousand of our enemies." Gabriel's plan included killing all the local whites except for those they considered potential allies: Quakers, Methodists, and Frenchmen, a reference perhaps to two men who plotted with Gabriel and to the unfounded rumors that French forces had landed at Old South Quay port on Blackwater River in Southampton County to collect debts from the United States and, potentially, help freed people. Like Nat, Gabriel became known to history through his enslaver's last name, and most books refer to him as Gabriel Prosser, a name he was not known to be called in his lifetime, according to the foremost historian of the rebellion. Gabriel was executed on October 10, eight days after Nat's birth.[82]

Gabriel's was the most famous but not the only rebellion in the years just before and after Nat's birth. In 1799, in Nat's own Southampton County, several enslaved people bound together in a coffle fought the slave dealers who aimed to drive them to Georgia for sale. Using sticks, knives, and pistols, five of the enslaved people killed the dealers and took their money. When the county patrol caught them, ten enslaved people were reportedly killed and five recaptured and tried before a Southampton court that sentenced four to hang and one to lashing and branding. It is hard to imagine that Southampton enslaved people did not speak of the hangings in Jerusalem, although it is not possible to know how long this memory persisted among the county's enslaved people.[83]

Arguably, this uprising was fueled by enslaved people's knowledge of the Haitian rebellion, as one scholar suggested. Without doubt, a separate Southampton County letter three years later showed the circulation of rumors about Haiti.[84] In February 1802, when Nat was a toddler, Southampton whites discovered a paper at Barrow's Store that claimed that enslaved people would follow "precisely" the plan that succeeded in Saint-Domingue by setting fires and murdering "thousands of whites." Although no one was ever charged, locals connected it to the murder of a white overseer at the hands of three enslaved people, who were caught and hanged.[85]

Then, twelve years after Nat was born, Virginia Black people took up arms once again in the War of 1812. There were signs that enslaved people discussed the potential for war even before the British attack. In March 1812, an enslaved man named Piedmont Tom learned about an impending invasion by the British "from the poor people in the neighborhood." Tom took heart from a conjurer's prediction and a recent fire at a Richmond theater. "God Almighty had sent them a little Hell for the white people, and . . . in a little time they would get greater." Celia, an enslaved woman he was courting, told Tom "they could not rise too soon for her as she had rather be in hell than where she was." To impress her, Tom killed his enslaver. After his capture, Tom relayed this story to a concerned group of magistrates, one of whom would two decades later confront Nat's uprising as governor of Virginia.[86]

When the War of 1812 began, the British at first warned officers against inciting insurrection among the enslaved people and limited soldiers to recruiting them as guides. For those guides, however, the British stuck to their prior practice of guaranteeing freedom in exchange for aid. "You must distinctly understand that you are in no case to take slaves away as slaves but as free persons whom the public become bound to maintain," the British secretary of state wrote to the commander of the Chesapeake in March 1813.[87]

Enslaved people once again interpreted the war through their own readings of history and faith, decamping from their enslavers' plantations to seek freedom with the British. This time, the numbers were smaller than in the Revolution, in large part because of geography; the British stayed closer to the Chesapeake Bay, fearful of getting trapped in up-country fighting. Still, 3,400 enslaved people in Virginia and Maryland escaped to the British lines during the War of 1812, the vast majority from plantations and farms in sight of the bay and its large rivers.[88] A smaller number fled from counties near Nat's Southampton, including neighboring Surry and Isle of Wight, which each faced the James River.[89]

Most of these fugitives escaped in family groups based on both kinship and neighborhood.[90] For example, on June 25, 1813, an en-slaved man—Anthony, he was called—was fishing in the James River when a British boat sidled up to his position and took him aboard. Two weeks later, three other enslaved men from Anthony's neigh-borhood, evidently with his encouragement, made their way to the British, too.[91] British ships beckoned them with bands playing, beat-ing drums, swinging lanterns, and the promise of freedom.[92] Many fugitives served as scouts, guiding British forces through the rivers, swamps, and forests in the night, helping them evade "several snares and ambushes," one British lieutenant recalled. "The country within ten miles of the shore lay completely at our mercy."[93]

Once again, flight was prelude to armed rebellion. One "pugna-cious" runaway from Norfolk informed a British lieutenant that he meant "to wipe off old scores with his master."[94] The British, following Dunmore's course during the American Revolution, in September 1813 offered enslaved people freedom in return for military service.[95] The next year the British organized four hundred Black men into a battalion of Colonial Marines, a force that inspired fear among the Americans and admiration from the British as they liberated family members and plundered plantations and farms.[96] Their raids laid the groundwork for the most spectacular British victory of the war, the burning of the American capital at Washington, D.C., an event widely discussed across Virginia, and one with symbolic meaning obvious to everyone.[97]

IN A RELATIVE BACKWATER like Southampton, it is not possible to know exactly what news circulated among white people, much less among those enslaved people who worked to keep their knowledge out of sight of their enslavers (and thus out of the records historians now consult). But it is easy to imagine that in the years around Nat's birth enslaved Southside people spoke of the Methodists who had fought for the British, of the Black generals in the great revolution in Haiti that so frightened the white people in Virginia, and of the smaller uprisings (and rumors of them) closer to home. If we cannot say with certainty what Nat heard as a young child, it is very likely he knew stories of Black men in arms, and possible that he knew acquaintances of the Methodist enslaved men who fought in British uniforms for their promised land. As Nat approached thirteen years old, it is likely that he heard about the Black soldiers who fought for the British in the War of 1812.

It is clear from the statements of Nancy Parsons, the governor, and other Black and white observers that stories of these past Black uprisings shaped white fears and Black hopes in the early moments of Nat's rebellion. That rebellion would be fought near ground where enslaved people eighteen years earlier had fled to the British to fight, and where enslaved people thirty-eight years before that had done the same. Much had changed between the time of Nat's birth and his rebellion, and those changes would be visible in the sovereignty Nat appealed to, not the sovereignty of the British king, but the sovereignty of the King of Kings in heaven. Still, some of the same religious principles that helped inspire and explain the Virginia and Sierra Leone rebellions between 1775 and 1812 would also inspire Nat and some of his followers. Nat was an unusual character, but his plans might well have seemed comprehensible to neighbors because events during their lifetime taught them to understand slavery not simply as a struggle but as a literal war, a war that people had fought on those same grounds not all that long before, a war that could be fought again.

2

Nat, Methodist

It's likely that Nat's parents expressed their hopes for their boy in the name they gave him: a diminutive of Nathaniel, meaning "gift of God." Nat was known by the diminutive in the records but was often referred to as Nathaniel by later Black orators, as the historian Kenneth Greenberg noted. Nathaniel was a name utilized in the white Turner family for white family members as well, so we cannot be certain that Nat's parents played the key role in selecting it, but even if not, we can perceive the ways that his devout mother and grandmother could have helped Nat understand his name's powerful biblical resonances as he began to encounter them in his childhood.[1]

Nat surely did encounter these biblical Nathaniels, for he was an intensely curious, literate, and faithful boy. "Religion was the subject to which [his mind] was directed," he later said. "Whenever an opportunity occurred of looking at a book," he would read, unless he was "devoting my time to fasting and prayer."[2] Whether or not his parents or enslavers made the coincidence of names explicit, a child's curiosity likely led him to contemplate other people with the same name in the Bible his family and his enslavers studied so fervently in their meetings. Perhaps those biblical figures were models for a young Nat. Models were not oracles, nor were they types that advanced the cosmological fulfillment of God's kingdom, but they were and remain ways that Christians ask the question of how to live a godly life.

In both the Hebrew Bible and the Christian New Testament, Nathans and Nathaniels present models of prophets in communication with God. In the Hebrew Bible, the Lord told "Nathan the prophet" of the covenant the Lord would make with King David: David should build a temple in Jerusalem to thank God for leading him "to be ruler over my people, over Israel." The Lord would then establish "the throne of his kingdom forever. I will be his father, and he shall be my son." Later Nathan bitterly scolded David for his affair with Bathsheba and the murder of Bathsheba's husband, giving voice to the Lord's disappointment. Still later, Nathan with the priest Zadok anointed King Solomon.[3]

The Christian Testament disciple Nathanael called Jesus both "the son of God" and the "King of Israel." Jesus replied, "Thou shalt see greater things than these . . . Verily, verily, I say unto you, Hereafter, ye shall see heaven open, and the angels of God ascending and descending upon the Son of Man."[4] John Wesley, the guiding light of early Methodism and namesake of many of the movement's branches, praised Nathanael's "integrity" for laying "him open to the force of evidence" that Jesus was a ruler both in heaven and on earth. Wesley glossed Christ's final words to Nathanael as a promise: "All of these, as well as thou, who believe in me now in my state of humiliation, shall hereafter see me come in my glory, and all the angels of God with me."[5]

Thus the name bespoke prophecy, the promise of God's return, and the fulfillment of God's kingdom in Jerusalem. For Nat, of course, an American Jerusalem lay a few miles up the Cross Keys Road, across the bridge that ran over the Nottoway River. The town itself was small and unimpressive, and we cannot be sure that Nat ever went there before his arrest, trial, and execution. But the town's name connected it to Nathan the prophet.[6] As a boy, Nat had models at hand for his own prodigious faith and religious gifts and for the place where he might fulfill them. For a child looking, as Nat said, for confirmation of "things that the fertility of my own imagination had depicted before," the coincidence might have felt auspicious, even prophetic.[7]

Of course many parents give their children portentous names, and few of them end up as prophets, much less rebel generals, but Nat's name was just one among many signs of his future. Much of our evidence comes from Nat's *Confessions*, but there are also references to his precocity in contemporary white sources as well as in the Black oral traditions. According to the *Confessions*, Nat's father and mother saw signs of his special talents when he was only a toddler. One day, when Nat was three or four years old, Nat told his playmates about incidents that had happened before he was born. "I stuck to my story" when his mother pressed him, Nat later recalled. Then she called over other people on the farm, and they "were greatly astonished." Years later Nat began the story of "that enthusiasm" that led to his uprising with that childhood "circumstance—trifling as it may seem, it was the commencement of that belief which has grown with time." The people around him said, "I surely would be a prophet, as the Lord had shewn me things that had happened before my birth. And my father and mother strengthened me in this my first impression, saying in my presence, I was intended for some great purpose."[8] In the record of his telling, Nat did not claim prophecy as an adult; it was put upon him from a young age by parents, family members, and white and Black neighbors who saw in him something unusual that he in turn reflected back to them. Family and fellow churchgoers prepared him to accept that calling. These people were the people known to Nat, the people who defined his neighborhood—in a rural area the region defined by a couple hours' walk, where people and places were familiar. Because people in rural neighborhoods saw and heard about one another from neighbors, their words mattered in a way that the views of people from beyond the neighborhood—strangers—did not.

Those neighborhood views were forged in early national Methodism, one of the most dynamic religious movements in U.S. history, and one that shaped Nat's view of God, himself, and the future of the world. In the years after the Revolution, Methodism expanded in the North and the South among white and Black Americans in both segregated and biracial services at places like Turner's Meeting House. It was a religion rooted in prayer meetings, services, hymn singing, study, reflection, and contemplation of biblical models and types. It was also a religion that seems to have inspired Moses Wilkinson to lead his neighbors to the British, the formerly enslaved Richard Allen to walk out of a white-dominated congregation and found a new denomination, Denmark Vesey to plot a rebellion, David Walker to call for war against slavery, and enslaved people in Guyana and elsewhere to go to war. It was a religion on fire, and that passion—or enthusiasm—coursed through Nat and many other Methodists. Because some pop culture (and scholarly) works followed northern abolitionists in assuming Nat was a Baptist, based on misconceptions of Methodism and a single baptism Nat later performed, and because Methodism became pacified over the mid-nineteenth century, it is easy to miss this aspect of his story.[9]

Methodism was a religion struggling over race, slavery, and freedom in ways that Nat's parents and neighbors would have understood. In the years before Nat's birth, Methodists critiqued slavery and urged followers both to free individual people and to lobby against the spread of the institution. But as slavery grew, and as independence severed American Methodists from their antislavery English codenominationalists, antislavery sentiment faded among white American Methodists, and the practice of manumission became rare just as Nat was born. By the time he was an adult, Virginia Methodism had accommodated itself to slavery, and some white Methodists embraced biblical defenses of enslavement even as they aimed to convert individual Black people. As Nat's family and Black and white neighbors considered whether his gifts would lead him to manumission, Nat absorbed religious practices that reinforced the power of prophets, the normalcy of enthusiasm, and the coming battle for the kingdom of God.

WE KNOW QUITE LITTLE about Nat's immediate family. The *Confessions* gives warm, general remembrances of his mother and grandmother and their role in shaping his life and his religious faith, but the search for their historical identity remains educated guesswork and supposition. Several historians, including David Allmendinger, believe his mother was named Anne, often called Nancy. A local historian stated seventy years after the fact that she had been abducted from Africa in her youth, though there is no concrete evidence this was true. If so, this raises questions about the role of West African religious faiths in Nat's life, and it is possible to trace resonances in some of his visions and practices, though Nat himself did not leave a record of this influence either in the *Confessions* or in the testimony of local enslaved people. According to one story, Nancy became a cook in the Turner family and through proximity learned to read in English and converted to the white family's Methodist faith. By some later local reports his grandmother was Bridget, but historians point to a different woman named Lydia as more likely to be his grandmother based upon her proximity to Nancy and young Nat. Even if this is so, we do not know if Lydia was Nancy's mother or mother-in-law.[10]

Nat's father is more elusive. In the *Confessions*, Nat says that both his father and his mother "strengthened him" in his belief that he "was intended for some great purpose, which they had always thought from certain marks on my head and breast." Nat also says that his father ran away when Nat was a boy.[11]

For information about Nat and his family, we must shift our attention to the records of the white Turners. The white Turners had moved into the region in the mid-eighteenth century following the property acquisitions of William Turner Sr. William's son Benjamin Turner Sr. split his 1,400 additional acres and ten enslaved people among his children and grandsons, leaving the rights to three enslaved people to his son Benjamin Turner Jr. and others to Benjamin Jr.'s brother Nathan. As white family members died, Benjamin Turner Jr. bought rights to four more enslaved people in 1793. The records of the white Turner family suggest that Nat's grandmother and mother might have been among the two enslaved people Benjamin Jr. purchased. That same year Benjamin Turner Jr. also purchased a man named Abraham who disappeared from the records in 1811, matching Nat's recollection of a father who ran away (or perhaps was sold away) around that year. If indeed the property records are correct and the entire enslaved family lived with Benjamin Turner Jr., then it is likely that this trio was Nat's biological family: grandmother Lydia, mother called Nancy or Anne, and a father named Abraham. They did not live alone. Benjamin Turner Jr.'s holdings grew eventually to thirty enslaved people before his death, placing him among the top 10 percent of the county's white population in wealth.[12]

Like all enslaved people, this Black family enslaved by the Turners spent their time at work. They farmed corn and tobacco and some cotton, raised cattle and hogs, and distilled brandy from the apples they grew. Slave-based agriculture paid in these years, and Benjamin Turner Jr. spent his profits on land and enslaved people, not material possessions. At his death in 1810, Benjamin Turner Jr. owned a modest house, a distillery, a barn, a stable, and the slave quarters, along with eight horses, ten saddles, nearly a thousand acres, and twenty-nine enslaved people.[13]

Benjamin Turner Jr. also owned seven walnut chairs and eighteen "sitting chairs," likely for the biracial Methodist classes and meetings in the house.[14] Until Nat was about seven years old, he and his family—including his beloved and pious grandmother—met in the home of their owner with "other religious persons who visited the house."[15] Other people who attended the Methodist meetings might have been Benjamin's brother Nathan, their neighbors Samuel and Sarah Francis, and John and Catherine Whitehead, along with an unnamed number of enslaved people.[16]

When Nat was seven, Benjamin Jr.'s son Samuel married Esther Francis, the child of neighbors and fellow Methodists. That fall Samuel and Esther moved eight enslaved people with them to a tract of land Samuel had recently bought. Among them were Nat, Lydia, and Nancy, a further suggestion (though of course not definitive evidence) that Lydia, then in her fifties, was the grandmother, and Nancy, then in her thirties, was the mother. With them were five other enslaved people, all children. For now, the enslaved people were not Samuel Turner's property, but they were subject to his control. Two years later, in 1809, just before Benjamin Jr. remarried, the father sold the land at a sharp discount to his son.[17]

The following year, in October 1810, three things happened that shaped Nat's upbringing. First, Benjamin Jr. deeded one acre to the local Methodist church for a meetinghouse. The deed stated that only Methodists could preach there. This would be the site of Turner's Meeting House, where Nat learned the faith. Then, five days later, Benjamin Jr. dictated a new will, splitting the rights to twenty-eight of the twenty-nine enslaved people among his sons, daughters, and wife, should they survive him. A month or two after that, Benjamin Turner Jr. died. He could have freed people in his will, but he didn't. He left Nat, Nancy, Lydia, and five others to his son Samuel.[18]

Samuel began the work of building that church, Turner's Meeting House, and also of expanding his holdings in enslaved people, many of whom in turn attended services there. In time Samuel, at least by local memory, became a church trustee.[19] The Turner families' simultaneous commitments to biracial Methodism and to enslavement shaped and tore at Nat. The white Turner family would lead him to Christ but not to freedom. It took time for this lesson to sink in, but it was becoming fearfully clear by 1810, at least in retrospect.

Perhaps Nat's father escaped not long after these transformations in October 1810, if indeed his father was Abraham. Abraham disappears from the records of enslaved people in 1811, roughly matching Nat's recollection of his father's flight. Nat never says what became of his father. Neighbors speculated for decades about his feat. Local whites believed that Nat's father was "very high-spirited" and was never recaptured. A Black oral tradition said that Nat's father had not run away at all but was taken by whites across the Meherrin River to neighboring Greensville County and sold to a slave trader heading south to Georgia's turpentine forests.[20]

In his private moments, Nat might have whispered prayers for his father to return to spirit them away. It was not inconceivable that his father was close enough to come back. It wasn't at all unusual for enslaved people to stay near their home places when they ran away, or even to run deeper into slave territory to check on extended family. If Nat's father was from Greensville County, perhaps Nat assumed he had gone there to check on his people. We have one potential analogue to ponder, a man with some geographic and perhaps family connections to Nat. In 1815 a twenty-three-year-old enslaved man called Arch, who was raised near Jerusalem, ran away from a jail in North Carolina. His enslaver took out an ad to offer a $25 reward to entice readers to capture and return him. That enslaver expected Arch to go by the name of Willis or James Turner, "both of which names he assumed on former attempts to pass as a free man," once by forging a pass. This man carried the scars of slavery: "He had the under part of right Ear cut off, and bears the mark of much whipping." The enslaver expected him not to run to the North but instead to "make for the lower part of the State again."[21]

The place of this man's raising and the choice of the Turner last name raise the possibility that this person not only paralleled Nat's father's choice but actually had been known to Nat's family, though we can never be certain. Still, the story suggests why Nat might have held out hope even as his father stayed gone, hope that his father enjoyed freedom and perhaps hope that his father would return to help them flee, too. He also likely felt dread that his father had already been captured and would never return. Perhaps his own feelings about his father's disappearance taught Nat the effects of such flight on the people left behind. Nat himself would run as a young man— but not far and not for long. And when he resisted slavery, he attacked it head-on, in a manner meant to save his family and everyone else.

IN BENJAMIN TURNER JR.'S house, and then in Turner's Meeting House, Black and white, family and faith, intersected. Neighborhood elders like Nat's parents and grandmother, unnamed Black women and men, and white people like Samuel and Sarah Francis, John and Catherine Whitehead, and Turner Newsom, along with Benjamin's brother Nathan, schooled Nat in the Methodist ways and praised him in a manner that would later seem to Nat a sign of his precocious and peculiar connection to God.[22] These were, Nat recalled in the *Confessions*, the people "by whom I had been taught to pray, both white and black."[23]

For Nat as for most early nineteenth-century Methodists, the method was in the meetings, not merely sites for sermons but participatory explorations of faith. While Methodism would turn toward Sunday schools and weekly services later in the nineteenth century, early Methodism grew from intimate Wesleyan societies, small classes of roughly a dozen people, and band meetings, where participants like Nat's family and the white Turners prayed, instructed one another, and held one another to account. Methodists might celebrate a love feast or Lord's Supper or hold "prayer meetings" under an elder or class leader who, according to Methodist *Discipline*, would ask them "how their souls prosper" and would "advise, reprove, comfort, or exhort as the occasion may require."[24] While Samuel Turner might have been the elder of Turner's Meeting House, Nat emphasized not the hierarchy but instead the general familiarity that prevailed among his family, their enslaver, "who belonged to the church, and other religious persons who visited the house."[25]

Up-country Virginia, including Southside, was fertile ground for Methodist and Baptist evangelizing like that taking place at Turner's Meeting House. As people moved deeper into the state, established Anglicans struggled to extend their older communities to these newer settlements.[26] Baptists led an awakening in Southampton County in the 1760s, and permanent Baptist congregations formed in 1774 at Mill Swamp and at the port at Old South Quay. A new congregation of Baptists opened in 1786 at Black Creek. Hebron Church on Flat Swamp, known also as Sturgeon's Meeting House and as Meherrin Church, was organized in 1788. An early nineteenth-century pastor at Hebron would be known as the "soldier preacher."[27]

The Methodist revival had been led by itinerant ministers, including the noted evangelist Francis Asbury, who preached in Southampton numerous times in the 1780s, likely in revivals attended by older people in Nat's childhood circle.[28] On the Brunswick Circuit that included Southampton, Freeborn Garrettson reported that prayer meetings lasted for six or seven hours and "five, eight, and ten are often converted at one meeting." At prayer meetings, "the power came down," and inspired followers then swelled class meetings.[29] A later 1801–1802 revival was not as strong in Southampton, perhaps because brandy and cider makers were becoming wary of the temperance message of some Methodist sermons.[30] Still, by the 1830s, there were Methodist churches at Mount Horeb, Barnes, Peete, Applewhite, and Clarksbury, which had originally been known as Turner. And the Christian church offshoot of Methodism organized two other congregations.[31]

Although the details of these revivals are scant, similar revivals in the era were marked by the proximity of Black and white converts. One Presbyterian pastor in eastern North Carolina remarked on a revival with two thousand people, including a "poor black man with his hands raised over the heads of the crowd, and shouting, 'Glory, glory to God on high.'" Near him was "another black man prostrate on the ground, and his aged mother on her knees at his feet in all the agony of prayer for her son" and a Black woman "grasping her mistress' hand." Next to them was a "little white girl." The historian Peter Hinks wrote, "At the height of these revivals the fundamental boundary between master and slave seemed to be disintegrating."[32]

After the revivals came regular church and class meetings that Nat would have attended, and at these Methodist churches the "pattern" had to be taught to children like Nat, the methods made, the habits acquired by repetition and imitation. The presence of God was not something that simply visited unsuspecting people, although at times it could be that; the presence of God was also a skill cultivated in practice. Thus Nat remembered "hearing the scriptures commented on at meetings."[33] Yet much of the teaching was implicit,[34] hinted at in sermons and class meetings,[35] modeled in the acts of other worshippers, and learned by repetition until peculiar practices became second nature. All the elements of what Methodists called public worship— hymn singing, scripture reading, preaching, and prayer—dramatized this evangelical experience.[36]

Methodists in this era wrestled with the balance between communal learning and individual relationships with God in ways that Nat would have absorbed and pondered. The experiences of contemporaneous Methodists, Black and white, offer some insight into how Methodists understood their personal connection with God. One such early nineteenth-century Methodist was Zilpha Elaw, a free Black woman. In Philadelphia in the 1810s, Elaw explained both the communal and the individual aspects of conversion. She compared the inspired example of her sister to iron sharpening iron. Members of the church "sat with her in their meetings, and received much edification from beholding the earnest devotedness of mind she manifested in the House of God." In turn Elaw's sister took her charge very seriously and "conducted herself very strictly and exemplarily in all her movements."[37] Still, it was not unusual for inspired Methodists to brush past the lessons of their lay teachers and to emphasize their individual relationship with God. "It was by the Lord alone that I was upheld, confirmed, instructed, sanctified, and directed," Elaw claimed.[38]

PERHAPS NAT LEARNED to read at these meetings, centered as they were on the Word, although the story persisted among Black Southampton County residents for generations that his precocious reading ability had arisen spontaneously in his walks in the surrounding woods. A white historian in 1900 wrote that it was "well known" that Nat's parents and his enslaver's son John Clark Turner, born a year after Nat (and conspicuously not attacked in the rebellion), had given him "instruction."[39] In the Confessions, Nat said he learned to read and write "with the most perfect ease, so that I have no recollection whatever of learning the alphabet" but that he simply began "spelling the names of different objects" in a book, showing off to the "neighborhood, particularly the blacks."[40] This reading prepared him to judge the claims of white congregants and, eventually, to develop his own interpretation of the Bible.

Even as a child, Nat thrived in these meetings, becoming adept at the imitation required of all aspiring Methodists, white and Black. He was, according to the Confessions, "observant of every thing that was passing,"[41] and he absorbed Bible passages and Methodist practices in these meetings.[42] Children like Nat typically watched adults repeat passages over and over, witnessed their jerks and writhing at moments of conversion, saw them clasp their hands and kneel, and learned the outward signs of approaching and experiencing God. In the process they also wrestled with a paradox: to find a living God, a Methodist could not just wait but had to prepare himself for God's visitation. These unusual experiences of God's presence were not distinct from the Methodist method but were to some degree their ultimate accomplishment, the most precious skill the method taught.[43]

The method was also in the music, the great concern of the Wesley brothers and of many of their followers around the world, and Nat would have frequently sung with white and Black Methodists at the beginning and end of services.[44] The Wesley brothers' *Collection of Hymns for the Use of the People Called Methodists* was a kind of self-fashioning evangelical autobiography, a mirror in which "real Christians" could recognize, model, and emulate Methodist piety.[45] In these hymns, Nat would have heard older Methodists praising and practicing fellowship, singing, "Let us each for other care, / Each the other's burden bear; To thy church the pattern give, / Show how true believers live."[46] The hymns also schooled Methodists in the quotidian ways of public worship and the private devotion to prayer, practices Nat seems to have absorbed rapidly and successfully.[47]

Prayer meetings were profoundly shaped by local people like the white Turners because official leadership was so thin. In the church hierarchy of Methodism, itinerant preachers traveled a "circuit" every four to six weeks. During the other weeks, the uninitiated and the spiritual strivers might take cues from their sisters and brethren and find themselves moved by the preaching to the point of "conversion," when a "mourning" and sinful Methodist might feel God's forgiveness. From there Wesleyans converted followers under the stewardship of the itinerant's local assistants, preachers, exhorters, and class leaders who presided over prayer meetings.[48]

In these meetings, the method turned upon prayer. Like other aspects of early nineteenth-century faith, prayer could appear to be something a believer simply did, and many believers in fact spoke of prayer in just these terms. But prayer like other forms of worship had to be learned through instruction and imitation until it came to seem natural. Prayers were calls for God's attention, and they had to be addressed in proper ways. The *Confessions* records only one of Nat's prayers, so we cannot know for sure what he typically prayed for. He was sorely in need of assurance, instruction, and guidance, and he, like many Methodists, likely prayed to approach a God who seemed near at hand.[49] "All my time, not devoted to my master's service, was spent either in prayer, or making experiments," Nat recalled.[50]

Between meetings, Methodists like other Christians found places of solitude to continue their prayer and contemplation. For Nat, that place was often the woods that surrounded his neighborhood, woods that served as pathways and barriers in this relatively rugged region. Four-fifths of the county remained woodlands, crossed by paths and roads that connected one farm to another.[51] Like his rough contemporary Joseph Smith in western New York and like Jesus in the deserts sometimes translated as wilderness, Nat found his personal vision in nature, where he could communicate directly with God.[52] For Methodist itinerants during the early republic like Zilpha Elaw, woodlands were the retreat for reflection and prayer, "seasons of sweet communion with my God."[53] Indeed, the woods would be the site of Nat's most astounding visions.

Nat's visions were unusual, but his method for approaching God was not; Nat's elders taught him and other converts how to detect the presence of God through their own stories of their encounters with the Lord. A sense of God's imminence, or even a feeling that God was speaking verses from the Bible, was part of the normal experience of religiosity for many awakened Americans, including those who would not consider themselves prophets.[54] Methodist hymns taught their singers to prepare to be seized by a "gracious Lord" who would "take possession" of them.[55] Charles G. Finney, the outstanding preacher in the Second Great Awakening, offered one of the most vivid descriptions of how he felt in God's presence. "The Holy Spirit descended upon me in a manner that seemed to go through me, body and soul. I could feel the impression, like a wave of electricity, going through and through me. Indeed it seemed to come in waves and waves of liquid love for I could not express it any other way," he recalled. "It seemed like the very breath of God."[56]

The pinnacle of the ecstatic experience of early Methodists was a vision of God, a noteworthy but by no means unheard-of or controversial event. Zilpha Elaw's long-sought conversion finally came when she had a vision during an imploring hymn. As she sang a verse beginning, "Oh, when shall I see Jesus," Elaw recalled, "I distinctly saw the Lord Jesus approach me with open arms."[57] These ecstatic religious experiences could be enfolded into normal religious practice, even by non-evangelicals, if they were limited to feelings of grace. Only if they turned to direct communication with God that went beyond repetition of the scripture did they edge into "enthusiasm."[58]

NAT'S EXPERIENCES WITH Methodism would come to seem unusual as the denomination changed in the United States, leading writers at times to confuse what made Nat distinct with what made the early nineteenth century distinct. In time, white Methodist practices would become more restrained and less ecstatic. In both the United States and Britain, white Methodists seeking respectability downplayed their enthusiasm and conformed to less evangelical practices. Sunday services and hierarchy would displace the centrality of the meeting, of the method. But in Nat's world, his quest for God and his devotion to prayer would have seemed comprehensible, even if precious and intense.

Black experiences with Methodism diverged over the nineteenth century from white people's. Although Methodism grew within prejudiced societies where slavery existed, its early manifestations broke down some racial barriers. The Wesleys wrote against slavery and prejudice, though their writing betrayed prejudices of their own. And eighteenth-century Methodist fellowships were often biracial, with people of different races belonging not just to the same denomination but to the same congregations and to the same services. There was nothing in the Wesleyan hymnal about segregation in heaven.

In fact Methodist ministers of color repeatedly pointed out the hypocrisy of white Methodists' prejudices, given the biblical and denominational teaching about brotherhood and unity. Critics like the Pequot minister William Apess were stinging as they deployed Methodist standards for judging white Methodists. Two years after Nat's rebellion, Apess appealed to "that God who is the maker and preserver both of the white man and the Indian . . . who will show no favor to outward appearances but will judge righteousness," and noted that Jesus and the apostles "certainly were not whites." Apess asked, "Did you ever hear or read of Christ teaching his disciples that they ought to despise one because his skin was different from theirs? . . . [D]id not he who completed the plan of salvation complete it for the whites as well as for the Jews, and others?" So why, Apess asked, "is not a man of color respected?"[59] Even if most Christians of color were not quite so outspoken, surely many contemplated those questions as they witnessed the cruelty of white American Christians.

For many Black Americans in the antebellum North—and some in southern cities—Methodism would divide between a white-dominated Methodist Episcopal Church and two Black denominations, the African Methodist Episcopal (AME) Church and the African Methodist Episcopal Zion Church. A key figure in the creation of the larger, Philadelphia-based AME church was Richard Allen, who converted at age seventeen to Methodism while enslaved, then purchased his freedom and gained authorization to preach at area churches, including Philadelphia's St. George's Methodist Episcopal. After whites segregated and abused Black members at St. George's, Allen helped lead a walkout that sparked the creation of a new church, and eventually the founding of a new denomination. A parallel movement in New York led to the creation of the smaller AME Zion. The AME spread quickly across the North and to some southern cities, including Charleston, South Carolina, where Denmark Vesey might have helped lead an AME church that might have included David Walker. Publicly Allen chastised white people for their support for slavery, reminding them that God would not forgive their sins. But he also insisted on their potential redemption and on Black people's need to love white people. Still, some dissenting Black Methodists claimed that Allen privately called white people "evil." David Walker likewise acknowledged white people's potential salvation while also stating that "the whites have always been an unjust, jealous, unmerciful, avaricious and blood-thirsty set of beings, always seeking after power and authority." While he called himself "divested of prejudice," Walker asked, "whether they are *as good by nature* as we are or not . . . [B]ut this . . . is shut up with the Lord."[60]

Nat gave no indication of his childhood questions about the moral nature of the white people who taught him Methodism. Surely, he must have wondered at their ability to profess love of Christ and love of God's creation as they enslaved their fellow believers. When he witnessed cruelty or the transfer of enslaved people from one site to another, so, too, might he have wondered whether white Virginians were—or even could be—Christians. Perhaps he pondered these questions at age thirteen in 1813 when he might have heard that enslaved people from nearby counties were escaping to the British lines and taking up arms against the slaveholders in the Colonial Marines. Yet he kept quiet about this in his *Confessions*.

The Methodism of Nat's childhood was torn by the issue of slavery. An enslaved person owned by awakened evangelicals had good reason to hope for manumission in the late eighteenth century, the years just before Nat was born. In that period Methodists lobbied for abolition—the end of slavery—and encouraged manumission: the freeing of individual enslaved people. While abolition failed, individual emancipation had a dramatic effect upon the neighborhood where Nat lived. By 1830, there were 1,745 free Black people in Southampton County, one of the larger populations in the state, though a small number compared with the county's 7,756 enslaved people. This number of resident free Black people did not include those people who had left the county following manumission. Some of those who remained lived around the Turners, carried the Turner name, and were well known to Nat and his family.[61] Some of these people worked on farms; others owned small amounts of property.

The first antislavery denomination in Southampton County was the Quakers who moved there during the early eighteenth century, before the evangelical revivals. By 1776, Southampton Quakers renounced slaveholding in the Black Creek Friends Meeting. Quakers remained unusually prominent in and around Southampton County, naturalizing the presence of antislavery talk in a slaveholding region.[62]

In the decades before Nat's birth, Black congregants entered Virginia Methodist and Baptist churches in large numbers, spurring debates about the righteousness of slavery. These struggles were doubly intimate, not only between pro-slavery and pro-manumission white members but also between white members and their growing number of Black congregants. During the Great Revival of 1785 to 1792, Virginia Baptists tripled their membership, and Black Baptists rose from 11 percent of the state membership in 1780 to 28 percent by 1790. The same trends shaped the Methodism that Nat grew up within. Methodists more than tripled in the state between 1786 and 1792. The number of Black Methodists increased by a factor of 9 between 1786, when there were only 379, and 1792, when there were 3,494. The proportion of Black Methodists to total Methodists rose from less than 10 percent to 21 percent in these years.[63]

In Southampton, the first non-Quaker sect to struggle over slavery was the Baptist Church. This debate began not long after David Barrow began preaching at the Black Creek Baptist Church in the 1770s. Although Barrow had enslaved people, he freed them by 1784. In 1786, Black Creek Baptist declared slavery unrighteous. What this meant in practice was harder to say, because more than one-third of the members continued to claim enslaved people. By the 1790s the church had turned against its antislavery stance, and opponents of slavery boycotted Communion in protest. In 1798, Barrow left the area for Kentucky. But the fires of antislavery evangelicalism had not been entirely extinguished at the congregation. In 1825, a different pastor shocked the church when he said that he would not administer the Gospel because "a Part of the church were slave holders." After debate the church expelled this pastor.[64]

For Methodists the struggle was more prolonged and perhaps more agonizing. Black Methodists largely remained within interracial churches governed by a broader conference organization that encouraged, even required, regional and national debates that the Baptists worked to submerge in individual congregation decisions. As Black preachers arose within Methodism, they at times preached to biracial groups. In turn, biracial class meetings and small congregations like Turner's made the questions immediately personal and visible.

In the years before Nat was born, American Methodists wrestled with the righteousness of slavery, torn between their leaders' opposition to slavery and their own place in an independent nation where slavery thrived. John Wesley's *Discipline*, his explication of God's will and of the obligations attendant on Methodists, prohibited buying and selling slaves and excluded slave traders from membership in the church.[65] In *Thoughts upon Slavery* in 1774, Wesley grounded his condemnation of slavery in natural rights, calling slavery in the West Indies a "violation of justice, mercy and truth."[66] During Britain's struggle with the North American colonies, Wesley sided with the empire and amplified his opposition to slavery. In a dozen essays between 1768 and 1782, he cast the monarchy as the only safeguard for religious and civil liberty, posed the struggle between the Crown and the North American colonies as a fight between order and mob rule, and chided self-styled Patriots for contending for their own liberties while holding slaves.[67]

These Wesleyan teachings against slavery, still important in the lifetimes of Nat's parents, likely helped shape his parents' hopes that Nat's special talents would earn him emancipation. Even as white American Methodists retreated from the Wesleys' Loyalism, they for a time continued their antislavery course.[68] In 1784, they added new rules to the *Discipline* that barred slaveholders from joining the church and gave Methodist slaveholders twelve months to manumit their slaves. The rules, however, granted an additional year for slaveholders in Virginia, home to more slaveholders as well as more Methodists than any other state in the fledgling republic. If the compromise with Virginia was characteristic of the evangelicals' ultimate resolution of the slavery question, this final outcome was not apparent during the 1780s, when antislavery seemed ascendant among both Methodists and Baptists. The English minister Francis Asbury and the U.S. bishop Thomas Coke agreed at the Baltimore Christmas Conference of 1784 to "extirpate this abomination from among us" and initiated a major Methodist campaign against slavery. In 1785, itinerant Methodist preachers in Virginia circulated petitions urging the state legislature to abolish slavery. The Southside circuit leader James O'Kelly led these attacks on slavery, working closely with Black Methodists and increasing Black membership.[69] The petitions from Methodists invoked the Revolution, arguing that "Liberty is the Birthright of Mankind."[70]

But these petitions inspired a bitter counterpetition campaign by pro-slavery activists who raised doubts about the loyalty and reliability of Methodists and Baptists. More than a thousand Virginians signed petitions supporting slavery, basing their arguments on biblical justifications. Bishop Coke was threatened by a "mob" with "staves and clubs." In fear for his denomination's future growth, and perhaps for his own safety, Coke decided it would be "prudent" to retreat from the attack on slavery and to avoid giving "much offense."[71] After independence, Freeborn Garrettson, a Chesapeake itinerant who had been imprisoned for his refusal to serve in the Patriot army, returned from Nova Scotia and retreated from his previously sharp antislavery stance, urging but not requiring manumission and accommodating those who refused.[72] Garrettson and Coke likely held to their prior beliefs even as they held their tongues; it was just simpler to pronounce slaveholding a matter of conscience than to continue facing intense hostility.[73]

In the decade before Nat's birth, Methodists beat a steady retreat. In the summer of 1785, the denomination's Baltimore Conference retracted the rules on manumission.[74] Meanwhile, across the sea, the Methodist founder, John Wesley, never let up his critique. In 1791, in the last letter of his life, Wesley urged William Wilberforce to persist in the abolition campaign against "that execrable villainy, which is the scandal of religion, of England, and of human nature . . . till even American slavery (the vilest that ever saw the sun) shall vanish away."[75] In 1798, Methodist bishops issued a revised *Discipline* that condemned slavery as an "enormous evil" but advised preachers to reinforce the holiness of enslaved people's obligations to masters when they ministered to the enslaved.[76] Still some prominent Methodists along with some Baptists continued manumitting enslaved people. In 1790 the Methodist minister Edward Mitchell freed fourteen people because it "is contrary to the Principals of Christianity to hold our Fellow Creatures in Bondage." Methodist ministers with antislavery zeal continued to encourage individual grants of freedom in some areas even as they found it impossible to make headway in others.[77]

While the national debate continued, there were signs that the movement was dying in Virginia. As whites brought more enslaved people into the piedmont and the backcountry, and as enslavers sold people farther south into the Carolinas and Georgia, it became much more profitable to keep enslaved people than to free them. A moment was passing. In 1792, James O'Kelly, discouraged by the stance of Southside Methodists, led a group out of the Methodist church, and many Black members went with him.[78]

In 1800, the year Nat was born, antislavery American Methodists made their last stand. At the General Conference, where the church adopted policies for Wesleyans nationwide, a prominent adviser to Bishop Francis Asbury suggested "that from this time forth no slaveholder shall be admitted into the Methodist Episcopal Church." Two other resolutions proposed that Methodists emancipate all children born to enslaved parents after Independence Day 1800 and manumit the rest of their slaves within one year. The conference voted down all three resolutions. That year, for the last time, Methodist groups urged state legislatures to abolish slavery.[79] The triumph of slaveholders in

Methodism was just one of their victories. The spread of slavery in Kentucky and Tennessee—newly admitted in the 1790s—was evidence of the growth of the slave-based economy and of slave state power in national politics, confirmed over Nat's lifetime by the admission of the slave states of Louisiana, Mississippi, and Alabama in the 1810s and Missouri in 1821.

As Nat became a precocious toddler and impressed his neighbors with his gifts, Methodists settled on a prudential compromise, making slavery a question of individual conscience, encouraging but not requiring manumission. The general conference that rejected the resolutions on emancipation put a bold face on voluntary manumissions as "a blow at the root to the enormous evil." The conference's address struck chords of republican principle and evangelical duty in a fulsome condemnation of slavery as "repugnant to the unalienable rights of mankind, and to the very essence of civil liberty, but more especially to the spirit of Christian religion." The church resolved to form committees "of the most respectable of our friends" to sponsor petitions in favor of legislation permitting manumission in states where it was not yet legally allowed. Where Methodists once lobbied to end slavery, now they lobbied simply for the right to emancipate individual enslaved people. By 1804, the general conference had withdrawn the call for petitions.[80]

FOR ALL THE EQUIVOCATIONS of the early nineteenth century, the Methodist position still created space for Black families like Nat's to bargain for individual freedom. Despite the shift against obligatory emancipation, skilled preachers like Garrettson could still turn sermons and testimony toward a hope that individual slave owners might be moved to demonstrate God's power by freeing their own slaves.[81]

In Nat's childhood, during the gradual Methodist retreat from manumission, his family appears to have opened a subtle high-stakes negotiation with the white Turners for Nat's freedom. To follow this, we have to read behind the lines of Nat's elliptical but revealing statements in the *Confessions*. His owners and their religious-minded visitors, he recalled, "noticing the singularity of my manners, I suppose, and my uncommon intelligence for a child, remarked I had too much sense to be raised, and . . . would never be of any service to any one as a slave." Evidence of Nat's precocious intellectual abilities, his seemingly effortless learning of the alphabet, and his uncanny knowledge of events that transpired before his birth generated a reputation that his abilities were "perfected by Divine inspiration." The parties to the negotiation were not equal, nor were the negotiations themselves formal or even necessarily explicit. But Nat's family appears to have endeavored to improve the balance of power by cultivating neighborhood support for Nat's manumission among white and Black Methodists. Nat's stories of his precocity were likely the foundations of his family's case as they talked up their beloved boy's spiritual gifts, spreading the word one feat at a time along with their own exalted interpretation of each act's prophetic import. The Methodists passed these stories along. The case for his manumission grew with his reputation for divine inspiration. So it was that Nat's family likely encircled the white Turners with Methodist believers in Nat's spiritual gifts.[82]

Nat's family had reason for hope. Despite the pro-slavery tide, Virginia remained a site of widespread manumission, especially among Methodists. Virginia had made legal provisions for manumission in 1782, and Methodists took advantage of them.[83] The Tidewater region that stretched to the edges of Southampton was the site of the largest number of manumissions at the turn of the century. By 1830, 13.5 percent of the Black population of the Tidewater was free.[84] In this region Methodists accounted for about half the religious people who manumitted slaves into the mid-nineteenth century.[85] Enslaved people in two counties adjoining Southampton—Isle of Wight and Surry—had some of the best chances of manumission of any county in the state. More than five hundred enslaved people in these two counties gained their freedom in 1782–1806.[86] Eighty-three enslaved people in Isle of Wight were freed by one owner alone in 1802.[87]

Traveling or itinerant ministers who rode circuit led the Methodist fight for manumission in their trips to Turner's Meeting House and
other Southampton meetings. In the historical record, these figures
often disappear behind the local preachers who tended to leave better records and longer-lasting impressions, but they played important
roles in spreading the faith. Although Virginia was exempted from
the early requirement that itinerants manumit slaves, in 1795 Virginia
itinerants voluntarily agreed not to hold slaves or ordain slaveholders.[88] Bishops persisted in urging preachers to speak against slavery
even as the church began to publicly back away from abolition.[89] On
itinerants, Methodists, too, retreated, opening up loopholes and by
1808 ending the requirement that enslavers hear about the church's
opposition to slavery and hopes for manumission.[90]

Manumissions were clustered around the sorts of intimate networks that enmeshed the Turner family and other Black and white
Methodists in their neighborhood.[91] In Isle of Wight County, just
east of Southampton, manumission followed kinship ties, as James
Gwaltney and then two of his adult sons emancipated people.[92] Manumissions by up to sixteen enslavers coursed through another clan of
intermarried families, some of whom had ties to Southampton: the
Johnsons, Outlands, Ducks, Butlers, and Jordans.[93] Notwithstanding
the rare concentration of Quakers in Isle of Wight, Methodists also
stood out among manumitting slaveholders in that county. Two Methodist brothers-in-law, Andrew Woodley and the preacher William
Blunt, both emancipated slaves. The minister David Bradley, a protégé
of the Methodist antislavery radical James O'Kelly, freed the people he
enslaved and witnessed manumissions by three other slaveholders.[94]

But the motives for these manumissions were changing exactly
as Nat was born. Manumissions between 1782 and the early 1790s
were often explained as acts against the institution of slavery, perfor-
mances of a holy obligation. Some of these enslavers freed all their
people, a sign of their opposition to the institution. Some then employed the freed people as workers; others kept close tabs on them;
others encouraged the freed people to leave the state. But between

the mid-1790s and 1806, manumissions became understood as ways of buttressing slavery by rewarding individual enslaved people, usually older slaves, for their loyalty. In part this defense of slavery even among emancipators reflected their own simple self-interest; they could make money selling younger enslaved people to Georgia or Alabama even as they rewarded a few middle-aged people for their service. Manumission became a prize, not a weapon.[95]

Legally, the routes for Nat's manumission were diminishing as he aged from toddlerhood into childhood. Emancipations had been based in a 1782 manumission law that permitted freed Black people to remain in the state. In the nineteenth century, the state's leading figures, fearful of the Haitian Revolution and Gabriel's rebellion, worked to stanch the growth of a large free Black community. Between 1803 and 1806, when Nat would have been between three and six years old, the legislature weighed stringent limits on manumission and eventually passed a law requiring that free people leave the state or risk sale. Support for these laws was especially strong in counties with high proportions of enslaved people, including the Turners' Southampton County. Delegates from those largely slave-occupied counties favored the law by a margin of ten to one and voted for a broader bill prohibiting all manumission by two to one. While Southampton's representatives split on the 1803 bill, they voted unanimously in favor of the 1806 effort.[96]

The legislature meant to slow manumissions, and that was precisely the act's effect. Manumissions declined markedly after the expulsion act. Some owners seem to have reconsidered the wisdom of emancipation out of fears for the future of expelled Black people or about the opinions of their neighbors.[97] Freed people could, of course, simply ignore the statute and remain in place, and many did, but theirs was a perilous existence, since the law opened the door to selling them back into slavery.[98] Over time the legislature narrowed the few exceptions, eventually permitting only those who could prove a particular act of meritorious service to remain freely in Virginia.[99]

Nat's family was apparently making an argument from a past era, suggesting that Nat deserved manumission not for his meritorious service but for his precocious intellectual abilities and spiritual gifts. His family retold stories of his intelligence, his uselessness in the fields. Nat seems to have sustained this effort during his adolescence as he tried to live up to his reputation's demands. The neighborhood's "belief was ever afterwards zealously inculcated by the austerity of my life and manners, which became the subject of remark by white and black."[100]

Despite the gloomy portents, Nat's family had reason close at hand to believe that local Methodists, including the Turners, were open to their pleas. One piece of evidence was a figure who attended Turner's Meeting House and was apparently well known to young Nat: Benjamin Turner Jr.'s brother Nathan. Like Benjamin Jr., Nathan inherited the rights to several enslaved people, but he died holding only two. Benjamin Jr. and Nathan's brother Henry went much further. Although Henry had died eight years before Nat was born, his decisions and the decisions of his children were likely known to Nat's mother and grandmother. The historian David Allmendinger suggests that Henry gave up market crops entirely, leaving no record in his estate of tobacco, corn, or cotton. Instead, he shifted his property to two mills and two stores. In his will, Henry freed ten people without any obligation and promised manumission to an eleventh if that enslaved person earned sixty pounds through hiring out. The process of emancipation dragged on as Henry's widow likely claimed a right to the enslaved people's labor, but by 1800, the year of Nat's birth, nine of the eleven people were free, and by 1806, when Nat was reading and showing off to area Methodists, at least ten of those eleven were free.[101]

That legacy continued among Benjamin Jr.'s nieces and nephews. Three of Henry Turner's four children never left a record of owning an enslaved person, according to Allmendinger. The fourth paid tax on a single enslaved person for 1812 and 1813, as Nat was becoming what we would call a teenager. And the people those Turners freed stayed close to home. At least eight free people of color took the last name of Turner, one buying thirty-six acres on the Flat Swamp, others living and working right in Nat's neighborhood, alongside families of freed people like the Artis family. By the time of Nat's rebellion in 1831, Henry Turner was among the most influential emancipators in county history measured by the number of formerly enslaved people who stayed in the county. We cannot know for certain the role of Methodism in turning Henry and his children against slavery, but we can understand why Nat's mother and grandmother clung to hope.

On Samuel Turner's land lived another person who might have interested Nat: a free Black man with the name that perhaps also belonged to Nat's father—Abraham Turner. While Nat's father was not freed, this Abraham had been enslaved by Samuel's uncle Henry and then made free by Henry's will. Freedom might turn on something as small as which of the Turner brothers enslaved a family. But Abraham was an emblem of a day gone by, not a time to come, surrounded as he was by dozens of enslaved people.[102]

Indeed, Benjamin Turner Jr. was not following the path of his brother Henry or even the more limited path of his brother Nathan. Instead, Benjamin Turner Jr. had expanded his holdings both in land and in enslaved people. His brothers and their families edged away from slavery, but he did not.[103] As Nat approached adulthood, it became clear that his family had failed to convince the white Turners. The lives of the white Turners suggest years when Nat's parents might have held out special hopes and found them disappointed. In 1807, Benjamin Turner Jr. decided on the future of Nat, but instead of freeing the child, he bequeathed Nat to his own son Samuel. Around 1809, Samuel made it clear that he meant to exploit the boy's labor and started working him in the fields.[104] He might be a prophet in training, but he would not be freed for his gifts.

In fact, Samuel married even more deeply into the world of enslavement. His wife, Esther, was the daughter of Samuel Francis, a landowner who lived three-quarters of a mile from Samuel Turner's father, running a farm with ten enslaved people of taxable age. Her family lived in a small house, sixteen feet square, saving their money for purchasing enslaved people. When Esther's father and one sister died, Samuel Turner administered the estate, giving him control of nearly fifty enslaved people for a time. When Esther's brother died in 1819, Turner once again served as executor, transferring to his family members the rights to the enslaved people.[105]

The estate of Samuel Francis, father of Nat's second "mistress," reveals the intimate geography of the rebellion to come. Samuel Francis died early in 1815; his daughter Esther followed either later that year or in 1816. Four of Samuel Francis's heirs would be among Nat's targets: his widow, Sarah; sons Nathaniel and Salathiel; and daughter Sally. Three of the enslaved people in Samuel Francis's will would figure in the uprising.[106]

In 1818, when Nat turned eighteen, Samuel Turner remarried another Methodist, Mrs. Elizabeth Reese Williamson, whose family owned 849 acres and about twenty-five enslaved people in the west of the county. She brought more enslaved people into the family holdings, as well as control of enslaved people held in trust for her daughter by a previous marriage. Moores, Reeses, Turners, and Francises, connected by marriage, continued to worship together at Turner's Meeting House, as did many of the people they enslaved. Together the families Samuel Turner was connected to held seventy-five enslaved people.[107]

Samuel lived in a relatively large house, a story and a half tall and perhaps forty feet wide, on grounds that included more than thirty enslaved people legally owned by different estates and in trust for different children. Samuel and his white family did not live a fancy life, saving their money for buying more enslaved people. In Samuel's lifetime, Virginia's economy began to turn from tobacco to cotton, and Samuel followed suit, dropping tobacco entirely, growing more cotton, and raising dozens of cattle and hogs.[108]

Around 1820, Nat reached another milestone when he approached what he called a "man's estate."[109] It was a peculiar turn of phrase on an enslaved person's part, with its echoes of law and property. The law did not recognize slave adulthood through such milestones as marriage and the ownership of property, but the law in some ways did denote crucial ages for enslaved people, including emancipation laws that set the age of male manumission at twenty-one.[110] Thus the campaign by Nat's family for their son's emancipation likely reached a milestone in the fall of 1821 as he approached the minimum age of manumission. A dream, long fostered and worried over, began to wither, with imaginable but untold effects on the spirits of Nat, his mother, and his grandmother.

Five months later, in 1822, Samuel Turner died, likely spurring another round of hope for Nat's family and other enslaved people. Samuel Turner died slowly, and enslaved people would have had time to wonder about what came next.[111] Of those owners who manumitted people, many did so through their wills, and enslaved people knew it. But Samuel left his land to his brother, and the rights to his enslaved people to his daughter Polly. Nat was listed first on the estate settlement, one of the two most valuable enslaved people in the tally. Listed, too, was Lydia, likely his grandmother, and Nancy or Anne, likely his mother.[112]

Everyone now knew that death would not bring deliverance. Six of Samuel Turner's family members died young between 1810 and 1820. Beyond the Turner family, one-third of the men who owned property in the parish in 1821 had died by 1831, according to the work of Allmendinger; half of the enslaved people of taxable age in the parish in 1821 had experienced the death of an enslaver by 1831. Almost one-quarter of all the land in the parish in 1831 remained under the control of estates. In the neighborhood, none of the 100 white people who owned enslaved people in 1821 and survived to 1831 recorded an act of manumission, and of the 101 enslavers who died in that period, only 4 attempted to free any people. Death swept through the neighborhood, but it no longer brought freedom.[113]

Nat then entered a time when he was passed among different family members. While he remained the property of Polly, Samuel's thirteen-year-old daughter, he was put under the control of Polly's aunt and uncle, Thomas Moore and Sally Francis Moore. Later in the decade, he possibly was hired to a neighbor, then put under the control of Sally Francis Moore's next husband. Seven people claimed legal power over Nat during his life, sending him as an inheritance, a gift, a loan, a sale, a hire out, a person controlled in trust. Several people could have freed him; none did. All were tied, most of them intimately, to the Methodist Church. Perhaps Nat's understanding of his future came down to a basic fact: like his father, but unlike his uncle, Samuel Turner had not manumitted anyone in his will.[114]

AS HE MOVED into early adulthood, Nat would have likely salted pork in the winter and waited out the freezes and cold snaps. Around March he would have begun to plant corn, then sweet potatoes, then cotton, then pea vines once the cornstalks were tall enough to support them, and then in late July or early August he would have begun chopping weeds and topping cotton. If agricultural work slacked in late summer, white and Black people held larger religious camp meetings in the county or across the state line in North Carolina. By August, the first apples and peaches were ripe, and the enslaved people went to work picking, then making cider and brandy, then corn fodder. They harvested peas and cotton bolls. In the late fall they shucked corn, often in large gatherings. Then it was winter again.[115] Nat and most enslaved people likely lived in log cabins, most no more than sixteen feet square, often daubed with mud to keep out the wind.[116] The cabins were near one another, and generally quite close to the house of the enslavers. Beyond the dwellings of enslaved people were pathways through the woods to other clusters of enslaved people that constituted the neighborhood, pathways that ran along creeks and swamps, areas difficult to farm.[117]

It is possible that around this time Nat's life changed in a marked way. Reports at the time of the rebellion and local Black memories point to Nat marrying in his early adulthood. Just after the rebellion, two correspondents from the area referred to "his wife," who had given up some of Nat's notes "under the lash." However, no other record from the period refers to her, including testimony from enslaved and free Black witnesses in the fall of 1831. The record of Nat's lengthy statements in the jail includes references to his mother, grand-mother, and father, among others, but not a wife. But then, seventy years after the uprising, a trained white historian who grew up in the area recorded that locals said Nat fathered a son named Redic.[118]

Over the twentieth century, scholars focused upon a woman some-times named Cherry, sometimes Chary, who appears in a number of documents recorded in Nat's neighborhood of Cross Keys, includ-ing in the will of Benjamin Turner Jr., who left her rights to Samuel Turner. Somehow she passed to the estate of Joseph Reese Sr., who had been a tenant at Benjamin Turner's plantation. The list of Joseph Reese Sr.'s enslaved people included a child named Riddick, proba-bly the youngest boy on the plantation. Then the 1870 census records a Cherrie Turner living in the parish, aged sixty-five, and also lists, just across the Meherrin River in Greensville County, a Black man named Riddick Turner, fifty years old. It is possible these are Nat's wife and child. If so, Cherry likely lived on the same farm with Nat for much of their young life, but then they were separated in 1817–1819, when Joseph Reese Sr. moved away. The Reeses headed seven miles north to Three Creeks. If so, it would make sense that this separation further angered Nat. But he did not say so.[119]

Other sources offer other suggestions. Lucy Mae Turner wrote a two-part published essay in the mid-twentieth century, claiming that Nat's wife was named Fanny and was Lucy Mae Turner's own grand-mother through Nat's alleged son Gilbert. A recent work of scholar-ship traces Nat's descendants through Sidney Turner, a farmer who bought land in the area and walked his grandchildren around the woods, pointing to sites where Nat was captured.[120] In the end, local memory, careful historical work, and deduction lead us only so far, es-pecially in a region with many people named Turner. And we can only speculate on how marriage and fatherhood shaped Nat's life. But we have much testimony from other enslaved people about the painful effects of separation from spouses and children.

It is also possible that there were whispers of rebellion in 1821 that could have shaped Nat's expectations. In that year, an enslaved man named Dread, whose enslaver lived in the parish, broke into a store in Jerusalem and stole extraordinary amounts of money—thousands of dollars by one report—and hundreds of dollars' worth of merchandise. One person said Dread hoped to persuade someone to buy his freedom. That same year, a farmer and his wife four miles southeast of town were murdered in bed, and two enslaved people were hanged for the crime. How much these events shaped Nat's view of slavery is impossible to untangle since there is no record of his referring to them. But events like these were common in the history of slavery; we know other enslaved people watched resistance carefully for signs of what worked and what didn't, what led to a pathway toward freedom, and what to a crackdown that threatened everyone.[121]

However marriage and fatherhood and local strife shaped him, Nat reached adulthood around 1821 or 1822. He seemed to recognize a sharp break in his own life story, perhaps a recognition that voluntary legal freedom was not imminent. Nat withdrew from the neighborhood to fast and pray. Having grown up amid a family campaign waged through faith for his manumission, Nat seems to have begun to wonder what his future held. He continued to pray on a particular passage of scripture from the Sermon on the Mount he had often heard at prayer meetings: "Seek ye the kingdom of Heaven and all things shall be added unto you."[122] Like most Methodists, Nat understood prayer to be a method for resolving the doubts and uncertainty in his heart. He prayed because he needed direction.

Likely Nat wondered what lay ahead for him. One path was to grow into the role of spiritually gifted man of color, a position that offered status and sometimes escape from hard labor, but also entailed grave, possibly unbearable, obligations to white patrons who demanded control over the sermons and the congregation. There was reason to think this path was available to him. Had Nat lived in a city and been able to preach in an AME church, perhaps he might have followed that route, although the early 1820s destruction of the Charleston AME church suggests the perilous nature of that work. But even in white-controlled Methodist and Baptist churches there was a pathway to the ministry. By the 1810s, as manumission faded among Methodists, Black preachers became more common. In the 1810s and 1820s, more enslaved and free Black ministers were licensed than at any time before the Civil War. And a number of churches in Southampton, both Baptist and Methodist, had large numbers of Black members.[123]

We might see one glimpse of that future in a book titled *The African Preacher*, set partly in Nottoway County at the mouth of the river that bisects Southampton. This biography was penned by a white Virginia Presbyterian minister, William S. White, and published by the Philadelphia Presbyterian Board of Publication in 1849. While it provides extensive details on the Preacher's adulthood, the biographical sketch is very limited. In some respects, the African Preacher's story was markedly different from Nat's; neither born in Southside Virginia nor raised in a biracial Methodist conventicle, the African Preacher was taken from his African family at about seven years old, sold into the transatlantic slave trade, bought at a landing on the James River in the 1750s, and only converted to Christianity as an adult in the 1780s.[124] Widely known as Jack or Uncle Jack, the African Preacher became an exhorter among slaves in his Virginia neighborhood and often traveled as far as thirty miles to preach, first as a Baptist and then as a Presbyterian. When his owner died, white Presbyterian admirers helped him raise the money to purchase his freedom.[125]

In some respects a figure like the African Preacher might have appealed to young Nat. The African Preacher was admired for his common sense, his character, and his biblical knowledge.[126] White ministers widely acknowledged learning from him, and laypeople sought out his counsel.[127] The African Preacher's oratorical powers gave him an authority to render judgments on white people that Nat might have appreciated, but the preacher had to rely on the art of indirection. Choosing the right targets for critique was important to the African Preacher's appeal, even his survival, and he reserved some of his sharpest words for unconverted men, already in low repute, comparing some to hogs.[128] As much as Nat might have enjoyed gaining such a purchase on white people, his spiritual abilities did not necessarily come with the African Preacher's discretion, nor his "meekness and humility."[129] It was not for Nat to be, like the African Preacher, "patient and submissive in the endurance of evil."[130]

Nor would Nat likely have embraced the African Preacher's willingness to silence disorderly enslaved people, nor the Baptist minister's role in punishing enslaved people. At nearby South Quay Baptist, enslaved members were disciplined in Nat's boyhood for hiding stolen goods, attending races, fighting, selling alcohol, drinking, and other minor infractions, including the expulsion of an enslaved woman for "disorderly conduct toward her master and mistress."[131] We don't know the full extent of the African Preacher's disciplinary role, but the biographer hinted at it when he claimed that "all feared him."[132] Nat evinced no interest in regulating other enslaved people in his neighborhood.

Perhaps Nat in the early 1820s still held hopes that his fasting and prayer would lead him to a calling in his family's Methodism. If so, he might have been following in the path of a formerly enslaved Virginian named George White. Born on the eastern shore of the Chesapeake and raised for a time on the bay's western shore, White was converted in New York in 1795 during a night watch service at the Bowery Church. White sought licensing as an itinerant preacher but was rejected four times. Fearing that he would never be accepted by the Methodist episcopate, White approached "the very borders of despair; yet the Lord soon revived my soul again, by revealing himself." To reach the Lord, White turned, like Nat, to fasting and prayer. "I neglected no means, which I thought would be beneficial to my own soul: but particularly fasting and prayer. And what I did myself, I exhorted others to do likewise." White's revelation came to him in a dream. "In my sleep, a man appeared to me, having under his care a flock of sheep." The man separated some of the sheep and asked White to look after them. "I told him I was no shepherd," but the man left them with White anyway. White tried to find out his name, but the man "replied that it was enough for me to know that he was a shepherd." The vision gave him the strength to apply for his license once again, successfully this time.[133] While White enjoyed a certain high stature, Nat would have seen how Black ministers like White were stifled in the Methodist church, especially enslaved ministers who answered not only to the church and circuit but also to their enslaver.

So as Nat approached a "man's estate" in the early 1820s, he kept to himself as much as he could, "devoting my time to fasting and prayer." He retreated in prayer to protect his neighborhood reputation for God-given gifts. "Having soon discovered to be great, I must appear so," he recalled, according to the *Confessions*. He "studiously avoided mixing in society, and wrapped myself in mystery." Whether these words are Gray's or Nat's, they pithily capture his dilemma. His neighbors continued to believe in his "Divine inspiration," but he had yet to make good on his parents' conviction that he might become a prophet. The studied display of self-control might not have secured his freedom, but it contributed to the belief that he was touched by God and it probably helped preserve his reputation. "The austerity of my life and manners," Nat said in the *Confessions*, "became the subject of remark by white and black."[134]

In his own fasting and prayer, Nat was trying to conjure the presence of God.[135] One of the psalms of David is a prayer by a fasting David to the Lord to take up arms—shield, spear, and javelin—and "fight against those who fight against me!"[136] Like David, Nat's fasting and prayer would bring him in his twenties to a very different revelation from George White's, and his story to a very different turn.

3

Nat, Fearful Prophet

In his early twenties, Nat faced the hard fact that his religious gifts might not exempt him from a lifetime of enslaved labor. His family's hopes for his manumission had been disappointed. What then lay ahead for him?

Nat looked to God for answers. To approach God, Nat reached back to a verse frequently invoked at the "meetings" at Turner's Meeting House: "Seek ye the kingdom of Heaven and all things shall be added unto you." He "reflected much on this passage, and prayed daily for light on this subject." Again and again, he repeated the verse. He wondered as he worked the field, praying at his plow.[1]

Then God answered. "The spirit spoke to me, saying, 'Seek ye the kingdom of Heaven and all things shall be added to you.'" This was Nat's first direct engagement with the Spirit, and in many ways his least surprising one. Later, Nat would see visions that the Spirit prepared for him, visions that went well beyond the words he first heard in his early twenties.

But in this first visitation, the Spirit did not say anything that disrupted the world, did not raise the specter of immediate revelation; the Spirit simply repeated the biblical verse. Still, the fact that Nat heard a voice speaking directly to him raised questions, especially in light of what the voice would later say. Nat recognized the consequences of his claims. When he told this to the local attorney Thomas Gray during the 1831 jailhouse confession interviews, Gray interrupted the tale with a simple but important question: "What do you mean by the Spirit?"

"The Spirit that spoke to the prophets in former days," Nat replied.[2]

With this phrase, Nat retrospectively placed himself in a line stretching back to the Hebrew Bible. He was a prophet.

But Nat's later confidence might have masked what appear to be his early doubts. While we know Nat and other prophets through their uncanny certainty—their confidence about things no human can normally say with assurance—Nat's life and the *Confessions* seem on closer look to be plagued by doubts as Nat pondered that voice he heard in the fields and wondered if he truly understood God's call. In the *Confessions*, Nat (or perhaps Thomas Gray) repressed those doubts, but they become apparent when the text is read carefully and with an eye to its omissions. When Nat did finally act in 1831, nine years after his first vision, the boldness of his strike erased observers' ability to grasp Nat's own worries, just as the explicitly voiced fears of the Hebrew Bible prophets are often overshadowed by the acts that come to define them.

Understanding Nat's early adulthood requires that we see him in both lights—as confident prophet and as self-doubting seeker. It is more difficult to keep hold of the doubting than the confidence. Nat spoke in the *Confessions* in the voice of certainty and glossed over his period of questioning. His fate by that point was sealed, and his conviction rose to meet it.

But Nat would not have been alone in his fears. In the Hebrew Bible, Nat encountered prophets who took bold action at the Spirit's command, but also those who struggled bitterly with doubt and disillusionment. If we read Nat through those types and through his contemporaries, we can gain a window—narrow and tentative to be sure—into what he might have thought and felt in the years he kept to himself, to glimpse anew certain moments in his own trial of faith, to consider the questions that preoccupied him, to hear echoes of what he left unsaid.

THE WORLD NAT was born into, the early decades of the United States' independence, was crowded with prophets, and also with skepticism about prophets. Nat's message was extraordinary, but it was not at all unique. The historian Susan Juster estimated there were "hundreds, possibly thousands," of self-styled prophets in eighteenth-century Britain and British North America, and they continued to be prominent after independence.[3] Nat was born five years before the other most famous prophet in U.S. history, Joseph Smith; twelve years after the prophet Robert Matthews, who founded the notorious "Kingdom of Matthias"; and within a decade or so of a number of less famous people who proclaimed themselves prophets who heard the voice of God. Like Nat, Matthews and Smith had their visions in the 1820s. Many lesser-known prophets likewise experienced voices from God in the first decades of the nineteenth century. Many were Methodists or Baptists, denominations that especially inspired prophetic claims in this period, others Presbyterians or even Quakers. There were "hundreds of strange religious events that occurred all across the United States from the 1820s through the 1840s," the historians Sean Wilentz and Paul Johnson wrote. "Young women conversed with the dead; male and female perfectionists wielded the spiritual powers of the Apostles; farmers and factory hands spoke directly to God; and the heavens opened up to reveal new cosmologies to poor and uneducated Americans."[4] In his early encounters with the Spirit, Nat was thus doubly typical—sociologically a man who shared experiences with other contemporary people and theologically a representative of a biblical type.

Types helped shape Christians' understanding of the relationship between the past and the present. The prophets in the Hebrew Bible prefigured their expansive recurrence in the Christian Testament and served as evidence of the existence of prophets in the world around them in the nineteenth century.[5] Paul, in his letters, made this connection directly, calling the Israelites in the wilderness "types of ourselves."[6] According to Augustine, "we are all aware that the Old Testament contains promises of temporal things" in the particulars of Israel's history, and "in these temporal figures there was the promise of future things, which were to be fulfilled in us."[7] John Wesley, the guiding spirit of early Methodism, routinely discussed typology in his notes on the scripture and considered the "spiritual gifts" of the "word of wisdom" in 1 Corinthians 12:8 "perhaps an extraordinary ability to understand and explain the Old Testament types and prophecies."[8]

Religiously awakened Americans found types useful because they provided both meaning and fluidity. Scholars debate whether New England Puritans actually deemed the Massachusetts colony a biblical type. But after the Revolution, Americans looking for national destiny sometimes turned back to the Puritan John Winthrop's clarion call to see their new Massachusetts colony "as a City upon a Hill," an exemplar of a godly community to all the world.[9] In what a Puritan minister called the "Analogical sence," early national Americans asked whether the New Jerusalem that would fulfill Canaan might be located in the new United States.[10] During the early republic, this analogical sense ornamented American letters with all manner of images and metaphors for American destiny.[11] The record is unclear, but perhaps that is why the little Southside Virginia town on the Nottoway River was given the name Jerusalem in 1791, only a decade after Cornwallis's surrender and four years after the writing of the Constitution.

In this early national period, perhaps no type struck deeper in the American imagination than the Israelite exodus, an analogy that could be used to sanctify escape from bondage of many different types and one of the most exhilarating types at hand for Nat. Writers from Hugh Henry Brackenridge to James Fenimore Cooper patterned the new nation after the exodus, making the enslavers the British Empire.[12] But the most creative participants in the typology of the exodus were African Americans. Like the Puritans and early American authors, they imagined the story of the Lord's chosen people in their own way, crafted to their own purposes. Many religious enslaved people saw themselves as a chosen people, though they configured America not as a new Canaan but as Egypt, and envisioned exodus as their own liberation.[13]

Few nineteenth-century Americans explored the Israelite exodus more thoroughly than David Walker, a free Black man, a near-exact contemporary of Nat's, a Methodist, and a rebel. In his *Appeal*, Walker drew a straight line from Moses to Jesus Christ to the United States. As God "handed a dispensation" to the Israelites through Moses, so he "handed a dispensation" to Europeans "together with the will of Jesus Christ." As the Israelites broke faith with God by "hypocrisy, oppression, and unbelief," so had "the Europeans" violated Christ's dispensation by slavery.[14] Thus, American slaveholders became types of Egyptians, crueler than Pharaoh, with "hardened" hearts.[15]

It is true that we cannot be sure exactly what Nat knew of each individual Bible story. But we do know that he attended regular Methodist meetings, that even less devout Christians had biblical references at hand that would now impress a scholar, and that the *Confessions* is full of a biblical language that the atheistic Thomas Gray never used in his own writings. We know what people like Nat heard and what they learned. And we know the connections he made, at least according to Gray's narrative. It is a leap, but not an unlikely one, to go from that general context to the specific case of a man all acknowledged to be unusually brilliant and unusually devout. As he pondered the Spirit's voice and words, Nat likely considered the patterns that he was being drawn into, lineages that could expand from Moses's crossing of the Red Sea to Black people's escape from slavery, from Christ's entry into Jerusalem to a new Jerusalem here on earth, perhaps very near at hand. If Nat was a prophet, then these stories of prior prophets were not simply a precursor or inspiration; they were patterns he was being called to reenact and to expand.

IF NAT WAS a prophet. We know that Nat received his first visitation around 1822. Yet, for roughly two years, he did not act. He prayed for further signs before doing anything or even quite believing what he had seen, and it would be nine years before he finally led his rebellion. His delay is a mystery to us, and perhaps was to him, too. As Nat prayed, he probably—like most other prophets—questioned God and himself. Had Nat heard correctly?

Was this why Nat waited to act? He did not tell Thomas Gray, or if he did, Gray did not record it. We can attempt to understand the silences in Nat's story by reading it alongside those of the other prophets who walked around the early republic and who peopled the Hebrew Bible and Christian Testament, and whose stories in some ways echo Nat's. While historians generally prefer a deductive method, this inductive reading of a life in context can offer clues that otherwise may disappear behind the myths and desires of later generations.

For many prophets, the path began, as for Nat, with a voice. Although Joseph Smith's experience started with visions of "a pillar of light," a voice quickly followed. "He spake unto me saying Joseph my Son thy sins are given thee, go thy way, walk in my statutes and keep my commandments." A Methodist minister scoffed at Smith not "because of the strangeness of Joseph's story but because of its familiarity. Subjects of revivals all too often claimed to have seen visions," as Smith's leading biographer states.[16] For Elijah Pierson, bereft as his wife sickened, it began with a voice in June 1830 that told him, "I have named thee this day Elijah the Tishbite, and thou shalt go before me in the spirit and power of Elias, to prepare my way before me." The next day, the voice returned as he traveled along Wall Street. Later Pierson would come to believe these calls corresponded to contemporary voices that spoke to Robert Matthews, founder of the "Kingdom of Matthias."[17]

Black, white, and Native prophets—like Tecumseh—were common in the early nineteenth century. Black prophets may well provide the clearer windows into Nat's self-understanding. Zilpha Elaw, an African American Methodist in Burlington, New Jersey, came to see herself as a prophet after hearing God several times. Sometimes the voice "whispered in my heart," a process that would not seem inherently strange to establishment Christians since it repeated verses she had studied.[18] Elaw heard the voice several times at raucous camp meetings and in silent prayer.[19] But in April 1828, Elaw's experience crossed the potentially dangerous threshold to direct revelation. Elaw was worshipping intently when "suddenly the Spirit came upon me, and a voice addressed me, saying, 'Be of good cheer, and be faithful; I will yet bring thee to England, and thou shalt see London, that great city, and declare my name there.'" She looked around to see who was speaking but found no one. She felt as if her "very blood" stopped and turned cold "in my veins: it was evidently the Spirit of the Lord," she recalled, "who had spoken to me."[20] The verse that the Spirit spoke to Nat also had great meaning for Elaw as she struggled to build her ministry: "Seek ye the kingdom of God and his righteousness, and all things shall be added unto you."[21] Pious intellectuals who refused the name "prophet" also spoke of hearing God's voice. Jarena Lee, a member of the African Methodist Episcopal Church who began as an itinerant exhorter in 1819, was urged on by an unseen voice at several spiritual crossroads.[22] Although Lee did not claim the voice was the Word of God, she followed its injunction to "go preach the Gospel!"[23]

After hearing the Spirit, Nat likely wrestled with recurring, all-too-human questions: Was he sure? Had he misunderstood? As much as Nat wanted to believe that God had chosen him, as much as his childhood training taught him this was possible, Nat could scarcely believe it. "I was greatly astonished" at the first revelation from the Spirit, Nat recalled, and "prayed continually, whenever my duty would permit." This was not simply an automatic turn to prayer but an effort, learned early in Nat's childhood, to summon God. After the first voice, Nat called for the Spirit in prayer again and again, for days, weeks, and months. Still the Spirit did not return. In the Confessions, Nat simply noted the passage of time, leaving us to discern what he made of the wait the Spirit imposed on him, what doubts he experienced.

Nat's own doubts were part of the passage almost every prophet went through. The worry, the waiting, they were a test. "God often hides the sensible signs of his favour from his dearest friends," John Marrant reminded Black Loyalist settlers in Nova Scotia during a funeral sermon, "and leaves them in such inextricable windings, that they know not what course to steer." Waiting for God was thus a holy act.[24]

THEN, AT LAST, probably in late 1823 or early 1824, the Spirit appeared to Nat again and repeated the words it had said before: "Seek ye the kingdom of Heaven and all things shall be added unto you."

This second revelation, Nat told Gray, "fully confirmed me in the impression that I was ordained for some great purpose in the hands of the Almighty."[25]

And yet. How sturdy was Nat's feeling of confirmation? How confident was he? While Nat did not speak of his own fear of death or of his uncertainty, we may see glimpses of it in his own account. The *Confessions* alludes to years of persistent doubt after his second revelation, doubt that it was the Lord who spoke to him. "Several years rolled round," he said, "in which many events occurred to strengthen" his conviction, yet in which he did not act. That very word "strengthen" betrays Nat's own doubts, for if he were "fully confirmed," why exactly did his faith need strengthening? Possibly Nat still held out hope for manumission, though there is good reason to suspect this seemed unlikely by 1823 or 1824. The plausible explanation is that he lacked faith even if he could not quite admit it. Nat described later actions confirming his "belief" in his chosen status because he was still looking for confirmation.[26]

As Nat pondered the praise Methodists laid on him in his youth—that he was too smart to be kept a slave, that he was too gifted to give good service, that he was destined to be a prophet—he began to see those attributes in light of "the things that had been shown me" by the Spirit. This call perhaps had, as with the biblical language of the injunction to Jeremiah, been issued "before I formed thee in the belly," when God "sanctified thee" "a prophet unto the nations."[27] As Nat looked back on his pride of place among the Methodists, he came to see his childhood not as the unrealized promise of freedom but as the prologue to the revelations from the Spirit. The type found him. His continued captivity did not disprove his special status; it gave him an avenue to act out the "great object," God's vision, "for which, by this time, I felt assured I was intended."[28] God, in short, had made him a prophet, too.

But what did prophecy mean? In our own time the claim of prophecy is less overwhelming because it is less specific. The Black prophetic tradition is so frequently invoked as to be a trope, and the word captures a sense of the urgency and discontent we might find in Nat, but its contemporary religious bases—and ultimate claims—seem thin and even unthreatening next to Nat's. Although cloaked in the language of brimstone, the word "prophet" today often invokes a kind of high-minded, well-spoken reformism. Nat was confronting something different: the possibility not that he might wish the world better but that he might be the agent of its destruction.[29]

For a time, Nat tried telling people about his calling. He began preaching around the neighborhood, talking about the Bible and spreading the word about his revelations among enslaved people, as if speaking the words aloud would make their meaning apparent. The telling might not have made the meaning clear, but it did accomplish other goals. Nat's stories about "the communion of the Spirit" and his "revelations" impressed his fellow slaves, and "they believed and said my wisdom came from God. I now began to prepare them for my purpose, by telling them something was about to happen that would terminate in fulfilling the great promise that had been made to me."[30]

But in this world, Nat's life was subject to the whims of other people, white people. After the death of Samuel Turner in 1822, Nat and Nancy and Lydia (likely his mother and grandmother) were assigned to Samuel's daughter Polly when she either married or reached adulthood. For perhaps a year, Nat remained on the land under the control of two men assigned to execute the will. Likely it was during this period of flux when he was "placed under an overseer." Nat, in the *Confessions*, does not say anything about the overseer. We can well imagine that the overseer beat him or was the cause of what his appointed lawyer later described as "a large knot on one of the bones of his right arm near the wrist produced by a blow."[31] Assuming that Nat's wife was Cherry or Cherrie, she likely had been moved away a couple of years earlier, according to the historian David Allmendinger, but still the reallocation of enslaved people with Samuel's death might have confirmed Nat's understanding that he might never live with his wife and child.[32]

Around 1823, Nat was put under the control of Captain Thomas

Moore and his wife, Sally, while their niece Polly—Nat's nominal owner—was under the guardianship of a different uncle and aunt. Thomas Moore would be Nat's master for the next four years, until his death in 1827. Although Thomas Moore did not inherit enslaved people, his wife, Sally Francis (sister of Samuel Turner's first wife), claimed three. Over time, Thomas Moore expanded his landholdings to more than four hundred acres and the number of enslaved people he controlled to about a dozen. One of those expansions of his property holding occurred around 1823, when Thomas Moore took possession of two people who would be crucial in this story: Nat and the enslaved man Hark, sometimes known as Hark Moore or as "Captain" Moore during the rebellion. They lived with about ten enslaved people in two or three rough cabins on Moore's isolated farm a couple of miles from the old Turner property. Nat would have occasion to learn of Thomas Moore's cruelty over the next years.[33]

ABOUT THIS TIME, Nat ran away.

Running away is such a common occurrence in the history of enslavement that it is tempting to brush past it. Yet it is worth pausing to consider the ways that Nat's decision made little sense in the narrative he told of his life, although it made perfect sense in a narrative of a more typical human life under slavery. Even as he promised his neighbors that some prophetic event would soon reveal his purpose, even as he championed his special role in the Spirit's plan for the world, Nat fled from his neighbors and perhaps even from the unique destiny that he believed was his. If Nat believed what he said, if he truly was confident that the Spirit planned to change the world through him, why did he run? We cannot say for sure, though it seems clear his prophetic call was a burden he would not bear lightly.

Nor can we say much about Nat's time away. In the *Confessions*, Nat said very little about why he ran or what he did while away. When he was gone, local enslaved people concluded that "I had made my escape to some other part of the country, as my father had done before,"

Nat told Thomas Gray. But Nat claimed that he stayed "in the woods" nearby.[34] Surely he prayed, an extension of his earlier retreats to the woods to seek the Spirit. Perhaps he kept tabs on his mother and grandmother and wife and son. Although the stories of escapees to the North are the most famous, many enslaved people remained around the farms where they worked and, especially, around their families. This does not fit the narrative of moving northward to freedom but did reflect the contradictory forces that bound many enslaved people: a desire to escape enslavement balanced against a desire to be around loved ones who remained enslaved in the neighborhood. Flight to the North meant abandonment of family, not to mention the danger of being caught in unfamiliar terrain. Nat would have known this well from the disappearance of his father. Perhaps he was torn between those desires, and perhaps he was torn between the urge to flee his prophetic fate and his need to face it.[35]

White people in the neighborhood later claimed that Nat hid in a small cave in the woods a mile and a half from the plantation, abjuring food like the prophets of old. Black tradition gave a bleaker story: Nat ran twelve miles west to Greensville County, where his father had been raised. Perhaps he hoped that he would find his father there, since he might have believed his father had escaped successfully. By this tradition, Nat learned that his father had not run to his freedom but instead been sold away to traders heading south to Georgia, perhaps to enslavement in the turpentine farms.[36] But we have no way of knowing if either tradition had a basis in fact.

Then, after thirty days, Nat came back. The decision to return may be even harder to understand than his decision to run away. For Nat, the reason was ominous but clear: The Spirit ordered him to. The Spirit reminded him that his first two revelations came with a condition: Nat must seek "the kingdom of Heaven." The Spirit told him something else that must have discouraged Nat. The Spirit told Nat that he had disobeyed God's will and would be punished.[37]

The Spirit saw that Nat had lowered his sights from heaven, had cast his eyes on earthly comfort, and now the Spirit chastised him.

Nat's desires had been "directed to the things of this world, and not to the kingdom of Heaven." The Spirit echoed the words Jesus used to chastise Peter as they entered Jerusalem: "Get thee behind me, Satan: thou art an offence unto me: for thou savourest not the things that be of God, but those that be of men."[38] Nat did not interpret this scolding for us, but we can imagine that he understood the Spirit to be castigating him for shirking the burden of his prophecy, for choosing his own freedom over the Lord's call.

The Spirit dispatched Nat back to his "earthly master" with brutally disappointing language. "For he who knoweth his Master's will and doeth it not shall be beaten with many stripes, and thus have I chastened you." This is a close paraphrase of the King James Version of Luke 12:47: "And that servant, which knew his lord's will, and prepared not *himself*, neither did according to his will, shall be beaten with many *stripes*." The next verse excuses those who "knew not" while emphasizing the punishment of the knowledgeable. "For unto whomsoever much is given, of him shall much be required; and to whom much was committed, more was asked of him."[39]

Chastisement by the Spirit was a common experience of Methodist evangelists. When Rebecca Jackson, a free woman in Philadelphia who would become an itinerant preacher in the African Methodist Episcopal Church, became downcast, she interpreted her moods as punishment for her failure to pray for an ailing friend. "I had disobeyed the Spirit, that had brought me out of Egypt," she recalled. So the Spirit sent her back.[40] Zilpha Elaw, struggling with a lingering illness in 1819, came to understand her sickness as divine punishment for her "sturdy . . . unbelief." She had left God no alternative "to severe and extraordinary means to bring me into subjection to his holy will."[41] Elaw saw these punishments not as personal failures but as part of God's plan of instruction. "The chastisement of God is often more profitable than His indulgence would be; His correction is kindness, and His severity mercy."[42] So, too, did Nat come to understand God's chastisement as righteous, as didactic.

If they knew of the Spirit's reference to his "earthly master," Nat's

Black neighbors might have asked: Had he returned because he thought he deserved to be a slave? In Nat's Southampton, as across much of the South, the word "servants" was commonly utilized to refer to enslaved people and did not occasion the status-splitting differentiation it did in the North or other societies with a greater mix of free and enslaved labor. Did the Spirit's injunction to obey his "Master's will" or risk being whipped mean that Nat was consecrated to slavery? Certainly a growing number of white Christians claimed that the Bible sanctified slavery as long as the slave owners took seriously their religious obligations toward the enslaved people.[43] The very verse from Luke that the Spirit used for Nat, the verse about knowing the master's will and doing it not, was one often used to justify slavery. The historian Patrick Breen notes that Lunsford Lane, an enslaved man from North Carolina, had heard white ministers preach that line over and over to enslaved people, so much so that Lane compared it to the "first commandment impressed upon our minds . . . to obey our masters."[44]

To Lane, and perhaps to some of the enslaved people around Nat, the meaning of that verse was clear: it was a sanctification of slavery, something that Nat (and many enslaved people) could not accept. Black Christianity (and for a time biracial evangelical Christianity) had been premised upon the opposite idea, that the scripture was liberating. Did Nat's return and his talk of servants reflect his absorption of a quiescent Christianity? Knowing Nat's future, this is hard to imagine. But from the perspective of 1820s Southampton, an enslaved man returning to slavery talking of the Spirit's injunction to do his master's will might have occasioned hard feelings—even a sense of betrayal—among his Black neighbors and acquaintances. This might well have been the charge murmured against Nat. If so, it does not appear to be a fair one. Nat never expressed any endorsement of slavery. His later actions suggested the contempt he held for most white Christians, perhaps especially for most white Methodists, and the hatred he had for slavery.

The Spirit sent Nat back to his owner not because the Spirit fa-

vored the enslavement of one man to another but because Nat had
not absorbed the most difficult lesson of discipleship: its crushing
of individual will. Discipleship did not make individualists. It made
people step beyond their selves. Nat had to discern the distinction
between being enslaved to a man and accepting submission to God.
The former, unthinkable. The latter, necessary, if he aimed to fulfill his
hopes for God's favorable judgment, for an afterlife that would sur-
pass any of the joys of the earthly realm.

Chastened, Nat returned home determined to be a better disciple.
In this he resembled the great Black Methodist Richard Allen. Allen
wrote that when we apply "our substance to the pomps and vanities
of this wicked world," "we deny God's right to what he hath thought
fit to place in our hands; and disown him as our master . . . In short,
the love of this world is a heavy weight upon the soul, which chains
her down and prevents her flight toward heaven." The answer, Allen
wrote, was to "seek the kingdom of God and his righteousness," and
then "both earthly and heavenly blessings" would be "added unto
me." Nat had learned the hard lesson that Allen wrestled with, as had
so many others: He had lost sight of God's kingdom. He had worried
over his earthly kingdom. He had given his all to a struggle with his
overseer. He had taken his eyes from heaven. But this was not the path
to righteousness.[45]

Nat's neighbors and acquaintances saw his escape and return differently, as a cowardly choice of slavery over freedom. If Nat hoped that
his fellow enslaved people would welcome him back, he was greatly disappointed. They rebuked him and they lost faith in him. He had proved
himself weak and foolish, not a man to be emulated. If they had Nat's
"sense[,] they would not serve any master in the world," they said. His
neighbors called into question whether he had that "sense" they had
claimed for him in the first place. Perhaps Nat was a fraud, or a fool.[46]

So Nat's neighbors "murmured against" him.[47] In this word, too,
we see a connection with the biblical prophets, especially Moses. Biblical prophets were themselves not immune to the whispered complaints
of their potential followers. The ungrateful Israelites "murmured"

against Moses and his brother Aaron for lack of food and water during the exodus, even after Moses and the Lord parted the Red Sea.[48] John Marrant likewise warned Black Loyalists that "indwelling sin excited a spirit of murmuring, under outward troubles."[49] Like Moses, like John Marrant, Nat struggled against a people with a short memory, a people who forgot his own election, his own vision, even their own recent praise.

So murmuring didn't prove that Nat wasn't a prophet. Even as the complaints diminished Nat, they kept him, at least in his interpretation, in the line of prophets, for the prophet's lot was to be scorned. Once God appeared to Elaw, she wrote, "I became so unpopular, that all our coloured class abandoned me except three. Like Joseph, I was hated for my dreams." It all proved that, in Jesus's saying, "a prophet is not without honour, save in his own country."[50] So, too, with the Quaker prophet John Woolman, who compared Quakers' dismissal of him to the Jews' treatment of their own prophets.[51]

Probably, Nat followed other prophets in castigating his people for their murmuring. When the Israelites complained about their thirst, Moses "cried out to the Lord," asking in anguish, "What shall I do with this people?"[52] As an answer to this question, a voice was not enough for many prophets, nor for Nat.

What many prophets longed for was a gift far beyond a voice: a vision. Visions answered a need central to prophets' lives but difficult to capture in Nat's own words: their doubt. If prophets were simply fanatics, certain of their calling, they would not need repeated injunctions. But many of them doubted the voice they heard, questioned their own memory, wavered on the actions the word seemed to demand of them, until a vision coaxed them forward. The Black Loyalists who fled Virginia for Nova Scotia and Sierra Leone described wild and exuberant visions. So, too, did Jarena Lee, and popular Methodist hymns. Zilpha Elaw "possessed no assurance of my acceptance before God" until "I distinctly saw the Lord Jesus approach me with open arms." "Thy prayer is accepted," Jesus said, "I own thy name."[53] With that, Elaw found her blessed assurance. She had further visions at a camp meeting, in chapel, in a barn, and in her dreams.[54] Although scoffers "ignorantly" denied accounts of "apparitions and angelic appearances," Elaw wrote, "the most extensive experience, instinct, belief, and credible testimony of persons of every nation, and of all ages" proved the visions were real.[55] It was a prevailing notion in nineteenth-century Pennsylvania, Elaw wrote, "that whatever a person dreamed between the times of twilight and sunrise, was prophetically ominous, and would shortly come to pass."[56]

FINALLY, SOME TIME after Nat returned from the woods, perhaps in 1824 or 1825, the Spirit bestowed a new gift upon him, and what a vision it was: "And about this time I had a vision—and I saw white spirits and black spirits engaged in battle, and the sun was darkened—the thunder rolled in the Heavens and blood flowed in streams." As Nat looked into the sky, he heard a voice saying, "Such is your luck, such you are called to see, and let it come rough or smooth, you must surely bear it."[57]

The vision was Nat's call, his command. But what was his fate? It was telling that the Spirit called Nat not lucky but unlucky. The vision was something that he would have to bear. A call was indeed a burden, as prophets knew. As Jesus bore his cross, a prophet bore the weight of his vision. Perhaps—as one scholar suggests—what Nat saw and interpreted was the occasional dust-induced red precipitation called blood rain and the play of the northern lights. But we should not rush to assume Nat was describing widely visible natural phenomena; neither his neighbors nor his interlocutors made this connection, as we might expect had they recalled this sight in the sky. We cannot ignore the possibility that his vision was uniquely his own.[58]

The burden was surely his alone, and what a burden the vision foretold, for it evoked the most violent images from the Gospels and the book of Revelation. Nat saw spirits in battle, a darkened sky, blood flowing in streams. The rolling thunder and streaming blood envisioned by Nat echo the apocalyptic vision of John of Patmos when he was guided up to heaven and beheld Christ. "Out of the throne proceeded lightnings and thunderings and voices," John wrote.[59] An angel wielding a huge scythe harvested grapes for "the great wine press of the wrath of God," and for two hundred miles "blood came out of the wine press, even unto the horse bridles."[60] The darkened sun in Nat's theophany shadows the apocalyptic discourses in the Gospels of Matthew (24:29) and Mark (13:24), and the Spirit's ultimatum paraphrases the proclamation of John the Baptist when John told the villagers around the Jordan River that "every valley shall be filled, and every mountain and hill shall be brought low; and the crooked shall be made straight, and the rough ways shall be made smooth."[61]

We do not know how long it took Nat to decipher this vision, but it seems clear that he knew the vision foretold a war. What kind of war, he might not have yet understood, but the battle between black and white spirits raised questions. Did the Spirit suggest that he must lead the enslaved people into war against the white people? As he faced that task, Nat froze again, probably because he knew what the Spirit asked of him and what the cost would be.

Nat understood the call to war because he was enslaved and because he was a Methodist. Methodists in the early nineteenth century saw belief as a form of warfare, and they did not interpret that warfare as solely metaphorical. Early Methodist theology and practice drew heavily upon spiritual warfare to explore conversion and faithful life. Even today's more quiescent Methodist hymnals bear traces of this militant Methodism in "onward, Christian soldiers, marching as to war." Charles Wesley struck some of the earliest chords in Methodism's martial tradition in a poem called "The Whole Armour of God." In 1742, John, Charles's older brother, used the poem to conclude the seminal Methodist document "The Character of a Methodist," and in 1780 included a shorter version in the widely distributed *Collection of Hymns for the Use of the People Called Methodists* in a section titled "For Believers Fighting." The hymn is now known as "Soldiers of Christ, Arise."[62]

In the war-torn colonies, a belligerent Christianity helped preachers connect the Bible to the surrounding world. Colonial preachers often used the Bible as a catalog of war stories, and Methodist ministers absorbed and repeated this practice. They looked to Exodus, Judges, Kings, and Jeremiah from the Hebrew Bible and Revelation from the Christian Testament for tales of God's conquest of the earth and of human hearts: the Lord's destruction of Pharaoh's armies; the heroics of Israelite women against the Canaanite army; the house of David's campaign against the rest of Israel after Solomon's death; the images of Jesus from Revelation not as loving savior but as warrior-king leading forces into battle against Satan.[63]

Awakened ministers used these passages to help make sense of the wars Americans lived through in the eighteenth century: bloody struggles to drive Indians off their lands and repeated campaigns with Spain and France, Catholic powers that represented Satan's forces on earth to some awakened Protestants.[64] The leading light in Virginia's Great Awakening, Samuel Davies, drummed up recruits for the Seven Years' War with a series of belligerent sermons in the Southside counties near Southampton, drawing widespread praise for his musical voice and his pungent critiques—from Jeremiah—of those "that keepeth back his Sword from Blood." In the war against French "Papists" and their "barbarous" Indian allies, "the Sword is . . . consecrated to God; and the Art of War becomes a Part of our Religion," Davies said. In the face of these enemies, "even the God of Peace proclaims by his Providence, 'To Arms!'" Virginians should give their enemies "Blood to drink in their Turn, who have drunk ours."[65]

When colonists turned those guns against the empire in the American Revolution, Patriot ministers used the same analogies to explain the war as biblical, even holy. The colonists became the Israelites, the British the Egyptians, George III became Pharaoh, and George Washington their Moses.[66] The occasional Patriot minister even preached from one of the chapters in Revelation that inspired Nat's ultimate vision of the Spirit.[67] While Jesus was the peacemaker in the Gospels, Revelation was a war text.[68] There, Jesus rode into battle upon a white horse with a "sharp sword" in his mouth to "smite the nations," and he conquered "the beast, and the kings of the earth, and their armies."[69] The preacher Samuel Davies reveled in the nineteenth chapter of Revelation as "one of the most majestic descriptions of Jesus," his eyes "a flame of fire," his raiment "dipt in blood."[70] When Nat saw a war of spirits in a fight against the serpent, he saw an image that Methodist ministers had been repeating over and over since before he was born.[71]

These images might have become even more common in Nat's childhood as American Methodists struggled to reconcile their Wesleyan faith with John Wesley's loyalty to the British Crown. Wesley's views were serious threats to Methodism's growth, even its survival. In Virginia the number of Methodists declined over the 1790s and early years of the nineteenth century. To prove their Americanness, some Methodists proclaimed their patriotism and their support of slavery. Virginia Methodists, originally more closely aligned with Britain than with their northern counterparts, turned more sharply against English churches and English practices, eager to prove they belonged in their new country, especially in the War of 1812.[72] Languages of divine combat became ways of fitting Methodism into the American vernacular. Methodist leaders and ministers routinely characterized those in the throes of conversion as caught in "holy violence," in which God slayed converts and then gave them new life, compared themselves to veterans "long in the field," and described their "whole armour of God."[73]

Like their white counterparts, Black Methodists used the language of warfare to integrate their faith into a belligerent early republic. George White, a free Black Methodist preacher raised for a time on the western shore of Chesapeake Bay, described conversion as feeling "as one wounded or slain in battle," and his post-conversion work as "warring a good warfare."[74] Jarena Lee, a free Black woman who preached itinerantly for the African Methodist Episcopal Church, blamed her early failings on the fact that "I had not yet learned how to war against temptation of this kind."[75] And Zilpha Elaw, the African American Methodist itinerant, recalled a preacher at a camp meeting around 1821 who proclaimed "this is the great day of battle against the old dragon and the powers of darkness."[76] This embrace of spiritual warfare rang through the work of Richard Allen. In 1801, before he founded the African Methodist Episcopal Church, Allen published a collection of hymns with so many militant images we might consider it an instruction book for God's soldiers for a "war in Christ's all conquering name."[77]

Perhaps the most thoroughly militant of these hymns was "Fighting the Battle of Christ." Methodists described the "alarm" the "trumpet sounds" that called "volunteers" to join the "band" behind Jesus, "our captain." "Come who will list with Jesus / a soldier for to make / And like a faithful subject / His armour on you take." Like the Israelites following Moses, they would "go together / with weapons in our hand / Let us begin the battle / Like David with his sling / Fight with courage stout and bold / For Jesus Christ our King." When the "foes are slain," they would "take the large possession / Where peace for ever reigns."[78]

Nat also would have understood the visions as a call to war because he was Black and enslaved. Like other Black evangelicals, Nat would have connected this ubiquitous language of warfare with the potential for the liberation of his people even as he also might have hoped for a paradise that encompassed racial divides. White Methodists might well reflect on their wars against Britain as they contemplated their metaphors of spiritual warfare, but Black Methodists often connected these words to the wars they must fight for their freedom. David Walker in the *Appeal* repeatedly warned slaveholders of God's punishment. "They forget that God rules in *the armies* of heaven and among the inhabitants of the earth," that Christ was "the King of heaven and of earth . . . the God of justice *and* of *armies*." Walker reminded his "Suffering brethren" that surely as the Lord gave them Christ to redeem the world, God "will give you a Hannibal" whose accomplishments would recall "the divisions and consequent sufferings of *Carthage* and of *Hayti*." This war would be a terrible one. "When God almighty commences his battle on the continent of America, for the oppression of his people, tyrants will wish they never were born."[79]

Although Methodists generally were tamping down this language of warfare by the 1820s and displacing it with a sentimen-

NAT, FEARFUL PROPHET 81

tal language that prized emotions, the lesson remained visible, even if only dimly, for those born in Nat's generation. Christianity was a fighting faith, and prophets were not merely mystics but also warriors. It was part of the method, and a part he likely paid close attention to. Men and women who did not convert were at war with God. Even after conversion, they had to fend off attacks from Satan, the Serpent.

When Nat saw the black and white spirits at war in the sky, he saw a vision of holy violence, a vision that made all too much sense. This vision carried a command: Nat should prepare for war, should prepare to kill, should prepare to die.

THE DATE OF Nat's vision may tell us something about his understanding of the broader world of slave revolts. Nat's vision came some time after the voices he heard in 1822, "having arrived to man's estate." We cannot be certain of exactly when Nat saw the spirits, but assuming it was 1823 or 1824, it is possible that his interpretation of his vision was also fed by rumors of a great event in 1822: the much-discussed rebellion scare in Charleston, South Carolina.

In early summer 1822, word began to spread across Charleston that enslaved people intended to rise, led by the free Black carpenter Denmark Vesey. Vesey was believed to be a class leader in the African Methodist Episcopal church in Charleston, honored today as a founder of Mother Emanuel AME Church in that city, though one scholar has pointed to evidence of Vesey's Presbyterianism. In class meetings, Vesey taught Exodus and the warfare verses of Zechariah: "Behold the day of the Lord cometh, and thy spoil shall be divided in the midst of thee. For I will gather all nations against Jerusalem to battle."[80] The religious inspirations were not simple: Vesey apparently worked with Gullah Jack, who performed Angolan rituals to bring success. Exactly what they planned will never be known for certain, but the stories that circulated were awe inspiring. In June 1822, white Charlestonians launched inquests where they tortured Black people into confessions. They testified to a broad plot to call up thousands of enslaved rebels to launch a holy war against whites and against slavery. The date for the rising, some testified, was July 14, anniversary of the French Revolution. Scholars still debate whether the uprising was, in fact, planned, or whether panicky white Charlestonians invented a conspiracy, perhaps to further the political agendas of some white elites. But white South Carolinians believed enough to execute roughly three dozen Black Carolinians.[81]

However elaborate Vesey's plans were, word of the testimony spread quickly. Vesey's name became an emblem of warlike resistance among enslaved people. David Walker lived in Wilmington during 1822 and perhaps had direct contact with Vesey and the conspirators, though this can't be established with certainty. Other Black Americans took inspiration from Vesey's boldness. Perhaps Nat knew a great deal about Vesey, or perhaps only a sketch of a story of an inspired Methodist leading a rebellion in Charleston. And, too, Vesey's rebellion was only one among what the scholar Peter Hinks called "a high incidence" of rebellions, plots, and rumors between 1820 and 1824 in southeastern Virginia and eastern North Carolina. Perhaps these stories spread through runaways and maroons hiding in the Great Dismal Swamp that spanned the border between the two states.[82] Whether or not Vesey directly inspired Nat's vision, the coincidence of timing suggests the militant, visionary strains in Black southern Methodism in this period, strains that animated Nat's belief in his own mission.[83]

STILL, NAT DID not act. Perhaps Denmark Vesey's fate—assuming Nat heard rumors of it—gave Nat pause. His doubt is all too human and yet also all too confounding. Any of us might well imagine waiting nine years to act upon a command from God, but few of us would understand that command in the emphatic terms that Nat did. By some lights, Nat appears so faithful as to be an unfathomable fanatic, yet viewed askance he seems hardly faithful at all.

But once again Nat's doubt gives us a window into his self, even into his soul, that he could not quite convey in words. In doubting, Nat followed the prophetic path, and in reckoning with that, we come to see the prophet anew, not as divine but as all too frail. Like Nat, Zilpha Elaw waited two years before taking up God's command to preach as an itinerant. Jarena Lee, a free Black woman who converted at Richard Allen's Bethel Church, waited eight years to act upon God's call.[84]

And so it was for the great prophets whose lives Nat typed. Perhaps only Abraham embraced his role without doubt, most vividly in the horrifying sacrifice of Isaac. But virtually every other prophet mumbled and tarried. The most reluctant of all prophets, Jonah, accepted his call only after Yahweh had a great fish swallow him and then vomit him onto a Mediterranean beach.[85] Amos denied he was a prophet, insisting he was simply a common herdsman and dresser of vines until a persistent critic forced him to acknowledge his call.[86] Moses's early life was defined by hesitation. Repeatedly Moses told God that he was unworthy, a poor speaker. He did not know God's name. God had not kept his promise![87] When Pharaoh punished the Hebrews, Moses blamed God. "O Lord, why hast though done evil to this people? Why didst Thou ever send me?"[88]

Consider, too, how astounding and awful Nat's commission was: a slave rebellion, a war of the races. For those, like Nat, born enslaved in Chesapeake Virginia, their understanding of Exodus as a war story might well have added to their sense that a slave rebellion was always that: a rebellion, thus a war. We can never know for certain exactly what memories of Chesapeake Black Loyalist soldiers in the Revolutionary War and Black soldiers for the British in the War of 1812 resounded across Southside Virginia and into the worldviews of Nat and of his neighbors. We cannot know for certain what they knew of Haiti, though there is reason to think they knew a good deal. Could they have known of the battles fought by former Southside enslaved Methodists in Sierra Leone? Of the Aponte rebellion in Cuba, with its mysterious connection to the perhaps prophetic book of paintings that José Antonio Aponte and his aide Trinidad Nuñez constructed and that Spanish officials worried over?[89] There is reason to believe that Nat and his followers knew enough of this history to know the fates of those who followed prophets, to know of the graves Moses Wilkinson and his followers left behind. Prophets were not always victorious, not even if they were righteous.

Nat had reason to worry about another issue that tormented other prophets. What would become of his family? Scholars struggle to pin down the exact nature of Nat's family life. Still, it is easy to imagine Nat, like other prophets, wrestling with a horrible question: Was he dooming his own loved ones? Zilpha Elaw wondered this during the two years she—a widow with a young daughter—delayed acting upon God's commission to preach "far and wide." Elaw imagined different ways the Lord might provide for her child, but the Lord did not "avail Himself of my short-sighted plans." So she began to doubt, to pray for confirmation. "Give me a token thereof by opening my way before me at the end of three months," she implored God. If not, then could God "remove from my mind" the commission to preach?[90]

The year after the Spirit spoke to Nat, a rebellion in Demerara, now Guyana, would have confirmed the potential and the dangers of warfare. Inspired by a belief that the British government had promised emancipation, by Methodist missionaries' nonconformist preaching, and by planters' efforts to ban church services, enslaved people in Demerara rose in August 1823. They were led by a church deacon named Quamina, who struggled with his own sense of divine mission and his own doubts. Thousands joined the rebellion, but the British eventually prevailed, executed dozens, and left their bodies on display. It is hard to know how quickly this news spread to Virginia, but it would not be surprising if white Virginians read about it in the frequent republications of international news in local newspapers and discussed it in front of enslaved people, seeding knowledge of the event and of its bloody aftermath, confirming the possibility and the cost of a holy war.[91]

AFTER THE VISION of the battle between black spirits and white spirits, Nat "withdrew myself as much as my situation would permit, from the intercourse of my fellow servants, for the avowed purpose of serving the Spirit more fully." In withdrawing, Nat might have acted strategically. With time, the freshness of his flight and return would fade. His neighbors might recover their faith in his visions, his mysterious powers. Nat had taken his chastisement to heart. If he would not yet strike, Nat would turn his attention from the world and devote himself to the Spirit.

In waiting on the Spirit, Nat was saying, in all piousness, a very unpious thing: he wanted more direction. And he had reason to hope. Hadn't other prophets received further assurances from Yahweh? God gave Hebrew Bible prophets knowledge, comfort, blessed assurance.[92] The Lord told Abram of Ur to "get thee out of thy country, and from thy kindred, and from thy father's house, unto a land that I will shew thee," and that then "I will make of thee a great nation, and I will bless thee." Still, even then Abram wanted to know more. Where was he going?[93] When Abram with his wife and their slaves reached Canaan, the Lord told him, "I will give unto thee, and to thy seed after thee . . . all the land of Canaan, for an everlasting possession."[94] Yet still Abram questioned how his descendants could inherit the promised land, since he had no children. God answered again, bidding Abram to look into the sky. His descendants would be as numerous as the stars, the Lord promised.[95] "I am thy shield," the Lord told Abram. Only now, after repeated explanations and reassurances, Abram "believed in the Lord," and the Lord understood Abram's belief as righteousness.[96]

What Nat would have done for the revelations God lavished upon Abram. For Nat received knowledge, but no assurance and precious little comfort. Nat waited and wondered, yet he would learn little more about his commission from the Spirit, even though he would learn something more about the Spirit itself. It would take him years to come to terms with this fact: he would not know what he wished to know. And thus he joined the list of prophets whom God called upon but disappointed, who stewed in anxiety and uncertainty as they wrestled with a commission they could not understand. When Moses complained that Yahweh did not tell him enough, the Lord responded that Moses had it better than the patriarchs. "I appeared unto Abraham, unto Isaac, and unto Jacob, as God Almighty," he reminded Moses, "but by my name JEHOVAH was I not known to them." Still Moses, like almost all the prophets, wanted more.[97] In Nat's own time, Jarena Lee replied to God, "No one will believe me." The voice responded, "I will put words in your mouth." But Lee feared Satan was speaking to her, and prayed to God to tell her whether she was deceived, begging for certainty.[98]

But against that fear, Nat might have pondered the possibilities. He could commence a *magnolia dei*, a mighty act of God. The Lord performed any number of miraculous, mighty acts during the exodus, and might perform any of them now in Southampton. Perhaps there would be plagues as upon the Egyptians—the locusts, the frogs, the boils, the dark storms, the deaths of the firstborn sons.[99] Or perhaps the Spirit would appear to the enslaved people and the white people of Southampton as Yahweh appeared to Israel at Mount Sinai and to the Canaanites at Jericho, before the collapse of the walls confirmed—at last—Joshua's leadership to his followers.[100]

Wondering about these biblical events, Nat might well have noted the mighty and miraculous outcome pledged at Sinai: the freeing of the enslaved. At Mount Sinai, Moses relayed God's words to Israel about the Jubilee that would take place on the day of atonement in the fiftieth year. In that yearlong Sabbath, the Israelites must leave the land fallow and settle their accounts "and proclaim liberty throughout all the land unto all the inhabitants."[101] The slave shall "depart from thee, both he and his children with him, and shall return unto his own family, and unto the possessions of his fathers shall he return." There, at Sinai, Yahweh taught Israel the lesson about slaves that the Spirit taught Nat: "For they are my servants . . . they shall not be sold as bondmen."[102] Nat belonged not to his earthly master but to the Spirit.

Nat revealed very little of his own feelings as he wrestled with the Spirit's words and his detractors' derision. Perhaps the prophet Jeremiah's agony suggests some of Nat's emotions. In a single prayer in one of the most heartfelt of all the books of the prophets, Jeremiah allows us to see a prophet torn between God's commands and a detractor's mockery. The revelations brought Jeremiah "joy and rejoicing," yet also "indignation" and "despair" and fury. "Why is my pain perpetual, and my wound incurable?" Jeremiah asked.[103]

The ultimate doubt would have come not from Nat's detractors, and not from Nat's own mortal mind or his weakened soul. The final doubt came from his certainty that whatever came next would be indeed terrible, even if also glorious. Nat surely imagined what would come, and what he imagined likely drew upon the unmitigated horrors the Bible provided for him as guides, as well as upon the terrifying toll of death and dismemberment in the history of slave rebellions in Virginia and neighboring states.

As Nat contemplated the potential for disaster, he might well have thought of a type very close to home: the biblical Jerusalem. So many of those biblical stories ended in Jerusalem, that holy city, the focus of prophets' desires and their worries. The Bible was full of predictions and predicaments for Jerusalem, of rescues and of obliterations at the hands of three conquering empires: the Assyrian, Egyptian, and Babylonian. All could be part of God's plan.[104]

In the prophets' messages about the suffering of the biblical Jerusalem, Nat might have found contradictory ways of reading the outcome of his own contemplated assault on Jerusalem. Some of the sins of Ezekiel's Jerusalem echoed Nat's critique of Southampton's Jerusalem. In Jerusalem, "the bloody city," as Ezekiel called it, mother and father were treated with contempt and the Sabbath was "profaned."[105] A man "lewdly defiled his daughter in law; and . . . hath humbled his sister," and "the city sheddeth blood."[106]

Nat's Jerusalem was its own bloody city, if a tiny one, and around it an enslaved woman was her own master's daughter, vulnerable to the sexual predations of the young master, her brother. Mothers and fathers were sold for debt at the courthouse door and flayed at the whipping post. The "princes," Ezekiel continued, "are like wolves ravening the prey, to shed blood, and to destroy souls, to get dishonest gain."[107] Was not the same true in Nat's Jerusalem? For that reason Nat might take solace in seeing the enslavers as the faithless to be destroyed, and hope in the vision of his Black neighbors come to save Jerusalem from the fallen.

But the Hebrew Bible also offered Nat terrible prophecies of what would become of Jerusalem. Jerusalem's impurity will be purged by fire, Isaiah warned, like a base alloy burned down to its constituent elements.[108] Jerusalem's people were good for nothing but to feed the flames of God's consuming anger, the Lord told Ezekiel.[109] Beyond fire, the Lord said that he would "send my four sore judgments upon Jerusalem," claims echoed by Jeremiah's "four kinds" of destroyers: "the sword to slay, and the dogs to tear, and the fowls of the heaven and the beasts of the earth, to devour and destroy."[110] Jeremiah suffered over these visions: "My bowels, my bowels! I am pained at my very heart."[111] "Woe is me for my hurt! My wound is grievous; but I said, Truly this is a grief, and I must bear it."[112] Perhaps Nat suffered, too, as he contemplated the suffering of the people of Jerusalem, Black people to be sure, but perhaps he suffered, too, over the agonies that awaited white people.

War could destroy everything. Or not. Sometimes Yahweh saved Jerusalem.[113] The most brilliant vision of what could follow the assault on Jerusalem was Isaiah's millennial prophecy of a new king arising from the ashes of war to renew the house of David. Many Black prophetic ministers, like John Marrant, saw the New Jerusalem in happier terms, as God's promise to them, the enslaved people.

Given these ambiguities, could Nat, the warrior on the road to Jerusalem, be certain which type he was fulfilling? Was he considering an attack on God's New Egypt or on God's New Jerusalem? Of course God sought redemption. But who, precisely, did God aim to redeem? David Walker, the great Methodist rebel, worried over this same question: Was God on their side? Much of the time, Walker, like Nat, answered yes, and urged other Black people to follow God's commandments to arise. They need not fear white people's superior numbers or superior education: "For why should we be afraid, when God is, and will continue, (if we continue humble) to be on our side?"[114] Still, Walker was not always certain what they might expect from

God—holy justice, detached indifference, or divine punishment—not when God "suffered our fathers" to be "enveloped" in "misfortunes" for "many ages." Sometimes, in his bleakest writing, Walker asked whether God was on the slaveholders' side. "Can the Americans escape God Almighty? If they do, can he be to us a God of Justice?"[115] Later in the *Appeal*, Walker wrote, "I am brought oftimes solemnly to a stand, and in the midst of my reflections I exclaim to my God, 'Lord didst thou make us to be slaves to our brethren, the whites?'"[116]

God could come to destroy the slaveholders, or to redeem them. To free the enslaved people, or to send them to their doom; to save Jerusalem, or to destroy it. This was the lesson of the Hebrew Bible: there was no single lesson. Types did not repeat. They expanded in ways that fit God's mysterious will. Nat's revolt would be his campaign to take his own Jerusalem, and that would require him to risk either outcome: his doom or the city's doom. Or perhaps both.

Nat carried this doubled sense of confidence and resignation with him to his grave. When Nat related his last revelation from the Spirit, Gray broke in again, speaking not just the skepticism of a white Virginian toward an enslaved rebel but also the confusion of a secular person: "Do you not find yourself mistaken now?" Surely Gray referred to the jail cell where he interviewed Nat, to the dead bodies of Nat's compatriots, to the enduring power of Southside slave owners, to the seeming failure of Nat's rebellion.

"Was not Christ crucified?" Nat answered.

4

Nat, Warrior

For a couple of years, Nat waited and wondered and watched. Then, in 1825, the Spirit answered Nat's yearning in a dizzying set of visions that led Nat to believe he possessed not merely access to God but special knowledge of Jesus's Second Coming. And the Spirit did not simply appear once; the Spirit came again and again, delivering more wonderful and terrible signs each time. Beginning in 1825 and stretching perhaps to the spring of 1828, the Spirit carried Nat from the political stories of the Hebrew Bible through the Gospels' apocalyptic heralds and finally to the battle for the fate of the world in the book of Revelation. This relay between what Christians call the Old Testament and the New was not a departure but a fulfillment of those older prophecies, part of the Christian Testament's claim of carrying forward the promises of the Hebrew Bible through types.[1]

Nat's sketch of these visions was often merely a sketch. He told his interlocutor that he had seen the mysteries of the universe, read the constellations anew, observed Christ's blood, learned secret languages and sciences, and heard God's commands. In 1825, Nat said, the Spirit "appeared to me, and reminded me of the things it had already shown me, and that it would then reveal to me the knowledge of the elements, the revolution of the planets, the operation of tides, and changes of the seasons." Then "the knowledge of the elements" was "made known to me." After that the "Holy Ghost" appeared and told him to look to the "Heavens," where Nat "saw the forms of men in different attitudes." Then he saw in the sky the "lights of the Saviour's hands, stretched forth from east to west." After this he "discovered drops of blood on the corn as though it were dew from heaven," then "hieroglyphic characters, and numbers, with the forms of men in different attitudes, portrayed in blood" on the leaves. Finally, on May 12, 1828, he heard a "loud noise in the heavens, and the Spirit instantly appeared to me and said the Serpent was loosened, and Christ had laid down the yoke he had borne for the sins of men."[2] These phrases are evocative but also maddeningly elusive. Even when Nat described earlier visions in detail, like the battling figures in the sky, they remain open to interpretation. Now that Nat simply alluded to them, it can feel as if we have no firm ground at all. Still, it is clear that these new visions helped steer Nat toward a claim so expansive that he—like any prophet—might have shrunk from its audacity, so vast that he might have evaded it in his jailhouse interview.

Thomas Moore shaped a good deal of Nat's mid-twenties, as Nat wrestled with his separation from his wife and son and with the visions that occupied his mind. On four hundred acres two miles away from the old Samuel Turner plantation, Moore had legal control—if not always direct title—over about five enslaved people of working age, including Nat and his future collaborator Hark, as well as a few enslaved children. It was in Moore's fields where Nat saw the blood on the corn and received his knowledge of the elements and planets. It was near Moore's fields, or perhaps in them, where Nat preached to his neighbors, mostly enslaved people held by different members of the extended Francis family.[3]

And it was likely that Moore whipped Nat, perhaps more than once, in these years when Nat experienced his greatest wave of visions. An 1831 letter by a local white man stated that "something like three years ago, Nat received a whipping from his master" for proclaiming that slavery should end and that Black people would be free. We cannot be certain that Moore was the "master" referred to, but he is the most likely culprit even though he died a bit more than three years before the uprising.[4]

We do not know exactly how Moore became aware of Nat's bold talk, but we have evidence that Nat's visions were becoming known in the neighborhood. The visions were part of his general reputation for strangeness, even if Black and white understandings of his eccentricities were surely distinct. The letter Thomas Gray likely wrote in September 1831, before Nat's capture and "confessions," stated that Nat had "acquired the character of a prophet," like "a Roman Sybil." Nat gained this power through "his divination in characters of blood, on leaves alone in the woods . . . He, likewise, pretended to have conversations with the Holy Spirit." In a sign of his "shrewdness," Nat had made these discoveries known to his Black neighbors but had not been "noticed by the whites."[5] A different letter referred to the "number of revelations" that Nat "says he has had, from which he was induced to believe that he could succeed in conquering *the county of Southampton!*" The author of this piece then included an aside to distance himself from the "superstition and fanaticism" that Nat displayed: "what miserable ignorance!"[6]

These authors tried to discredit Nat by tying him to religion; some later interpreters have tried to save Nat by distancing him from those same religious motivations. But within the world of his early national Methodism, Nat's claims were not necessarily shocking; they made a certain kind of dangerous sense.

For believers as immersed as Nat in early national Methodism, the message of his visions was becoming clearer, even if it was also becoming terrible and astounding: Nat's warfare for Jerusalem would lead to the Second Coming of Christ. He was called to begin not just another in a string of God's battles for the world but the final apocalyptic struggle that would culminate in Christ's return and a new epoch. At stake was not only the end of slavery but also the end of the world. The Spirit did not tell Nat to make a new nation; it told him to fulfill his type by helping inaugurate a new age.

WHAT GAVE NAT'S visions coherence during his years on Moore's farm was their invocations of the book of Revelation, perhaps the strangest book of the Bible, and certainly the most difficult to assess. Revelation presents nothing less than the end of the world following Christ's return and a bloody battle for control of the universe. Unlike other books of the Bible, which narrate a fallen world, Revelation is a story of the Messiah's return, his judgment of humanity, and his reign on earth.[7] The story is lavished with a congeries of images, brilliant in color, epic in scale, shocking in their import, and horrifying in their violence. For Revelation is a war story, a story of Christ's campaign to destroy Satan.[8]

Revelation is told as the visions of John of Patmos in Asia Minor (present-day Turkey). John was a Jewish follower of Christ in the second generation after the Crucifixion. John lived with the painful knowledge that Rome sacked Jerusalem in 70 CE, sending Jews into exile. To explain that catastrophe, John looked to the stories of the Babylonian threat to Jerusalem in the prophecies of Ezekiel, Daniel, Isaiah, and Jeremiah.[9] John of Patmos echoed Hebrew Bible imagery, phrasing, divine judgments, and promises of redemption to explain the world he saw around him and the world to come.[10]

Nat drew upon a literal, not metaphoric, understanding of Revelation, an understanding that was surprisingly, even disturbingly, robust among early American Christians, particularly Methodists. Methodists repeatedly tied Hebrew Bible warrior stories to the apocalyptic vision of Revelation to make the Bible a story of past wars that served as types of the final battle to come. Early national Christian prophets thus explained how the Hebrew Bible would come alive through the return of the warrior-king Jesus Christ, heralded perhaps by prophets typed after John the Baptist. Congregations sang its most awful images in war songs. "My way is full of danger," a "faithful soldier" sang in a Virginian's camp meeting hymnal. "Now I must gird my sword on, / My breastplate, helmet and my shield, / And fight the host of Satan."[11] In his much-reprinted 1801 collection of hymns, the Black Methodist Richard Allen published several songs combining the stories of the Hebrews and the Christian Revelation. Several popular Methodist hymns survey the images from Revelation that the Spirit showed Nat:

> The sun may be darken'd,
> The moon turn to blood,

The mountains all melting
At the preference of God.
Red lightning's a blazing,
Loud thunders may roar;
All this cannot daunt me
On Canaan's sweet shore.[12]

Revelation was the proof text for several characteristically Wesleyan practices. Methodists fell down during conversion as if God had struck them dead, reenacting John of Patmos's reaction when he saw Christ's eyes "as a flame of fire" while "out of his mouth went a sharp twoedged sword."[13] Revelation also offered "the people who sing"—as John Wesley once termed the Methodists—a warrant for hymnody in the twenty-four elders who burst into song.[14]

Revelation gave sanction to Methodists' well-studied preoccupations with blood and death, preoccupations that shaped the visions the Spirit gave Nat. Even John of Patmos's angels praise God for giving sinners "blood to drink."[15] In Revelation blood is drunk by God's enemies in Babylon, runs in the fountains and rivers, falls from the sky, and colors Christ's robe.[16] Methodist hymns portrayed Jesus's blood-dipped robe, the "blood-washed throngs," and the blood that flowed from Jesus "to cleanse us."[17]

Nat's absorption in Revelation was typical of many early national Methodists. During the Revolutionary War, an enslaved woman named Elizabeth (whose amanuensis did not see fit to record her surname) was not quite thirteen years old when she discovered her "spiritual eye" and witnessed visions that echoed the second cycle of Revelation, especially the opening of the seals.[18] Still enslaved in Maryland, grieving for her mother, who had been sold twenty miles away, Elizabeth saw before her "an awful gulf of misery." A "director, clothed in white," led her "by the hand" down toward "an awful pit," where she "began to scream for mercy." Grabbing a strand of silver hair, she was lifted "above the fiery pillars," until the "Saviour" bid her "peace, peace, come unto me." The Saviour led her to the open door of heaven as "indescribably glorious light" flowed from his hands in a vision saturated with images from Revelation.[19]

So, too, did John of Patmos's visions help give Nat's their structure, their transcendence of material events, their explanations for the world's mysteries, and their quickening pace.[20] Neither John nor Nat paused for long to interpret what he had seen.[21] And both heard the words of the Spirit.[22] The sensorium of Nat's visions is John's, bright with stars, wet with dew, drenched in blood. Neither slaveholders nor Roman soldiers are named in either John's or Nat's descriptions, perhaps because the promise was not the end of one system but the end of the world. In Latin, "revelation" means apocalypse, and the two men spoke with a single voice, a voice that prophesied the millennium and worried over eschatology, the teaching of the end-time.[23]

For all its terrible imagery, Revelation brought good tidings of a sort. What "must shortly be done," in the angel's assurances to John, is a victory of the weak over the strong.[24] The forces arrayed against God will be formidable but not victorious. Ten new-crowned kings in league with "the beast"—Satan—will "make war with the Lamb, and the Lamb shall overcome them."[25] Voices from heaven then announce the millennium: "The kingdoms of the world are become the kingdoms of our Lord, and of his Christ; and he shall reign for ever and ever."[26]

John's vision of a new Jerusalem must have tantalized Nat. He surely took to heart Revelation's promise of "a new heaven and a new earth," the "holy city, new Jerusalem, coming down from God, prepared as a bride adorned for her husband." In Revelation, Jerusalem became not the site of cruelty to Isaiah, Jeremiah, and Ezekiel but a wondrous place of justice.[27] The names of the twelve tribes were to be etched into the city gates, but the city was to be open to "the nations," and the leaves on the tree of life used "for the healing of the nations."[28] In the New Jerusalem, the servants of God and Christ "shall reign for ever and ever."[29]

Beyond this New Jerusalem, Nat might have longed for another promise of Revelation: an intimate and unmediated relationship with

God. Until Revelation, Moses was the only figure in the Bible to lay eyes on the Lord. But in the promise of the New Jerusalem, all the "Servants" of God "shall see his face."[30] Even as Revelation announces a military campaign, it also proclaims a romance. The angel who takes John to see the New Jerusalem calls the city "the Bride, the wife of the Lamb."[31] What would follow that encounter was not terror but love, a love far more profound than any earthly passion. At camp meetings, Methodists sang of this erotic love between the faithful and the Savior: "King Jesus takes her in his arms, / Transported with his lovely charms, / She thus begins to sing."[32] A prophet was once consigned to earth; now he could be a sibling of angels, even a bride of Christ.

BUT THESE REVELATIONS did not lead Nat to launch his assault. According to Gray, Nat described the Spirit's visits as elusive. "It would then reveal to me the knowledge of the elements, the revolution of the planets, the operation of the tides, and changes of the seasons." Nat might not yet have understood the particulars of these promised visions, but he knew they were a sign of God's special favor, a favor God withheld from many others.[33] That specific favor was not yet evident, so Nat like other Methodists worked to perfect himself. "I sought more than ever to obtain true holiness before the great day of judgment should appear," Nat recalled. "And from the first steps of righteousness until the last, was I made perfect."[34] Methodists of the period held to a belief in perfectionism, the faith that conversion or "justification" opened a further path to sanctification. Although some Christian sects looked to faith alone or expected that converts would continue to sin, many American Methodists absorbed John Wesley's message that "you, therefore, must be perfect, as your heavenly Father is perfect."[35] They sought to live out the "second work of grace" from Paul's charge to the Corinthians to "cleanse ourselves from every defilement of body and spirit."[36]

While some Black Methodists like Jarena Lee and Sojourner Truth (when she was still known as Isabella Van Wagenen) found perfection immediately, other Black Methodists, like Nat, followed most white Methodists' longer, slower path to holiness.[37] Rebecca Jackson passed six months between her justification and her moment of sanctifying grace.[38] For Nat the journey had taken almost his entire life. From his abstemious youth, he held himself apart from the misdeeds of other neighborhood boys. After his revelations of 1825, inspired by the Spirit's hint of knowledge to come, Nat struggled even more earnestly for perfection. "I began to receive the true knowledge of faith," he recalled.[39]

Now, approaching perfect holiness, Nat felt God's presence in a new way: "The Holy Ghost was with me." Nat's phrase called back to Christ's commission to his disciples in the last lines of Matthew. After the resurrection, the disciples repaired to a mountaintop in Galilee, where they had a vision of Jesus. Christ directed them to evangelize "all nations, baptizing them in the name of the Father and of the Son and of the Holy Ghost." Then Jesus—to Matthew the embodiment of God's presence—assured them, "I am with you always, even unto the end of the world."[40] In John of Patmos's vision of the New Jerusalem, Jesus promises likewise that "God himself shall be with them."[41]

God's presence meant something quite specific to the biblical prophets, and thus might have meant something similar to Nat. It meant that God would see them through war. Moses urged the Israelites to take courage as they attacked a superior army "for the Lord thy God is with thee."[42] In his commission to Joshua, God tells him, "As I was with Moses, so I will be with thee; I will not fail thee, nor forsake thee."[43] In Jeremiah's theophany, Yahweh likened being a prophet to going to war, telling Jeremiah that the kings and priests and people of Judah would all "fight against thee; but they shall not prevail against thee; for I am with thee, saith the Lord, to deliver thee."[44]

Knowing now that the Holy Ghost was with him, Nat might have sensed the answer to the question that plagued all prophets: What would be his fate? The strength Nat gained from his answer was one that other Black Methodists like Zilpha Elaw and Sojourner Truth experienced when they felt calmness in the face of angry mobs. We might well imagine that Nat's heart swelled like Truth's at God's presence and that, like her, he called out, "Oh, God, I did not know you were so big," and saw himself "brightened into a form distinct, beaming with the beauty of holiness, and radiant with love."[45]

NAT'S CONFIDENCE IN the Spirit was eventually rewarded with a new vision, one that extended his knowledge of the universe in new directions. Nat discovered something incredible: the stars in the sky formed the body of the risen Christ. "Behold me as I stand in the Heavens," the Holy Ghost said to Nat. Nat now saw the constellations with new eyes. What the "children of darkness" called Ursa Major and Ursa Minor were not the Great Bear and Little Bear, or the Big Dipper and Little Dipper. Those constellations were, Nat saw, "the lights of the Saviour's hands, stretched forth from east to west, even as they were extended on the cross on Calvary for the redemption of sinners."[46]

This was a joyous vision: Christ had come again, already, and waited only for people on earth to recognize him. Thus Nat became akin to the post-Crucifixion apostles who saw Jesus on the road from Jerusalem. They "were terrified and afrighted, and supposed that they had seen a spirit." Only when Jesus showed the disciples his hands did they realize they were in his presence. Nat, too, had to see Jesus's hands in the night sky to realize that Christ had been with him all along.[47] John of Patmos also had seen "seven stars"—for the seven churches of Asia Minor—in Christ's hands in his first vision.[48]

The Spirit had graced Nat with rare knowledge—the actual presence of the Savior—but still Nat wanted further confirmation. "I wondered greatly at these miracles, and prayed to be informed of a certainty of the meaning of them," Nat said. "Shortly afterwards," Nat's prayers were answered with another cycle of revelations. While he was "laboring in the fields," he recalled, "I discovered drops of blood on the corn as though it were dew from heaven."[49]

After this vision, Nat followed the prophets' path into the woods, where visionaries often waited upon God. There, he saw blood on the leaves, "representing the figures I had seen before in the heavens." This time, Nat did not name the figures in the heavens because the Holy Ghost had done it for him, telling him, "Behold me as I stand in the heavens." The blood on the leaves, then, connected the stars in the hands of Christ to Nat's original commission to launch the battle between white and black spirits where the "blood flowed in streams" down into this world. Blood flowing from the sky ran through Revelation, especially John's second cycle of visions, and also Methodist songs like Richard Allen's "See! How the Nations Rage Together," with its bloody moon, its fiery falling stars, and its "leaves almost appearing / Awake!"[50]

Local enslaved people later told white investigators about some of these visions when they were interrogated (and likely tortured) in the weeks between the rebellion and Nat's capture; Nat's "confessions" to Thomas Gray thus expanded on an already-circulating story in the county. Before the jailhouse interview, Gray had likely suspected that the blood on the leaves was a con, suggesting in a letter that Nat would arrange the leaves "in some conspicuous place, have a dream telling him of the circumstance; and then send some ignorant black to bring them to him, to whom he would interpret their meaning. Thus, by means of this nature, he acquired an immense influence, over such persons as he took into his confidence."[51]

Later scholars tied these images to existing natural phenomena. One historian carefully connected Nat's heavenly visions to specific weather events. Another noted that a weed called the Blood of Christ or Christ Weed contains red veins and was said locally to have grown beneath Christ's cross. This weed had been put inside hats for good luck or used for conjuring. Perhaps Nat in his desire to draw in Black followers played upon these stories.[52] Or perhaps white interrogators, seeking to avoid executing people their neighbors enslaved and counted as assets, deceived themselves into blaming foolishness for Black people's support for Nat, not genuine belief.

Whatever the case may be, Nat at last began to tell what he had seen in the cornfield, speaking "to many, both white and black in the neighborhood." Knowing what was to come, we may find it strange that these bloody visions would not alert Nat's white neighbors. But this is hindsight at work. Prophets narrated their visions; they did not interpret them with precision. The very open-endedness of revelation invited hearers to insert themselves—their own circumstances, fears, aspirations—into the interstices between the force of God's expressed will and the prophet's enigmatic language. Blood was so ubiquitous in white and Black Methodism that perhaps the image was not shocking. Methodists sang of blood and prayed for it, and why should they think an enslaved person's vision of it foretold a literal slaughter? After all, there were far more prophets than rebels in the early nineteenth century. Nat became distinct from his times not when he had his vision but when he acted on it by leading a rebellion.

IN THE WOODS, on a break, Nat soon had another vision. "I then found on the leaves in the woods hieroglyphic characters, and numbers," Nat recalled, "with the forms of men in different attitudes" or postures, "portrayed in blood, and representing the figures I had seen before in the heavens." An 1831 letter by a white man in the county also noted that Nat's wife held papers "filled with hieroglyphical characters . . . traced with blood; and on each paper, a crucifix and the sun, is distinctly visible."[53] The hieroglyphs point to another inspiration: a nineteenth-century fascination with Egypt as a source of secret knowledge, an esoteric learning that could be available to only an enlightened few. This absorption with Egypt inspired Nat's contemporary prophet Joseph Smith, among many others.[54]

As to the numbers in Nat's visions, Nat's papers included figures traced in blood, "6,000, 30,000, 80,000 &c," according to the letter.[55] Nat studied those numbers in blood long and hard, and he apparently left them for safekeeping with his wife. Some of the numbers could represent Nat's estimate of the people he would have to kill to take control of the country. And the digits likely had meaning drawn from the patterns in John of Patmos's vision and other ancient Judaic and early Christian apocalyptic texts. There patterns of numbers express a belief in the order of time and space.[56] We do not know the numbers referred to in that "&c," but it is possible they were the sevens that frequently recur in Revelation: seven mustering armies, seven seals, seven stars, seven bowls of God's wrath, the seven-headed dragon, and the seven-horned Lamb representing "the seven Spirits of God sent forth into all the earth."[57] Or perhaps they were the fours that occur in the four horsemen of the apocalypse,[58] or the twelves that spill out from the seventh seal: 144,000 soldiers mustered for Christ's first battle against the dragon Satan, dispatched in 12 battalions of 12,000 men.[59] Nat might have had reason to contemplate these soldiers, for they received the protection that Nat sought when the angels placed a seal on their foreheads.[60]

As Nat searched for answers in numerology, he was part of a fusion in American evangelicalism between math and scripture. Most famously, around 1818, about seven years before Nat's vision of the numbers, a farmer in northern New York named William Miller began calculating the precise date of Christ's return. Miller obsessively read the Bible and tried to resolve contradictions by turning days into years, horns and beasts into empires and tyrants, and Revelation prophecies into Babylonian and Roman history. Miller reckoned that the end-time would begin by 1843. He was at least the fourth visionary to set that year for Christ's return. Only in the summer of 1831, as Nat set his own revolt in motion, did Miller begin to preach on his calculations and their revelation. Twelve years later, Miller's followers would bring this association between numerology and prophecy to an end point or turning point when the Millerites faced Great Disappointments in 1843 and then again in 1844, as Miller's predictions seemed not to come true. In the aftermath, those Millerites developed alternative explanations and became the Seventh-Day Adventists still popular today in a domesticated form.[61]

Revelation disappoints those like the Millerites who seek an appointed time for Christ's return. When the fifth seal was opened, the martyrs gathered under the altar before God's throne, demanding to know, "How long, O Lord, holy and true, dost thou not judge and avenge our blood on them that dwell on earth?"[62] In reply God gave them a white robe, signifying his favor and the promise of resurrection, but sent no answer, telling them to "rest yet for a little season."[63] Only when, as one scholar writes, "the number of their fellow servants and their brethren should be complete" would God punish their antagonists.[64] Until enough believers died for the faith, the altar would not be avenged.

Nat seemed able to live with this uncertainty, waiting for more instead of demanding answers. "And now the Holy Ghost had revealed itself to me, and made plain the miracles it had shown me," Nat recalled. The Holy Ghost reminded Nat of all that he had been given. The stars were not the constellations but Christ's hands outstretched across the night sky as on the cross outside Jerusalem. Nat had prayed for understanding of what these visions meant, and his prayers were answered by the blood on the forest leaves. Christ's return was nigh. These visions also contained a revelation about the revolt that Nat, ever the prophet, did not spell out explicitly in the *Confessions*.

From the beginning, Nat had surely yearned to know a simple fact: Whose blood flowed in the vision of black and white spirits? One answer was that it was the black spirits' blood. Another was that it was the white spirits'. Or, possibly, it was both. For Nat, a great deal—his success and his very life—turned on the answer to that question. If it was white people's blood, it might foretell his triumph; if Black people's blood, his doom. Yet the revelations from the Holy Ghost suggested another answer altogether, one that followed from the Spirit's original admonition to Nat to attend not to *the things of this world* but to *the kingdom of heaven*. The blood that sketched the figures of the black and white spirits might be the spirits' own blood, or blood that would be shed by the participants in the revolt. But the stream of blood and the drops on the corn and leaves were something different, the Holy Ghost revealed: they were the blood of Jesus Christ, shed to make a new age.

"For as the blood of Christ had been shed on this earth, and had ascended to heaven for the salvation of sinners, and was now returned to earth again in the form of dew—and as the leaves on the trees bore the impression of the figures I had seen in the heavens," Nat recalled, "it was plain to me that the Saviour was about to lay down the yoke he had borne for the sins of men, and the great day of judgment was at hand."[65] This was the good news: The Savior was returning for the apocalyptic battle against Satan. The battle between black spirits and white spirits would be the start of the battle for God's kingdom. And the Savior would be on his side.[66]

It was a beautiful vision, and a terrifying one, too. It foretold not simply the end of slavery but the end of the world.

NAT'S VISIONS DID not bring him honor in the neighborhood. Perhaps because of his earlier escape and return or perhaps because of the skepticism prophets always face, Nat did not attract many disciples. Possibly people were mystified by him. Or maybe they were afraid.

One follower, however, raises a profound question about Nat's understanding of the war to come: Etheldred T. Brantley, a white man and a drunkard. Brantley, a former overseer, was seeking God among the Baptists when he became aware of Nat's preaching. Despite Brantley's reputation, Nat was deeply gratified to have a follower. Nat claimed that he "had a wonderful effect" upon this sinner, who then "ceased from his wickedness." Nat saw his own power reflected in Brantley's life and on the overseer's very skin, which suffered from a "cutaneous eruption, and blood oozed from the pores," Nat said. By following Nat's example of "praying and fasting," Brantley "was healed" after nine days. Nat's story was partly corroborated in September 1831, weeks before Nat's capture and confession, in an account by the local attorney William C. Parker.[67]

Having healed Brantley, Nat claimed a mantle that went back to the Bible. In the Hebrew Bible, Moses's prayers cured Miriam's leprosy, and other prophets restored followers. Nat might have seen his healing through its association with the most famous healer in the Bible, Jesus Christ. Christ had healed many people—blind men, lepers, a paralyzed person at Capernaum, a bleeding woman, a man with dropsy, a disabled woman, deaf people, and a man with a withered hand, among others. While some powers belonged only to Christ, healing was something his disciples could carry out in the present day. Healers were common, respected figures in enslaved communities, and many formerly enslaved people believed in healing practices rooted in West African religions and folkways. Nat would have had a wide repertoire of spiritual traditions to draw from, and we cannot know for certain whether he saw himself syncretizing these beliefs or following one specific line. Nor is the distinction always clear in the stories of enslaved healers who practiced both Christianity and West African rituals.[68]

It may initially seem strange that a Black prophet would take joy from converting and healing a white overseer. But Zilpha Elaw also related her satisfaction at converting a belligerent white person. One Christmas Eve, as Elaw gave a sermon, the "most profligate drunkard in that vicinity" at first taunted her, then fell into tears and dropped to his knees. The next day, Elaw learned of the depth of the man's response and of his sins, for this man, too, was an overseer. Elaw returned to the chapel with "swords sharpened," hoping to convert him, and was pleasantly surprised to see the overseer "clothed, and in his right mind."[69]

So, too, did Nat take on the work of converting the overseer Brantley, whatever judgments Nat had reached about slaveholders. The "Spirit appeared" to Nat again and said that he and Brantley should be baptized "as the Saviour had been baptised," and Nat went to work. The baptism should be a public event, a ritual acknowledgment of his prophetic status, but "the white people would not let us." Nat's account was partly corroborated by a local attorney's claim that "pre-

tending to be divinely inspired . . . he announced to the Blacks, that
he should baptize himself on a particular day, and that whilst in the
water, a dove would be seen to descend from Heaven and perch on his
head,—thus endeavoring to collect a great crowd." The attorney likewise claimed the "assemblage" was blocked, but that Nat completed
Brantley's baptism anyway. We cannot be certain which white people
blocked the gathering. It was not necessarily the congregation at Turner's Meeting House, where Nat worshipped as a child, nor was it necessarily that of any other Methodist church. Brantley might well have
preferred his own Baptist church, and Nat would have been within
the teachings of Methodism to offer to baptize a convert in the convert's own church.[70] Black people in Southampton later claimed that
Nat asked the Methodist church to baptize Brantley but was refused,
leading him toward Brantley's Baptists in his final years. But Nat did
not say so, even though Gray, an atheist, might have been interested
in raising doubts about another evangelical sect.[71] What Nat did say is
that he and Brantley went to Persons Mill Pond, just west of Persons
Methodist Church and about four miles west of the Moore farm, and
there a crowd gathered to watch them.[72]

In the *Confessions*, Nat avoided most expressions of emotion, but
he was overjoyed by what came next. When Nat and Brantley walked
to the pond, "we went down into the water together, in the sight of
many who reviled us, and were baptized by the Spirit." This seemed
to echo the story of John the Baptist as he baptized Jesus, though not
in every respect. The heavens did not open up over them, as they did
over John the Baptist, but Nat was not Christ, nor did he ever think
himself so. Still, the Spirit's arrival to baptize Brantley was a public
display of Nat's status. Nat absorbed the Spirit's presence as a confirmation. "After this I rejoiced greatly, and gave thanks to God."[73]

Nat did not comment on the crowd of onlookers beyond the fact
that they "reviled" him, and he gave no indication that the baptism
changed their views. This might have discouraged a lesser person, but
Nat well understood that a prophet was often treated dismissively or
derisively. He had seen this when he returned from his thirty days of

laying out and found that fellow enslaved people murmured against him. Had not Jesus preached in Nazareth that "no prophet is accepted in his own country"? Didn't the stories of Jeremiah and other prophets confirm this?[74]

Some time later Nat began preaching that "blacks ought to be free, and that they would be free one day or other," according to the report in the Richmond newspaper. For his freedom talk, Nat was whipped, likely by Thomas Moore.[75] The whipping surely outraged him, and it might have humiliated him. Perhaps it confirmed his perfection in the face of the world's sinfulness, the association between his suffering and Jesus's. But we do not know: in the Confessions, he did not mention Moore by name.

In the middle of 1827, Nat's life changed again. Thomas Moore died unexpectedly, without leaving a will. Control of the enslaved people would be shuffled again. Moore's land belonged to his widow, Sally Francis Moore, during her lifetime, and to their little son Putnam in his estate. Moore's widow claimed the use of Hark and two other enslaved people, her son legal possession of six others, including Nat. Once again Nat belonged to a child, and once more his rights were controlled by an estate.[76]

Now Nat had a reputation, although it isn't clear how seriously the white people took it. Sally's brother Salathiel Francis lived across the road from her in his own cabin. A local historian suggested that Salathiel warned Sally about Nat. But we do not know if other white people, or other members of the Francis family, harbored the same fears, or even if Salathiel warned his sister at all.[77]

Whatever their opinion of Nat, the Francis family was exerting increasing control over him. They had also come to control much of the neighborhood. Sally and Salathiel's brother Nathaniel Francis lived two miles northeast along footpaths that crossed the different Francis farms. Together the Francis family holdings totaled nearly 1,300 acres and almost forty enslaved people, sixteen of them over fifteen years old, the rest children. Among those enslaved people held by different Francis family members were not only Nat but also other figures who would be important in the rebellion, including his chief lieutenant and his "executioner."[78]

In 1828, it is possible that Nat lived not on one of those farms but on nearby land rented out to Giles Reese, a debt-plagued thirty-year-old man who had married into the Turner family. Giles Reese had leased the farm bordering Sally and Salathiel. The Reeses were Methodists, too, but troubled ones. Giles Reese had been charged with assault twice, and other Reeses were in and out of legal disputes. But the family remained part of the broader Methodist network of enslavers, and Reese cousins probably claimed ownership over Nat's wife and son during the 1820s. Possibly Cherry and Riddick had moved back to the Cross Keys area with a member of the Reese family around 1826, and Cherry might have worked on the farm that belonged to Nathaniel Francis, Sally Francis Moore's brother.[79]

Nat might have lived with Giles Reese between Moore's death and Sally Francis Moore's remarriage. If so, he was living with Reese, near his wife and son, when the Spirit appeared to him again in 1828.[80]

ON MAY 28, 1828, Nat had another vision. "I heard a loud noise in the heavens, and the Spirit instantly appeared to me and said the Serpent was loosened." Perhaps the noise and the sight were the products of a large meteor's path through the sky, as one historian suggests, and some people elsewhere saw serpent-like trails behind the great meteor storms of that year. But if anyone else in Southampton saw such a thing, we have no record of it, and we should not exclude the possibility that Nat was describing not an interpretation of an existing natural phenomenon but a purely personal vision. The serpent's appearance confirmed his earlier understanding, for the serpent was the enemy that fought God in the Hebrew Bible and Jesus in the Christian Testament. It was the serpent who alienated humans from God in Genesis by tempting Eve, who led Eve and Adam to hide themselves from the Lord, and who warred with Christ in the battle that leads to the millennium.[81] After Christ descended from heaven on a white horse, cloaked in his blood-soaked robe, his eyes aflame, a sword between his teeth, the archangel Michael sealed up the serpent, "which is the Devil, and Satan," for a thousand years.[82] John of Patmos then "heard a loud voice saying in heaven, Now is come salvation, and strength, and the kingdom of our God, and the power of his Christ."[83]

So, too, did the Spirit tell Nat to prepare for battle. "Christ had laid down the yoke he had borne for the sins of men," the Spirit told him, "and that I should take it on and fight against the Serpent, for the time was fast approaching when the first should be last and the last should be first."[84] Nat's vision called back to the book of Matthew, where Jesus told the Pharisees in the coast along Judaea, "the last shall be first, and the first last: for many be called, but few chosen." Soon thereafter, Jesus entered Jerusalem.[85]

Standing near the road to his own Jerusalem, Nat saw in this vision the resolution to his fears and his doubts. If he were waiting to understand what type he might have to reenact and expand upon, he now had something close to an answer. He had cultivated his relationship to the Spirit, retreating to the woods in solitary prayer, telling of his visions, puzzling over meanings, and seeking knowledge and assurance.[86]

Now the Spirit cast the battle against the white spirits in the great train of events that would culminate with Christ's thousand-year reign in the kingdom of God on earth. When Nat launched the revolt, his oracle revealed, he would defeat the serpent, and the millennium would begin.

Nat's insistence that the millennium was "fast approaching" brought the apocalypse into historical time in this world. Like other early American Methodists, Nat suggested that Hebrew Bible narratives were harbingers of a future that was *possible*, not just metaphorically, but concretely. For all that Revelation dwelled in vagaries and phantom imagery, John of Patmos insisted he depicted a real future. "Come up hither," Jesus bade John of Patmos, "and I will shew thee things which must be hereafter."[87]

The Spirit's words evoked the biblical Jerusalem, Revelation's

New Jerusalem, and the county seat of Nat's Southampton, all at once. Jesus himself had paused on the way to Jerusalem and said, in Mark's language, "Many that are first shall be last, and the last first."[88] Twice in Matthew, we read something similar, once in the parable of the vineyards, which might have been especially poignant for enslaved Southampton people who worked distilling brandy. Now, outside Nat's own Jerusalem, the Spirit gave Nat the same message in almost the same words. The time was fast approaching when the first should be last and the last should be first.[89]

Still, Nat did not quite act, because the time fast approaching had not yet arrived. Nat explained this need to wait as the Spirit's own injunction. It was only a matter of time, the Spirit told Nat, before it revealed "when I should commence the great work."[90]

THREE YEARS PASSED between the revelation of May 12, 1828, and the revolt of August 1831. The Spirit's visit led Nat not to action but to another mysterious period of hesitation. It is possible he paused because he hoped to gain followers, though it seems he didn't actually tell anyone of his plans for quite a while. It is possible that Nat paused because of the shift in his living conditions, hired out to neighbors who might or might not have governed his everyday movements. It is also possible that he had more time to visit his wife and son.

But then Nat's domestic situation changed again. In October 1829, Sally Francis Moore married Joseph Travis, a man from outside the area with no close relatives in the county, in a ceremony at the Methodist church. It is difficult to say much about Joseph Travis. He was roughly Nat's age, and he had married to great advantage, having no land of his own. He tried to keep the Moore farm raising corn, cotton, cows, and hogs through the work of seventeen enslaved people, six of whom were children. According to Gray, Nat said that Travis "placed the greatest confidence in me" and was a "kind master." One local historian claimed, presumably based on stories of older residents in the late nineteenth century, that Nat was "often called Nat Travis," but no other source records this. The Travises lived in a two-chamber, one-story house, with a front door that opened into a hall that served as dining room and sleeping area for Putnam and white boarders. There was a kitchen where a young, enslaved child named Moses slept. Then to the left was Joseph and Sally's room. From the dining room, a staircase led to a small upstairs attic. The other enslaved people slept in cabins near the house. In 1831, Sally became pregnant, and by summer the baby slept with them in a cradle.[91] Perhaps something about this situation gave Nat pause.

IT IS ALSO POSSIBLE that Nat and other enslaved people were aware of rumors about an 1829 debate over the future of slavery in Virginia, a debate that they might have interpreted as a sign for hope. The debate was about the allocation of power within the commonwealth, as determined by the number of seats each county received in the state legislature. The basic question was the same one that had divided the U.S. Constitutional Convention decades earlier: Should areas with enslaved populations get credit for those people when setting their number of representatives? In Virginia this question was complicated by limited voter eligibility and by refusals to reallocate legislative seats as more of the white population moved into western counties. Over the 1820s, anger in the western region boiled over. By January 1828, legislators, under pressure, agreed to call a popular referendum on a constitutional convention, but only those already qualified to vote under the existing, restrictive laws could cast ballots. Even so, the convention resolution passed. At the convention, James Madison himself presided over a committee that recommended opening access to voting to all white male householders and equalizing representation.[92]

The convention ended in a compromise that expanded representation and suffrage, but not to the degree that westerners wanted; one-third of Virginia's adult white male taxpayers still could not vote, nor could anyone directly cast ballots for governor or for judges. The state reallocated seats based on the 1820 white population but did not include any mechanism for future revision, ensuring that the western counties would become more disadvantaged as they grew. The new plan still gave the eastern Tidewater four more delegates than a strict democratic apportionment would have. The vote was sharply divided; fifty-four of the fifty-five votes for the new plan came from easterners, while westerners cast thirty-four of the forty no votes.[93]

While the debates were over technical matters of representation, the language was contentious, even bitter, in ways that enslaved people might have taken as evidence of a deeper divide among white Virginians. Western representatives considered themselves oppressed by the slaveholding Tidewater aristocracy, while eastern delegates feared the growing power of western white people, most of whom owned few if any enslaved people. Whether deliberately or in panic, eastern delegates portrayed western demands for more representation as a campaign against slavery. One planter warned that there "exists in a great portion of [the western part of the commonwealth] a rooted antipathy" to slavery. If white western Virginia delegates held power, Richard Morris, a delegate from Hanover County, just north of Richmond, wildly predicted, "a sword will be unsheathed, that will be red with the best blood, of this country, before it finds the scabbard." The relationship "between master and slave, is one, which *cannot* be left to be regulated by the Government." Many Tidewater delegates believed that democracy and slavery could not be reconciled, that the only way to save slavery was to limit democracy.[94]

The wild language of these arguments, reprinted in state newspapers, might well have taught enslaved people that the political order was cracking. One local historian believed that enslaved people in neighboring Isle of Wight learned of the debates and thought they turned on emancipation, not representation. This historian thinks Nat "doubtless" heard the same rumors. If so, it would have resembled— as the historian James Sidbury notes—other moments when enslaved people hoped that debates among white people might create space for them to act. Sidbury points to the 1795 Pointe Coupée rebellion in Louisiana, when enslaved people incorrectly believed the king of

Spain proclaimed their liberation. These Virginia rumors might also mirror the connections enslaved people made between the contentious 1800 presidential campaign and Gabriel's rebellion in Richmond, and between Rufus King's bitter denunciation of slave power in debates over Missouri's statehood and Denmark Vesey's alleged rebellion. From one vantage these enslaved people seem simply wrong; southern whites rarely debated state-enforced emancipation, focusing on the allocation of power among white voters. From another vantage, however, enslaved people and their free Black allies were assessing the opportunities presented by conflicts among white people. Perhaps Nat, too, was watching in 1829, waiting to see what would become of the debates among distant white people, debates that could at least in theory transform his world. Perhaps he looked for signs that other white people, not just Brantley, could be saved.[95]

But maybe Nat's actions make better sense in light of the fate Nat saw for himself, a fate he might have guessed from the lives of Jesus Christ and other biblical prophets. Nat, contemplating himself on the road that led to his Jerusalem, hearing the words that Christ spoke on his road to the original Jerusalem, might have asked himself, yet again but even more concretely, whether his own death was inevitable. Christ knew for a certainty he would die, according to the Gospels of Matthew, Mark, and Luke.[96] When the Spirit showed Christ's outstretched arms in the stars of the sky, Nat might have seen his own future.

Christ's death in Jerusalem did fulfill the prophecy, but in a way that would be painful for a prophet to contemplate. Jesus was mocked and misunderstood and betrayed by the very people he aimed to save. Even those onlookers who cheered his arrival misunderstood him; they believed he had come to restore the Davidic kingdom.[97] Other prophets read Christ's experience on the road to Jerusalem as a metaphor for internal conflict and persistence. The preacher Elizabeth quoted Luke 19:41: "And when he was come near, he beheld the city, and wept over it." Just before the 1823 revolt in Demerara, in what is now Guyana, the parson John Smith read Luke's account to eight hundred enslaved congregants. So, too, might the enslaved people of Demerara or Elizabeth or Southampton weep over their fate, even as they approached it.[98]

Defeating the fear of death was an act of faith for evangelicals, but it took work to achieve this state of fearlessness. A line of 1 Corinthians portrayed death's diminishing effect and was repeated in a popular hymn collected by Richard Allen and many others: "O Death, where is thy sting?"[99] Yet, didn't death still have a sting, even for Jesus? Jesus became "sorrowful and very heavy" as he waited at Gethsemane. And didn't Jesus pray, "Father, if thou be willing, remove this cup from me"?[100] No one could expect any more of Nat. Because martyrs eventually die, it is alluring to make of them fanatics who care nothing for their own lives, but prophets did not act haphazardly or without forethought. They acted in dreadful knowledge and in dreadful fear. Nat's death was one of the possibilities the Spirit alluded to in the admonition that he would have to accept whatever happened, *come rough or smooth*.

In 1830, as Nat waited for his sign, several published copies of David Walker's *Appeal* were found in the Richmond home of a free Black person. Like Nat's *Confessions*, the *Appeal* shook the world, and continues to shake the world today with its dire critiques of slaveholders and its invocations of war. Amid all that bravado, Walker acknowledged the painful position of prophets like Nat: they had to strike without knowing exactly how God would intervene, or even whether the enslaved people's rebellion would succeed. It is tempting to imagine Walker's *Appeal* making its way to the highly literate Nat, but there is no such evidence. After word of that discovery spread through Richmond, Virginia's legislators—like legislators in other states—made it illegal for free Black people to gather together and teach themselves to read or write.[101] If enforced, this would have curtailed free Black people's experiences in both biracial and all-Black religious gatherings, though there is no sign of enforcement in Southampton.

Like Walker, like the prophets of old, Nat would have to act on faith alone. That faith could not promise him either survival or success, only that his actions were part of God's plan. Like Abraham on the altar with Isaac, Nat would have to offer not only himself but also his family and his neighbors as lambs for the slaughter. Only after Abraham obeyed God's order to sacrifice Isaac did the Lord reveal that this was a test, not a command Abraham would be required to carry out. So, too, might Nat launch his rebellion and only then understand God's ultimate task for him, whatever that might be. One day, surely, the land would be his people's, as Canaan eventually belonged to Abraham's descendants. But how? And when? And what role would his own actions play in this? Nat had to reconcile himself to the fact that he could not know, not any more than Abraham could. All he could know for certain was his own risk and his glimpses of God's mysterious will.

THE SPIRIT TOLD Nat to expect a sign to launch the revolt, and so Nat must have waited in hope and fear for thirty-three months. During this period, revivals spread across Virginia, and hundreds of thousands of white and Black Virginians went to camp meetings. In early 1831, at revivals in Buckingham County, pastors preached on the "great day of wrath" and the sixth seal of Revelation. The historian Wayne Durrill attributes the general discussion of apocalypses to the mix of economic hard times, revivalism, and political turmoil in Palestine, where Egypt's wresting of control from the Ottoman Empire led thousands of Jews to the Holy Land, raising some evangelicals' expectations that the return of the Jews to Israel would inaugurate the apocalypse.[102]

There were also signs of a changing world closer to home. In February 1831, one of the Reese family, John Reese, fell terribly behind on loans he had taken from his neighbors to pay for land near the extended Francis holdings. On February 5, Reese met with three men to discuss the debt: John Clark Turner (brother of Samuel Turner); Henry Moore (brother and executor of Thomas Moore); and Nathaniel Francis (Sally Francis Moore Travis's brother). As surety for his loans, John Reese offered three of the enslaved people he controlled, pledging his creditor could sell them at auction if Reese fell behind on payments. One of those he put up as collateral was Riddick, likely Nat's son. Even though the creditors accepted Reese's collateral, they still moved ahead with the land sale, and the buyers they found were, conveniently enough, themselves. Both Nathaniel Francis and Henry Moore bought land. John Reese was now a tenant.[103]

Seven days after this meeting, on the morning of February 12, 1831, Nat saw his sign, a solar eclipse, a message in biblical times and the present day. Four times in the Hebrew Bible, a dark sun warns of God's unhappiness. Isaiah and Ezekiel pointed to solar eclipses as proof of God's punishment of the Babylonians and Egyptians for holding Jews in slavery. The "day of the Lord cometh . . . [T]he stars of heaven and the constellations thereof shall not give their light: the sun shall be darkened in his going forth . . . And I will punish the world for their evil," Isaiah wrote.[104] In the books of Matthew and Mark, the disciples asked, "What shall be the sign of thy coming, and of the end of the world?" Jesus answered that after the "tribulation" the "sun shall be darkened, and the moon shall not give her light, and the stars shall fall from heaven."[105] In John of Patmos's vision of the opening of the sixth seal, "the sun became black as sackcloth of hair, and the moon became as blood, and the stars of heaven fell unto the earth, even as a fig tree casteth her untimely figs."[106]

The great eclipse of 1831 had been predicted in almanacs, and in some places business was suspended so people could watch it in trepidation and excitement. It was the first significant annular solar eclipse in Virginia in twenty years.[107] The day before the eclipse, one editor reported that an "old shoe-black" had told a person on the street "the world is to be destroyed to-morr; the sun and moon are to meet . . . and a great earthquake was to swallow us all." The day after the eclipse preachers frequently employed Luke 21:25 as a text: "There shall be signs in the sun."[108]

In fact, the spectacle was anticlimactic across many parts of the United States. But it was an impressive sight in Southside Virginia. For two hours at midday, a partial shadow fell over Southampton, just east of the total eclipse visible between Richmond and Norfolk.[109] The partial eclipse might have brought to mind the partial eclipse in Revelation when an angel inaugurates the fourth plague upon the earth at the blast of a trumpet: "The third part of the sun was smitten, and the third part of the moon, and the third part of the stars; so as the third part of them was darkened, and the day shone not for a third part of it."[110]

The Spirit told Nat to "conceal" his task "from the knowledge of men" until the sign appeared, and thus a seal was placed over his lips. Perhaps like Rebecca Jackson, the free Black visionary in Philadelphia, Nat kept his secrets jealously, hoping to gain God's favor by silence even as he also preached the Word.[111] But a seal is broken when it is time for God's actions to enter again into the world. In Revelation, an angel calls out, "Who is worthy to open the book, and to loose the seals thereof?" Only the Lamb—only Christ.[112] So, too, must God's revelation leave the secret property of the prophets' hearts and go out into the world.

The seal had been placed over Nat's lips, and the eclipse was a command to break that seal. In John of Patmos's revelation, breaking the seals unleashed afflictions of the end-time: wars of conquest, death, famine, disease, an earthquake, the bloodied moon, the blackened sun.[113] In John's last vision, an angel tells him, "Seal not the sayings of the prophecy of this book: for the time is at hand."[114]

The eclipse in February 1831 meant Nat's time was nearing, too. "And immediately on the sign appearing in the heavens, the seal was removed from my lips, and I communicated the great work laid out for me to do, to four in whom I had the greatest confidence," Nat said, according to the *Confessions*.[115] The Spirit had revealed all it intended. Now, at last, it was time to speak.

5

Alarm in the Neighborhood

Nat spoke only to his Black neighbors. His early followers included men who lived nearby and whom Nat had known well for years. To find them, he turned to the same neighborhood that had raised him, those enslaved men who had viewed him as special. After the attacks but before his capture, Thomas Gray wrote to a Richmond newspaper that Nat "had acquired a great deal of influence over his neighbourhood acquaintance."[1]

By 1831, Nat had a wide "acquaintance" within the neighborhood, especially for a plow-hand. Nat learned the neighborhood not by trade but through church and the geography of his owners, passing from one white person's legal control to another. A rural neighborhood might be stitched together geographically by paths, institutionally by families, farmland, and churches. In the area around Cross Keys, a handful of white Methodist families had intermarried, passed enslaved people and land to one another, executed one another's wills, offered credit to one another, helped one another in busy farming seasons, lent enslaved people to one another, and attended services and class meetings together. The enslaved people held by these families thus had moved from one of the white nuclear families to another, mixing among enslaved people from nearby farms, establishing their own networks through marriage, work, church, and gossip. Nat was visibly and meaningfully known to many of the enslaved people in the immediately surrounding area, not just by name or by sight, but by knowledge of his past behavior. Those were the people he told.[2]

Nat began by confiding in four men "in whom I had the greatest confidence" about "the great work laid out for me to do." These men were known to whites as Henry Porter, Hark Moore (sometimes called Hark Travis), Nelson Edwards, and Sam Francis, although we cannot be certain that the men attributed those last names to themselves. They were all men of the neighborhood who likely had worked fields. They, like Nat, were all in their thirties and had lived in the neighborhood for more than five years, some much longer. Each of them came from farms with fifteen to thirty enslaved people, mostly owned by Methodists. Some of them likely had attended Methodist services with Nat and with Nat's enslavers and their family members. Henry might have been enslaved by Richard Porter on a farm two and a quarter miles east of Nat's residence, with about thirty other enslaved people. If so, the historian David Allmendinger suggests, he might have lived in the neighborhood with Nat as a boy, been sent five miles north when his original enslaver's daughter married, then returned after the death of that husband. Nelson had lived two and a half miles northeast of the Travis farm on a plantation with twenty-eight enslaved people. It's possible he had been born farther away and been moved into the neighborhood when he was fourteen when his enslaver's widow married Peter Edwards. Sam had fallen under the control of Sally's brother Nathaniel Francis in 1820, on a plantation located between the Travis place, where Nat lived, and the Edwards and Porter plantations, where Henry and Nelson lived. Hark, probably short for Hercules, was by most accounts the most physically impressive and probably the most intimately known to Nat, having been under the control of the same enslavers for years and working and living alongside him. A white man called Hark "a regular black Apollo" and "one of the most perfectly framed men he ever saw."[3] Perhaps Nat thought of them as his version of David's "three mighty men," the elite inner circle of David's fighting force against the Philistines.[4]

We do not know exactly when they began to plan, but Hark and Nat might have begun to speak concretely in February when their family members were at fresh risk of being used as collateral. The others had perhaps listened to Nat's prophecies in the neighborhood. Perhaps they had not been part of the crowd that murmured against him. Perhaps they showed the respect that Nat felt was warranted a

man called by God.[5] Some enslaved people in other distant neighborhoods claimed later to have known of Nat's plans, but Nat disagreed.
Nat was not surprised that other people might have been moved by
the unjustness of slavery and the tidings in the skies, but he did not
take credit for a broader plan.[6]

Nat had kept quiet a long time because he understood a lesson of
other enslaved people's revolts: too much talking exposed them to betrayal. This happened to Denmark Vesey in Charleston and to Gabriel
in Richmond. A newspaper report said that Nat had told one of his
allies that "the negroes had frequently attempted similar things, con-
fided their purpose to several, and that it always leaked out." Therefore, Nat decided "their march of destruction and murder, should be
the first news of the insurrection." They met and planned, but they
kept quiet between February and August 1831.[7]

Nat did not tell the white man Etheldred T. Brantley, whom he had
baptized in 1828. Some later testimony suggested they held hopes
distant white people would recognize the holiness of Nat's cause and
convert, but it is impossible to be certain. For the beginning, at least,
their plan was for a religious war that was also a race war.

BEGINNING IN FEBRUARY 1831, they started preparations for "the
work of death" that was to commence on the propitious day of July 4.
The fact that Nat chose a national holiday raises questions that he did not
answer. Did Nat select July simply from practicality? Perhaps he judged
that white people would be drunken or sleepy that evening, vulnerable
and unsuspecting after the customary militia parades and celebratory
dinner in Jerusalem. Perhaps he hoped that the enslaved people would
be freed from work by the festivities, able to rest and to prepare. But
maybe Nat was moved by a different spirit, by the winds of Atlantic
revolution. Other African American rebels had timed their actions to
important dates in Atlantic history. The Charleston rebellion allegedly
plotted by Denmark Vesey was scheduled to begin on July 14, the anniversary of the date the French stormed the Bastille, and Vesey was

deeply aware of the history of Atlantic revolts. In Vesey's Charleston, South Carolina, there had been rumors in the 1820s of a July 4 attack. A pamphlet there argued that the "Fourth of July belongs *exclusively* to the white population of the United States" and Black people should be excluded. "In our speeches and orations, much, and sometimes more than politically necessary, is said about personal liberty, which negro auditors know not how to apply, except by running the parallel with their own condition. They therefore imbibe false notions of their own personal rights, and give reality in their minds to what has no real existence."[8] As enslaved and free Black people assessed their own revolutions, they frequently dressed themselves in revolutionary garb, quoted revolutionary sayings, and in other ways attached themselves to auspicious times and dates, perhaps to claim the nation's sense of destiny for themselves, perhaps to signal the hypocrisy of Independence Day. Maybe Nat, too, reflected on the potential for either redeeming or revealing the destiny of the United States on July 4, but if so he left no record. What else Nat did in the interim, we cannot say.

July 4 came and went, with no attack. In the last of the puzzling delays that shape Nat's story, he did not strike. The work of planning and the fear for his fate stopped him in his tracks. "Many were the plans formed and rejected by us, and it affected my mind to such a degree, that I fell sick, and the time passed without our coming to any determination how to commence," he told Gray. Beyond this mention of his sickness, Nat did not speak of anxiety or fear. Coincidentally, on that day a famous Virginian died: James Monroe, the governor who decided upon the executions in Gabriel's 1800 rebellion and the envoy who negotiated the Louisiana Purchase, extending slavery.[9]

Meanwhile, Nat and his compatriots formed "new schemes" and rejected them, waiting perhaps for one more sign. That sign came in August 1831, when a series of atmospheric disturbances created unusual sights in the sky. Coincidentally, several volcanoes erupted in the West Indies, Washington state, southern Italy, and the Mediterranean Sea, expelling ash into the atmosphere. At about the same time a hurricane struck Barbados and turned toward Louisiana. The hurricane's disruptions created a peculiar atmospheric effect. The Bermuda sun turned blue; on Cape Hatteras, ship sails seemed tinged blue as well. In Virginia the air appeared vaporous and red on Saturday, August 13. "About mid-day, the sun shining through this body of vapor had a silvery appearance similar to that which it wears when shining through a vanishing fog, & I observed it to give an unusually ghastly appearance to the countenances of persons," a white observer wrote. "Between three and four o'clock, the position of the sun, with respect to this body of vapor becoming changed, it assumed a greenish blue appearance." Then, "as the sun descended below the body of vapour, which was about fifteen or twenty minutes before its setting, the vapor reflected an intensely red light" and a spot appeared on the sun "visible to the unprotected eye." This blue sun allegedly convinced some people around Fredericksburg, Virginia, that "war is at hand."[10]

This sunspot, then, was finally the Spirit's call to act. Nat had received portents and visions and words, and now an eclipse and a sunspot. The "sign appeared again, which determined me not to wait longer," Nat said.[11]

Nat was not the only person caught in a swell of religious excitement. On the next day, Sunday, August 14, an event suggested the ferment among the region's Black people. That day, a large gathering of Black people apparently met near Barnes Church, on the southern edge of the county near the North Carolina line. A letter written in late August by a prominent white militia leader stated that "the prevalent belief is" that Black attendees "were observed to be disorderly, took offence at something (it is not known what)," and that "the plan of insurrection" was "then and there conceived."[12] It is impossible to know if the white militia leader had intelligence of some kind of conflict at the gathering that helped push Nat to act. Possibly Nat himself spoke. The text that was believed to have been discussed was from Revelation 6:2: "And I saw, and behold a white horse: and he that sat on him had a bow; and a crown was given unto him: and he went forth conquering, and to conquer."[13] Some whites later believed that Black people wore red bandanna handkerchiefs around their necks at that gathering, though it is likely this is a reading backward of the handkerchiefs worn during the insurrection.[14]

With Henry and Hark, Nat decided upon August 22, itself a propitious date in Atlantic revolutionary history. Forty years earlier, on August 22, 1791, large numbers of enslaved people on Saint-Domingue launched an attack upon plantations in Plaine-du-Nord that started what became known as the Haitian Revolution. How conscious was Nat of this date? Certainly African Americans knew of the "black republic" in Haiti, in part because of the fearful whispers of plantation owners and white politicians. Was the day August 22 widely associated with this rebellion among antebellum Black people, enslaved and free? Some scholars have raised the possibility that the Haitian Revolution was celebrated on that date in some African American communities, but there remain grave doubts about how widespread the practice was in the slave South.[15] Both July 4 and August 22 were Mondays, and it is possible that Nat simply planned to wait until the day after the Sabbath to give him time to celebrate the Lord's day and then six days for fighting before the prescribed day of rest the next Sunday.

Whether Nat arrived at Monday, August 22, through the Haitian Revolution or through his response to the sunspot, on Saturday, August 20, he, Henry, and Hark decided to host a dinner the following day "for the men we expected, and then to concert a plan, as we had not yet determined on any." Early on Sunday, Hark brought a pig and Henry brandy to Cabin Pond, less than a mile north of Joseph Travis's house. They were joined by Nelson and Sam, who had collaborated since February, and by two other men from the neighborhood. One was Jack Reese, the brother of Hark's wife. The other was Will, enslaved on the same plantation as Sam, a farm owned by Nathaniel Francis, the brother of Sally Francis Moore Travis. Will had lived in the neighborhood since his birth in the 1790s on the farm that belonged to Samuel Francis Sr., and thus had lived near Nat since 1807 and had been raised among Methodists, though Will's own faith is unknown. Will would join Henry and Hark in the rebellion leadership.[16]

As the men prepared the food, there was no Nat. He stayed away, he said, for "the same reason that had caused me not to mix with them for years before." Possibly Nat still felt the need to distinguish himself. Likely he prayed during the morning on Sunday, recognizing the Sabbath.[17]

Finally, at three o'clock on Sunday, August 21, Nat "saluted them on coming up." Seeing men he did not expect, Nat asked Will "how came he there." Will answered that "his life was worth no more than others, and his liberty as dear to him." Will pledged he would obtain freedom "or loose his life." With that, Nat placed "full confidence" in Will. Jack, however, was young and uncertain, only about twenty-one years old. Although claimed by the Reese family, Jack had been hired out and was just returning to his home plantation, probably visiting his wife, when Hark—his sister's husband—drew him in. But Jack "was only a tool in the hands of Hark," Nat believed. Nat had little confidence in him, for good reason. With this band gathered, Nat and the others made their plan to meet at Nat's home plantation, the Travis farm, later that night. According to Nat, "it was quickly agreed we should commence at home" and "until we had armed and equipped ourselves, and gathered sufficient force, neither age nor sex was to be spared, (which was invariably adhered to.) [sic]"[18]

Jack's account of the meeting differed from Nat's. When Jack later confessed, he claimed that the meeting was contentious. According to Jack's confession, Nat took the men away "one at a time" and held "long conversations with them." When the men said they would "rise and kill all the white people," Jack objected and "denied the possibility of effecting it" because their "number was too few." Hark then answered that "as they went on and killed the whites the blacks would join them." Nat agreed and suggested that they only had to kill the eighty thousand white people he believed lived in the area, and then the region would be theirs. It is certainly possible the meeting was contentious. But Jack had reason to emphasize his skepticism once he was captured and was seeking mercy.[19]

Finally the time fast approaching had arrived. It was time to act, and time to kill.

THEY WOULD BEGIN around midnight just after the Sabbath ended, at the farm where Nat lived. Having agreed, they waited until dark. Or, really, they did not wait but ate roast pig and drank brandy. What, precisely, the men anticipated on that night, we cannot say for certain. Nor can we know Nat's thoughts as he watched his followers, but Nat likely feared both that they would get drunk and that they would lose heart if they stayed sober.

After midnight, they began to make their way to the Travis house, the house that now belonged to Joseph Travis and his wife, Sally Francis Moore Travis, and her child Putnam Moore. Nat knew this place intimately, having lived there during his twenties under Thomas Moore and then again in 1830–1831 when Joseph Travis married Sally and apparently brought Nat back from his hiring. Nat went to pains to deny personal motives toward Joseph Travis, calling him "kind" and saying, "I had no cause to complain of his treatment of me."[20] And yet Nat and his band attacked Travis first. If we take Nat's words seriously, Nat struck not because of a personal grudge but upon the command of the Spirit. He might well have hated Travis, but he did not need to hate Travis to hate slavery or to believe that God had called him to act.

It was less than a mile through woods and undergrowth from their final feast to the Travis farm. There they found Austin, an enslaved man from a neighboring farm. The enslaved men "all went to the cider house and drank, except" Nat. The orchards around Southampton produced hard cider and apple brandy and other fermented and distilled liquors, and it is no surprise that the conspirators stopped several times to drink, whether seeking celebration or courage amid their anxieties. Nat held himself back, probably for the same reason he had kept the men waiting at the planning dinner. Nat was not like the men; he showed them that, and they knew it, whether they judged him favorably or ill for those differences.[21] Nat's standoffishness raises the question of when we should define a rebellion by its abstemious leader and when by his less abstemious followers, with their own motivations. Nat could not have rebelled without these followers, but it's also clear that Nat's role was indispensable. His followers needed him to be the one who could see higher meaning beyond the moments of death, to sketch a narrative that made those actions holy.

There had not been a service at Turner's Meeting House that day, so along with several of their neighbors the Travises had been away at a Methodist meeting, possibly hearing a sermon by Sally Travis's uncle George Powell, who preached to "seek first the kingdom of God, and his righteousness," a slightly differently worded version of the verse of Matthew 6:33 that Nat had heard and prayed upon as he waited for the Spirit. Then the Travises returned and barred the door for the night. Moses, the thirteen-year-old enslaved child at the Travis home, said he was awake when the men approached and he saw Jack sitting outside "with his head between his hands resting on his knees." But "Hark would not let [Jack] go." Later, Moses saw Jack in the yard, "sick." Inside the house, Putnam Moore and an apprentice were sleeping in the hall parlor, and Joseph and Sally Travis in the main bedroom with their infant in the cradle.[22]

As the band approached the house, Hark, who lived there too, carried an ax to the front door "for the purpose of breaking it open." But the group thought better of this plan, for "it might create an alarm in the neighborhood." So they decided to "enter the house secretly, and murder them whilst sleeping." Hark laid a ladder against the chimney, and Nat hoisted himself through a window into the attic and walked down the stairs. There, Nat unbarred the door "and removed the guns from their places." Before, the band had only axes and hatchets. Now they had firearms.[23]

They faced their first choice: Would they kill everyone? This was a decision they had settled during their dinner. Until they "gathered sufficient force" and "armed and equipped ourselves," they would indeed do so. "Neither age nor sex was to be spared." This decision was easy to make in principle but hard to carry out, and it would be tested a number of times.

As they collected guns, they discussed who would kill Joseph Travis. "It was then observed that I must spill the first blood," Nat said later. He did not say who observed this, but it is notable that he did not put the words into his own mouth. Nat was not shy about claiming credit for his own actions, and his disappearance into the passive voice gives a window into the views of the small band of men around him. They likely wanted to see if Nat meant what he said. Was he all talk, as perhaps some in the neighborhood thought of this strange, sometimes furtive, yet loquacious man? Perhaps this echoed the moment when the great warrior Gideon told his oldest son to kill two enemies and the son refused. The enemies taunted Gideon, saying, "Come, do it yourself," and "As is the man, so is his strength." At that moment "Gideon stepped forward and killed them, and took the ornaments off their camels' necks."[24]

So Nat, "armed with a hatchet," and Will, with an ax, entered Joseph Travis's dark room. Nat could not see in the gloom, so he swung the hatchet, and it "glanced from his head." Joseph Travis "sprang from the bed and called his wife." Here, the band faced their first true obstacle. Could they act before the Travis family awakened and before someone rushed for help? "Will the executioner," not Nat, settled that problem. With a "blow of his axe," Will "laid him dead."[25]

Sally was sleeping beside her husband. This was a woman Nat had known since childhood and with whom he had lived off and on for eight years, yet he said virtually nothing about her in the recorded version of the *Confessions*. If he explicitly denied personal motivation for killing Joseph Travis, he made no such claim about Sally. This killing he described briskly. Will killed her, "the work of a moment." They killed two other family members while they slept. As the men left, they took "four guns that would shoot" and "several old muskets" that were presumably less effective, along "with a pound or two of powder." Possibly Nat picked up a sword that had once belonged to Thomas Moore, Sally's former husband and one of the men who previously controlled the rights to Nat.[26]

After they left the house and "had gone some distance," one of them remembered that the Travises had another child, a baby born to Sally sometime that year, "a little infant sleeping in a cradle." This child's existence tested the men's commitment to "murder the family." Would they kill a baby, even at the risk of losing time? The answer was yes. Henry and Will "returned and killed it," Nat said. The infant's body was taken from the cradle, beheaded, and then put in the fireplace. Allmendinger suggests this placement of the body was meant to show anyone who entered the house "that slaveholding was a capital crime that corrupted blood and for which there could be no pleas of innocence."[27]

This doubling back to kill a baby remains one of the most troubling moments of Nat's rebellion, one that Nat's later admirers struggle to understand. Why did a process of liberation necessitate not just individual killings but a determination to kill everyone, even children? For those who understand Nat's rebellion as a war, however, the act of killing is unsurprising. If slavery was war, as scholars often say, then there need be no elaborate explanations for killing the enemy during conflict. Many human societies do this.

Yet war is not only killing. War also organizes violence by containing it. Laws and codes of war, formalized and written down decades after Nat's rebellion, emphasize the difference between soldiers, who are fair game, and civilians, who generally are not. Of course these lines were not drawn universally. Anglo-American wars against "uncivilized people," whether Indigenous Americans or South Asians or Africans, often turned to wholesale slaughter, sometimes through ostensible claims of reciprocity. This fact suggests some analogies. Did Nat consider all white people, even infants, to be barbarians, warriors striving to sustain slavery and thus fair game? This is plausible and rings true with some other slave revolts in the American hemisphere.[28]

Or was it hatred? Slave owners by and large understood that en-slaved people hated slavery, because they recognized that enslaved people were—despite their legal status—human, if not equals. But enslavers hoped their individual relationships with slaves would save them from this enmity. Some later interpreters looked for deeply per-sonal interpretations of Nat's murderous rage—his psychological state, the breakup of his family, potential abuse of his wife, sexual jealousy, anger at a father or father figure. These psychological explanations are compelling but for one fact: Nat himself was reluctant to kill. A local white historian later wrote down stories that Nat told whites after his capture, which said that killing the master's family was the most diffi-cult task Nat ever had to perform.[29] Whether this statement is accurate or not, it remains true that Nat was strangely uninterested in personally delivering blows. The Travis killings remind us of this. Who "observed" that Nat "must spill the first blood"? Why was Nat's first blow so inef-fective and Will's follow-up so immediately successful? Why did Nat step back and let Will complete the work, and why did Nat stay away again when Henry and Will returned to kill the "little infant sleeping in a cradle"? These do not seem the acts of a man in a rage.

We cannot answer for certain, but one thing we can tell from the narrative is that Nat personally avoided killing. Of the fifty-five peo-ple the rebels killed, Nat killed only one. Nat's reluctance might have been part of his general desire to separate himself from his follow-ers, to hold himself to higher standards of purity. While some bibli-cal warriors delighted in personally shedding blood, some—like the "prophetess" Deborah—issued orders to others. In a song preserved in Judges, Deborah sings, "So let all thine enemies perish, O Lord: but let them that love him be as the sun when he goeth forth in his might." Then the song of Deborah ended with an observation Nat might have cherished: "And the land had rest forty years."[30]

Nat's reluctance also might have stemmed from his deep knowl-edge of the white people they first encountered. Nat had close, even intimate, relationships with the white people in his immediate neigh-borhood. He had lived with Sally and her children for years; it is possible that this intimacy made him slow to harm them, even as he recognized his holy obligation to do them harm.

To understand why Nat and his band killed everyone, we do not need to look to psychology or personal history. An answer lay in Nat's own religious experiences. Early Methodists and other early national evangelicals often discussed a particularly thorny aspect of the Bible: the Israelites' blood-drenched wars against the Canaanites. After the exodus, as the Israelites passed over Jordan and confronted new enemies, the Lord pledged to "drive them out and destroy them quickly, . . . for the wickedness of these nations the Lord thy God doth drive them out from before thee." The Lord commanded Moses and his successor, Joshua, to go to war against the kingdoms that occupied the lands of Canaan.[31]

In Canaan, the Israelites practiced what biblical scholars call *herem* warfare, taking no prisoners, killing men, women, and children.[32] In the attack on Ăi, Joshua stationed five thousand men between Ăi and Bethel, leaving one detachment near Bethel. When the king of Ăi led his army and the inhabitants out of the city, Joshua's detachment circled behind and put Ăi to the torch. At the signal of the smoke rising up from the city, the main army under Joshua turned upon the king of Ăi, his army, and all his people "and smote them, so that they let none of them remain or escape."[33]

We cannot know for certain that *herem* warfare weighed upon Nat, but we do know that it mattered to the enslaved people at the auspiciously named Bethel Chapel in Demerara in what is now Guyana, about eight years before Nat's rebellion. There, congregation members discussed the Israelites' wars against the Canaanites, not only to pursue the common analogy of enslaved people to Israelites, but also to learn from the Israelites' path to power. Their discussions were prompted by the preaching of John Smith, a former itinerant evangelical preacher who had been sent to the colony as a missionary. At Bethel Chapel, Smith read the book of Joshua, where the story of those campaigns is told. Afterward, some of the men went back to the plantation Chateau Margot to read these verses for themselves.

"They said the people of Israel used to go warring against their enemy," recalled a deacon from Bethel who lived on the estate. Soon they would rise up against their enslavers in an evangelically inspired rebellion.[34]

Nat did not mention Ăi, but there was no shortage of other examples of *herem* warfare from the prophets. It would have been enough to know the stories of how the Israelites fought. The prophets, read literally, promised not simply deliverance for an enslaved people but power through a form of warfare that can look to us like genocide. When Moses gave the law to the Israelites, he told them to execute the ban upon seven peoples: the Hittites, Amorites, Perizzites, Hivites, Jebusites, Girgashites, and Canaanites. "Thou shalt smite them, and utterly destroy them; thou shalt make no covenant with them, nor shew mercy unto them," he said.[35] In the wars Joshua and the Israelites waged for the promised land, they aimed not to conquer the people but to exterminate them.[36] Extermination resolved two closely interrelated problems on the path toward the promised land. One was what to do with the people who were already there, the people who had occupied the land since Abraham's time. The other was how to rule as a relatively small, if brave, band. An answer lay in destroying the people already there.[37]

The most famous execution of the *herem*, or the ban, came at Jericho, in the moments after the walls came tumbling down. Over six days, Joshua's warriors had marched around the city followed by the priests and the ark of the covenant. On the seventh day, they circled the city seven times, the priests blew their rams' horns, and the Israelites shouted until the walls of Jericho crumbled.[38] In popular versions of "Joshua Fought the Battle of Jericho" and in some nineteenth-century versions of the related song "The Trumpeters," the story of Jericho ends here, with the crumbling walls. In the Bible, however, the arrival at Jericho is simply the opening salvo. "Shout, for the LORD hath given you the city," Joshua told the Israelites. "And the city shall be accursed, even it, and all that are therein, to the Lord." One woman in Jericho and her household would be spared for helping Joshua's band, but everyone else should be killed.[39] The Israelites obeyed. "They utterly destroyed all that was in the city, both man and woman, young and old, and ox, and sheep, and ass, with the edge of the sword."[40]

In the southern campaign, Joshua submitted seven cities to the ban.[41] At Makkedah, Joshua "utterly destroyed . . . all the souls that were therein; he let none remain." At Libnah, he "smote it with the edge of the sword, and all the souls that were therein; he let none remain in it."[42] Then he laid siege to Lachish, and on the second day he "smote it with the edge of the sword, and all the souls that were therein." When the king of Gezer brought an army to defend Lachish, "Joshua smote him and his people, until [the king] had none left him remaining." Although the narrative exalts Joshua as the peerless successor to Moses, the campaign is not his alone. "Joshua passed unto Eglon, and all Israel was with him," then to Hebron, and to Debir, and "they smote" each city "with the edge of the sword, and all the souls that were therein he utterly destroyed."[43] The description of Israel's barbaric southern campaign is brief, less than twenty lines, but it is all the more stunning for its compression and austerity.

The Israelites practiced *herem* warfare because it was an act of worship, a sacrifice to Yahweh, a tribute to God's power and glory.[44] When Joshua first received the divine command in a vision at Jericho, he fell to the ground face-first in "worship." Yahweh's messenger in turn told Joshua to remove his sandals, for he was standing on "holy" ground in Jericho.[45] Jericho, Joshua tells the Israelites, "shall be accursed . . . to the Lord" by being destroyed, and some recent translations trade "accursed" to the Lord for "devoted to the Lord for destruction."[46]

Herem was a way to serve the Spirit, even an obligation. In the first book of Samuel, God punished Saul for refusing to carry out the *herem*. Through Samuel, God told Saul to "utterly destroy" Amalek and "all that they have . . . both man and woman, infant and suckling, ox and sheep, camel and ass." Saul killed most of the Amalekites but spared their king and "the best of the sheep, and of the oxen, and of the fatlings, and the lambs, and all that was good, and would not utterly destroy them." The Lord then informed Samuel that Saul was unfit to be king, "for he is turned back from following me, and hath not performed my commandments." Samuel denounced Saul, for "rebellion is the sin of witchcraft." Although Saul begged forgiveness, Samuel butchered the Amalekite king, then named David to replace Saul.[47]

Nat's Bible did not leave aside *herem* warfare with those lines of Joshua but invoked it in the woe sayings of classical prophets like Ezekiel and Jeremiah and Isaiah, this time turned against the Israelites as punishment for disregarding God. In Ezekiel's vision, God commissioned six men armed "for slaughter" to "smite" Jerusalem and "slay utterly old and young, both maids, and little children, and women."[48]

The Demerara people were not the only 1820s Black evangelicals to be drawn to Joshua's conquest and its reverberations. In 1822, as Nat was having his early visions, enslaved people around Charleston apparently heard Denmark Vesey describe the Israelites' destruction of all the people—men and women, "young and old"—and of the livestock in Jericho.[49] Vesey repeated this at work as a carpenter, at home on Bull Street, at taverns, and by some testimony at class meetings of the AME church established there.[50] Vesey also read the chapter from Exodus concerning slavery and violence: "He that stealeth a man, and selleth him, or if he be found in his hand, he shall surely be put to death."[51]

Vesey and his followers planned to put the principles of the *herem* into practice, at least according to the contested testimony given to interrogators. Witnesses said that Vesey and his lieutenant Peter Poyas estimated that it would take thirty minutes to kill all the white people in the Georgetown district. Then the Georgetown rebels were, according to one recruit, to "kill all the whites between there and Charleston." Poyas was meant to cut off surviving white Charlestonians and meet the other warriors along the bays south and east of town.[52] "All the Ministers were to be killed except a few who were to be" shown those verses about *herem* and asked, "Why they did not preach up" those passages.[53]

In 1829, David Walker gave the Methodists' martial spirit perhaps its most belligerent expression, one that hinted at *herem* in its predictions of bloody and vengeful violence. Scholars often note that

Walker's *Appeal* drew from seemingly contradictory impulses toward Christian charity and inflamed fury. Read through the Methodist obsession with warfare, the contradiction dims, and Walker's belligerence appears at least as holy as his potential for forgiveness and hope. Tyrannical slaveholders would tremble precisely because enslaved people would carry out God's plan of destruction. "I know that the Blacks, once they get involved in a war, had rather die than to live, they either kill or be killed," Walker wrote.[54] In other passages, Walker warned "you Americans" that "unless you speedily alter your course, *you* and your *Country are gone!!!!!!* For God Almighty will tear up the very face of the earth!!!"[55] More prosaically, Zilpha Elaw thought of Joshua when a camp meeting began with a clarion call to battle.[56]

Perhaps Nat envisioned a general race war of complete destruction, perhaps he imagined white people in farther regions as converts or even slaves, perhaps he imagined that God could create a beloved community once the Canaanites had been destroyed. But most likely, he simply did not know. The Spirit offered suggestions but not certainty. When the prophet-warrior Gideon concluded his campaign by slaying "the men of the city" of Penuel, his followers said, "Rule thou over us, both thou, and thy son, and thy son's son also: for thou hast delivered us." But Gideon refused. "I will not rule over you, neither shall my son rule over you: the Lord shall rule over you." In turning from prophet to warrior, Nat began the process; the Bible suggested a plan; God would conclude it.[57]

THE DEAD SAFELY behind them, weapons in hand, Nat and his followers paused to drill. Nat took his role as military commander seriously, drawing upon a widespread understanding that slave rebellions were wars, an understanding shared across much of the Black Americas in this period. This general belief was reinforced in the Chesapeake and Southside by the fighting of Black Loyalists in the Revolutionary War and the War of 1812 and in popular chatter of rebellions in Jamaica and Haiti and Cuba and Guyana and elsewhere, all of them rebellions that led to armed battles. With the four guns and several muskets, Nat gathered the men in the barn near the house.[58]

There they "paraded," working through the drills that Nat understood they would have to execute in their battles ahead. Nat knew that they could not survive disorganized. "I formed them in a line as soldiers," and he led "them through all the manoeuvres I was master of."[59] We do not know precisely where Nat drew his military knowledge, simply because such knowledge would not have been unusual. He came from a region where U.S. and British forces had warred once within his lifetime, once not long before, in an era when battlefield combat shaped much of the Americas. Enslaved people also saw whites on their July 4 militia musters. To set their identity as an organized band, Nat's followers made a banner and put on symbolic clothing to stand in for a uniform. A letter written after the rebellion said the banner displayed a red cross in a white field. They "wore red caps" or ornamented their hats "with red bands of various materials." They made "blood-red" sashes and draped them around their waists and over their shoulders. A very unsympathetic local white historian called their outfits "ludicrous and fantastic," but these visual representations of a common cause were nearly universal in military bands, used to inspire loyalty among their members and fear among their enemies.[60]

Hark and Nat were the only adult enslaved men on the Travis farm, so they took just one additional person with them as they moved on: the thirteen-year-old Moses. Under Nat's command they marched about six hundred yards to the nearest neighbor. This property belonged to Salathiel Francis, Sally Travis's brother and by at least one account the person who had warned Sally about Nat. In moving from Sally Travis to Salathiel Francis, Nat was not simply attacking a neighbor. He was also attacking the Francis family that was at the center of slaveholding and of Methodism in the neighborhood.

Sam and Will knocked on the door. When Salathiel Francis asked who was there, Sam replied that he was carrying a letter for the house.

Francis came to the door; then "they immediately seized him, and dragging him out a little from the door, he was dispatched by repeated blows on the head." Francis was the only white person on the property, so they moved on.[61]

Already we can see signs that, like any military band, they were learning as they proceeded. They shifted from breaking in to luring white people out. Nat did not narrate his reasoning, but it's quite likely that they knew Salathiel Francis, a bachelor, would be alone, and thus had fewer worries about encountering resistance or waking others. No one was there to scream when he died. So, too, might Nat have reflected on the ways that Joshua lured enemies out from their cities in order to ambush them.[62] They were killing, but they were killing with purpose and strategy.

But we can also see signs that they were struggling to attract recruits. At the Travis place, Nat and Hark were the only adult male enslaved people, so it is not surprising that the company didn't add more volunteers. But the problems at Salathiel Francis's farm were more worrisome. None of the people enslaved by Salathiel Francis were part of the original group of collaborators, and it is possible that none of the adult enslaved people at Salathiel Francis's farm joined up, either. While there might have been an unnamed recruit, two prospects identified by Allmendinger did not join: the adult enslaved man Red Nelson and the free Black man Emery Evans, who also lived on-site. It was, as the historian Patrick Breen notes, a particularly bad sign that they could not persuade Evans, because one of every six Black people in Southampton County were free and the company would need their support to win.[63] Later in the day, as they reached other plantations, Nat and his band would find some willing recruits and supporters, but also some among the enslaved and free Black communities who refused to join them or tried to thwart them.

Then Nat led the band two miles to the nearest farm of any scale, what he described as Piety Reese's place, though it was under the control of her son John Reese. The Reeses were cousins of the Turner family and had long been entangled with them in the Methodist church, in legal documents, and in slaveholding. Jack sometimes lived there. Among the twenty-one enslaved people on the small plantation were also likely Hark's wife (and Jack's sister), as well as Cherry and Riddick.[64]

The band marched, "maintaining the most perfect silence." Perhaps knowing that there were multiple white people at home, Nat's army did not call the whites to the door. "Finding the door unlocked, we entered, and murdered Mrs. Reese in her bed, while sleeping." Reese's son John sprang awake to say "Who is that," and then the band killed him, too. Jack, whatever his reservations about the enterprise, apparently took John Reese's shoes and socks. Perhaps they also took some of the family's eight horses. It is possible that two enslaved men from the Reese plantation joined up with them.[65]

Now they turned to Nat's former owner Elizabeth Turner. This was not their only option; two other widows lived closer to the Reese plantation, and both claimed ownership of enslaved people, but Nat and his band went a mile farther to Elizabeth Turner's place, referred to by the name of her late husband, Samuel Turner, Nat's second owner. Nat was leaving a trail of his personal motivations, having moved from the plantation of his current master to his mistress's brother to his former mistress. Elizabeth Turner lived with an overseer and eighteen adult enslaved people, nine of whom had been on the plantation when Nat last lived there in 1822, around the time his likely grandmother Lydia died.[66]

It was nearly sunrise now, and first they checked the still, where Henry, Austin, and Sam found Hartwell Peebles, the white plantation overseer. "Austin shot him," Nat said in the *Confessions*. Apparently, Elizabeth Turner and another white woman, a visiting cousin named Sarah Newsom, were standing on the porch. Nat's band rushed toward them, and the women barred the door. But Nat and his band were prepared. "Will, with one stroke of his axe, opened it." Will killed Elizabeth Turner with "one blow of his axe." Nat used his sword on Sarah Newsom. "I struck her several blows over the head," but he was unable to kill her "as the sword was dull." Instead, Will "dispatched her also." One of the enslaved members of the band, possibly the young boy Moses, later told a prosecutor that Sarah Newsom "shed tears" at the involvement of Hark, who was enslaved by her brother.[67]

It may seem strange that Nat depended upon a dull sword when Will carried an ax and others used guns. Perhaps Nat carried the sword simply as an emblem of his leadership, as generals and others often did. Perhaps he understood his sword was an ineffective killing tool and used it to spare himself the duty of drawing final blood. But Nat likely was conscious of the deep symbolic meaning of swords in the Hebrew Bible, including Yahweh's warning to Moses in Deuteronomy about the "sword without" that "shall destroy both the young man and the virgin."[68] The *herem* is repeatedly symbolized by the sword, as when the prince of the army of Yahweh appears to Joshua in the guise of a man with a "sword drawn in his hand."[69] Swords recurred in the classical prophets as the first of Ezekiel's "four sore judgments" and Jeremiah's "four kinds" of destruction, which included the "sword to slay."[70] While contemporary people routinely quote Isaiah's prophecy of beating swords into plowshares, Isaiah had a more robust sense of swords and their usage, threatening Judah that it would "be devoured with the sword" if it did not turn to obedience.[71] More prosaically, many biblical warriors smote with swords, including one of David's "mighty men," and the people in Zechariah fashioned "as the sword of a mighty man" to attack upon the sound of the Lord's trumpet.[72] Perhaps the sword John Brown obtained from George Washington's great-grandnephew carried similar meaning for that religiously inspired warrior at Harpers Ferry almost thirty years later.[73]

But Nat didn't count on the sword; his band used other weapons, and he remained clear-eyed about their challenges and necessities. Like all commanders he worried about supplies; carrying out God's will did not mean solely looking to heaven for the Lord to provide. At Elizabeth Turner's house, as at others, the men went in "search for money and ammunition." They had gathered at least nine horses by this point. They also laid waste to "property." Perhaps as they collected their material, they reenacted the destruction of prophetic times to usher in the new world, to purge this land of white enemies, or perhaps the men grabbed things they desired.[74]

Enslaved people on Elizabeth Turner's plantation responded in vastly different ways, showing the range from enthusiasm to horror in Black people's reactions. Some enslaved people had lived on the plantation with Nat, so he was not a stranger, nor was his band. Two young men joined willingly: Sam and Jordan, both in their twenties. A third, Davy, who also had lived at the plantation with Nat for at least four years, "took no part in murdering his mistress and family," Moses later testified. Davy, they forced, perhaps the first or second impressed warrior, depending on how one interprets the story of the boy Moses. The addition of those three, and of an adult man from one of the smaller farms they bypassed, raised their numbers to fifteen. From records of later attacks, it is very likely that they also received encouragement and supplies from enslaved women in the neighborhood, though not from all of them either. The record of the women on these first plantations is murky, perhaps reflecting the protectiveness of the enslaved men toward their wives, sisters, and neighbors. Of the fifteen men and boys in the fighting band, eleven or twelve were directly linked to the first four families they had attacked. Only three had no connection—Henry, Nelson, and Austin—and the Porter and Edwards plantations those three lived on were not far away, and already in their sights.[75]

It was Monday morning, August 22, daylight now, and Nat contemplated what to do. The nearest place of account was the Whitehead farm, but the Bryants were also not far, and they might have debated which to attack first: enslavers like the Whiteheads or white people without slaves like the Bryants. They passed homes belonging to two local white women with smaller farms without attacking, perhaps adding one enslaved man who rumor later suggested had joined on the promise the band bypass his enslaver's family.[76]

They decided to split in two. Nine men on horseback rode toward the Whitehead house. The other six "were to go through a by way to Mr. Bryant" and then rejoin the larger group at the Whitehead place. It was to be only a brief split, but already it tested the band's discipline and leadership. Could a small, cohesive group divide temporarily and yet remain unified in their future operations?[77]

And who exactly made this decision? Nat did not claim either to have made the choice or to have listened to his followers, so we must remain uncertain. Perhaps he saw the need to move quickly as the sun rose. Or maybe the men themselves disagreed about whom to attack first, and Nat resigned himself to appeasing both sides.

However the decision transpired, six men split off on foot toward the house of Henry Bryant, perhaps led by Hark. There they completed "the work of death assigned them," Nat later allegedly told Thomas Gray. That work confounds efforts to portray Nat's band as solely or primarily motivated by revenge against enslavers. Neither Henry Bryant nor his wife, Elizabeth, nor his mother-in-law, Mildred, nor his child owned an enslaved person in 1831, but they were all killed. Perhaps Hark's band was motivated by some personal or past slight. Or perhaps, some of the band were warming to the idea of killing all the white people.[78] What may be most striking is that the band that attacked and killed the Bryants did not include Nat. Hark could carry out the *herem* without him.

NAT RODE ON HORSEBACK with Will and perhaps seven others about one mile east to the Whiteheads. Catherine Whitehead was a widow in her fifties, one of the wealthiest slaveholders in the region, and resided about a mile southeast of Elizabeth Turner. Twenty-seven enslaved people worked her 1,245 acres, along with eleven white family members. Catherine Whitehead had tripled her slaveholdings over the previous twenty years by forcing the enslaved people to farm cotton, and she had the accoutrements to prove it, including one of the most valuable houses in the region.[79]

Nat's reasons for selecting houses were shifting. The Whiteheads did not own any of the people who plotted with Nat. But the White-heads were a visible symbol of slavery and its expansion. The plantation was also a rich source of potential recruits. And then there was another possible motivating factor: six or seven of Catherine Whitehead's grown children lived with her, including a son, Richard, who was a Methodist minister. Several of the Whiteheads, including the daughter Harriet, apparently were still asleep as the band approached.[80]

At the Whitehead house, Nat and the others encountered the Methodist minister Richard first, out "in the cotton patch, near the lane fence." They called him over into the lane, and "Will, the executioner, was near at hand, with his fatal axe, to send him to an untimely grave." Some stories claimed that Richard Whitehead pleaded for his life and Nat showed no mercy. Of course Nat showed no mercy to anyone, but these stories suggested he was particularly angry at the Methodists who had raised him and then abandoned him to slavery and refused him the right to baptize the overseer Etheldred Brantley. Perhaps he was particularly angry at this minister, the living embodiment of the betrayal not just of Nat's future but of his faith. Almost all the people killed early in the assault were Methodists, though Nat's world was so dominated by Methodists that it is difficult to untangle their faith from the family histories that made them alluring targets; Methodism and slaveholding had become almost indistinguishable in his neighborhood.[81]

While the band attacked Richard Whitehead, three of the adult male enslaved people fled, according to later trial transcripts. Two returned an hour later, asking if Nat's company had left. Those two, Jack and Andrew, then followed the trail of Nat's band to a house up the road. There, Venus, an enslaved woman, told them the band was still farther ahead, and Jack and Andrew left in pursuit, but never caught up with the company. A third enslaved man, Tom, also ran away but apparently made no effort to find Nat, and might have run up the road informing white people that Nat's company was coming.[82]

As the band moved toward the Whitehead house, they saw "some one run round the garden." Thinking it was a person from the "white family," Nat "pursued them." But it wasn't a white family member at all. "It was a servant girl." So Nat left her and "returned to commence the work of death." While Nat was busy chasing the enslaved girl, his followers attacked, and came to believe they had killed all but two of the Whitehead family members. Those two were Catherine Whitehead and her daughter Margaret. "As I came round to the door, I saw Will pulling Mrs. Whitehead out of the house, and at the step he nearly severed her head from her body, with his broad axe." Nat, for the only time in the rebellion, took upon himself the work of killing, hunting down "Miss Margaret" where she had "concealed herself in the corner, formed by the projection of the cellar cap from the house." Margaret Whitehead ran, but Nat caught her and began to strike her with the sword. When that failed, "I killed her by a blow on the head with a fence rail." Nat's remarks are the only record of the killing of Margaret Whitehead.[83]

Many have made a great deal out of this moment, none more so than the twentieth-century novelist William Styron, who invented a dramatic backstory to explain Nat's killing in his prizewinning novel *The Confessions of Nat Turner*. But what distinguishes the event may be much more simply explained: Will was not near at hand. When Nat struck Margaret Whitehead with the sword, it failed, as it had before. But this time, Nat could not rely on Will to finish the work, so he at last laid down the symbolic sword for something more powerful: a fence rail. It requires no complex psychoanalysis to explain these facts. Nat did not relish killing, but he did utilize his sword. When Will wasn't nearby, when Nat was forced to choose between killing and permitting an escape, he killed, as he knew he had to.[84]

Inside the house, one of the Whiteheads had in fact survived. When the company burst into a room where several adult sisters slept, one of them, Harriet, hid between the beds, she said later, "whilst her sister and the entire remainder of the inmates of the house were murdered in a few feet of her." An older enslaved man named Hubbard helped her away from the house after the company left. Later, Harriet would save Hubbard's life by telling murderous white militia what he had done.[85]

AT THIS POINT the men from the Bryant expedition returned, and the band regathered. There were fifteen corpses behind them. They had cut a bloody swath through their neighborhood. They had collected material and ammunition. They had trained and drilled. Their attack had already succeeded in killing more white people than most U.S. slave rebellions. Their ability to divide and recombine shows that even as Nat's eyes were on the heavens, he and his followers' actions were determined by the ground beneath their feet, their neighborhood's footpaths and roads, the lanes and the places where water blocked forward passage.

And they had an unexpected opportunity to add more men. Two enslaved hunters happened to arrive at the Whitehead house during the attack. Both had been claimed by white Turner family members at some point in their lives. Joe was thirty and claimed by Samuel Turner's younger brother John. The other man's name was Nat, and he had been owned by a cousin of Benjamin Turner Jr.'s. He lived on a nearby farm, hired out to John T. Barrow, brother-in-law of this Nat's now-deceased owner. The two men joined Nat's company, although it is not clear if it was by choice. An enslaved man in the house thought Joe was reluctant, although there was no such claim about the second Nat. However it happened, the company was probably seventeen men and boys strong.[86]

Now the company had to figure out what to do next. Should they fortify themselves in this terrain they knew so well? Or should they push into neighborhoods where they were much less confident of the terrain and the populace? We do not know how they debated this action. Probably Nat—like Jonathan in 1 Samuel—hoped that "the Lord will work for us" and intervene to reveal a plan.[87]

They split again into two groups, one large detachment with Nat, Will, Henry, Sam, Nelson, Austin, the other Nat, and young Moses heading due north toward Richard Porter's house and then to Nathaniel Francis's farm. We don't know why Nat left with this group, but it is notable that as long as Nat was with Will "the executioner," there would be little need for him to lead the killing. The other group, probably led by Hark, moved northwest along the White Meadow Road and then a byway toward Howell Harris's plantation and Augustus Doyel's rented house.[88]

This was a much riskier division than the one Nat's crew had just navigated. The distances were far greater and the odds of reunification far lower. Possibly Nat worried about the loss of personal control over all the men. But they all recognized the problem of time. At some point word would go out in the neighborhood, and the white people would call for reinforcements. And, too, Nat's followers might not have been willing to listen to him. Some of them might have had their own reasons for splitting off, their own scores to settle, their own people to rescue.

As they rode out in the morning light, other people were riding in behind them. The screaming had attracted the attention of a schoolteacher named John Williams, sometimes called Cherokee or Choctaw because of his long hair, who lived nearby in a rented house. Riding up to the Whitehead house, Williams saw the dead bodies, Richard in the field, the mother near the porch, the daughter Margaret by the fence, and four more in the house. In his rush, he did not realize that Harriet remained alive. Williams rode off to spread the word around the neighborhood. Perhaps one enslaved man was also traveling the roads, warning white people.[89]

TO GET TO the Porter house and then beyond to Nathaniel Francis's, Nat's detachment had to turn from their eastward trajectory, shifting almost ninety degrees to the north. This added time and, potentially, confusion. But the targets could not be avoided.

Richard Porter was thirty-eight and had lived most of his life near Nat's neighborhood, growing up on a farm within sight of Benjamin

Turner Jr.'s plantation, close enough that he likely knew Nat from his childhood. Although born to an enslaver, Richard Porter did not own land, a horse, or a significant number of enslaved people as recently as 1827, paying taxes on only one enslaved person of age. But that changed when he married a wealthy widow, Eliza Barnes. Through her property and guardianships, he now controlled 1,310 acres and thirty enslaved people. Eliza had deep ties to the Turner, Francis, and Reese families that shaped Nat's world. She grew up in the neighborhood, her sister married Samuel Turner's brother-in-law Edward Reese, and her father married Benjamin Turner Jr.'s second wife. When John Reese lost his land, raising fears that he would lose the enslaved people held as collateral, Richard Porter was one of the lenders and one of the witnesses to the deeds. Henry, one of Nat's key collaborators, lived on the Richard Porter plantation.[90] The morning's attacks focused on the enslavers of the original collaborators and the largest enslavers in the neighborhood. The Porters were logical targets.

At the Porter family house, Nat saw the grave challenges ahead. The house was empty. The Porters had escaped. Which meant they knew. "I understood there," Nat later told Thomas Gray, "that the alarm had already spread." Word was out. They could not count on surprise. Soon they would have to prepare for a counterattack. Nat decided to double back himself and warn the other band. He sent his detachment toward the Francis house, promising to join them there.[91]

Allmendinger believes the news reached the Porters at about 6:30 a.m. Monday. One later story suggested that an enslaved girl named Mary told first the Porters and then Howell Harris down the road. Possibly rumor had spread through multiple paths in a densely interconnected area. Allmendinger suggests that Harris might have by this time already set off on horseback toward the town of Jerusalem with the news that the enslaved people were in rebellion, stopping at the former congressman James Trezvant's home just outside town by 8:30 a.m. and reaching the county courthouse in Jerusalem fifteen minutes later. There, at least three attorneys, the court clerk, a deputy sheriff, and the tavern owner were present to learn the news. These were prominent, well-connected men, and they began their preparations for a counterattack that Nat knew would be coming.[92]

But there was also good news for Nat's band at the Porter plantation. There were probably five adult enslaved men there, and four of them joined. This would be one of Nat's most successful recruiting missions. Possibly the success here was tied to the presence of Henry, one of the original collaborators who brought brandy to the planning dinner. Henry would be called a "general" and "paymaster" of the force in later testimony.[93]

The other crisis they faced was also a product of their success: the more houses they cleared, the farther away they were from home. They were leaving the neighborhood they knew. Neighborhood lines in a rural area were just as constructed and complicated and personal as they were for people in cities. Rural neighborhoods were harder to trace, shaped by paths and private roads and cut throughs, but their evanescence does not make them less real. Like other people, Nat and the enslaved people of Southampton knew the area close at hand extremely well in terms of both the people and the landscape. But beyond the distance that could be covered in an easy walk, the world became less certain, especially for those who worked primarily in the fields.[94]

Nat referred to this separation in space and in knowledge by a simple distinction between this neighborhood and "that neighborhood." As he separated from the men at the Porter house and went in search of those who headed toward Doyel and Harris, Nat promised he would meet them back "in that neighborhood." He was venturing from one field of battle to another, and he seems to have known it.[95]

Nat responded to these threats like a military commander. Expecting an attack, he hoped to consolidate his lines. Like many campaigns, his began with the benefit of surprise, but surprise never lasted. Now they had to find other advantages. They would have to fight together.

Meanwhile, the smaller group had found Augustus Doyel (sometimes Doyle) in the road. Doyel, like his neighbor Howell Harris, owned relatively few enslaved people, but had been expanding his credit and debt in the neighborhood, likely signaling his goal of further acquisition of rights to property in people. The band killed him probably about the same time the main group reached the Porter house. Doyel's wallet would later be found with Hark, the likely leader of this band. Around this time, Jack, Hark's brother-in-law, fled toward the home of Jordan Barnes, who had hired him that summer. There, Jack would tell Jordan Barnes what had transpired, but not his own role. Two others also fled, including Joe, the hunter owned by the Turners, heading toward the house of a neighbor. At some point the band apparently learned from enslaved people that Howell Harris was not at home and so turned around. They were heading back toward Nat, when Nat came upon them in the road.[96]

Now Nat raced with these men to catch the first group on the road from Porter's house. While Nat was gone, that band kept moving forward, suggesting that at least the leaders—Sam and Will and Nelson—shared a sense of purpose and tactics. They headed a mile north toward the plantation of Nathaniel Francis. This was a plantation deeply tied to slavery in the neighborhood and to the formation of the rebellion plan. Among the people enslaved at Nathaniel Francis's plantation were Sam, an original plotter, and Will "the executioner." Nathaniel Francis was also at the center of the Methodist family ties that bound the neighborhood enslavers together. His sister Sally had been Nat's enslaver, directly or through marriage or guardianship, since about 1822, and she had been the first target with her husband and children. Sally and Nathaniel's brother Salathiel, across the road from Sally, had been the second. They had family and marital and church connections to the Turners and to the Reeses, repeated targets of the band. Nathaniel Francis and his mother, Sarah Francis, would be next in their sights.[97]

Nathaniel lived on the farm with his young wife, Lavinia Hart Francis, six free Black people, and fifteen enslaved people, including Sam and Will. With marriage and guardianship of his two young nephews, Nathaniel had improved his family holdings, more than doubling the number of enslaved people of taxable age between 1820 and 1831, lending his money to neighbors with their enslaved people as security. Lavinia had brought control over enslaved people to the marriage, as the historian Vanessa Holden emphasizes, including an enslaved woman named Ester.[98]

But the Francis family would not actually be the next to be killed. Although Nat never noted these attacks and likely did not know about them, the band encountered two other white people on the way, possibly on the lane leading to the Francis house. They were Louisa Williams and her infant, the wife and child of the school-teacher John Williams, who had sounded the alarm. We do not know the details of the killing, and some accounts placed their bodies at the Williams house. While Thomas Gray included their names in the appendix of the dead in the *Confessions*, Nat never referred to them, a sign he did not learn of their deaths.[99]

After the band killed the Williamses, they headed toward the Francis house, which was missing two of its key targets. Nathaniel Francis and his mother, Sarah Francis, were gone. An enslaved boy held on the Travis plantation might have warned Nathaniel early that morning that there were dead white people there, leading Nathaniel and Sarah to go check on his sister, her daughter. However this warning arrived, it is notable that Nathaniel's first thought was not protection for his nuclear family; as he went to check on his sister, he left behind his wife, Lavinia, now eight months pregnant, Nathaniel's two orphaned nephews, and the overseer. The band killed the Francises' overseer and the young nephews. Years later, white people said that the boys were decapitated and the overseer shot. Meanwhile, Lavinia Francis hid in the closet, testifying later that she heard the shrieks. At one point, the band opened the closet looking for her, but left without finding her. Perhaps they assumed she fled with Nathaniel and Nathaniel's mother.[100]

After the band left, two enslaved women, Charlotte and Ester, stayed behind to prepare food for the company of enslaved rebels, one of the signs of women's role in the revolt covered up in much testimony but recently analyzed by the historian Vanessa Holden. As they worked, the women began to argue over who would receive

Lavinia Francis's belongings. But Lavinia Francis was not dead. She had passed out from the terror and the heat. When Lavinia Francis woke and walked downstairs, she startled Charlotte and Ester, who reacted in exactly opposite ways to the survival of their enslaver. Charlotte lunged at her with a knife, but Ester stepped in between them, holding Charlotte off while Lavinia grabbed cheese and fled to the woods. Just as enslaved men were divided in their response to the attacks—with some joining enthusiastically, others reluctantly, still others fleeing, and a few aiding their enslavers—so, too, did enslaved women display a range of reactions, based on motivations we can only guess at. Charlotte and Ester joined together to cook food for the company, a contribution surely mirrored in other households by other enslaved women we don't know about. But on the question of killing, they came to different conclusions. Nat depended on other enslaved people flocking to his banner, and many did, but many others either did so only halfheartedly, avoided it altogether, or even resisted the rebellion.[101]

Moses, the boy impressed into the group at the Travis plantation, would later testify that the insurgents forced three more teenagers at the Francis plantation to join, putting them on horses and keeping them "constantly guarded by negroes with guns" under threat of being shot if they fled. One adult enslaved man, Dred, apparently joined of his own volition, giving the band a total of six enslaved people from the fifteen at the Francis plantation, including the leaders Sam and Will.[102]

All that Nat said about the Francis house was that, coming up the road with the other detachment, he calculated that the main group had already completed "the work of death and pillage," so he moved onward toward the house of Peter Edwards, "expecting to find them there." The Edwards farm was just north of the Francis place, the house half a mile up a dirt track. Like several of his neighbors, Peter Edwards had made his fortune through marriage and slaveholding. As Edwards reached adulthood, his father owned only two enslaved people and five acres. By marrying, Peter Edwards gained guardianship over three stepchildren and twenty-one enslaved people in

1817, a number that had grown to twenty-nine by 1830. One of those bondsmen, Nelson, was an original leader of the company. Another, Austin, had already joined.[103]

The attack on the Edwards house would have completed the work of taking the home plantations of each of the original members, and likely Nelson was looking forward to the chance to bring their combined plan to fruition. But the Edwards family had fled, perhaps drawing conclusions from the absence of Nelson and Austin and the swirling gossip. Some of the enslaved people at the Edwards home might have been hiding out as well. Even though there were eight enslaved men between the ages of sixteen and thirty-six, and two of those were already embedded in the group, one as a leader, only two of the remaining six adult men joined up, Sam and Jim. As Nat rode up to the Edwards house with the detachment, he was "expecting to find" the main company there, but they were already gone.[104]

Still in search of the main part of the company, Nat and the detachment rode up the road to the house of John T. Barrow. Barrow's house lay in a stretch of interconnected families on the way to Jerusalem, and Barrow's wife, Mary Vaughan Barrow, connected several of the next targets in the Barrow, Vaughan, Harris, and Parker families. John Barrow was about five years younger than Nat and had inherited enslaved people as he reached adulthood, owning thirteen by 1830. After his father's death, his mother had married Newit Harris, who lived three-quarters of a mile in the other direction. John Barrow had likewise improved his financial status by marrying Mary Vaughan, daughter of a wealthy widow, niece of one of the richest men in Southampton, and sister-in-law of James W. Parker, a magistrate whose house would play a crucial role in the uprising. Like the Turners, the Barrows had family members who had taken another path in relation to slavery. His father's cousin, David Barrow, was the Baptist minister who freed his enslaved people in 1784 and published a pamphlet calling on all Baptists to renounce slavery, then fled the state. In 1828, John Barrow's brother drew up a deed promising to emancipate an enslaved woman named Susan at his death. But John Barrow seemed to have no such qualms; in conjunction with Salathiel Francis, he had secured debts for his brother and taken four enslaved people as collateral.[105]

As the company approached, John Barrow loaded his guns and told his wife to run through the garden. The other Nat, the one who had joined later, began to shoot, according to Barrow's wife, Mary, and Barrow fired back in the first exchange of the day. Perhaps, Allmendinger speculates, John Barrow struck Will "the executioner," because he is not mentioned after this in the *Confessions*. The other enslaved people charged forward through the gunfire, and Barrow began to swing his gun at them, but, Gray later wrote, "he was overpowered and slain." One story suggested that Barrow shot from behind a window and that an enslaved person reached through with a razor and cut his throat. Barrow's brother-in-law George Vaughan came up to the house during the shooting, perhaps hurrying across a shortcut, and was killed by gunfire. About twelve enslaved people were held at the Barrow plantation, four or five of them adults. The two who joined had both arrived three years earlier, given to John Barrow by his mother-in-law. One was an adult man named Moses, not to be confused with the boy Moses brought in at the start of the day.[106]

The other was Lucy, an enslaved woman about twenty years old, and named by the historian Vanessa Holden as one of the most committed enslaved female rebels. As Mary Barrow, the wife, fled into the yard between the house and the kitchen, Lucy held her for capture until an older enslaved man pulled Mary Barrow free. Later, the young boy Moses would testify that he saw Lucy "in company with the insurgents." Afterward, Lucy would be the only enslaved woman tried as an active rebel.[107]

A little later, Nat and the trailing detachment found John Barrow's dead body and headed after the main company. That group could have taken George Vaughan's shortcut to get to Jerusalem more directly, but they turned away from town to go about three-quarters of a mile to the plantation of Newit Harris, John Barrow's stepfather. Newit Harris had lived on the old Barrow plantation since he married John Barrow's mother in 1810. Harris, unlike the Baptist Barrows, was a

Methodist and an even more prosperous enslaver. By 1830, he owned forty-nine people, giving him the seventh-largest number of taxable enslaved people in the parish, the largest house between Cabin Pond and Jerusalem, and the most valuable carriage. He was a cousin of the Turners, as was his wife, John Barrow's mother. Harris was approaching sixty, the leading elder in a combined clan of Harrises, Barrows, Vaughans, and Parkers tied by kinship, slaveholding, and sometimes religion to the Turners. He had been a magistrate, a captain of the militia during the War of 1812, and an estate executor, many times.[108]

It was here at Captain Newit Harris's house that Nat finally caught up with the rest of his men. They numbered at least twenty-eight (and perhaps as many as forty), and many were on horseback. Maybe Nat thought of this large band as the "thirty" who fought with David.[109]

The men "shouted and hurraed as I rode up." But Nat quickly saw the reason for their cheers. While some were loading their guns, others were drinking. And then there was further bad news. Captain Harris and his family had escaped, surely to spread the word to their white neighbors. The men captured the money and valuables and destroyed the rest of the house.[110]

In the Harris yard there were other signs of problems. Although they had a large band, they did not have success in recruiting. There were seven enslaved men between sixteen and thirty-six on the Harris plantation, but none joined the rebellion. Later the story spread that Harris had escaped because an older enslaved man named Ben helped hide his owner in the Angelica Swamp behind the house. There were also stories that enslaved men hid from Nat's company to avoid impressment.[111]

An enslaved man named Aaron might have tried to convince Nat and the company of the futility of their plans. The story spread afterward that Aaron heard Nat's band speak about the need to kill 80,000 white people in order to control the country. It is hard to know precisely what this 80,000 number referred to; there were 6,500 whites in Southampton County, about 700,000 in the state. Perhaps 80,000 was their estimate for Southside or some broader region. Aaron apparently believed that Nat's band thought there were 80,000 white people in the entire United States and warned them of their error. If Nat and his followers "had seen as many white people as he had seen in Nor-folk," they would understand they could not win, the story suggested. Nat and his leaders were not dissuaded, but it is not hard to imagine that some of the reluctant followers, not to mention those forced into joining, heard something like this with dismay and began to calculate their path to escape.[112]

Nat and the rebels had reached a turning point. Word was out in the neighborhood. Now they were a large and loud band, incapable of quiet approach. It was also bright daylight, between nine and ten in the morning. And they were moving beyond their neighborhood.

AT THIS POINT, Nat reformulated his strategy. No longer did he rely upon stealth and silence. He turned to concentration and might. "I ordered them to mount and march instantly." Perhaps he considered biblical stories of combining forces like the injunction from 1 Kings to "number thee an army" and "fight against them in the plain, and surely we shall be stronger than they." They were trying to cover sig-nificant ground to get to James Parker's home and its gate, almost within sight of his ultimate goal, Jerusalem. It was about eight miles away, and time was of the essence. They started northeast toward Bar-row Road. Then they turned east, aiming to follow Barrow Road until its end six and a half miles away, half a mile from the Parker gate, and not much farther than that from Jerusalem.[113]

Jerusalem was their destination, but they continued to stop on the way, perhaps according to plan, perhaps by chance. They covered a good deal of terrain, about three miles, before they reached the Levi Waller plantation. The Waller farm on the north side of Barrow Road included a house, a shop, and a school that roughly ten children at-tended, some living with the Wallers. In 1830, the Wallers kept eigh-teen enslaved people, four of whom were men between twenty-four and thirty-six. The Wallers lived on the edge of several other neighborhoods, but they did have a tie back to Nat's life: Levi Waller had lent Benjamin Turner Jr. the money to buy the tract of land where Nat lived for fifteen years, and Levi Waller knew Nat by sight. The Wallers had also been married by a Methodist minister. For these reasons, Allmendinger suggests that Nat and his band always intended to stop at the Waller house.[114]

Now that Nat was back with his band, it is once again possible to narrate the battles through the words that Thomas Gray said that Nat told him, as it is not with the houses attacked while Nat was trying to catch up. Nat described himself as a commander plotting tactics. He "took my station in the rear" and placed "fifteen or twenty of the best armed and most to be relied on, in front." Those men he sent to approach the houses "as fast as their horses could run." Nat had two goals now: "to prevent their escape and to strike terror to the inhabitants" so the rebels could "carry terror and devastation wherever we went." From the rear, Nat watched the work of death unfold, mostly out of sight of the attacks, holding back perhaps like a general. "I sometimes got in sight in time" to view the "mangled bodies as they lay, in silent satisfaction, and immediately started in quest of other victims."[115]

Perhaps an hour earlier, around 10:45, Levi Waller had heard that the band was on their way. He sent his son Thomas to bring back the seven students and the teacher William Crocker from the schoolhouse, a quarter mile from the main home. He then dispatched Crocker to load guns, while Levi Waller stayed at the still, working. There were now seventeen white people around the house, including nine family members. But they were no match in weapons or tactics for Nat's company. As the band rode up at great speed, some of the family tried to escape into the adjacent Buckhorn Swamp, and Levi Waller hid in the tall weeds. An enslaved man named Dred, whom the band picked up at the Francis plantation, came to look for Waller. But Alfred, an enslaved blacksmith on the plantation, distracted Dred as Levi Waller snuck away. From a hiding place in the nearby swamp, Levi Waller watched three enslaved people, perhaps led by Sam and including Daniel and Aaron of the Porter plantation, go inside a log house where Levi Waller's wife and four-year-old daughter had been hiding. Sam came out carrying Mrs. Waller's scissors. Levi Waller later said he saw Nelson knock one of the people's "brains out with the but of his musket." Hark walked around with a gun, answering to the name Captain Moore, a name that signified Hark's stature, the group's military organization, and the way enslaved people could be known by the name of people who owned them later in life. Then Nat rode up and ordered Sam from the Edwards plantation (not the Sam who was a leader of the group) to get on his horse. Sam seemed reluctant and was wiping his eyes, perhaps in terror or sorrow, but he obeyed. Some of the men began drinking their brandy. Davy, enslaved by the Wallers, changed into clean clothes, drank with Nat's company, and rode off in high spirits. Alfred, the blacksmith who had saved Levi Waller, rode off with the company, too. It is not easy to reconcile Alfred's saving of Levi Waller and his decision to join the band, but perhaps he was simultaneously driven by ambition to fight slavery and the desire to save the enslaver he knew, or perhaps he was just hedging his bets.[116]

At that point, Levi Waller walked out to inspect the carnage. The dead included his wife, Martha; a daughter also named Martha; a son, Thomas; six other children under fourteen; and an unidentified young woman. Their baby remained alive but died not long after. Six people survived: Levi Waller himself, the teacher William Crocker, three of Waller's sons, and a student named Clarinda Jones who hid, cheating death, she later said, "because the Lord had helped her."[117]

Now Nat and his band were moving quickly. A mile east, they passed a farm belonging to a man who claimed fourteen adult enslaved people, but they did not stop. They also passed by four small properties that together housed one enslaved person and seven free Black people. Davy, the enslaved man who joined them at the Waller plantation, testified later that Nat said he would not kill "very poor people" because they "thought no better of themselves than they did of the negroes."[118]

Because Nat spared some white people, including one Turner family member who might have been his playmate as a child, some scholars doubt the centrality of the *herem* to Nat's plan. Kenneth Greenberg noted Nat's skipping of the houses of the very poor as proof that "slaughter" was a "temporary tactic." Greenberg and David Allmendinger state that at least one witness, and perhaps Nat himself, suggested that Nat aimed to begin sparing women and children after they captured Jerusalem.[119]

But such decisions might in fact be in keeping with the biblical *herem*, if not with indiscriminate slaughter. Even those brutal oracles, Jeremiah and Ezekiel, stopped short of promising the complete annihilation that Joshua visited upon the Canaanites. Sometimes they proclaimed that God would use some enemies as slaves. Ezekiel prophesied that God would renew his covenant with a saving remnant, those who eschewed the sins of their fathers, and Jeremiah likewise envisioned scattered remnants who would survive.[120] Moses distinguished between Canaanites, whom they "shall utterly destroy," and people "very far off from thee," whom they should enslave.[121] For this reason the Gibeonites in Canaan pretended to be "from a far country" in order to avoid complete destruction. The Bible offered models for mass killing but also for restraint, when strategic. It is possible Nat still hoped that white people farther away might reconcile themselves to God's kingdom, and quite likely that Nat simply did not know and awaited further instruction while he completed his task of killing the white people in his path to Jerusalem. Even at his most prophetic, Nat understood his tasks as concrete. Losing precious time for indiscriminate killing would not bring him closer to his destiny in Jerusalem.[122]

Nat's band had not stopped killing; they had only become more selective. They soon reached a group of three farms, all belonging to the Williams family: Jacob Williams, his nephew William Williams Jr., and his sister Rhoda Worrell, all Methodists. In formation, the company approached William Williams's house, killing him and two little boys. "While engaged in this, Mrs. Williams fled and got some distance from the house, but she was pursued, overtaken, and compelled to get up behind one of the company, who brought her back," Nat allegedly later told Thomas Gray. They showed her the "mangled

body of her lifeless husband" and told her to "lay by his side." Then
they shot her dead. They marched around the bend to Jacob Williams's
plantation and charged again. As the band approached, a visiting overseer began to run, but was "pursued, overtaken, and shot." Jacob's
wife, Nancy, and her three small children were killed in the kitchen.
Other members of the band attacked the house of the plantation overseer, Caswell Worrell, and killed the overseer's wife and child. They
had not found the owner of the plantation or the overseer Worrell,
both of whom were at work, Williams in the woods and Worrell in a
farther field. Only one enslaved person here joined the rebels, another
man named Nelson, who stepped over the dead bodies "without any
manifestation of grief," according to notes taken during testimony.
During and after the events, an enslaved woman named Cynthia continued to cook, perhaps making food for the rebels as Charlotte and
Ester had done earlier in the day.[123]

After passing by the third Williams farm, where Rhoda Worrell
held no enslaved people, and then two other small farms, they turned
sharply left onto the long lane to Rebecca Vaughan's house. Rebecca
Vaughan, another Methodist, lived in the house with two sons, sixteen
and twenty, an orphaned niece, and nine enslaved people. Her niece
had grown up around Cabin Pond, living near Nat for a few years. Perhaps this tie drew the company up the lane. It is possible that Nat did
not follow them all the way, because he apparently told Gray nothing
of the attack. An enslaved person later told a white editor from Richmond that Nat's company galloped up and surrounded the house.
While Rebecca Vaughan begged for her life, they shot her, then shot
the niece near the doorway. One son was shot as he climbed a fence.
Then the enslaved people drank the brandy from the still and cursed
its taste. As they left, the company impressed two enslaved people, but
both quickly slipped away.[124]

They had come a long way—twenty miles—in the short time of
twelve hours, and they had accomplished a great deal. Several enslaved people had joined them, bringing their numbers close to sixty
by Nat's estimation, though perhaps closer to the thirty-three that

Allmendinger suggests. They had attacked people at fourteen houses and approached four others where the whites had fled, killing a total of about 55 people out of the estimated 106 white residents of those eighteen households. They were mounted on the horses they had taken and were "armed with guns, axes, swords and clubs." They had gathered a good deal of money and valuables.[125]

They had done their work of destruction well, carrying out the Spirit's command to bring "terror and devastation." Perhaps this terror was an earthly strategy, a way to utilize fear to throw enemies off balance. And perhaps it was a rage long repressed, now unloosed. But perhaps it was also the work of the prophets, bringing waste to the sinful land, preparing for God to enter and call up a new world.[126]

They had done much, but Nat still might not have known for certain what the Spirit intended for them to do next, or what the Spirit might do for them. Perhaps Nat considered Ahaz, the king of Judah. As Syria threatened an attack, the Lord told Ahaz, "Ask thee a sign of the Lord thy God; ask it either in the depth, or the height above." But Ahaz answered, "I will not ask, neither will I tempt the Lord," fearing his people would "weary my God also." Immediately after, Isaiah delivered the news that a child named Immanuel would be born one day to a virgin.[127] Always there was longing to know, fear of testing the Lord, and hope that restraint would lead the Lord to reveal even greater prophecies.

Still, there were reasons for concern. They had probably lost Will "the executioner" to injury or death. At least four enslaved people had fled. On at least three plantations, enslaved men they hoped to recruit had instead run away. And several recruits, maybe a quarter, had been coerced. They had rushed through several farms and left survivors and had missed several families they had targeted while leaving other people inexplicably untouched.[128]

They did not know when and how God might intervene, and they were entering areas they did not know nearly as well. As this fearsome band rode to the next farm, they paused and debated what to do next.

6

Parker's Gate

Nat and his company rode down the lane from the Vaughan house, then turned northeast on the Cross Keys Road toward Jerusalem. Soon they came to a gate. Beyond the gate was an eastbound path across a field and some woodlands to the home of Vaughan's son-in-law, James W. Parker. Parker was an alluring target, a wealthy and powerful man with 23 enslaved people and seven horses. A former magistrate, he was a protégé of the county's most prominent leader, the former congressman James Trezvant, and a member of a broader pool of families through the Vaughans that claimed 121 enslaved people. But Parker had no close ties to the neighborhood around Nat's home and Cabin Pond and might not have meant much to Nat. And Parker had likely already fled, "gone to Jerusalem," Nat thought.[1]

The company could pass by the gate and continue on Cross Keys Road about two and a half miles until it merged with Belfield Road and reached the bridge to Jerusalem. It seemed a propitious time to assault the county seat. Nat and his company were numerous, battle hardened, well armed, and on horseback.[2]

Should they fight, or should they march onward to Jerusalem?

To Nat, the answer was obvious. What was the military objective in attacking a house from which white people had likely already fled? Perhaps Nat thought of the prophet-warrior Gideon, who asked the Lord, "Wherewith shall I save Israel? Behold, my family is poor." The Lord told Gideon not to tarry: "Go in this thy might, and thou shalt save Israel . . . Have not I sent thee?" The Lord expected action, not delay.[3]

But the men had other objectives. Some had "relations" at the house, perhaps partners, children, or parents whom they wished to recruit or rescue or at least visit. The rebels who joined later in the revolt lived closer to the Parkers and belonged by law to white families intimately connected with them, which suggests that they would have had the strongest ties to the enslaved people there and thus the strongest motives. The historian David Allmendinger wrote that the enslaved adult man Moses who joined at the Barrows' might have insisted on stopping since he had connections with several of the enslaved people there.[4]

Some of the men proposed an attack. Nat objected, but they went anyway. Nat is evasive on the exact nature of his command at this point. He said, according to Gray, that "it was agreed that they might call and get [Parker's] people." Who, exactly, agreed and on what terms, we do not know, only that Nat "objected" and the men went ahead. Whether Nat was being ignored or was strategically agreeing to demands he could not successfully resist, he was losing control of his men, and he knew it.[5]

Nat had another destination in mind, one that loomed large in his understanding of his earthly and prophetic mission: Jerusalem. "My object was to reach there as soon as possible," he said. As some of the other rebels rode over the fields to the house half a mile off, Nat waited at the gate, watching impatiently. The men were gone too long for Nat's taste. We have no way of knowing whether they celebrated reunions with brandy and cider or pillaged or simply took a few minutes to give their families time to gather their things. We can imagine that for Nat the wait was interminable. If Nat ever reunited with his own wife during the battles, we have no record of it. His way was forward.[6]

Time was of the essence. The approach to Jerusalem was not favorable. Had the company moved forward and merged into Belfield Road, they would have descended into a wetland and crossed two small bridges before reaching the wide but shallow Nottoway River and the narrow plank bridge that led to the county jail and the public grounds. If whites were alert, they would find it easy to block the narrow bridge.[7]

Nat might not have fully appreciated the difficulties of the approach to town, because he had little personal experience in Jerusalem. The map that Gray described as being in Nat's hand showed the way to Jerusalem but not the layout of the town. It was a three-hour horseback ride from the houses where Nat lived, and it is uncertain how often, or even if ever, he went into town. Allmendinger suggests that it is possible Nat traveled with Samuel Turner to the courthouse on one of Turner's visits to administer estates, or with Thomas Moore when Moore went to serve on juries. Possibly, Nat accompanied Joseph Travis on March 21, 1831, when Travis went to the grand jury. But it is possible Nat had never been to Jerusalem at all. Most townspeople seemed unaware of him or what he looked like. Nevertheless, a local white woman said that Jerusalem clearly remained their goal, saying, "They show a great desire to cross the river." Thomas Gray, in the period before Nat was captured, wrote that taking Jerusalem "was with him, a chief purpose, and seemed to be his *ultimatum*."[8]

Nat had both earthly and biblical reasons to desire Jerusalem. Jerusalem was the place where the roads from Murfreesboro, North Carolina, and Belfield joined and then carried onward toward Norfolk and the great harbors of the Chesapeake. Sitting on the shallow Nottoway River, which divided Southampton County in two, Jerusalem was a small town listed at 293 residents in the census but probably generally holding closer to 250 once enslaved people were counted at the plantations where they worked outside town. There were 8 free Black people and perhaps 140 enslaved people in or close to town, along with 103 whites in nineteen households. There was a tavern, a jail, a courthouse, a horse racing track, some lawyers' offices, and a stable. That was about it. Small as it was, it was by far the most significant settlement in the little county, and Nat had reason to hope he could recruit the enslaved people there, and perhaps some of the free Black people.[9]

In seeking to capture the enemy's seat of power, Nat was behaving like many early nineteenth-century generals; thirty years later, U.S. generals spent several years trying to capture southern cities before learning to focus their efforts on destroying the Confederate army itself. So there was no mystery in a nineteenth-century commander trying to take a city. Nat also believed there was ammunition in the militia's arsenal, though authorities had earlier moved the weapons to the state capital.[10]

There was another reason for Nat to yearn for Jerusalem: the Southside terrain gave him few other choices. Nat's Southampton was carved by the river-fed swamps that separated the county into fingers of habitable land. These low-lying swamps had their military uses; they were advantageous places to hide. But the swamps were no place to wage a prolonged rebellion, because they lacked the higher ground that rebels in places like Jamaica's Great River valley used to defend their position and hold off the white militias in the so-called Baptist War later in 1831. A stronghold in the mountains projected strength and attracted potential recruits. A band hiding in the swamps was laying out, near defeat. In Virginia, as in Jamaica, the enslaved rebels avoided the swamps until their cause was lost.[11]

Still, taking Jerusalem was risky; it lay on a road that would allow for greater communication and movement, surely bringing in a larger force to oppose him. For that reason, Nat's choice can reinforce the perception that he was a fanatic or even a fool. But if we see him as a military leader assessing his own terrain, the reasons to head for town appear clearer: every other choice suggested an acceptance of defeat. Joshua did not prevail by retreating into the wilderness. He won by seizing the cities. It was "by Jericho" that Joshua encountered the "captain of the host of the Lord." Perhaps it was in warfare against a city where Nat would meet the Lord. The books of Joshua and Judges are elusive on exactly whether Joshua captured Jerusalem, but they can be read to suggest that his forces had taken the city.[12]

To find a place they could defend, they would have to conquer it, and on flat land the most likely defensible space was a riverside town. It is possible that Nat understood something about the history of sieges, and the ways that towns could be quite resistant to capture, if fortified, and so wished to take Jerusalem before it could prepare for him, and then to use the town as a site for defense against the attacks to come. The Bible describes both successful and failed sieges of Jerusalem, events that could be read favorably or unfavorably by Nat. The second book of Kings describes the Assyrians' efforts to take Jerusalem. But unlike the leaders of other cities, the Judaean king Hezekiah refused to surrender. Through Isaiah, the Lord pledged that the king of Assyria "shall not come into this city . . . For I will defend this city, to save it, for mine own sake, and for my servant David's sake." That night the angel of the Lord "smote in the camp of the Assyrians an hundred fourscore and five thousand: and when they arose early in the morning, behold, they were all dead corpses." If Nat took Jerusalem, could the Lord favor him in his defenses in the same way?[13]

Perhaps Nat's motivations could be reduced to a name, Jerusalem. Perhaps he was drawn there by something profound, something that resists secular explanation but is suggested by the biblical prophecies that influenced his worldview. What name illustrated the overlap between biblical and present time more clearly than Jerusalem? The name invoked both the county seat now just three miles away and the great promise of the biblical prophecies. Jerusalem, in its coincidence in the Bible and Southampton County, allowed Nat to locate divine intervention in space as well as time. Joshua's war of annihilation suggested *how* southern slaves could escape their Egypt. Nat's visions suggested *when*. And the name Jerusalem suggested *where*.

It was in Jerusalem where the Lord visited Isaiah in a terrifying, intimate way, "sitting upon a throne, high and lifted up, and his train filled the temple." The seraphim cried, "Holy, holy, holy is the Lord of hosts," and one of the seraphim placed a "live coal" upon Isaiah's mouth to purge his sin and iniquity. The Lord said, "Whom shall I send, and who go for us?" Isaiah responded, "I, here am I; send me." The "word of the Lord" came to Zechariah in Jerusalem, and came to Micah there, too, telling Micah "the Lord cometh forth out of his place, and will come down, and tread upon the high places of the earth."[14] Methodists and other awakened evangelicals moved from that historical Jerusalem to the "new Jerusalem" the Spirit showed

John of Patmos, and sang of that hope in their songsters. This New Jerusalem would be a wondrous, heaven-sent city, a place of justice, a place where Nat might even enter an unmediated relationship with God.[15]

Yet it would be a mistake to presume that Nat was confident that good tidings would await him in Jerusalem. Perhaps the Spirit was sending him there to overthrow the Babylon of slavery in the United States and would aid Nat's rebellion by fire, by sword, by tribulations of the end-time, by catastrophes visited upon their enemies. But perhaps Nat was being sent there to die, like other prophets mocked in the city, like Jesus himself, who said "it cannot be that a prophet perish out of Jerusalem."[16] The apostle Paul refused to weep when he learned that he would be killed if he went to Jerusalem, telling the other apostles, "I am ready . . . to die at Jerusalem for the name of the Lord Jesus."[17] Nat surely knew he was no Messiah, but he was a prophet. Nat did not know the role he would play in bringing about God's kingdom; he knew only that he must fulfill his duty, and his duty lay in Jerusalem, not at Parker's gate.

"AFTER WAITING SOME TIME FOR" his company, Nat "became impatient, and started to the house for them," leaving six of his men as guards. Nat did not recount what he discovered of his men's activities or how long it took for him to drag them away or what tactics of persuasion he used. We do know that eight people living at Parker's plantation were later tried as participants in the rebellion, suggesting that the recruiting efforts had made headway.[18]

The only thing that Nat told Gray, or at least the only thing that Gray recorded, was what Nat encountered when he came back from the Parker house with his band. "On our return we were met by a party of white men, who had pursued our blood-stained track." The war was about to take on a different aspect: a pitched battle between Nat and organized white forces.[19]

The white response came in waves: first impromptu gatherings of white men in town who, learning of the attacks, rode to discover the facts and confront them; then messengers to other counties, some deputized for the purpose and others simply running for their lives and raising the alarm in neighborhoods not too far away; next the arrival of loosely organized bands from Jerusalem and surrounding counties; then, finally, the coming of regular state militia and federal military forces. Each of these groups faced different conditions and attempted different actions, ranging from indiscriminate slaughter to efforts to calm the populace to formal legal proceedings. These differences brought tension and sometimes open conflict, yet they also revealed white people's powerful advantages: their communication networks, their access to military weapons and organizations, and their ability to call upon a near-uniform determination to defeat the rebellion.

At Parker's gate, Nat and his band eventually faced two white militia companies, one he seemed to overcome, another that thwarted Nat's plans. The first posse that approached Parker's was only about eighteen men strong when they encountered Nat on the pathway. Those men were the initial party to leave from Jerusalem when someone—perhaps Howell Harris—brought warnings that morning. They were not a formal militia but something more like a posse comitatus. Only one member of the group was identified by name, the cavalry lieutenant Alexander Peete, who claimed thirty-one enslaved people and more than a thousand acres, but some of the others have been deduced by historians. Allmendinger suggests that three men almost certainly joined on hearing the news: Thomas Gray, who would later interview Nat in the jail cell, might have been at his home office in town; James French, another young lawyer, was probably at the tavern; Aubin Middleton, a militia captain, was likely in Jerusalem for work as clerk and coroner, though he lived on a plantation near the Waller farm and owned seventeen enslaved people. Neither French nor Gray owned an enslaved person. The group picked up perhaps eight recruits in town, then added more after they rode across the bridge toward Cross Keys, possibly with Harris as a guide. Sampson

Reese, Elizabeth Turner's brother and Piety Reese's nephew, joined, along with—perhaps—the husband of Samuel Turner's sister Nancy, James Bryant, and two men from farther west. Some called them a militia, others a white patrol or a posse or the citizens of the county. They worried less about the source of their authority than their purpose: to be the advance guard of a larger force mustering to destroy the rebels and the rebellion.[20]

These men had been retracing Nat's steps, following rumors and patchy information but struggling to find the rebels. They arrived at the Whitehead house about the same time Nat reunited with his company near the Harris plantation five miles ahead. They found "the blood hardly congealed, in the houses they had left," Thomas Gray later wrote. They rode toward the Waller farm, and there Bryant apparently moved the infant daughter from sunlight to shade. When Aubin Middleton broke off to check on his family, Peete became the captain. Along Barrow Road, they met the enslaved blacksmith Alfred, who had saved Levi Waller, then rode off with the band, perhaps under duress. Later neighborhood stories suggested that Alfred fell off his horse and snuck away from Nat's company. This first town company, led by Peete, wrestled with how to deal with Alfred. They did not wish to kill him nor to leave him able to assist the rebels, so "he was disabled by cutting the longer tendon just above the heel in each leg" and left there.[21]

It was around two o'clock in the afternoon when this company of about eighteen townsmen rode up to Parker's gate and saw the Black guards. The white men fired at one of the sentries, perhaps Daniel, enslaved by the Porters. Under assault, the sentries rode back toward the Parker house, running into Nat and the rest of the company heading in the other direction. Nat might have had a moment of shock at the timing and location of the encounter, but he would not have been surprised by the idea of a confrontation with white people. He had begun a war, and it would proceed like a war. He expected it would play out in battles where he would be called to command, where his men would be driven to kill and to die. Perhaps he hoped that God would intervene as the Lord intervened when Satan and his forces threatened the "camp of the saints" in Revelation and "fire came down from God out of heaven and devoured" Satan's forces.[22]

Perhaps Nat was relieved at the prospect of facing open combat. It helped return him to the biblical story of the God-sent commander. It helped clarify who was the enemy, and perhaps it clarified, too, who should be in charge. After the killing of children and women, it would be less disturbing to kill men at arms, men who could be nothing but enemies. But it would also be much more dangerous. As Nat looked ahead to the battle to come, he might well have felt fear of what his obedience to God would cost him. But if he felt this, he kept quiet.

Shifting abruptly into command, Nat "ordered my men to halt and form, as they appeared to be alarmed." Again, we see Nat shifting from prophet to commander, turning his lessons in tactics and formations to good account. Some whites mockingly called Nat "general," but an officer he was, confronting his men in disarray, ordering them into formation. Beyond making them into a line, we don't know much about Nat's specific tactics at this point. Possibly he thought about the order of battle and reflected on God's biblical injunctions to attack first, not to lie in wait. Over and over, the Lord told his followers, "be not afraid," for "the Lord thy God is with thee, which brought thee up out of the land of Egypt . . . [L]et not your hearts faint, fear not, and do not tremble."[23]

We can surmise that Nat was a better commander than his opponent, Peete, who quickly lost control of his men. Peete had ordered his troops to hold their fire until the rebels were within thirty paces, but one of them disobeyed, firing when the rebels were a hundred yards away. A local historian suggested that James French's colt startled, causing the young attorney to fire his gun and the horse to bolt forward. The fear and jitters were widespread. About half the white men were already retreating at the sight of the rebels. Maybe, to Nat, it appeared as if the Lord confused the white men, as when God led the enemies of Gideon to "turn on each other with their swords."[24]

Discovery of Nat Turner
(Schomburg Center for Research in Black Culture /
Photographs and Prints Division / The New York Public Library)

Nat Turner and His Confederates in Conference
(The Miriam and Ira D. Wallach Division of Art, Prints and Photographs /
The New York Public Library)

Horrid Massacre in Virginia, from *Authentic and Impartial Narrative of the Tragical Scene Which Was Witnessed in Southampton County* (New York, 1831)
(Library of Congress Rare Book and Special Collections Division)

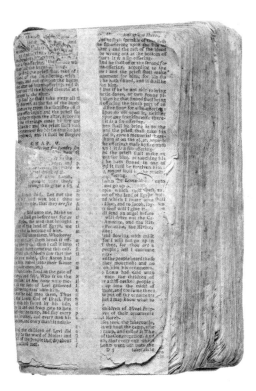

Pages from Exodus and Psalms
in Nat's Bible

(Smithsonian National Museum of
African American History and Culture)

•••• The following photographs were taken in the late nineteenth century, with identifications based on a combination of local memory and records. Some buildings had been altered in the interim, so they may not represent the structures as Nat saw them. (All photographs from the collection "Speech and Photographs Relating to Nat Turner's Insurrection," Accession #10673, University of Virginia Library, Charlottesville, VA) ••••

Belmont, the home to several generations of Blunts, as it was during the residency of Dr. Simon Blunt, son of Dr. Samuel Blunt

Home of Mrs. Catherine Whitehead

Cypress Bridge over the Nottoway River,
three miles southeast of Jerusalem, VA

Home of Nathaniel Francis

Home of Richard Porter

Blackhead Sign Post

The Doyel (sometimes Doyle) farm

Parker's gate

Home of Salathiel Francis

Benjamin Blunt's lane and residence,
Belmont

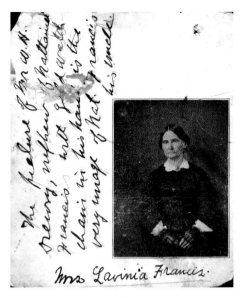

Mrs. Lavinia Francis

Persons Mill Pond, the site of Nat's baptism

Nat's cave

Nat's Methodist church

Battlefield (James W. Parker's field)

Seeing the white men's panic, Nat ordered his men to "fire and rush on them," knowing the importance of turning a retreat into a rout, and they raced forward on horseback and on foot. A few of the white men "stood their ground" until the rebels cut the distance in half; then they "fired and retreated." For about two hundred yards Nat and his men chased and fired, galloping past wounded bodies.[25]

Upon reaching the top of a little hill, Nat and his men discovered that the situation had turned. There, approaching, was a second party of white men that Gray described as a small posse who came separately from Jerusalem. Hearing the noise, this second group halted Nat's charge and perhaps saved Peete's fleeing band.[26]

This second posse was led by two prominent men: the former congressman and county militia colonel James Trezvant, who owned forty-eight enslaved people on a plantation between Jerusalem and Parker's gate; and the less wealthy but highly respected William C. Parker, an officer in the War of 1812 and a local attorney (not James C. Parker, who owned the plantation where they fought). Likely they had about the same number of men as Peete's company, roughly twenty, doubling the size of the white forces. "We arrested their progress," Trezvant later said of his second white company. "Several were shot in this skirmish."[27]

The battle turned from a rout into a pitched stand. Nat assessed the new conditions. "As I saw them re-loading their guns, and more coming up than I saw at first," Nat knew the battle was shifting against him. Several of his "bravest men" were wounded, and others began to flee across the field. Soon Nat's band was in retreat, the whites in pursuit. "Hark had his horse shot under him, and I caught another for him as it was running by me," Nat allegedly told Gray. Some of the enslaved people abandoned the battle, likely including the three enslaved boys from the Francis farm and the teenager Moses from the Moore farm. His men in flight, Nat fled, too.[28]

Luckily for Nat, the white companies did not pursue him. Puzzlingly, the second band headed back to Jerusalem. They were not confident they could defeat Nat head-on, and they feared his next move, so they returned to prepare the town to face an attack. The first group, including Thomas Gray, rode through the region looking for the rebels for almost twenty-four hours but never again found them, a reminder of the grave difficulty of obtaining information in rural areas. This delay gave Nat breathing room. He kept about half his force with him, maybe as many as twenty men and boys.[29]

Already Nat was seeing the whites' numerical advantages. A well-ordered plan could dissolve in the face of reinforcements, no matter the general's tactical aptitude. This attempt on Jerusalem had failed, so he must find another. Nat used his deep knowledge of the terrain to formulate a new strategy. Once again he thought as a commander moving across ground controlled by his enemies. He could not simply race up the road to town; the white people were waiting for him there. But he also could not bring himself to turn back or settle for a different objective. His destiny, as the Spirit had told him, lay in Jerusalem.

Instead of the road, Nat's path would be a "private way" across properties to his east. With about twenty men, he aimed to cross the Cypress Bridge over the Nottoway River, three miles below Jerusalem. He would gather forces to attack Jerusalem "in the rear," catching the townsmen from behind as they guarded the bridge from Cross Keys and left open their southern and eastern approaches. Maybe Nat thought of David against the Philistines in the valley of Rephaim, where the Lord told David not to go straight on but "fetch a compass behind them, and come upon them over against the mulberry trees." Or perhaps Nat thought of the time when Gideon approached Karkor in a roundabout way and "smote" the unsuspecting army. Beyond the Bible, this turning maneuver was a common military strategy. Often it was an effective way of bypassing defenses and catching the enemy at an angle and by surprise. It was always difficult to execute, however, because the attacker moved great distances in hopes that the defenders did not pivot a short way. If it worked, it could lead to a rout. If it failed, it exhausted the attacker and gave the defenders time to entrench.[30]

Like all plans, it depended not just on its strategic design but on its implementation, and Nat faced conditions that made him recalculate. Along the private way they found two or three enslaved men who had been with the company at Parker's. They told him the other fighters had scattered "in every direction." For a while Nat tried to "collect a sufficient force to proceed to Jerusalem" from the men and women along the private way, but he could not recruit enough. Then the Cypress Bridge was guarded by more white men than Nat intended to attack head-on. So, again, he maneuvered.[31]

Nat intended to take Jerusalem, but he did not intend to launch an attack that would fail. God's backing did not alone ensure success. Yes, God might command the sun to stand still as the Lord did for Joshua, or the earth to shake as the Lord did for Saul, but still warriors had to be strategic and wise to prevail. Even when "the Lord was with Judah" in the Israelites' battles against the Canaanites, the Israelites prevailed only in the mountains, not the valley, because the people there "had chariots of iron." Thus the Lord's favor was simultaneously all-powerful and often tied to conventional tools and tactics of war. Instead of separating his identities as a prophet and as a general, Nat seems to have combined them, to have understood that his prophecy would require generalship. To a remarkable degree, against extraordinary odds and with no training, he succeeded in turning himself into a commander who could formulate plans, command men in formation, and improvise when conditions changed.[32]

The whites were surely gathering in force against him, perhaps a sufficient force to defend against any attacks. It was time for Nat to balance the scales, to find his own reinforcements. The first place he would look for them was among the men who had been with him when they reached Parker's gate. "I was sure they would make back to their old neighborhood," Nat said. So Nat began to head there in hopes of calling upon his old fighters, "make new recruits, and come down again."[33]

Along the way Nat and his men stopped at several houses, searching for white families "to gratify our thirst for blood," according to Gray's dubious wording. They passed the farm of Elizabeth Thomas, a widow who claimed twenty-eight enslaved people and whose young son George would be a future U.S. general and Civil War hero, and then Nancy Turner Barrett Spencer, the sister of Nat's former enslaver Samuel Turner. But the white families had already fled. Nat had lost the advantage of surprise. He then led his band back to the Rebecca Vaughan and Barrow plantations.[34]

Nat successfully gathered additional men. By his count, he gained perhaps twenty new fighters to join the twenty already with him. That night, these fighters—the historian Patrick Breen estimates their numbers that evening at thirty-six—rested in a wood at the edge of the plantation that belonged to Thomas Ridley, a major in the militia, home to some part of the 145 enslaved people Ridley claimed. The overseer had apparently fled, leaving Nat momentarily safe. They were four miles west of Jerusalem, at the edge of multiple plantations that could be fertile grounds for recruiting. At least four of the enslaved men who lived on the Ridley plantation joined his re-formed company. Perhaps from them, Nat learned that many white people had gathered at the Ridley plantation house for safety, but he did not expect them to attack in the night, and they did not.[35]

That evening, Nat placed sentinels and lay down to sleep. He did not leave a record of his thoughts or his dreams, but he might well have imagined his entry into Jerusalem, the divine city, so near at hand, so frustratingly beyond reach. His plans for Jerusalem had fallen apart at the hands of his own men, who did not listen to his commands to proceed forward, and at the hands of the whites, who had gathered in force. Still, he had kept his men together and added new fighters, and he had his plans to catch Jerusalem by surprise. There, he likely believed, was his destiny.

MEANWHILE, WORD OF the rebellion spread among Black and white people in the region, bringing out new would-be rebels among the Black population and a much larger number of eager combatants among the white people of Southside and the adjoining counties in North Carolina.

Black people, both free and enslaved, analyzed the stories that began to circulate. For some, the attacks confirmed things they believed
were coming. An enslaved woman named Beck testified later that enslaved people talked of the rebellion ahead of time at the plantation
where she lived at the border of Southampton and Sussex Counties.
She claimed there was plotting among the Black members of the biracial Raccoon Swamp Antioch Baptist Church she attended with her
enslaver, and that the uprising was discussed the night before the rebellion began. Once the rebellion was under way, she allegedly heard
enslaved people gossiping at a neighboring plantation, saying that the
enslaver there "would be cropped before the end of the year." Later,
however, lawyers cast doubt on her story, and many white people dis-
believed it. A few miles away, on the Blunt estate, a man named Ben
headed to a nearby farm and told a man named Sam that "there was
going to be a war." An hour later, a white farmer confirmed "the negroes are behind the killing of the white people." "Ah," Ben said to
Sam as the white man left, "did I not tell you there would be war?"[36]
Other Black people tied the attacks to conflicts with Britain in their
own lifetime, including the claim by the enslaved person Hardy that
"the English were in the County killing white people . . . ought to
have been done long ago." So, too, did Ned, claimed by the estate of
Charles Stuart, talk of a British invasion.[37]

Nat did not hear that conversation between Ben and the farmer,
but surely he hoped that word of the attacks would draw dozens, then
hundreds, then thousands, of enslaved supporters, the way that the
"prophetess" Deborah's army attracted ten thousand supporters to
Kedesh. Such a large group was not forthcoming, but sometime during
the day on Monday, August 22, another potential band of supporters might have headed out in search of Nat's company. The group
included two enslaved young men who had left the Whitehead plantation during Nat's attack. When they returned, other enslaved people
told them that Nat expected them to join his band, so they glumly
rode along Nat's route, some among the half a dozen or so enslaved
people searching for Nat in the neighborhood. At the Porter farm,

Venus, an enslaved woman, told them that the Porters had fled and that the rebels were not far behind. Then they visited Thomas Haithcock, a free Black man. Haithcock advised them to follow Nat's orders and left with them. Later in the day the young men turned themselves in to a white farmer. But Haithcock remained at large.[38]

If Nat's band could attract free Black people like Haithcock, there was an additional pool of potentially hundreds of recruits from the more than seventeen hundred free Black people in the county. While many free Black families lived with whites, and thus might find it more challenging to operate, about fourteen free Black households lived on land owned by themselves or by other free Black people. Nat might also have hoped to attract people from the mixed-race households on the Cheroenhaka (Nottoway) reservation; there twenty-three free Black families lived among the other residents on Indian land, as the historian Vanessa Holden found. While the overwhelming majority of Nat's followers were enslaved men and boys, there were other Black and mixed-race free people he might have hoped to call upon if he could demonstrate his strength.[39]

AMONG WHITE PEOPLE the word spread more widely but for the first day slowly. Perhaps the first groups of whites outside the county to learn of the uprising were in Murfreesboro, North Carolina, fourteen miles away. The schoolteacher John Williams had returned to his house from checking on the Whiteheads and learned that Nat's company had killed his wife, Louisa, and their child. Williams headed off to alert white people in the more populous (and easily reached) town across the state line, arriving in Murfreesboro on Monday afternoon. In Halifax, thirty miles away, the first evidence of a warning came later Monday. Richmond, Suffolk, Norfolk, Edenton, and other places forty to sixty miles away didn't record warnings until Tuesday morning, or even after that. A historian estimates that the news traveled at three miles an hour, an "astonishingly feeble pace." By dusk Monday, the first outside support was on its way as a company of guards with an artillery piece crossed the Meherrin River into Southampton from neighboring Belfield, Virginia. But their effects would not be felt until Tuesday. So, too, would that be true of the Petersburg militia that arrived about midnight Monday. The white people's advantages of numbers and communication would become evident, but not until Tuesday or Wednesday.[40]

In the meantime, the Cross Keys region of Southampton County southwest of Jerusalem was largely abandoned by white people, while Jerusalem became a refuge and an armed camp. "The country we have passed through is completely deserted and the inhabitants have absolutely left their doors even unbarred," wrote a volunteer from Norfolk. But in Jerusalem, another white fighter wrote, "every house, room and corner in this place is full of women and children, driven from home, who had to take [to] the wood, until they could get to this place." A newspaper editor who arrived Thursday estimated that between three hundred and four hundred women and children "sought refuge" in Jerusalem, filling the small white town well beyond its capacity, with the "farms most generally left in possession of the blacks."[41]

Just after midnight, as Monday turned to Tuesday, word of Nat and his company's whereabouts filtered into the town of Jerusalem, stirring fear and dissension. This gossip was accurate about location but not size. Captain Parker believed there were two hundred enslaved soldiers at Ridley's Buckhorn Quarter, a huge overestimate, while Parker had only sixty white men combined. Still, Parker suggested they take thirty or forty men from town to attack Nat's company, but "those who had families" in Jerusalem "were strongly opposed to it." If the men left, couldn't Nat's band slip past them in the dark and attack a defenseless Jerusalem? Parker "acceded to the suggestions of those who had so much at stake." Even a full day into the rebellion, the Black fighters seemed to have some advantages.[42]

THAT NIGHT, NAT'S sleep was brief, if he slept at all. Nat was soon roused by a "great racket." His sentinels believed—inaccurately—

that they spotted a force en route to attack them and gave "the alarm" to the sleeping band at Ridley's. It was all one big mistake, a panic. Again Nat tried to command. His men were in disarray, some mounted, others "in great confusion." He sent a few to "ride round and reconnoitre," knowing that a fighting force could not blunder forward without knowledge of its terrain and its enemies. But this tactic backfired. As these sentinels returned from scouting, the sound of their horses' hooves spooked Nat's men. Becoming "more alarmed," "not knowing who" was coming, about half fled in different directions, leaving Nat with a remnant of twenty. Still, Nat might have reflected on the time the Lord told Gideon that he had "too many" recruits, as the Israelites would "vaunt themselves against me, saying, Mine own hand hath saved me." Therefore the Lord urged Gideon to send home everyone who was fearful, then everyone who drank water in a certain way, eliminating all but three hundred of his original force of thirty thousand. By the three hundred men "will I save you," the Lord said. Perhaps Nat's remaining band would be enough; perhaps the Lord would work not through numbers but through miraculous force.[43]

It was still a little before dawn on Tuesday, but there was a full moon, so Nat set off with his remaining forces. The need again was for men. They headed west, away from Jerusalem, toward the neighboring plantation of Dr. Samuel Blunt. His 1,500 acres were home to sixty-nine enslaved people, including up to twenty men of fighting age. This time, however, Nat miscalculated. Assuming that the Blunt family had left for the Ridley house, Nat approached openly, without any efforts at stealth. It was about five in the morning, but the Blunt family—and some of the enslaved people there—had prepared for an attack. Blunt armed two neighbors, his son, and an overseer. But he also went further, counting on enslaved men he trusted, men who assumed positions that allowed them to see who was coming. They spied a band of perhaps twenty-five men, they estimated, led by Moses, the adult man enslaved by the Barrows. Moses, seeing an enslaved young woman carrying a white child run from the house, leaped off his horse to chase them. Moses caught her but then was captured himself by Frank, an enslaved man claimed by the Blunt family.[44]

The rest of Nat's company was coming up behind, not necessarily aware of Moses's flight. Perhaps they were even clamoring, the way that Gideon's forces chanted about the sword of the Lord as they attacked. To see if any of the Blunts were home, Hark fired a gun. They had their answer right away. Five of the white men—all but the older Blunt—fired, striking Hark and driving him off his horse. Nat's band was only a few dozen yards from the house, but, seeing their situation was dire, they "retreated," Nat later said. Nat did not mention Hark's injury. As they backed away, it is possible they were harassed by the enslaved people at Blunt's plantation. Some accounts suggest the enslaved people actually drove Nat's company off; Blunt gave the white people credit for the victory but did say that the enslaved people chased after the fleeing rebels "with shouts and execrations."[45]

Nat once again looked for help to Cross Keys and the small neighborhood around Cabin Pond and the Turners' old plantations. He was well aware that his commanding authority might slip as he left his own neighborhood, bringing in fighters who did not know him or his calling. He must return to the people who believed in him to "rally the neighborhood I had left." So back toward home (and away from Jerusalem) he went, in defeat but not in despair, in hopes of preparing another assault. Nat and his fighters retraced their steps of the previous day, the path of their bloody fight through the neighborhood. Along the way, Nat sent two enslaved men to recruit in the more distant plantations of the Newsom and Allen families fifteen miles off. These were potentially prime recruiting grounds, the first- and fourth-biggest plantations in the region. Nat seemed to understand that he needed to gain access to the largest slave quarters in the parish in order to prevail; the Newsom, Allen, Ridley, and Blunt holdings were four of the six biggest plantations by the number of enslaved people.[46]

If there was to be a time when the enslaved people would rise en masse, it would have to be now. In fact, sometime on Tuesday, the free Black man Thomas Haithcock discovered another small band of people seeking to join Nat's company. After his two companions from Monday disappeared, Haithcock came across another free Black man who was willing to fight, William "Billy" Artis. Artis, along with his wife, Cherry, and sons, had recruited enslaved people on a farm belonging to the estate of the late Benjamin Blunt. At some point Artis rode past the Blunt plantation, waving his hat and yelling he "would cut his way, he would kill and cripple" as he went. Early Tuesday, Haithcock and four enslaved boys visited Peter Edwards's plantation and told the Black people that "Gen'l Nat would be there on Wednesday or Thursday." But if Haithcock ever caught up with Nat's band, he did not stay.[47] Nor did another band of Black rebels wandering around the neighborhood, scattered remnants of the company who had been with Nat at the failed attack on Dr. Samuel Blunt's house. They were seen around Cross Keys on Tuesday, but not again with Nat.[48]

THE STRUGGLE TO attract Black recruits outside the neighborhood doomed Nat's rebellion. In some ways his recruiting succeeded extraordinarily well; Nat gathered at least forty men and boys and one woman, and perhaps a few more than that. Although he gained more men closest to home, there were signs that he could recruit enslaved men at the larger plantations if he could reach them in force. But this was a problem. There are scattered indications of enslaved people on more distant plantations hearing about the uprising and expressing interest in fighting, if the company reached them. Beck testified that on Tuesday she heard an enslaved man named Shadrack say that he would join if the band came their way. Although lawyers later cast doubt on Beck's testimony, there is little doubt that some enslaved people were willing to join a band at their doorstep, but not willing to risk running toward the fighters. There was safety, and confidence, in numbers and in proximity.[49]

Perhaps Nat's recruiting was doomed by the very thing that fueled his early success: surprise. Knowing that other rebels, especially

Denmark Vesey, had been stymied by traitors who told whites of their plans, Nat deliberately kept his counsel close. This meant that white people did not know of his attempt beforehand. But it also meant most Black people did not know either. Nat faced an almost impossible quandary. He needed time to prepare Black people to fight, but he could not risk letting time pass. He had calculated that it was better to risk confusion than to give up on surprise.[50]

By Tuesday morning, that decision was coming back to haunt Nat. His reliance on surprise meant that his rebellion depended on success to attract new people. The longer it took for him to draw large numbers of soldiers, the more time it gave neighboring whites to respond. On Tuesday morning, the first band of white cavalry from Greensville County reached the neighborhood of Cross Keys, presumably armed with their own guns. They did not know where Nat was, but they rode through the area. During the day, they visited several plantations that Nat's band had visited.

At the Waller plantation, the Greensville cavalry found Levi Waller binding up the legs of Alfred, the enslaved blacksmith who had perhaps helped Levi Waller escape. The previous day, Captain Peete's posse, finding Alfred, had crippled him but left him to live. When the Greensville cavalry arrived, their commander apparently took Waller's solicitude as evidence of the laxity of neighborhood slaveholders and decided to teach these white people a lesson. Denouncing Levi Waller, the cavalry commander ordered Alfred tied to a tree and shot to death as a "beneficial example to the other Insurgents," Levi Waller later wrote.[51]

When the Greensville cavalry reached the Whitehead plantation and discovered the dead bodies strewn across the property, they sought similar retribution against enslaved people there. As the enslaved people begged for mercy, the Greensville cavalry prepared to kill them. One of those enslaved people was Hubbard, the blacksmith who had saved Harriet Whitehead's life. He led the way to her hiding place, proof positive of his good intention, but she was gone. Confused, Hubbard suggested that Nat's company had discovered and killed her. But in fact Harriet Whitehead had simply crawled away. Hearing the Greensville cavalry accuse Hubbard, she "ran out and saved him by relating the circumstances of his conduct in aiding to save her life."[52]

Meanwhile, Nat and the remnants of his company rode six miles back toward Cabin Pond, where they had begun. They were about halfway home when, after sunrise, they reached the lane to Newit Harris's plantation. Nat had just sent the enslaved men Curtis and Stephen to go out recruiting at the large Newsom and Allen plantations, so the company's numbers were even smaller than before. When they reached the house of Captain Harris, they discovered a "party of white men."[53]

This was the Greensville cavalry, the first reinforcements from outside the county, the first true sign that whites were preparing a massive counterattack. Some later believed that Will "the executioner" was shot here by the Greensville cavalry, but Will might already have been killed the day before at the Barrow plantation.[54]

Nat's company was outnumbered and outgunned, and there was nothing to do but flee for their lives. Because they did not have hills, they could not run to higher ground. Because there were no mountains, they could not form a maroon redoubt and dare the whites to attack, the way enslaved rebels did in Jamaica. All they could do was scatter and hide. Nat headed to the woods, to the swamps. He knew the backwoods and swamps meant survival, but also an acceptance of his weak position. He was not heading there to take a stand. He was heading there to recalculate.[55]

As the men fled on their horses, Nat was left with only two followers, Jacob and the other enslaved rebel named Nat. Not enough to attack. But here, on his own ground, he could not easily be captured either. They knew the area extremely well, and they were known to the enslaved people in this vicinity, so they had less reason to fear they would be betrayed. That day they hid in the woods, waiting out the white militia, waiting for night.[56]

When it was near dark, Nat sent Jacob and the other Nat to find his original collaborators, Henry, Sam, Nelson, and Hark, whose injury might have been news to Nat. The message was a simple one: gather where they had begun Sunday at Cabin Pond, where they had eaten their preparatory dinner, where the men had drunk and talked of what was to come, where Nat had prepared himself for his destiny. Nat meanwhile would prepare himself again. It was a setback, but did not every warrior-prophet face defeat? Saul's early battles against the Philistines went poorly, and the Hebrews hid in caves, thickets, rocks, high places, and pits, while some crossed over Jordan. Those who remained with Saul were "trembling" until the Lord turned the tide and "saved Israel that day."[57]

Nat made his way through the woods to Cabin Pond, and he waited. But he never saw Jacob or the other Nat again. Jacob returned to the Porter plantation, where he lived, and he was captured there the next day. The other Nat hid for a week before being caught. Nat, the commander, did not know this for certain, but as Wednesday passed, he became suspicious. Again we do not know Nat's thoughts in this moment of defeat. But he had no shortage of prophets to type himself after, prophets who suffered and were left alone and whose faith in the face of this ridicule was rewarded by the Spirit. Perhaps Nat waited for the Spirit to tell him what to do. Perhaps he devised his own plans for another assault on Jerusalem. Perhaps like Gideon he did not separate the prophetic and the strategic. Almost surely he prayed "without ceasing" and even tried to "in every thing give thanks," as Paul directed the Thessalonians in the Christian Testament.[58]

Wednesday night he heard voices, but the voices did not belong to Hark or Henry or Nelson or Sam. They were the voices of white men, who were "riding around the place as though they were looking for some one." The whites knew where he was. None of his collaborators had joined him. Nat considered these facts and reached his conclusion. "Jacob and Nat had been taken, and compelled to betray me." Nat might also have heard gunfire from Peter Edwards's plantation, not far away. And so "I gave up all hope for the present," Nat said. He understood that this phase of his campaign was over. It had failed.

He had not reached Jerusalem and would not do so in this moment. Yet he did not give up hope forever. Perhaps Nat immediately began plotting. From his actions it appears likely that he did what he had always done: he waited for instruction from the Spirit.[59]

Nat spent Thursday taking provisions from the Travis farm, where he had begun with the attack on his enslaver three and a half days earlier. Then, retreating into the fields not far from the pond, a mile from Benjamin Turner Jr.'s old plantation, where he had spent his boyhood days, Nat dug a hole under a pile of fence rails, a hole he called a "cave," and there he concealed himself and marked days on a stick.[60]

7

Vengeance

As word traveled across the region on Monday and Tuesday, Southampton County white people mobilized themselves and called for support from their networks in adjoining counties in Virginia and North Carolina, the state government, and the federal military. In the process, they proved the potency of the warning that the enslaved man Aaron allegedly gave to Nat: the white population was much larger and better connected than the rebels understood. Over the next week, these mobilizations first put down the rebellion, then turned to other work: terrorizing and punishing local inhabitants for a while before trying to restore order by restraining the wildest among the armed whites and shifting from murder to murder trials. Instead of a monolithic white response, Southampton displayed competing visions for the future.

For the Southampton white posses and the Greensville company, the first work was rounding up the participants. Several enslaved people were captured Tuesday, including the older Moses, James and Sam of Peter Edwards's plantation, and Curtis and Stephen of the Ridley plantation, taken by John Clark Turner while those two men were en route to the vast slave quarters at the Allen plantation.[1]

The leaders began to be counted over the next two days. Hark, wounded Tuesday morning, was arrested with a pocketbook, powder, shot, and silver either on Tuesday or on Wednesday. Jack, who had been coerced by Hark into participating, was arrested quickly, perhaps on information from the white man who had hired his labor. The young boy Moses, impressed into the group at the Moore plantation, was in custody by Wednesday. Nelson was seen in the Edwards orchards on Wednesday but fled. When the militia caught him on Thursday, they killed him and by one story beheaded him and gave his skull to a militia unit from Norfolk as a souvenir. Henry, the paymaster, was killed about the same time, his head severed and taken to Cross Keys, presumably to be displayed as a warning. By Thursday, an editor from Richmond said that thirteen prisoners were in jail in Jerusalem and all the leaders were accounted for, except for Sam, Will, and, of course, Nat. Will had likely died in an earlier battle. For the moment, Sam and Nat remained at large.[2]

As it became clear that the rebellion had been put down and most leaders captured, many Southampton white people sought revenge against specific enslaved people. Nathaniel Francis, reunited with his wife, Lavinia, learned that Charlotte had tried to kill his wife. In a rage, Francis tied Charlotte to a tree and shot her. John Williams, the long-haired schoolmaster who had lost his family, was "almost insane with grief" and wished to "kill every negro . . . in sight." Theodore Trezvant, whose brother's plantation was not far from Nat's route allegedly shut the post office in Jerusalem and went "out killing negroes." At dawn on Wednesday, an alarm spread of a possible uprising, and in the confusion a local posse killed a Black enslaved man on his way to visit his wife.[3]

But white Southampton men quickly began to debate the propriety of killing minor participants. Enslavers especially tried to protect their property from bands of white vigilantes. On Tuesday, James turned himself in to his owner, Peter Edwards. Edwards, judging James guilty only of complicity, asked a militia captain to "prevent his being shot if I could." That captain tied him to the side of the house for safekeeping, but "a party rushed up and shot him—he fell dead." Nathaniel Francis revealed his own judgment when, after killing Charlotte, he embraced the enslaved woman Ester, who had helped save his wife's life. But these distinctions meant little to men from outside the neighborhood. A mob "almost killed" him for defending Ester, then murdered her. The historian Patrick Breen argues that the brutality of the Greensville militia and some poorer Southampton white men provoked Southampton enslavers to try to rein in the chaos and protect the lives of the people whom they claimed and for whose loss no one would compensate them. As Peter Edwards put it, "It is not to be supposed that juries would award damages against persons that they might think were acting under a sense of duty and with a view to the public safety."[4]

Thus, enslavers had a vested interest in saving the lives they could. For local white people who did not own slaves, the need for restraint often seemed less clear, and some participated in mass murder, driven by revulsion and fear but also—for some—by a wish to drive all Black people from the lands poorer whites coveted. For more distant white people who rode to the rescue but found a county already returning to peace, there was no reason for restraint at all. Some, in fact, seem to believe they needed to teach the white men of Cross Keys a lesson about how to govern enslaved people. Of course the ultimate price of these campaigns of revenge was paid not by elite white men but by the Black people they tortured and killed.[5]

By Wednesday, many white people were flooding into the county. The white men arrived in waves, but, with the exception of the Greensville company, they showed up after Nat's rebellion had been largely defeated. Over Tuesday and Wednesday, militia appeared from Petersburg, Richmond, Lafayette, Norfolk, Portsmouth, Prince George, and Halifax, many gathering at Richard Darden's tavern between Jerusalem and Cross Keys.[6]

FIRST IN THE lower part of Southampton County, then in Jerusalem and the rest of the county and in adjoining Isle of Wight, whites spread the word that a band of enslaved people were on the march, attacking and killing whites. The whites who gathered were not simply an assortment of pale-skinned people but men with kin and church ties to Cross Keys. White Southsiders responded to a call coming from their own extended kin or fellow congregants.

These white mobilizations revealed some fundamental differences between the power of white and Black Southsiders. As in many agrarian societies, white Virginians built community upon foundations of kin, family, geographic proximity, and church. White people were hardly alone in utilizing these tools. Black Southsiders worked hard to sustain similar networks, especially intimate and extended familial relationships, but they struggled with a dire power imbalance: they could not prevent enslavers from selling away their family members and bringing strangers into their midst.[7]

Ties were stronger and much more geographically extensive among white Southsiders precisely because the system of slavery had been constructed upon communal networks. White neighborhoods were larger, sometimes looser, but much wider ranging. White Virginians drew upon a common racial calculus—trust no one of the other race and look for allies with similar skin—but they faced fewer complete strangers, and they had more reason to trust in the reliability of whites who joined their battle, if defined not as a struggle between denominations or political parties but as a race war. While Nat paused as he left the neighborhood and paused again at Parker's farm, white Virginians mobilized across larger spaces.

One of the institutions that whites used to mobilize was the militia. Many of the 850 men who organized over Tuesday and Wednesday were part of the unwieldy but important system of militias that had developed in slave colonies and states to suppress rebellions. Every imperial European power turned to militias to deal with the lack of regular forces to deploy against foreign invasion, Native peoples, and slave rebellions, and most expanded these militias after the Seven Years' War between 1756 and 1763. For reinforcement, Spanish colonies relied on Black militia members to supplement Spanish-descended free men in areas like Florida and Peru that had relatively small enslaved populations and, at times of crisis, in places with significant slavery like Cuba.[8]

But English colonies like Virginia generally resisted Black service in the militia, relying upon their larger white settler populations. As early as 1678, colonists in Nevis, Montserrat, St. Kitts, and Antigua were divided into military "divisions" and assigned to military officers. Over time, some English colonies incorporated Black members, including in Jamaica and Barbados. But most did not, and everywhere the militia was controlled by planters. And everywhere poorer white men complained about their service, their heavy uniforms, their expenses, and the deference they were expected to show. Throughout the empire, observers feared that militias would not be able to defend white people against a slave revolt or an invasion. It isn't surprising that militias were often weak; one colonial militia muster went so awry that enslaved people openly mocked the effort.[9]

In colonial Virginia, militias existed more in theory than in practice until the Revolutionary War, when militias became a home protection force that supplemented but never displaced the regular army. But the militias did not distinguish themselves even when operating close to home. After fifty insurgents ran unopposed through April and May 1778, Governor Patrick Henry lamented the militias' ineffectiveness in a letter to the legislature. The regiments in the counties adjoining the insurrection, "like too many other Militias in the State," were rendered useless by a near "total want of discipline." Still the Revolutionary-era militia did provide some home guard service and, in propaganda, was celebrated for its work against the British. This service helped solidify their place in the new national society, such that they were enshrined in the Bill of Rights and in many state constitutions and laws.[10]

In Nat's lifetime, white Southsiders were reminded several times that the militias were a last line of protection. In the War of 1812, both formal and informal militias mustered in defense of the Chesapeake and of slavery. Militias helped block enslaved people's paths to British ships, serving more as a slave patrol than as a fighting force.[11] So, too, did militias resurface as a potential line of defense in slave revolts like Gabriel's rebellion and the Denmark Vesey conspiracy scare. Even so, militiamen often responded to calls with skepticism, overwhelmed by their own work and the number of false alarms. In the Demerara revolt, for example, John C. Cheveley, a militiaman who had arrived two years before the 1823 rebellion, had already gone to bed when the bugle sounded for muster. A neighbor told him "the negroes were all in rebellion." Still, Cheveley thought, "Oh, never mind them it is all nonsense, keep where you are." But then he did muster in order to avoid getting "into trouble for skulking" and feeling like a coward.[12] No militiaman in Southampton or Isle of Wight left an account like Cheveley's. But they likely felt the same mix of emotions as they wondered whether this was another false alarm or whether they would face actual danger.

As Nat's men attacked on Monday and Tuesday, the word spread through white networks: mobilize or die. This was no drill. Men who lived in the immediate vicinity often stayed home to protect their houses or gathered at nearby plantations or Jerusalem for safety; many—like the men in Jerusalem Monday night—were wary of riding out and leaving their homes exposed. Therefore, the call to arms depended upon a broader imaginary neighborhood, an appeal to men who lived nearby but were not themselves in immediate danger.

The response in Southampton turned on credibly calling out men from neighboring counties, near enough to care, far enough to leave their families safely at home. This kind of mid-distance communication was possible because of the long-standing family-based structure of white Virginia society, which stood in contrast to other Anglo-American colonies like Jamaica or Demerara. And it depended upon the personal testimony of people like John Williams, who had seen the dead with his own eyes, who had lost his own family, who could overcome skepticism of yet another rumor that turned to dust. Once the militia gathered, the overwhelming majority of them were not from Southampton County at all but from neighboring Isle of Wight, or from farther away. Among the many advantages white Southsiders possessed, these networks of communication and affiliation, imperfect though they could be, were perhaps the most significant. The 850 white fighters who gathered in the area were referred to as militia, and many of them undoubtedly were, operating with a sense of duty developed in their training. But the group might well have included men who were not part of an organized militia or who had mustered independently upon hearing the news, called out not by formal duty but by the urge to help.

Some of the members of these militias were literally family members. Of the many men who arrived from Isle of Wight, more than a quarter shared surnames with members of the South Quay Baptist Church in Southampton, including half of the sixteen officers.[13] Those people with ties to Southampton could in turn call upon large extended kin networks to build a sense of solidarity. Almost three-fifths of the Isle of Wight militiamen (324 of 564, or 57 percent) shared a surname with at least one other member of the regiment. Of the 88 men who mustered with Captain Joseph Holland's company, three-quarters (66) shared a surname with at least one other member, and eight family names accounted for half the company, including eight Hollands.[14] Another quarter (23 of 88) of the men were married to a woman whose maiden name matched the surname of another man in the company. Five Bradshaw men and their in-laws, 18 altogether, encompassed one-fifth of the company.[15]

These ties of mobilization were powerful because they were enduring; white families could keep their kin groups close to home for decades. Of the men from Isle of Wight who turned out against the British in 1812, 7 out of 10 (432 of 599, or 72 percent) shared a surname with at least one man who turned out to fight Nat a generation later. The Dardens contributed 7 men in 1812, 9 in 1831; the Daughtreys, 7 in both years; the Hollands, 9 in 1812 and 14 in 1831; the Turners, 17 in 1812 and 18 in 1831.[16]

These kin groups sustained themselves through not simply family feeling but long-standing, cultivated property ownership. The ties of property and marriage that bound the white Turner/Francis/Reese/Porter family or the Barrow/Vaughan/Harris/Parker family were by no means unique; many white Southsiders lived near property belonging to kinsmen. Consider the Vick family, yeomen who lived around St. Luke's Parish in the lower half of Southampton County. Of the fourteen Vick households on tax lists, ten owned no enslaved people of working age, three owned between one and five, and only one owned more than five. If this family could not rely on large-scale slaveholding to build wealth, they could rely on one another. Of the sixteen Vick households in St. Luke's Parish, at least fourteen had acquired part of their land from someone else named Vick; half had received all their land from a family member. Nine of the sixteen households received tracts "by will" or from the "Estate" of someone else named Vick. Jordan Vick, for example, bequeathed the only fifty-three acres his son John owned in the 1820s; Matthew Vick divvied up the ninety-seven acres he inherited from another Vick between himself and John's brother Joel, who later received another bequest from a Vick relative, and then in turn passed on land to Bolling Vick, just as the Francises and Turners had passed land and people among white family members.[17]

Most white landowners in St. Luke's Parish had property near kinfolk. More than three-quarters of all landowners (350 of 446, or 78 percent) shared a surname with another landowner in the parish. More than two-fifths (197 of 446, or 44 percent) lived within a mile of another household with their surname, and one-quarter lived on property adjoining that of someone with their surname (116 of 446, or 26 percent), based on the distances recorded in Virginia land tax records. These figures, while intriguing, should be viewed with caution; we cannot assume that *all* of the people *lived* on the property so designated, because some households owned more than one tract of land, some tracts were not contiguous, and not all white people with the same last name were related. Still, if we consider landowners who shared a surname with at least one other landowner, three-quarters (263 of 350, or 75 percent) owned property within five miles of another person of the same name. They were not simply in the same county; they were in the same neighborhoods. All of these landed property transmissions, so crucial to white yeomen's sustenance of family connections, were unavailable by law to enslaved people, who were moved around against their will.[18]

Marriage was another crucial way white people built extended family ties and property. Women were binding links in the transmission of landed property even when they did not own it outright themselves. They could hold usage rights, or they could be the vehicle for transmission of land from the family of a bride's parents to the family of her husband. The Vicks, for instance, intermarried with the Jordans. In 1820, John Vick received forty-two acres from Patience Jordan "By Marriage," a conveyance of land from the Jordan family to her husband's household.[19] As the Jordans intermarried with the Vicks, three households of Jordans in the parish lived within three miles of ten different Vick households by 1831. While enslaved people experienced deep intimate ties solemnized in ceremonies like jumping the broom and shared deep emotional connections with kin and with unrelated people they treated as kin, the legal forms of marriage, and the way those forms shaped property, were unavailable to enslaved people in Southampton.[20]

Many of the whites who flooded into Southampton with guns were bound by ties formed in churches that crossed neighborhoods and counties. According to a membership list for South Quay Baptist Church in Southampton between 1775 and 1827, the congregation was largely composed of a few families who lived in proximity to one another; eight families constituted a third of the members. This was quite like the arrangement, as far as we know, at Turner's Meeting House, where Nat learned to pray from other Turners and Francises.[21] While the quasi-legal model of church discipline in the minute books suggest an individual should be arraigned before the unified congregation, the covenant of the church placed discipline within the context of households, and thus under the control of men. Members promised to "watch over our Families under our care" to ensure that they kept the "Lord's Day holy" and behaved "to becometh the Gospel of our dear Redeemer Jesus Christ."[22] Through churches like South Quay, extended kin groups not only reinforced their ties with one another but also constructed powerful, if sometimes contentious, ties with other extended kin groups. Once again, enslaved people practiced fervent religious ceremonies, but they struggled to replicate the large and broad, if often thin, bonds of expanded kin groups that turned white neighbor-hoods into webs of interconnections. To be sure, it is likely white people would have rushed to the aid of whites they did not know, but the extended family ties across the region likely made it easier to gather men in a hurry and to persuade them to take the threat seriously.

These organizational imbalances, along with the generally equal number of Black and white residents in the area, blocked Nat from forcing the kind of crisis that transformed other slave rebellions into larger wars, like the 1823 Demerara rising and the 1831 Christmas attacks in Jamaica. There, enslaved rebels attracted large numbers of followers that overwhelmed local white militia and gave them con-trol over their home region, until more-distant white forces arrived. Nat likely hoped for a similar expansion, and he utilized many of the same combat tactics and strategies those rebels did. But he faced much graver odds. In Jamaica, Black people far outnumbered whites in many regions and could draw upon longer communication net-works. There, the rebels encircled the militia and forced them to re-treat, opening up possibilities for Black rebels to claim larger militia stores, arm themselves, and attract more recruits. In Demerara, the white militia confronted three thousand to four thousand Black reb-els converging on the whites at Bachelor's Adventure from two dif-ferent directions.[23] With fewer Black people in the neighborhood and better-connected white enemies, Nat could not win the recruitment battle once his initial advantage of surprise was gone; within hours, he was facing larger and larger forces of opponents, and his followers, seeing this, ran for their lives.

ONCE NAT FLED to the woods, he probably did not know what was happening in the county. But he could guess. As usual, whites re-sponded to a slave rebellion by launching a campaign of terror, one with both judicial and extrajudicial wings. They aimed to show Black people in Virginia and around the world that white Virginians were firmly and forever in charge.

From the beginning, local elites aimed to focus their revenge upon the guilty, while outsiders and poorer whites seemed more likely to terrorize the entire slave population. Later in the week, as the rebellion was irrefutably quashed, other divisions emerged, especially between those whites who wished to take vengeance privately and those who wanted to convey captured prisoners to Jerusalem for trial. Some of these divisions mapped the contrasts between proximate and far-flung whites, between elite and poor, between those who had a property interest in the enslaved people in the region and those who did not. Some mapped a growing legal effort to constrain the violence of slavery within the (extremely broad) limits of the law, to make southern society appear civilized and law-bound in the eyes of the world, an effort to bind together Southampton elites and the highest-ranking officers from Richmond. But this legalism was contested by those who claimed the right to punish as a people's right, not the special province of the courts. Both the wild campaigns of terror and the turn toward legal resolution have their analogues elsewhere in the Atlantic. While some whites sought a race war, elite slave owners across the Atlantic world generally tried to stop rebellions, demonstrate their own grotesque and terrifying power, then retreat into legalistic conclusions that ended the rebellion moment and restarted the normal time of mundane life. The rebellion thus could be the state of exception, the trial the return of the state of peace. At least in theory.

After the posse broke the rebellion at the Blunt house and realized that Nat was not preparing an immediate counterattack, a new phase began. Now the militia shifted from a military operation to a campaign of terror. The terror the militia inflicted upon the neighborhood was deliberate even if it was probably not planned. Black people had tried to claim their own form of control, of what we call sovereignty, over the land, and white people intended to demonstrate who made the rules on this ground, who must be obeyed, and who must obey. Terror takes its power from its seeming randomness; it could land on anyone, and one's own actions were no defense. The goal was to inspire enough fear to restructure the political calculations of the terrorized.

In the immediate aftermath, bands of white people from surrounding counties unleashed a wave of terror that began in Southampton but moved far beyond its borders. On Wednesday, a search party shot down Austin, enslaved by the Edwards family, when they saw him "standing in the yard by himself perfectly defenceless." A company from Murfreesboro, North Carolina, killed Moses, Aaron, and Jacob, all enslaved by the Porters, in a field near the Whitehead plantation. At least one white observer heard that the Murfreesboro company divided up the men's possessions.[24]

Sometime during the week, Billy Artis, the free Black man who had formed a band to support the rebellion, was discovered hiding near his house and was shot. Although some initial reports claimed he had been killed, others said that he survived this shooting and was "lurking about the neighborhood." By Friday, September 2, he was found dead, with his hat on a stake near him "and his pistol lying by him." Some assumed suicide, though others suspected he had died of his wounds.[25]

This stage of terror continued over Wednesday as larger numbers of white militia arrived, including the Roanoke Blues from Halifax County, North Carolina. This company reached the county Tuesday night but, fearing they faced a force of a thousand, slept outside the county's bounds and crossed after sunrise Wednesday.[26] These militia arrived with their own sense of panic; many came from regions on a high level of alert, where enslaved people fell victim to paranoia or gossip. In the Blues' Halifax County, stories spread of an enslaved man named Sam who was decapitated and whose head marked a crossing between the towns of Scotland Neck and Palmyra. In Murfreesboro, where Williams the schoolteacher had brought the news, refugees poured in with wild stories of a Black-white alliance, a company of 150 Black soldiers, and a plan to march into North Carolina, reports that drove the town into a frenzy. On Thursday, an unnamed Black man was shot down outside town. Whites in Murfreesboro cut off his head, stuck it on a pole, and planted the pole at a central cross street, then threw his body away. That same day, an enslaved carriage driver was put to death because of a complaint that he had behaved impudently. Stories spread that four Black men's heads were posted on roads heading into the cities of Wilmington and Fayetteville, North Carolina.[27] Whether every individual story was true, or whether some represented imprinting of a true story onto other geographic locales, the stories were proof of the wide radius of fear and rage among white Virginians and North Carolinians.

The indiscriminate killing provoked a backlash from self-interested Southampton elites, who wanted to protect their investment in enslaved people, and from the state leaders who began to arrive from Richmond. A Richmond newspaper editor, John Hampden Pleasants, wrote of his time in Southampton that "it is with pain we speak of another feature of the Southampton Rebellion . . . We allude to the slaughter of many blacks, without trial, and under circumstances of great barbarity," including "decapitation." This editor remained mostly in Jerusalem, talking to local people, and estimated that between twenty-five and forty people had been killed indiscriminately, some by Southampton men wild with rage, others by bands from neighboring counties.[28] A Methodist minister from a nearby North Carolina county wrote on August 27, "Many negroes are killed every day. The exact number will never be known."[29] A young man from the North living in Sussex County wrote that the militia "have been for four days and four nights hunting them out and killing them, like so many wolves!"[30] A free Black woman in northern North Carolina later said, "The white people that had no slaves would have killed the colored, but the masters put them in jail to protect them from the white people." Bands of whites "came to my mother's and threatened us," and one "put his pistol to my breast, and said, 'If you open your head, I'll kill you in a minute!'"[31]

This was exemplary violence, meant to cow a population into

quiescence. A Hertford County militia captain wrote, "It is nearly requisite for some time yet to show in full force, that the blacks may have view of power which can be speedily used against [them]. The impression must be made on their fears through the medium of their eyes and bodily feelings."[32] Some of this exemplary violence was deliberately and vividly cruel. One woman wrote that whites cut the ears off an enslaved person and tied him to the belly of a horse that dragged his body into the woods.[33]

The militia from Murfreesboro, North Carolina, might have committed the most gruesome forms of exemplary violence: decapitation and display. The Murfreesboro cavalry company killed a number of Black people as it rode through the Cross Keys region, perhaps as many as forty, though the historian Patrick Breen places the number closer to eight. Allegedly, one Murfreesboro company massacred a Black man said to be a "Methodist minister" for his alleged complicity. "They burnt him with red hot irons—cut off his ears and nose— stabbed him, cut his hamstrings, stuck him like a hog, and at last cut off his head, and spiked it on the whipping post for a spectacle and a warning to other negroes!!" a northern visitor to the area wrote. Not all the stories can be verified, but at least one of these people's heads, after decapitation, was "spiked" to a post at the intersection of Barrow Road and Jerusalem Highway for a spectacle and a warning. That crossing was known for decades as Blackhead Sign Post. Throughout the Atlantic world, such beheadings were mementos of power that settlers used in the aftermath of victory and then displayed as macabre icons. The New England settlers displayed the skull of Metacomet (or King Philip) for years on a pole in Plymouth, Massachusetts; white South Carolinians similarly showed off the skulls of enslaved rebels after the Stono rebellion; white Louisianans lined the route to New Orleans with skulls after the 1811 German Coast rebellion. The land of the United States had been covered in these skulls, signaling the power of white men over the land and over the other people there.[34]

Pinning down the number of people killed in these first days is impossible, and historians' estimates have varied from 24 to hundreds. Certainly, there was a great deal of talk about broader massacres among the white people in the region, and undoubtedly many whites committed horrid atrocities. The most careful recent counts of extralegal killings suggest between two and three dozen murders in the fields and crossroads, based on readings of census and estate accounts. To some degree the larger, earlier estimates of 120 or 200 might have been based on exaggeration, perhaps a deliberate exaggeration by enslavers seeking to inspire fear that in turn formed the basis of critique by antislavery writers and then historians. In part, those exaggerations may come from expanding the geographic and temporal radius and attributing any mention of any atrocity in the region to Nat's rebellion, thus forgetting the everyday nature of violence in a system of slavery.[35]

Across the Americas, more rebels than slaveholders generally died in slave rebellions, and the Southampton rebellion was probably no different. The trials and the record in the *Confessions* emphasized the fifty-five dead whites. We do not know precisely how many Black people died in the Southampton revolt, but it seems likely the number approached or exceeded that, once we add in the people executed and the people killed farther from Southampton. This mirrors the numbers in rebellions in Jamaica and Demerara and Cuba. Rebellions were held up as extraordinary acts of violence by Black people against white, but they summoned up extraordinary, generally more brutal, violence by white people in retaliation.

Within hours, the former congressman James Trezvant and other local elites reacted against the violence of the white militias rampaging through the county and asked state and federal governments to intervene. On Monday morning, Trezvant wrote to Petersburg with news of the rebellion and a request for help from Richmond; that letter arrived in the state capital early Tuesday morning. About noon Tuesday, town leaders—likely including Trezvant—asked the young lawyer Thomas Gray, back from riding with the posse, to carry news to the federal forces sixty miles away in Norfolk. Gray arrived at the

USS *Natchez* very early Wednesday morning. Soon, larger, more organized forces were on their way, numbering about three thousand people, including four militia companies from Petersburg, two from Richmond, one from Norfolk, and one from Portsmouth, plus federal sailors from both Norfolk and Fortress Monroe, and additional militia artillery, joining the militia from neighboring counties already in the region. The Richmond editor John Hampden Pleasants rode eighty-one miles with the Richmond companies, arriving at Jerusalem exhausted but ready. But already there were too many people in Jerusalem with too little to do. "Jerusalem was never so crowded from its foundation," Pleasants wrote, between the hundreds of troops and the hundreds of women and children who crowded the tiny town.[36]

These state elites preferred other ways of demonstrating power, ways that would not threaten so much slave property or undermine their self-image as defenders of law and enlightenment. The militia brigadier generals Richard Eppes, appointed by the governor to direct the militia in Jerusalem, and William Henry Brodnax, who oversaw forces just west of Cross Keys, helped limit the terror and steer the response toward legal trials. To be sure, not all these late-arriving forces were so restrained. One group of marines allegedly marched through the north end of the county with the "head of a rebel" on a sword, and a Richmond militia company purportedly killed an enslaved man as they reached the Southampton County line as a brute display of power. In general, however, the farther-flung forces soon became instruments of restraint. For Eppes and Brodnax the indiscriminate killing of enslaved people was a violation both of the legal order and of the rights of enslavers to their property.[37]

These outside generals, as well as local elites like the former congressman Trezvant, tried to persuade the militias to bring captured rebels to jail instead of murdering them, a shift from extralegal terror to legal hegemony. An enslaved rebel who called himself Marmaduke was already in jail Thursday. Marmaduke, who might have also been known as Tom and might have been enslaved by the Reese family, had allegedly shot Rebecca Vaughan's niece. Nevertheless, he was brought in alive, a sign that the white response was shifting. Pleasants, with awe and perhaps fear, wrote of the "magnanimity with which he bears his sufferings." Marmaduke died Friday of his wounds. Sometime Wednesday, Hark was captured near the Blunt plantation, where he had been shot during the raid. He, too, was held for trial. Between Thursday and the following Tuesday, six more enslaved people were brought alive to the jail, including the other Nat. Even before the county was quieted, the turn toward judicial processes was under way. To keep angry whites from killing the prisoners before the court had a chance to, the magistrates asked for an armed guard.[38]

Eppes and Brodnax worked methodically to stop the campaign of terror in the countryside. Their reasons are interesting to contemplate. They seemed genuinely taken aback by the vigilante violence and wanted to reestablish order as men of the law. But they also heard planters' complaints that they were losing thousands of dollars' worth of property as enslaved people were killed. Eppes echoed this concern that "killing must be attended with a total loss to their neighbors, and friends of the value of the property." Then there was the ultimate question of who was in control: until order was restored among white people, the time of the rebellion would still be under way, and thus they would be living in a world of Nat's making. By Eppes and Brodnax's lights, Nat began the rebellion, but they would claim the right to declare it over.[39]

On Wednesday, Eppes proclaimed the rebellion suppressed and began sending troops back home. On August 28, the Sunday after the rebellion began, Eppes ordered local whites to cease all "acts of barbarity and cruelty" and "abstain, in future, from any acts of violence to any personal property whatever, for any cause whatever, unless the person by whom the violence is done" was "in arms or otherwise refusing submission." Those whites who continued to commit violence "shall be punished, if necessary, by the rigors of the articles of war," a threat with genuine teeth. "No excuse will be allowed." Eppes also encouraged people in Jerusalem to return to their farms. Pleasants cheered this restraint of "great barbarity" that had revealed the "sanguinary temper of the population . . . The presence of troops from Norfolk and Richmond alone prevented retaliation from being carried much farther."[40]

But not all local white people accepted Eppes's claim that peace was restored. The day after Eppes's order, on Monday, August 29, some local whites wrote to President Andrew Jackson asking that federal troops be sent back to Southampton. Others in Norfolk pleaded with Virginia's governor, John Floyd, for arms. Eppes dismissed these requests as needless, and Governor Floyd wrote that he was "disgusted with the cowardly fears" of local white people.[41]

WITHIN DAYS OF the defeat of the rebellion, state and county leaders faced the question of the rebellion's breadth, a question deeply entwined with the stories people told about what the rebellion was and what it meant. Now that the rebellion had been suppressed, they asked how widely it had spread. To answer this, they tried to fix its geographic limits. Elites sought to define the rebellion as particular, not general, neither a warning to nor an indictment of the entire South.

This work of confining the rebellion took place in a contest of stories, a contest between those who thought the rebellion was an isolated, onetime event and those who believed it was part of a general slave uprising. For a week after the insurrection, rumors coursed along the roads and rivers of southern Virginia, rumors claiming that three hundred or four hundred rebels had crossed west from Southampton County into Greensville County, which sat between Southampton and Brunswick. On the second day of the revolt, families in Brunswick County, more than forty miles west of Jerusalem, raced to their county seat of Lawrenceville for safety. Others suggested that a giant band of enslaved people was on the march from Wilmington to Raleigh. Three days later, as the rebellion ebbed and militias began to return home, commanders in two adjoining counties, Surry and Nansemond, asked for arms from the state to put down what they feared was a coming insurrection. In North Carolina, there were rumors of potential risings in Duplin and New Hanover Counties, sparked by a large religious revival among Black Methodists.[42] One white diarist wrote, "There was a peculiar feature displayed in the late insurrection. Most of the culprits were members of the methodist church, some of them in high repute for honesty. On some plantations, in fact it is almost a general rule, they set down a negro who joins the church for a rogue and one who becomes a preacher for an arch villain." Wilmington's Front Street Methodist Episcopal Church in the fall of 1831 issued a public statement denying Methodism's connection with the alleged rebellions.[43]

What fed these rumors was Nat's disappearance, and elites were eager to catch him. In the early days, companies searched nearby counties for him, but soon stories spread of his flight to other regions, and Cross Keys people seem to have returned, startlingly quickly, to their daily lives. Still, the folkloric Nat became a repository for the fears of white people. Every act of defiance in any crevice where slavery lived might suggest that the Nat rebellion was at work, at least to those whites who wished to manipulate those fears. This panic would inspire a wave of legislation across the South, aimed at disarming, separating, and in some cases expelling free Black people from society and at constructing more effective militia and slave patrol systems. As long as Nat remained at large, the idea of him loomed everywhere.

These stories threatened the stability of slavery, and planters knew it. These fears could lead some whites to massacre enslaved people who belonged to other whites, could spark complaints about the growth of slavery, could threaten the sense of a shared racial project that existed—tenuously—alongside the divisions of class that shaped white southern life. Enslavers knew they depended upon the fearful vigilance of poorer white people, but they also needed to keep that fear within boundaries or else risk their own property, the viability of their legal system, and the region's reputation among northern and English trading partners.

Therefore, several local and state elites began telling stories of the rebellion's narrow scope, stories that emphasized the peculiar figure of Nat and the anomaly of the Cabin Pond rebellion. Fixing the geographic limits of the rebellion was one of many tasks of suppressing it, part and parcel of capturing rebels, slaughtering Black people, putting the accused on trial, expelling collaborators, and hanging perpetrators. To quash those fears, authorities delineated the lines of the rebellion and reassured white people outside the rebellion's zone of terror that it did not affect them, tried to convince them the legal system would suffice. The same day that militia officers in Surry and Nansemond appealed for armaments, Eppes wrote in a newspaper that "no great concert among the slaves" had prevailed. Eppes exonerated "all slaves in the counties around Southampton" of any prior knowledge about the revolt. During the week following the rebellion, editors and correspondents discredited reports that exaggerated the rebellion's size and scale. These newspaper accounts did not minimize the insurrection; they still estimated its participants in the hundreds. But they did isolate it.[44]

An important propagandist for the narrow definitions of the rebellion was Pleasants, the editor of the Richmond *Constitutional Whig*. Pleasants had accompanied the Richmond militia to Jerusalem, then published several pieces on the rebellion. He argued that the best way to dispel fears about the revolt was to define its size and geography. On August 25, during the first trials, Pleasants wrote that "for the first time" "we learnt the extent of the insurrection, and the mischief perpetrated. Rumor had infinitely exaggerated the first, swelling the numbers of the negroes to a thousand or 1200 men, and representing its ramifications as embracing several of the adjacent counties, particularly Isle of Wight and Greenville." But Pleasants located the origins of the rebellion more narrowly, and more precisely, in the region southwest of Jerusalem "in the neighborhood of the Cross Keys." The following week, Pleasants disposed of readers' questions about the immediate causes of the rebellion as relatively unimportant. "A more important inquiry remains—whether the conspiracy was circumscribed to the neighborhood in which it broke out, or had its ramifications through other counties." White people debated the extent and nature of enslaved people's neighborhoods as a way of measuring their own safety and plotting their response.[45]

THE PARTICIPANTS' TRIALS demonstrated the legal system's role in spreading the story of the rebellion's narrow geography. Those trials told of particular individuals motivated by a peculiar, charismatic man to commit specific acts in a small neighborhood, acts that would lead to legally sanctioned punishment, not vigilantism. These trials commenced quite quickly. The last of Nat's close compatriots, Sam, was captured on August 30 and brought into town by Nathaniel Francis, his enslaver. Like the wounded Hark, he was held for trial.[46]

The trials themselves raise interesting questions. If slave owners could slaughter the offenders, why did they bother to bring them to court? One reason lay in the very rumors that circulated of a widespread, general rebellion by the enslaved people. The trials were the next step in the battle to establish the story of the rebellion. In a world where rumors moved quickly, the trials were an effort to constrain that talk. Of course there were other motivations as well. The trials were dominated by a small number of local lawyers, men with ties to the state government and the state bar and with a great deal invested in their vision of the sufficiency of the law to resolve problems and sustain order. They knew their standing in the state and wider world depended upon what they saw as a civilized response, and they probably absorbed their commitment to law not as self-interested performance but as belief. While we may today see enslavers as lawless, it is undeniable that many planters were also extraordinarily devoted to the triumph of forms of law.[47]

Knowledge about the rebellion increased daily in late August and early September as county leaders conducted an inquiry. This county inquiry was led by the former congressman Trezvant, the postmaster (who was Trezvant's brother), the county clerk, the sheriff, and the attorneys William Parker, James French, and Thomas Gray, working with Brigadier General Eppes and the prosecutor Meriwether Brodnax, the brother of Brigadier General Brodnax. A few days later, trials began, helping broadcast information about what had been a chaotic and fragmentary story. By August 31, nineteen of the main participants were either in jail or in places where the authorities could easily bring them in. Eleven others were dead. Of the sixteen people David Allmendinger defined as minor participants, including the enslaved woman Lucy, all were either in jail or in places where they could be summoned except for Billy Artis, the free Black man who would soon be found dead. By mid-September, Thomas Gray had written a list of forty participants, an impressive count but hardly a general uprising. Somewhat more than a dozen other people openly aided or sympathized with the company. The numbers told a story: in a county with more than 7,700 enslaved people, the rebellion was not general.[48]

Both before and after the trials, most of the charged survivors were held in the small jail just past the bridge into Jerusalem on the public grounds near the courthouse, the clerk's office, and the rooms utilized as offices by attorneys. There were four cells inside, divided by iron bars fixed to the ceiling. Although the rooms were supposed to have stoves for warmth, a later inspection stated that only one stove worked. In the jail, the company was gathered again as they awaited their fates.[49]

Two of the captured men shaped the stories that circulated: the reluctant Jack and the boy Moses, enslaved at the Travis plantation. Jack, desperate to prove that he was an unwilling participant, described the gathering at Cabin Pond, Nat's speech, and his brother-in-law Hark's role in forcing him to join the rebellion. But Jack does not seem to have described the killings, knowing those details would personally implicate him. Moses, also eager to save himself, described the attacks from his vantage point near the back, holding the horses. In fact, Moses had seen more battles than anyone else, including Nat. A guard said that Moses spoke "free and voluntarily," eager to show his own disagreement with the rebellion.[50]

Their testimony sustained a growing effort among county elites to construct a story of the rebellion, a story that emphasized Nat's eccentricity. This began immediately. On the Wednesday after the rebellion, even as militia roamed the county, the town postmaster had begun to construct a chronology of the attacks. Over the next days, the white survivors Mary Barrow and Levi Waller added details, as did some enslaved people who did not participate. As the number of inmates rose past forty, more confessions followed with more details of the rebellion. The former congressman James Trezvant and the prominent attorney William Parker both constructed roughly accurate calculations of the total number of participants and of the dead. With more information, the postmaster added more details, sending on September 5 a list of fifty-five white victims and the order in which they were killed. Thomas Gray, one of the defense attorneys for the cases, came to the same number, though Gray did not initially share the postmaster's chronology.[51]

To obtain information from more reluctant prisoners, white jailers and interrogators turned to their usual tool of torture. Ten years earlier in Southampton, officials suspended an enslaved person by the thumbs before having him drawn and quartered. They might well have used similar methods this time, though there is no record of it. They did acknowledge using the "lash" to make people speak. Torture was a common device in trials of conspiracy, and historians have wrestled with the wisdom and ethics of our use of statements taken under duress. Scholars have debated the testimony taken under torture in the Denmark Vesey uprising in Charleston nine years earlier, with some suggesting that those statements give an utterly fallacious account of what happened. So, too, have historians noted the difficulty of assessing statements taken under torture after a later uprising scare in Natchez, Mississippi, where some Black people might have invented details to make the torturers stop.[52]

Although these are pressing issues for scholars, not all of them apply to the Nat rebellion. Unlike the Vesey or Natchez alleged uprisings, the Southampton attacks were not a scare; they were a fact, and authorities had to check confessions against the bodies and evidence left along the route. Some key leaders like Hark and Sam apparently did not give any useful information even if they were tortured. Finally, Nat's statement, once it came, was surely given under duress but not necessarily under direct torture, given that he gave similar accounts multiple times over his final days, even before he reached the jail in Southampton and often with many people watching. Undoubtedly, some rebels covered up details of who killed whom or cast blame on the safely dead to divert attention from themselves, but in general the evidence in the field and in the testimony lines up.

What is more striking are the things that people did not say, especially about the role of enslaved women in supporting the rebellion. If there was deception, it was likely for the protection of women who had not yet been accused. Nevertheless, white people understood the role of women in the rebellion. One of those "under the lash" was the woman described as Nat's wife, who was whipped until she talked and turned over documents. If the woman was indeed Cherry, it is possible she was brought in on August 30, a week after the rebellion, perhaps by her enslaver Nathaniel Francis, who carried Sam to town on that day. Under torture she turned over a "map" "descriptive of the county of Southampton" that was said to have been drawn by Nat with pokeberry juice. Thomas Gray wrote, the papers "are filled with hieroglyphical characters, conveying no definite meaning," some written in blood. There was a "crucifix and the sun" with figures on it, and also some men's names, "short of twenty," perhaps his recruiting plan or a target list. Otherwise we know almost nothing about his wife's actions in those weeks. There are gaps, as well, in information about other enslaved women along the route, except for those like Ester and Charlotte who became visible to the whites as symbols of treachery or of loyalty.[53]

On August 31, a week after the state militia commander declared the insurrection suppressed, the trials began. The trials of enslaved people followed a particular format called a court of oyer and terminer, developed in England for people accused of treason or rebellion. Courts of oyer and terminer did not follow common law, require indictments, or include a jury. Instead, a panel of judges heard the case. This kind of court had been used in Salem Village, Massachusetts, for people accused of witchcraft. Virginia had placed capital crimes committed by enslaved people under oyer and terminer, and enslavers began to use this system to protect their investments (and thus, from self-interest, the lives of their enslaved people) as courts of oyer and terminer could bypass the middling and resentful white who often formed the pools for juries. The judges for oyer and terminer courts were appointed by county magistrates, often large slaveholders who sought to reserve political power for the propertied elite. In Jerusalem, the three most active judges—the former congressman James Trezvant among them—sat on at least twenty rebellion trials each and lived on plantations with an average of thirty-nine enslaved people. In turn the clerk who recorded the trials claimed property rights over forty-seven people, and his brother, the county sheriff, over thirty-three. Oyer and terminer courts also granted enslaved people rights available only to white people in regular trials, including the right not to testify against themselves, the right to plead not guilty, and the right to hear formal charges against them. Peculiarly perhaps from our vantage, but logically from the planters', oyer and terminer courts preserved some rights for these enslaved people as a way of precluding middling whites from interfering with the property claims of wealthy white people, and in the process incurring claims for reimbursement for executed enslaved people, expenses in turn likely to be paid by the county's largest taxpayers.[54]

The treatment of free Black men under investigation suggests some specific differences from the treatment of enslaved people. Five free Black people were brought to formal justice for their roles in the Southampton revolt, and the court followed different procedures for them. Instead of a court of oyer and terminer, they were brought in front of the county court. This may seem meaningless, since the same men sat on the county court as on the courts of oyer and terminer, but the process was quite different. The county court decided only whether there was sufficient evidence to try them in front of the superior court. One of the five, Arnold Artis, was then released. Four others were held until the spring of 1832, when passions had cooled. At that point, three were acquitted, including Thomas Haithcock, who had recruited people to join the rebellion, and Exum Artis, who had threatened to shoot an enslaved man for trying to warn whites. The only person convicted by the superior court was Berry Newsom, a free Black man who stayed home during the rebellion but was heard to say that "if Capt. Nat came on," he would become a "soldier." Newsom was the only free Black man convicted, and he was hanged that spring.[55]

The courts of oyer and terminer that tried enslaved people moved quickly but not haphazardly, returning a range of verdicts over seven weeks in the late summer and early fall of 1831. Not all the fifty cases brought to court went forward; seven were dismissed without a trial. The trials themselves were conducted on normal oyer and terminer processes with Meriwether Brodnax serving as prosecutor and reading charges. In each case, at least five magistrates were present, often more. They heard sworn evidence from a total of fifty-one witnesses, the clerk recorded the proceedings for the governor, and the court appointed lawyers for the accused. A total of twenty Southampton men served as judges, fourteen of whom owned more than twenty people in 1830. Four of them had served in the state legislature, two as sheriff, one—James Trezvant—as congressman. The court appointed less wealthy but still-established lawyers for the enslaved people: the War of 1812 hero William C. Parker and James French handled most of the cases. Others went to the less established but still prominent Thomas Gray, who would interview Nat in November. These lawyers' arguments, and the court's desire to demonstrate its commitment to legality, led to a wide range of outcomes: The Southampton court convicted thirty of the forty-three who were eventually tried, releasing thirteen. The court recommended eleven of the convicts for commutation and sale out of state, and a twelfth was commuted as well. That left eighteen enslaved people sentenced to be hanged.[56]

Commutation requests put the record into the hands of the governor and his council, who had to offer a recommendation on the case. Perhaps the most challenging commutation discussion turned on Jack, Hark's brother-in-law. Magistrates agreed on his guilt, but divided over whether to recommend commutation of his death sentence and condemn him instead to sale out of the state. Gubernatorial commutation was deeply entwined with slave rebellion in Virginia; it had arisen after the twenty-five death sentences in the 1800 Gabriel conspiracy created a fiscal crisis when the state had to compensate enslavers for executed people. The next year, the legislature empowered the governor to commute and deport enslaved people for sale beyond the commonwealth. When the divided verdict in Jack's case rose to the governor's council, the council recommended execution, and Governor Floyd accepted their judgment. After that, the council and governor essentially accepted commutation for all those who were forced to join the company, became separated from it, committed no crime, and showed no sympathy for the rebellion. In the case of three young boys who joined at the Nathaniel Francis farm, the local court actually recommended commutation even before the defense lawyers asked for it.[57]

The sentences told a story about Southampton, a story that white elites hoped would not only be defined by rebellion and terror. Thomas Gray and other people in the area publicized those findings of innocence or requests for commutation to the world—in the case of Gray, in the final pages of the *Confessions*—to prove the rationality and justness of the Southampton court. The mix of verdicts told the world that Southampton remained a place governed by law, its elite respectable members of an enlightened age. White Virginians thus followed a pattern in Demerara, Jamaica, Cuba, and elsewhere, as the frenzy of counterattacks was quieted by trials held under surprisingly exacting rules of evidence and advocacy.

The trials also told a story about the geography of the rebellion, showing where the danger lay, and thus where it did not. The lawyers, especially Thomas Gray, had struggled to piece together the precise narrative of the events, and some believed there had been several scattered rebellions—something closer to a general rising. But the testimony of the impressed enslaved boy Moses helped convince Gray and others that in fact a single group had divided in two. Moses's early impressment and his vantage from the back of the group where he held the horses gave him unprecedented awareness of the scope of the rebellion and credibility in defining it. In the end, Moses was one of the rare enslaved people who traveled with the band for a long period of time and still received a reduced sentence of deportation and forced sale, not death.[58]

One enslaved person challenged the interpretation of a narrow rebellion. A woman named Beck, also called Becky, offered the most concrete evidence of a broad uprising in her trial testimony. Beck testified that a week before the rebellion she overheard two enslaved men say they would join rebels who came to their vicinity. Another man ventured that his master had "crossed him and he would be crossed" before the year was out. According to the trial record, Beck said she had heard three other men say much the same "some time previously in the neighborhood." The defendants, Beck noted, lived about a mile from her owner's plantation, well north of Nat's neighborhood. She also discussed earlier talk of a possible uprising at Raccoon Swamp Antioch Baptist Church, where eight or ten enslaved people allegedly plotted back in May. Because Beck lived across the county line in Sussex, her testimony resulted in some trials being held there and played a key role in the conviction of nine enslaved people by the county's court of oyer and terminer.[59]

There is good reason to take Beck's suggestions seriously. Scholars like Peter H. Wood and Scot French have suggested it is possible that Nat's rebellion was tied to a broader conspiracy, as has some (but not all) local folklore. But there are also reasons to doubt this. Many local elites did not believe Beck. The Southampton court disregarded Beck's testimony until the governor upheld some Sussex cases, leading to an apparent reevaluation of her trustworthiness in a few cases. Even in Sussex, confidence in Beck's testimony waned over time. When one of the condemned men escaped, local authorities did not actively pursue him and later offered to recommend his commutation to the governor, with eighteen local whites publicly questioning Beck's credibility.[60]

Later, Nat denied that he had been part of an "extensive or concerted plan" and answered queries with a damning question: "Can you not think the same ideas, and strange appearances about this time in the heaven's might prompt others as well as myself to this undertaking?" Rebellions were local and sporadic, but discontent with slavery was universal.[61]

THE STORY OF the rebellions ended, like most stories, in death. Sixteen enslaved people were executed over August, September, and October 1831. Daniel from the Porter plantation was convicted on August 31 and hanged six days later. Then nine other men were sentenced on September 2 and 3: the adult Moses from the Barrow plantation, Curtis and Stephen from the Ridley plantation, Davy from the Waller plantation, Nelson from the Williams plantation, Davy and the other Nat from Elizabeth Turner's plantation, Sam from the Francis plantation, and Hark. After that, on September 5, Dred from the Francis plantation and Nathan from the Blunt plantation were condemned to death, along with the reluctant Jack from the Reese plantation, who had been brought in by Hark and whose initial verdict was divided. Jack and five others were hanged September 12, followed by Hark and Sam three days later. Then, on September 19, two more were sentenced: Joe from the Turner plantation and Lucy from the Barrow plantation, the only woman to be executed, presumably for her efforts to prevent Mary Barrow from escaping. On October 17, Sam from the Edwards plantation was convicted, the last before Nat. (Ben of the Blunt plantation, the last enslaved man to be hanged, would not be killed until December, the free Black man Berry Newsom not until 1832.)[62]

Probably the executions occurred at midday in the commons near the courthouse and the jail. It is unclear how many people attended, whether white people seeking the solace of vengeance or enslaved people a final look at a loved one. As with much of the history of Southampton County, the details are elusive. We do not know the feelings of the condemned people as they were sentenced to die or as they were hanged. But we can say what the executions meant to white elites: the trials sought to conclude the rebellion. To signal the end of the rebellion, dead bodies must be displayed for the public as a symbol of the past reality and present nullity of the rebellion, of the endurance of white power, of the futility of revolt. No doubt white Virginians worked hard to create such a display in their public hangings, and hoped the executions of Sam and Hark and the others would toll the end of the rebellion and of rebelliousness. Bodies were potent symbols, especially the bodies of people like Sam and Hark.

But still the bodies hanging from the scaffold could not end the story. The hanging of Sam and Hark could not represent the actual conclusion of the rebellion. Only one body could demonstrate conclusively that the rebellion was over, and only one person could signal the story's end.

That body belonged to Nat, and Nat was not on the scaffold. In fact, no one could be sure where Nat was. In the absence of an ending, stories spread widely and wildly that he had been seen across Southside Virginia, across the South, even in free territory. In one county or another, people claimed to have captured a man they believed to be Nat. But these were all just rumors.

Nat's actual body hid near a fence, but his legend walked the earth. To end the story, to kill the legend, Southside planters needed to find the body, and so even as they proclaimed the success of their trials, they searched and they hunted.

8

The Book of Nat

For ten weeks, no one knew where Nat was. Many people thought they knew, and they didn't hesitate to share their theories as though they were facts. As time passed, Nat became an almost-magical figure, untethered to the soil, able to fly freely across the country. A month after the rebellion, a Richmond newspaper published a report that Nat had been spotted in Botetourt County, 180 miles west of South-ampton. Perhaps, they speculated, Nat was heading north. Others heard rumors of Nat taking part in other alleged rebellions as white southerners for a time stitched together every act of resistance into a concerted uprising and sought a single scapegoat. If it were so, the problem might lie not in the system of slavery but in the actions of one individual enslaved person.[1]

More plausibly, others suspected Nat was hiding in the Great Dismal Swamp to the east, the roughly million-acre wildlands that spanned southeastern Virginia and eastern North Carolina. There, a boggy terrain with dense stands of reeds, shrubs, and woods offered an opportune, if often unlovely, hiding ground. People of color had been fleeing into the swamp for a century or perhaps more. It re-mained a mysterious area to many white Virginians, a place beyond their control. And so, naturally, they imagined Nat hiding there, near at hand, but impossible to capture. How else could they explain the mystery: Nat, the most sought-after man in the country, had been nei-ther apprehended nor seen.

But for ten weeks, Nat apparently did not travel very far at all. He remained on the Francis place, less than two miles from the Travis property where the revolt began, right in the Cross Keys neighbor-hood where he grew up, quite close to Cabin Pond where he met his

conspirators. Both gossipers and later historians have enjoyed spec-
ulating about longer flights, and we can never know for certain of
his movements. But his words, at least as allegedly recorded by Gray,
were clear: he had not run to the North nor to the swamp nor even to
nearby North Carolina. As white people worriedly scoured news of
resistance across the Atlantic states, some of them tried to blame Nat,
but these claims all proved groundless. Rebelliousness, to the degree
that there actually was an unusual amount of resistance in the ensu-
ing months, might have the same general cause as his—the horrors of
slavery, the desire for freedom, God's inspiration—but it did not have
the same instigator.

We might assume that Nat stayed in hopes of receiving the support of the neighborhood, but he did not suggest he expected or received much aid from the people who had known him the longest. By
his statements, as recorded by Gray, he did not seek their help even
though he was close enough to hear them, almost to touch them. He
did all he could to remain out of their sight. For the first six weeks,
Nat ventured out from his hiding place only for food and water. After
that long stretch of complete solitude, he crept through the woods to
"eaves drop the houses in the neighborhood" during his final month.
Nat insisted no one had laid eyes on him until the meat in his "cave"
was sniffed out by "a dog in the neighborhood."[2]

It is possible that Nat was untruthful, that he had talked with and
received help from people in his old neighborhood. It would be surprising if it were not so, and it would not be at all surprising if Nat
kept this information from his interlocutor to protect his neighbors—
perhaps especially his wife—from the persecution that rained down
upon his former allies, now murdered, executed, and exiled. So there
are reasons to suspect that he must have received help, reasons rooted
both in Nat's own narrative and in historians' assumptions that enslaved people formed unitary, cohesive communities where everyone
supported one another.

Yet it is worth checking that assumption against the facts about
enslaved communities. Historians have indeed recovered extraordi-

narily strong bonds among some enslaved people, the deep networks of kin groups and clans and fictive kin that they fashioned, and the crucial role of women in constructing those ties. Yet scholars have also explored competition and suspicion within enslaved worlds as clans and neighbors fought for control of scant resources and viewed rivals or outsiders with caution, even suspicion. Enslaved people made the same calculations as other people when confronting rule breakers; even when they agreed with the motivation, they might decide it was safer to pretend not to agree or safer still to turn in the offender. So it was not surprising that enslaved people testified about the activities of other enslaved people, sometimes under physical torture, sometimes under the general torture of being an enslaved person. Nor was it surprising that enslaved people did not automatically aid one another. Enslaved people's bonds of solidarity were real but not easily forged and not always intact in moments of great strain.[3]

Nat well knew the limits of that solidarity. He understood that other rebellions were defeated because some Black participants told whites what was coming. Within his own neighborhood, he had first acquired, then lost, a reputation as a prophet. As white Virginians offered rewards for help and threats for obstruction, Nat likely feared that his neighbors would turn him in. His own neighborhood had turned against him once and might turn against him now. And he might also have feared that seeking help from those neighbors would expose them to a death he had chosen for himself but would not choose for them. Perhaps this was an act of skepticism, perhaps of love and self-denial.

Around Thursday, October 13, a dog discovered Nat. It had been more than seven weeks since he fled into the woods. A couple of nights later, the dog returned, accompanied by two people whom Nat identified only as "negroes." Nat begged them not to expose him, but "they fled from me." Now Nat faced another crisis: Should he have faith in those men? He answered it in his actions: "knowing that they would betray me," he left his cave and moved to another hovel. It seems likely that Nat felt abandoned by his neighborhood, even if he did not put too fine a point on it in the *Confessions*. In calling these men betrayers, Nat might have simply been turning to the most available word, or perhaps he was referring to the repeated references in the Christian Testament to Jesus's knowledge that Judas would betray him.[4]

Nat had reason for concern. On Saturday, October 15, an enslaved man named Red came to Jerusalem to say he had seen Nat in the woods. We do not know if Red acted out of fear or anger or greed. We know only that the authorities were closing in around Nat, and it appears that other enslaved people were part of the threat he faced.[5]

WHAT OCCUPIED NAT'S mind in those ten weeks in hiding? Perhaps Nat beseeched the Spirit for guidance. Maybe he begged to see the Lord he loved. Perhaps he pleaded for the assurance given to Elijah. Once again, Nat did not share this side of his conversation with the Spirit. We can only read into the types he guided himself by if we wish to guess what he felt in these moments of trial.[6]

We might suppose that Nat felt terribly alone, abandoned by the God he hoped to obey and even perhaps to meet. Yet the history of prophets was replete with messengers from God who suffered in isolation. This suffering did not prove that a prophet had failed. Suffering might instead demonstrate that a prophet had served the Lord faithfully, in service of something the people were not able to understand. The suffering might also serve as a testing ground for the prophet. Perhaps God was measuring Nat's faith in the face of adversity. Perhaps Nat could not enter Jerusalem until he had shown his faith even in the worst defeats.

What example shone brighter than the Savior's? Faithful people did not lightly compare themselves to Jesus, but they saw in him a model that illuminated their way. If they could not be Jesus, they could aspire to be like Jesus. Nat would embrace that comparison, to a point, after his capture.

As Nat contemplated his suffering in his cave, he likely considered the temptation of Jesus. For Matthew, this temptation followed a crowning moment in Jesus's life, his baptism by John and anointing by a voice from heaven. Then the "Spirit" led Jesus "into the wilderness to be tempted of the devil." Jesus fasted forty days and forty nights, and afterward he was "hungered." The "tempter" appeared to Jesus and said, "If thou be the Son of God, command that these stones shall be made bread." Jesus refused, answering from Deuteronomy 8 that "man shall not live by bread alone, but by every word that proceedeth out of the mouth of God."[7]

We do not know precisely what Nat ate in his roughly seventy days in the woods. But it is likely that he went hungry, even if he did receive occasional assistance from neighbors. We cannot say for certain that Nat saw his fasting in the woods as a purification ritual, akin to Jesus's in the wilderness, but we do know that the comparison to Jesus was on Nat's mind.

For prophets, the sacrifice of hunger might be rewarded with further tests. Jesus's fasting did not deliver Christ to the Lord's embrace. Instead, the "devil" took Jesus to the "holy city," Jerusalem, and placed Jesus on a "pinnacle of the temple," taunting Jesus to leap, daring God to send angels to save him. Jesus then quoted Deuteronomy 6:16: "Thou shalt not tempt the Lord thy God."[8] Still Jesus was not rewarded. The devil led Jesus to an "exceeding high mountain, and sheweth him all the kingdoms of the world, and the glory of them" and promised all these kingdoms to Jesus "if thou wilt fall down and worship me." Instead, Jesus rebuked the devil: "Get thee hence, Satan!" Jesus quoted Deuteronomy 6:13: "Thou shalt worship the Lord thy God, and him only shalt thou serve."[9]

Then and only then did the "devil" leave Jesus. "And, behold, angels came and ministered unto him." Still, it was some time before Jesus made his entrance into Jerusalem. Nat knew the Bible well enough to realize that salvation did not come cheaply. Nor would the apocalypse. If the Spirit intended to use him, the Spirit would test him.[10]

Before his rebellion, Nat had hoped that he was at the end of his purification, that he was prepared at last to do the will of the Spirit and meet God. But perhaps only now did he enter fully into the period of temptation, of the testing required to enter Jerusalem. If such had been required of Jesus, how could it not be required of Nat?

If Nat saw himself primarily as an Atlantic revolutionary or a vengeance seeker, we might expect the scales to have fallen from his eyes just then. He might well drink a cup of bitterness that he had failed. But we have no reason to think that Nat understood his motivation in those conventional ways, much less that he lost his faith. We have many reasons to believe that he saw his suffering as proof that God continued to hold him, and to test him.

If Nat in his cave looked to the history of prophets for solace, Elijah might have been an especially meaningful type. Elijah was a powerful figure to awakened Christians because he had appeared to Jesus at the moment of transfiguration, thus crossing from Hebrew Bible to Christian Testament.[11] In the book of Kings in the Hebrew Bible, Elijah killed all the prophets of Baal, then fled to a cave on Horeb, the "mouth of God." There, the Lord gave Elijah gifts: a vision, a voice, even a listening ear. Nat might have yearned for an opportunity Elijah had, a chance to vent.[12] After Elijah complained, the Lord delivered a promise with a specificity that the Spirit had thus far denied to Nat. The promise came with a command: "Go, return." Elijah had to go back, as Nat would have to. But then Elijah would begin a new era by anointing new kings, choosing a new prophet, slaughtering the unfaithful, and ascending into "heaven by a whirlwind."[13] Like Elijah, Nat had been forsaken and hunted by people who professed to follow the Lord but instead violated the commandments and oppressed the Lord's people. Could Nat hope for Elijah's triumph for himself?

Even King David hid in a cave at Adullam to save himself from Saul. From that spot David attracted "everyone that was in distress" or "in debt" or "discontented," then launched his counterattack; waiting had been the prelude for God's victorious deliverance.[14] Psalm 57, allegedly penned by David in the cave at Adullam, begged God to "be merciful unto me . . . until these calamities be overpast," and then rejoiced that the enemies who "have digged a pit before me" had "fallen themselves."[15] In his prayer from the cave in Psalm 142, David "poured out my complaint" and "my trouble" to the Lord. "There was no man that would know me: refuge failed me; no man cared for my soul . . . Deliver me from my persecutors, for they are stronger than I. Bring my soul out of prison, that I may praise thy name."[16] In the eleventh book of Hebrews, which opens with the definition of faith as "the substance of things hoped for, the evidence of things not seen," the prophets suffered "in dens and caves of the earth." Some of the prophets saw the fulfillment of their hopes; others "died in faith, not having received the promises, but having seen them afar off, and were persuaded of them, and embraced them, and confessed that they were strangers and pilgrims on the earth."[17]

As always, Nat might have seen many paths ahead in the biblical types he pondered. They, too, had been defeated. They, too, hid in caves. Some emerged as kings, like David. Others as mighty and powerful prophets like Elijah, with protégés who carried forward their work. Some faced only earthly defeat but still were victorious in heaven. Jesus became the Savior of the world. Nat could not know if his time in the cave foretold his return as a victorious warrior-king, his recognition as a prophet, his anointing of a successor, or his own further mortification and suffering. But he knew that defeat, even terrible defeat, did not prove that he was wrong about the Spirit, only that his mission was not yet over. So he waited.

AFTER NAT'S DISCOVERY by the neighborhood dog on Thursday, October 13, the neighborhood search assumed a new intensity. In the weeks between the rebellion's suppression and October 13, it is not clear how often or resolutely people looked for Nat. But from mid-October through his capture, people pursued him "almost incessantly." In fear Nat scrambled to a new hiding place. He did not detail these final weeks in hiding, but we can imagine his fear and also his contemplations about what he would do upon being captured. Nat might have considered fight, flight, suicide. Still, he hid.[18]

On October 27, two weeks after the dog's discovery, Nathaniel

Francis saw Nat step out from among the fodder stacks in his fields. The two men knew each other very well. They had grown up together and attended Turner's Meeting House. They were also closely tied by the events of the rebellion: Nathaniel Francis had missed being attacked by Nat by mere chance; he and his mother had gone to check on his sister Sally Francis Moore Travis and his brother Salathiel, both killed in Nat's earliest attacks. Nathaniel Francis's house was attacked, but his wife, Lavinia, narrowly escaped, hiding in the attic while Nat's company killed two of their nephews and the white overseer. It was at Nathaniel Francis's house that the enslaved woman Charlotte tried to kill Lavinia Francis, who then was saved by the enslaved woman Ester. Red, the enslaved man who discovered Nat and reported his whereabouts to town, was now the property of Nathaniel, his former enslaver Salathiel Francis having been killed. So, too, had Nathaniel Francis claimed Will "the executioner," now himself dead. Few people were more closely intertwined with the rebellion and its aftermath than Nathaniel Francis. A neighbor wrote that Nat stood "with a smiling countenance, and without showing any hostile intention." Nathaniel Francis drew his gun, Nat his sword. Nathaniel Francis fired, and the shot passed through Nat's hat. Nat fled with a ham, leaving sweet potatoes and shoes behind in his den.[19]

Now the search for Nat became widespread, almost frantic. For three days, the white neighborhood searched for Nat. Finally, on Sunday morning, October 30, fifty men with dogs were tracking Nat through the Francis property while Nat hid "in a little hole I had dug out with my sword, for the purpose of concealment, under the top of a fallen tree." That day, a young white man named Benjamin Phipps saw a head pop out from a hole or "cave" beneath pine branches. Phipps "cocked his gun and aimed at me," Nat said.[20]

Nat neither fought nor fled. "I requested him not to shoot and I would give up." When Phipps demanded his sword, Nat "delivered it to him." In his ten weeks in hiding, Nat "had many hair breadth escapes," which he did not relate, whether from concern for Gray's time, as he said, or fear of betraying allies. But now Nat surrendered.[21]

Why didn't Nat take this opportunity to end his ordeal with a clash of arms? Nat might have worried that ambushing Phipps would be cowardly, unworthy of either a warrior or a prophet. Perhaps he had in mind those military commanders who fought valiantly but surrendered their swords at the final defeat. Perhaps Nat simply was hungry or exhausted. Perhaps he wished to live more days, as most humans do, even prophets. Maybe it was as simple as this: it was Sunday. Nat launched his rebellion just past midnight as a Sunday turned to Monday. He took seriously the commandment to keep the Sabbath holy even at that moment of crisis. Perhaps now, too, he was reluctant to attack on the Lord's day.

By local legend, Nat was captured with a Bible in his hands. This would be in keeping with the importance he attributed to the Bible, though as with many details surrounding his life, it is hard to separate fact from fiction. Whether or not he held the Bible in his hand, it is clear from the words he said that day and the days following that he kept it in his mind and in his heart.[22]

In his time in the woods, especially in those last weeks, he had the chance to reflect on what would come next. He might have thought on the examples the Bible offered him and especially of the great prophet Elijah. When Elijah was discovered, he did not flee or fight; instead, he asked his discoverer to tell the angry king where he was hiding. The way to the kingdom ran through surrender. So, too, had David resisted the opportunity to ambush Saul when Saul confronted him in a cave in the wilderness.[23]

And so Nat began what would be a trip of fifteen miles along the same roads he had taken in August toward Jerusalem, once again surrounded by bands of armed men, but this time the men were white, and their intention was to bring him to his death. Phipps fired into the air, and other white men gathered around him, identifying Nat. They took him to Peter Edwards's plantation a mile to the north. There they tied him up, and celebratory shots in the air drew a hundred "much excited" people. Nat did not know precisely what fate would befall him, though of course he would have known that the whites intended to kill him eventually.[24] At the Edwards's house, an enslaved woman who might have been the mother of Henry the paymaster might have run "out and struck Nat in the mouth, knocking the blood out and asked him, 'Why did you take my son away?'" according to a story repeated a century later by the woman's grandson, Henry's nephew. Nat replied, "Your son was as willing to go as I was."[25]

Nat was "said to be very free in his confessions," the Norfolk Herald reported, and a neighbor said Nat spoke for "more than an hour." Unlike the Confessions, these "confessions" were not recorded at great length, but the reports confirm the general outlines of the story Gray later recorded. Nat spoke at great length about religion. "He still pretends he is a prophet, and relates a number of revelations which he says he has had," the Herald wrote of these confessions at the Edwards house. A neighbor who joined the crowd wrote likewise that "Nat pretends to have been destined by a Superior power to perform the part which he did in the late bloody tragedy, and affirms that since 1826, he has constantly acted from a Divine impulse." According to some reports, Nat showed off the bullet holes in his hat.[26]

Word spread through the county, moving up the same roads that Nat's company had followed. By the evening, people in Jerusalem knew of his capture, and they "were firing guns by way of rejoicing."[27]

SURRENDER BROUGHT NAT at last to Jerusalem. The next day, Monday, October 31, Nat and a band of armed white men began to move the fifteen miles toward the county seat. At least one person heard that Nat was attacked and he was "conveyed alive" only with difficulty. The historian Patrick Breen suggests Nat was tormented by the people who came to see him and only survived because Phipps needed to convey him alive to town to collect a reward. But the historian David Allmendinger credits other reports that "not the least personal violence was offered to Nat." It may seem strange that the crowd did not tear him limb from limb, as they might have in August, but time had shifted perspectives, as victory and the passage of days would later lead a surprising number of white Virginians to become fascinated by John Brown, once held safely in jail. Now, a postmaster from Murfreesboro wrote, "no doubt public curiosity is on tiptoe to hear his confession." So they bore Nat safely into Jerusalem. Along the way he was once again "very free in his confessions."[28]

Of course Nat entered Jerusalem not as a hero but as a prisoner. Still, as he was led past the houses they had attacked two months earlier and then past Parker's gate—where they fought against white militia—and then across three bridges that carried the marshland and the Nottoway River, Nat might have reflected that he had at last entered the sacred city. Nat's unnerving calmness in his jail cell may reflect the mysteries of his personality, and also the intensity of his faith. He knew his type. Where else but in Jerusalem should a prophet suffer?

Nat was brought to the town in chains, guided through a phalanx of hostile white people. He first was taken to the courthouse, where he was examined by the former congressman James Trezvant and the magistrate James Parker, the same Parker who owned the gate where Nat's band first confronted the white posse. To them, he confessed again for almost two hours, apparently along similar lines as his statements at the Edwards plantation. Trezvant wrote that Nat gave his "opinions about his communications with god, his command over the clouds, &c &c which he had been entertaining as far back as 1826." Parker wrote that Nat spoke "with great candour," describing "the signs he saw; the spirits he conversed with," "his prayers, fastings, and watchings," and "his supernatural powers and gifts." Although Nat referred to the transformations in his life around 1826, he told Parker that "the idea of emancipating the blacks" had not occurred to him "until rather more than a year ago." Another attorney, William Parker, was there; soon he would be appointed Nat's lawyer.[29]

At three o'clock they took Nat to the town's four-chambered jail, just off the public grounds. Back in late August and early September, there had been fifty people crammed into the jail pending trials, but now there were only six: the four free Black men; the enslaved man

Sam who had been owned by Edwards and was scheduled to die in a few days; and the enslaved boy Moses, waiting to be deported and sold out of state. This left room for a crowd to gather around. In jail, Nat continued to answer questions, including about the money taken from white people. Someone recorded that Nat said, "You know that money was not my object." Other accounts stated that Nat continued to confess, showing "great intelligence and shrewdness of intellect, answering every question clearly and distinctly, and without confusion or prevarication," a Norfolk newspaper wrote. He told them he had devised the plan by himself and only revealed it to "5 or 6" others a few days beforehand. He had been led by a "revelation." Nat once again spoke about his ability to "command the thunder" and read "upon the leaves of the trees" and was "induced to believe that he could succeed in conquering the county of Southampton . . . as the white people did in the revolution." He spoke of the "*dark appearance of the sun*" that told him it was time to act and of the attacks along the way. He did not speak of doubts or regrets or repentance, even though it might have gained him some small favor from his audience.[30]

We don't know Nat's feelings in these moments, not even in the limited, imperfect way we might think we know his feelings at other moments. We can well imagine that he enjoyed the opportunity to talk about his prophecy. And we can also imagine that he found solace in the biblical prophets who were also imprisoned: Joseph, Samson, Hanani, Jeremiah, the kings Zedekiah and Jehoiachin, John the Baptist, Paul, Peter, and of course Jesus himself. In Ecclesiastes, Nat might have read that "out of prison he cometh to reign."[31] He might have known Psalm 68, where David proclaims that God "bringeth out those which are bound with chains," or Psalm 146, where "the Lord looseth the prisoners" and "raiseth them that are bowed down: the Lord loveth the righteous."[32] In Revelation, the "Son of Man" commanded John of Patmos to tell people in Smyrna "to fear none of those things which thou shalt suffer," even if "the devil shall cast some of you into prison, that ye may be tried; . . . be thou faithful unto death, and I will give thee a crown of life."[33] Jail was no surprise for a prophet.

Sometime later that day, another visitor came to the jail: the local lawyer Thomas Gray. Gray was born in 1800—the same year as
Nat—to one of the wealthier men in the county, a man who in 1820
owned 2,408 acres and twenty-three horses and claimed fifty-seven
enslaved people. Thomas Gray made a quick start in his own life,
owning 400 acres and fourteen enslaved people over age twelve by
the time he turned twenty-one. His holdings of enslaved people grew
to twenty-three people over age twelve by 1827, and in 1828 he became a justice of the peace. In 1829, he bought a town lot and more
acreage, and in 1830 helped found the Jerusalem Jockey Club. But
his family's financial fortunes took a wrong turn over the 1820s; his
father and brothers went deep into debt, and his father's holdings of
enslaved people fell from fifty-seven to eight between 1820 and 1831.
In turn, his father and brothers dragged Thomas Gray into debt with
them as he took loans to pay for his family's land. Over the decade,
Thomas Gray lost his land and his horses and his claim over enslaved
people. To stay afloat, Gray moved to town and opened a legal practice, living on Main Street by late 1830. In the middle of the trials, his
father died, leaving nothing to Thomas but passing a part of his estate
to Thomas's young daughter. When Nat's rebellion began, Gray was a
man moving into middle age with few prospects.[34]

Gray had been among the first to head out with the town posse
on Monday, August 22. The next morning, he rode around the Cross
Keys neighborhood examining the dead bodies in the Travis house and
the remains of the infant in the fireplace. At the Waller house, a young
white girl named Clarinda Jones stood looking at the pile of dead bodies. Lifting her onto his saddle, Gray took her home. On Tuesday evening, he rode to Norfolk to ask the U.S. commander on the *Natchez*
for federal help. He returned from Norfolk on Thursday, August 25,
renting his office to General Eppes's quartermaster. It is possible he
gave information to the Richmond editor John Hampden Pleasants
that day or the next, because Pleasants included estimates of the number of dead white people in his dispatch published in the Richmond
Whig the following Monday. With the former congressman Trezvant,

the town postmaster, the county clerk, the sheriff, the prosecuting attorney, General Eppes, and two other attorneys, Gray helped direct the legal inquiry into the rebellion. While other lawyers represented dozens of defendants, Gray brought forward only a handful of cases before his father died and he himself became sick, costing him needed lawyers' fees.[35]

On October 31 in the county jail, Gray asked Nat if he could return and speak with him the next day. Gray was sitting across from one of the most notorious men in the United States, and he apparently saw the story of the rebellion as his path to some type of windfall. Gray was well placed to see this opportunity: Through his participation in the posse, his ride through the neighborhood, his role in the inquiry, and his defense of Moses and other enslaved people, Gray had an unusually precise—although not completely accurate—understanding of the rebellion. Through his discussions with Pleasants, he had probably formed an idea of publishing. Gray had learned more about Nat through Nathaniel Francis on Francis's trip to town. He read the documents given up and the statements made under torture by Nat's wife. Allmendinger argues persuasively that Gray was likely the author of a letter the Richmond *Whig* published on September 26, 1831, from Jerusalem, a letter composed on September 17. If so, Gray had a genuinely deep interest in the case; he wrote the letter as he struggled with malaria and his father's imminent death.[36]

The letter was a broad overview of the rebellion, an argument that the rebellion had been narrow, contained, and anomalous, not a general indication of problems with slavery. While the atheistic Gray faulted "coloured preachers" and white pastors who "fill up their discourses with a *ranting cant* about equality," he attributed the rebellion not generally to religion but specifically to the "fanaticism" of Nat. He took solace in the small number of men in Nat's band of fighters and the even smaller group of plotters. Gray paid "passing tribute to our slaves, but one they richly deserve" for their loyalty to the enslavers. Nat's motivations were personal, and Gray reported for the first time that "something like three years ago, Nat received a whipping from his master, for saying that the blacks ought to be free, and that they would be free one day or other." In September 1831, before Nat's capture, Gray was not certain how seriously to take Nat's religion, dismissing Nat as "no preacher" but a fraud who wrote on the leaves, then sent "some ignorant black to bring them to him" to gain "an immense influence. He, likewise, pretended to have conversations with the Holy Spirit; and was assured by it, that he was invulnerable." Gray granted that Nat was smart; Gray had seen the papers that had been "given up by his wife, under the lash," with their hieroglyphical characters and figures. Over time Gray became more and more convinced that Nat's uprising was confined to the area and that innocent enslaved people elsewhere were being unjustly persecuted.[37]

Gray's chronicle was not the only one to go out from the town's lawyers in September. Another came from William C. Parker, the War of 1812 hero and the leader of one of the town posses. Parker learned details about the rebellion in his rides through Cross Keys, his service with Gray in the inquiry, his defense of enslaved defendants, and his likely discussions in town with Nathaniel Francis and Sarah Francis. Shortly after Gray's letter to the Richmond *Whig*, Parker wrote to a rival newspaper, the Richmond *Enquirer*. Parker had new information about Nat's religious activities, mentioning the baptism of Etheldred Brantley for the first time. He focused on Nat's idiosyncrasies, calling him a "would-be Prophet" who tried to "deceive, delude, and overawe their minds." But Parker was less confident about the scope of the rebellion. He doubted there was a concerted plan but still suspected that "the subject has been pretty generally discussed among them, and the minds of many prepared to cooperate in the design." Nevertheless, Parker rejected the idea that the county needed outside help and dismissed requests for a "regular standing force" in each county. But he did go beyond Gray in calling for more rigorous local volunteer companies and patrols.[38]

These two men, Gray and Parker, would play crucial roles over the next days. William Parker, one of the two most utilized attorneys in the uprising, would be Nat's lawyer at trial. In the interim, Gray would be his interlocutor, perhaps at times even his scribe. While they differed in their experience with the law and their understanding of the rebellion's scope, Gray and Parker shared a belief in the need to resolve the rebellion through the legal system, not mass violence. It is easy to scoff at the self-deception involved in celebrating a legal system while profiting from a social order that depended on violence, but it is clear that the participants took their commitment to the law seriously. The court named Parker to represent fourteen defendants, including Hark, and he handled their cases at least plausibly well, gaining four acquittals and two commutations, with eight executions. Gray represented only five, including Sam from the Francis plantation, the reluctant Jack, and the impressed boy Moses. Of these, all five were convicted, but Jack was originally recommended for a commutation, which was later denied. The boy Moses received a commutation; the others were executed. Clearly both men despised the defendants; just as clearly, both believed legal formalities had to be upheld, even—no, especially—in moments of crisis.[39]

ON TUESDAY, NOVEMBER 1, Gray returned to speak to Nat. Gray hoped not only to make money but also to puncture the "exaggerated and mischievous reports" that "greatly excited the public mind." Those rumors spread because the other participants had explained what happened but not why; the motives remained "wrapt in mystery." By emphasizing motives, Gray aimed to define the rebellion, to make it a singular event.[40]

We can see a glimpse of Gray's opening question in Nat's first recorded words: "You have asked me to give a history of the motives which induced me to undertake the late insurrection, as you call it." Nat answered in a roundabout way. "To do so I must go back to the days of my infancy, and even before I was born." That first day, Allmendinger suggested, the two men likely talked about Nat's history, creating the basis for the long section that leads up to the events of

1830–1831. The following day, when Gray returned to the jail, they likely discussed the rebellion itself. On Thursday, Gray "began a cross examination."[41]

Nat had reason to see Thomas Gray as his enemy and to doubt Gray's willingness to transcribe his statements, represent him fairly, or take him seriously. Even if Gray did transcribe accurately, his motives would be profit for himself, not Nat's cause or Nat's family. Yet Nat spoke at length to Gray. At his trial, Nat either—by Gray's account—explicitly affirmed his "full confession to Mr. Gray" or—by the account of the clerk—obliquely stated that "he had nothing but what he had before said" without specifying whether he referred to his prior comments to the lawyers upon being brought to town or his statements to Gray or both. Even acknowledging the likelihood that Gray exaggerated, none of the sources of the trial showed that Nat expressed doubt about Gray's portrayal of the events.[42]

Why would Nat speak to Thomas Gray, given what Nat knew about white people? It is tempting and for some has been irresistible to imagine some kind of understanding between the two men. On the other hand, it seems plausible to argue that Gray's writing may not reflect anything meaningful about Nat, neither his motives, nor his beliefs, nor even his language, but was merely a fiction of Gray's creation. But that argument runs aground on the other evidence we have of Nat's time in Jerusalem: Gray's account overlapped a great deal with what Nat told other people and with the testimony of other enslaved defendants.

Even if we accept the general veracity of Gray's quotations, we do not need to seek explanations for Nat's volubility in any emotional bond between the men. The reasons for Nat to speak would have been clear to anyone who read the Bible. In the end, what did prophets do? They left books. Many books of the Hebrew Bible were named for the prophets: Joshua, Samuel, Amos, Hosea, Isaiah, Micah, Zephaniah, Jeremiah, Nahum, Habbakuk, Ezekiel, Obadiah, Haggai, Zechariah, Malachi, Joel, Jonah. Other prophets were featured centrally in books not named for them, notably Elijah and Elisha. Jesus, of course, left testaments written down by others. Gray sought a financial windfall, but Nat might have sought a far greater reward.

It is only remarkable that Nat spoke to Gray if we forget that Nat had spoken to everyone since his capture. We can say with certainty that Nat wanted to tell people why he led the rebellion. Nat likely understood his time with Gray, limited as it was, would be the best chance he would have to put his words into the record. Imperfect as the *Confessions* might be, it would be the only book of his prophecy he could bequest to later readers. Nat understood the power of prophetic literature to shape lives and actions because he had lived that power in his own life, typing himself after the prophets of the books of the Bible he studied. Or perhaps he simply believed that a record of the Spirit's visions and words would remind people that the Spirit remained present on earth and would one day act upon God's enemies.

Of course the book of Nat was not written by Nat. Such was true of other books about prophets. But the particular question of what parts, if any, of the *Confessions* represent Nat's voice remains troublesome and has been a central concern of most recent studies of Nat.[43]

The *Confessions* derives much of its power from its seemingly unmediated account of Nat's story, but some words attributed to Nat were certainly Gray's. Many of these interventions are plainly marked as queries Gray addressed to Nat or with parentheses and brackets. Some of these expressed Gray's opinions of Nat, distilled in his parenthetical reference to "these barbarous villains." Other interventions come with no helpful marks of Gray's hand, but they have a pattern, and it dovetails with Gray's expressed opinions of Nat. Thus Nat is supposed to have referred to "our blood-stained track" and to a failure "to gratify our thirst for blood." These statements sound improbable coming from Nat, not least because the narrative reveals his reluctance to attack people. Exact body counts at different farms and the forces of whites rallying against the rebels are also more likely Gray's than Nat's. Some words seem unusually legalistic for any layman, white or Black, like "divest"; others assume a vantage that appears to be from outside Nat, such as when he is referred to as a "gloomy fanatic."[44]

But it is also clear that Gray did not invent crucial aspects of Nat's story. Other jailed members of the company had discussed Nat's visions in their testimony. White neighbors remembered his religiosity and his efforts to baptize the overseer. Court records verify the general trajectory of Nat's ownership, though he did not name all the steps along the way. Then there were the documents and the statements elicited from the enslaved woman described as Nat's wife, reported weeks before Nat's capture. Through the impressed boy Moses's testimony and reconstructions of the route, local people had pieced together much of the narrative of events of August 21 and 22. Then, too, Nat himself had told parts of this story to many people along the route to Jerusalem in the days after his capture. While those stories lacked the detail of the *Confessions*, they generally overlapped and sometimes named the same important dates as turning points in Nat's understanding of his call.[45]

Still, the *Confessions* added a new voice and a new set of facts to the great deal that was already known about the rebellion. After careful review, Allmendinger found that the *Confessions* contributed 116 details that had not previously appeared, some mundane, some momentous, some flattering to Nat, and some—like the infanticides—deeply disturbing. The voice that conveyed these details might not have been Nat's, but there is no reason to think it is Gray's. Gray was notoriously skeptical of religion and legalistic in his own writing, but the *Confessions*, as Allmendinger put it, slips into a voice "less 'classical' and more 'biblical' . . . more Lucan than lawyerly." While Gray likely learned about Nat's religious practices and beliefs from Sarah Francis, who worshipped with the Turner family during Nat's childhood, from Nathaniel Francis, and perhaps from John Clark Turner, it seems unlikely that he was channeling their voices or that Gray could have produced those cadences and claims on his own.[46]

It is this religious sensibility that Breen responded to when he critiqued the *Confessions* as "simplistic" for its portrayal of Nat's religious fanaticism. It is worth taking seriously the idea that Gray found religious motivations a convenient foil; they allowed him to separate the rebellion from broader discontent among enslaved people, lambaste religiosity in general, and blame preachers in particular. Yet Gray, for all his general skepticism, treated Nat's beliefs with patience and even respect in the *Confessions*, a respect not found in the letter he had likely written before Nat's capture. Additionally, there was nothing unusual in Gray's interpretation of the religious basis of Nat's rebellion. Nearly everyone who knew anything about the area or about the man made this association. A present-day dissatisfaction with that religious interpretation, and thus a need to pin the religious talk on Gray, may say more about current scholarship's wariness of treating religion as a genuinely motivating factor, not just a vehicle for the expression of other motivations. It is simpler, and perhaps more reassuring, for essentially secular scholars to treat religion as the means by which people act out their interests or secular ideologies or cultural repertoire, rather than to treat religion as an end in itself. To give religion that kind of motivating power is to admit that the material and linguistic assumptions that still animate much historical scholarship cannot adequately explain human behavior.[47]

The gap that may puzzle readers the most is the complete silence around Nat's wife, presumably the woman identified as Cherry. Gray had heard about her, perhaps had even seen her interrogated, and had read the materials she provided. It seems hard to imagine him not asking Nat. And it also is hard to imagine Nat not mentioning his wife and son in a narrative in which he is recorded as discussing his mother and grandmother, as well as numerous other personal details. Perhaps Nat was wary of mentioning sex, or even ashamed of having lived an unchaste life. But it seems unlikely he would have internalized white demands for legal marriages, given his clear-eyed understanding that it was white people who denied him the power to be married under the law. Perhaps Nat and his wife had become estranged by his solitude, but if so, it would be somewhat puzzling that she still held his papers. Perhaps Nat asked Gray to keep his wife out of the *Confessions* as a way of protecting her, a final gift. Perhaps Cherry's enslavers also wished her role suppressed so she would not be executed. If so, Gray kept that bargain.[48]

After Nat relayed his story, Gray began to cross-examine him "and found his statement corroborated by every circumstance coming within my own knowledge or the confessions of others whom had been either killed or executed, and whom he had not seen nor had any knowledge since 22d of August last." Perhaps we might read this as confirmation of the facts Nat gave, or perhaps as confirmation of Gray's presumptions, but it was likely some mixture of the two.[49]

Gray closed this section with some judgments of Nat, judgments that reflected Gray's change of heart. He no longer believed Nat was a fraud. No more did he mock Nat for allegedly painting leaves in the woods and sending the gullible to discover them, as he had in the September letter to the Richmond newspaper. Now he asserted Nat's sincerity, even as Gray considered it mad. "It has been said he was ignorant and cowardly" and aimed to steal money, but Gray dissented. "It is notorious, that he was never known to have a dollar in his life, to swear an oath, or drink a drop of spirits. As to his ignorance, he certainly never had the advantages of education, but he can read and write," having learned from his parents. "For natural intelligence and quickness of apprehension," Nat was "surpassed by few men I have ever seen." Gray also denied that Nat was a coward. "He is a complete fanatic, or plays his part most admirably. On other subjects he possesses an uncommon share of intelligence with a mind capable of attaining any thing; but warped and prevented by the influence of early impressions." Gray was struck by the way Nat told the story: his "calm, deliberate composure," "the expression of his fiend-like face when excited by enthusiasm." He was "clothed with rags and covered with chains; yet daring to raise his manacled hands to heaven, with a spirit soaring above the attributes of man. I looked on him and my blood curdled in my veins."[50]

Perhaps nothing in their exchange remains quite so challenging to contemplate as a moment when Gray apparently interrupted Nat. Nat was in the midst of describing one of his most vivid encounters with the Spirit, the moment the Spirit told him that the "Serpent was loosened, and Christ had laid down the yoke he had borne for the sins of men, and that I should take it on and fight against the Serpent, for the time was fast approaching when the first should be last and the last should be first."[51]

In the middle of perhaps the most extraordinary of Nat's many amazing statements, Gray intervened not with a request for more information but with doubt that a skeptic like Gray must have found overpowering, even more so as he came to admire Nat's intelligence.

"Do you not find yourself mistaken now?" Gray asked. Perhaps he gestured to their drab surroundings. Nat sat in front of him in rags, likely chained, his compatriots mostly dead, his cause silenced. The import of Gray's words was obvious. If Nat was favored by God, where were the signs of God's favor? Was the first last and the last first?

And so Nat answered, "Was not Christ crucified?" This fallen world would murder a prophet, as the Hebrew Bible recounted the ancient murdering of those prophets, as Jesus's world murdered him. Nat was not casting himself as the Messiah but typing his life after the models he knew. Sometimes God rewarded prophets with victory. But evil always rose up against faithfulness, at least until the end of this world.[52]

Why, precisely, should Nat expect this evil world to permit him to live, when the world had crushed so many virtuous prophets before him? If the atheistic Gray was troubled by this line of inquiry, he did not say so. But it is a question that has troubled the memory of Nat since 1831. And it is a question that should trouble us still.

9

Legacies

From late August through November 1831, the leading white men of Southampton had tried to teach the world that the law was sufficient to protect slavery. This meant restraining the violence of poorer white neighbors and asserting the elites' monopoly over punishment. They sought to show that slavery was compatible with the highest evidence of civilization in Anglo-American life, the law. They accomplished this, in their eyes, by putting participants on trial and then hanging them. Now it was time for the ultimate test of the law's power to deliver punishment: the trial of Nat.

Nat went to court Saturday, November 5, probably in the morning. Thomas Gray was there, perhaps looking haggard from writing up notes from his three days of sessions with Nat. Already, he had drafted the main sections of the *Confessions*, and he might have completed the entire work. But Gray was not at the trial as Nat's lawyer. The court assigned as Nat's attorney William Parker, the War of 1812 veteran who commanded the town posse against Nat. This may seem like a setup, and perhaps it was, but Parker was also a more established and successful lawyer than Gray and had gained more acquittals than any lawyer on the cases except for one.[1]

Form mattered, and not just in the appointment of a qualified lawyer. Instead of the usual five magistrates, this morning there were ten, including the former congressman Trezvant. The presiding magistrate, Jeremiah Cobb, had designed the jail where Nat had been held. One of the magistrates claimed sixty-three enslaved people and almost 3,400 acres of land; another was a Quaker who would soon be active in the region's colonization efforts. Two were doctors, one the son of the county's wealthiest family. One magistrate was James

Parker, at whose gate Nat's company first clashed with the county posse. The court clerk kept the record, and Gray was there as an observer, writing his own notes.[2]

To preserve the power of the law, the court called out a "sufficient additional guard to repel any attempt that may be made to rescue Nat alias Nat Turner from the custody of the Sheriff." While this reads as an effort to prevent his escape, it was also an effort to block whites from lynching Nat before the county could put him to death. The leading figures in the county intended to kill Nat, but in a manner they considered respectable.[3]

Then the prosecutor, Meriwether Brodnax, brother to one of the militia leaders, read the charges, and the court asked Nat for his plea. Nat answered, "Not guilty." According to the clerk's notes, he said nothing else. But Gray wrote in the *Confessions* that Nat told his lawyer, William Parker, "he did not feel so," probably meaning he did not feel guilty of the crimes. After that, Levi Waller and James Trezvant testified. Waller spoke of the company's attack on his house, saying that Nat, "whom he knew very well," "seemed to command the party" and had given orders. Trezvant described their interrogation on October 31, when Nat admitted personally attacking Joseph Travis and Sally Francis Moore Travis and killing Margaret Whitehead. Trezvant added that Nat described "incoherent and confused opinions" that he had developed over the past five years and that led him to "commence the bloody scenes." With that the prosecution rested. The defense declined to present a case.[4]

After Cobb announced the court's unanimous guilty verdict, he asked Nat to give any reason why a "sentence of death should not be pronounced against you." The clerk noted that Nat "said he had nothing but what he had before said." Here we face another divergence between the court records and Gray's published account. Gray suggested that Nat's *"Confession as given to Mr. Gray"* had been read to the court, but the clerk's records do not say this and leave unclear whether Nat was confirming his statements to Gray or to Trezvant, or both. Gray's account states that Nat said, "I have made a full confession to

Mr. Gray, and I have nothing more to say." The difference suggests that Gray might have been inflating his own record's importance in the trial, but it's not clear that much rides on these differences in wording.[5]

Cobb pronounced the sentence: hanging "until he be dead" in six days. Again, Gray's account expands on the clerk's, quoting Cobb at some length as he scolded Nat for "plotting in cold blood, the indiscriminate destruction of men, of helpless women, and of infant children . . . when they were asleep, and defenceless; under circumstances shocking to humanity." In Gray's account, Cobb seemed to quote from the *Confessions*'s description of Travis as an "indulgent" master. Then, by Gray's account, Cobb sentenced him to be hanged "until you are dead! Dead! Dead and may the Lord have mercy upon your soul." Afterward, six magistrates signed a statement that "the confessions of Nat, to Thomas R. Gray, was read to him in our presence, and that Nat acknowledged the same to be full, free, and voluntary." Assuming this is true, it is possible the reading had occurred prior to the trial, thus explaining the discrepancy between the trial's official record and Gray's account. The court set Nat's value at $375 in case his owner were ever to be compensated, though the legislature never allocated funds to repay local enslavers (nor did the militia members pay their lodging bills).[6]

Nat was ordered to be hanged on November 11, 1831, but we know quite little about his final days in jail. Perhaps he experienced them alone, withdrawing from society as he saw the end, granting himself time for contemplation and the preparations that some sick people seek in their final hours. Perhaps he had visitors, white or Black. He might have considered the life of Jesus, the question he had posed to Gray: "Was not Christ crucified?" When "a band of men and officers" came to arrest Jesus, Jesus answered—according to the book of John—"I am he," and urged his followers to put their swords away. Jesus asked Peter a question that might have steeled Nat: "The cup which my Father hath given me, shall I not drink it?" In the book of Matthew, Jesus says, "Thinkest thou that I cannot now pray to my Father, and he shall presently give me more than twelve legions of angels? But how then shall the scriptures be fulfilled, that thus it must be?"[7]

Perhaps Nat, having said so much, now said no more. In this, he would have been following Jesus's model. When Jesus was interrogated, he defended his beliefs but refused to name his own place in the coming of God's world. "My kingdom is not of this world," Jesus told Pilate, according to John. "To this end was I born, and for this cause came I into the world, that I should bear witness unto the truth. Every one that is of the truth heareth my voice." When Pilate pleaded for Jesus to explain himself, Jesus replied, "Thou couldest have no power at all against me, except it were given thee from above: therefore he that delivered me unto thee hath the greater sin." Luke presents one more condemnation of the world from Jesus's lips, reporting that Jesus told his female followers, "Daughters of Jerusalem, weep not for me, but weep for yourselves, and for your children. For behold, the days are coming, in the which they shall say, Blessed are the barren, and the wombs that never bare, and the paps which never gave suck. Then shall they begin to say to the mountains, Fall on us; and to the hills, Cover us."[8]

ONE REASON WE know so little about Nat's final days is that Thomas Gray left Jerusalem. Gray worked incredibly quickly during the days before the trial, writing as he interviewed, and now he moved just as rapidly toward publication. While we don't know if he feared particular people scooping his story, Gray certainly was aware of the interest of journalists and of other local attorneys, so time was of the essence. Finishing his writing on November 5, the day Nat was condemned, Gray headed to Richmond, arriving there by November 7. Three days later he applied for a copyright near Washington, D.C. The following week, he was in Baltimore, working with printers. On November 22, less than three weeks after Nat's trial, the book was published, and it was for sale the next day in Norfolk.[9]

That little pamphlet was a sensation at the time and has been ever since. Newspapers estimated the first printing at a staggering fifty thousand copies, though that number would be impossible to verify or for Gray personally to finance. Thomas Gray hoped his pamphlet would be both profitable and useful. But it is not clear that the book made Gray much money. By 1835, Gray was bankrupt and arrested for debt. Having lost his house and land, he used political connections to gain appointment as U.S. consul in Tabasco, Mexico, but never took the post. After working as an attorney, with little sign of success, in and around Norfolk, he died in 1845. His obituary claimed that he was a "scoffer of religion," but a local Methodist pastor said that Gray confessed his sins on his deathbed. Whether this was an opportunistic claim by a minister, or a sign of Gray's change of heart—motivated by whatever causes we might imagine—we cannot know.[10]

We do know that Gray was not present on Friday, November 11, around noon, when Southampton's sheriff led Nat to the same tree where the other soldiers in his company had been hanged, near Jerusalem's public grounds and not far from the very bridge that Nat had hoped to storm. The *Norfolk Herald* described his execution as solemn: Nat "betrayed no emotion, but appeared to be utterly reckless in the awful fate that awaited him and even hurried his executioner in the performance of his duty!" An account in the *Petersburg Intelligencer* claimed that Nat "exhibited the utmost composure throughout the whole ceremony." This newspaper stated that "although assured that he might, if he thought proper, address" the crowd, he "declined," and "told the Sheriff in a firm voice, that he was ready." It is impossible to get a clear sense of the scope of the crowd, since the two accounts present exactly opposite claims. The Norfolk newspaper stated that only "a few people" witnessed his death, but the Petersburg paper said an "immense crowd assembled," which seems probable. Later, local people said that Nat warned the crowd that after his death "the sky would grow dark and it would rain, but the rain would be for the last time," and that indeed a terrible storm was followed by an even more terrible drought ended only by "ardent prayers," but there is no contemporary evidence for this.[11]

Again, we do not know whether Nat's final thoughts turned to his wife and son, or his fighting friends, or his memories of his mother and grandmother. He might have tried to sustain his focus on the ultimate model for religious suffering: Jesus on the cross. Certainly the story would have prepared Nat for the degradations people may visit on a holy person. In accounts of the Crucifixion, soldiers force a crown of thorns on Jesus's head, and Jesus is made to carry the cross to the place of execution, Golgotha. The soldiers cast lots for his garments and his coats, but Jesus remained composed. Luke states that Jesus promised a follower, "Today shalt thou be with me in paradise." Matthew and Mark show Jesus in doubt, saying that he called out, after nine hours, "Eloi" (or perhaps "Eli"), "lama sabachthani," "My God, my God, why hast thou forsaken me?" At this point, by one account, the onlookers tormented him by pressing vinegar onto his lips. "It is finished," Jesus said, "and he bowed his head, and gave up the ghost."[12]

Nat died, though whether in silence, castigation, or lamentation we cannot be sure.

NAT'S BODY REMAINED under the control of the very people who had enslaved and executed him, and they treated his remains with contempt. At some point, Nat's Bible was presumably put away for storage, where it would remain for eighty years. His body, they handled far more crudely, passing his corpse to medical students who dissected it, probably beheading and skinning him. Some were motivated by medical curiosity, horrific as it seems, others by a gruesome desire for revenge, as they made "grease of the flesh." Stories have ever since circulated about the ways Nat's body was defiled after his death. While not all the stories can be verified, there is significant evidence for horrific mistreatment, as the historian Daina Berry has recently shown. "We can be certain that something happened to" Nat's body even if the "exact nature of that terrible something remains lost," another scholar put it.[13]

People spoke of seeing a "money purse" made from his skin. A local man boasted later in life about tanning Nat and said that "portions" of Nat's body "are now extant in the 'curiosity shops' of many residents in and about Southampton." Nat's skull fell into the hands of local doctors, then medical schools, where it became part of the traffic in skulls of enslaved people for use in nineteenth-century medical training. Perhaps it was displayed in a northern college well into the twentieth century. If white Virginians reckoned with the gap between the lawful proceedings and the brutal aftermath, they kept their worries to themselves. Gray, unsurprisingly, was silent on this topic. A pamphlet about the triumph of the law could not dwell on revenge, and Gray aimed to offer lessons in policy, not mob behavior. Besides, Gray was not there to see this, too busy marketing his book around Washington, D.C.[14]

The abuse of Nat's body drew upon the racist animosity of Southampton white people and the long-standing Anglo-American tradition of defiling bodies as punishment. While this defilement reaches back to old English customs, it found particularly gruesome expression in the United States. The history of white people's treatment of the bodies of Native peoples is replete with medical experimentation and also with the transformation of skin or other body parts into souvenirs. Perhaps most grotesque is the defilement of the bodies of the people who were lynched and whose remains were often preserved as mementos. These mementos had admonitory qualities; the defilement was a warning to people who considered rising up. But they also had a strange kind of talismanic effect. If the skulls of killed rebels staked upon the road were demonstrations of white people's power to the enslaved people, the display of Nat's body in white spaces demonstrated a different kind of power, a display that the proud owner might utilize to reassure those white people, and perhaps also to reassure himself.[15]

IF DESECRATING NAT'S body was meant to rob it of its power, the example of Nat's life, insurrection, and death showed the enduring power of his life and example upon the world, although people who encounter Nat in the pages of the *Confessions* or in the many reproductions of his life in nonfiction and fiction have taken away starkly different lessons.

Thomas Gray hoped his pamphlet would promote legal reforms to buttress slavery. Gray feared that exaggerating the scale of the rebellion would undermine popular support for slavery. The attacks "greatly excited the public mind, and led to a thousand idle, exaggerated and mischievous reports" that made a "deep impression, not only upon the minds of the community where this fearful tragedy was wrought, but throughout every portion of our country, in which this population is to be found." Gray intended the pamphlet to be an "awful" but "useful" lesson about the ways enslaved people might become "bewildered and confounded, and finally corrupted" by religion. Thus Gray blamed not the system of slavery but the proselytizers of Christianity.[16]

Gray's solution was the law, as befitting a lawyer's publication. The pamphlet was "calculated also to demonstrate the policy or our laws in restraint of this class of our population, and to induce all those entrusted with their execution, as well as our citizens generally, to see that they are strictly and rigidly enforced. Each particular community should look to its own safety, whilst the general guardians of the laws, keep a watchful eye over all." The challenges to slavery were serious but not overwhelming; Gray did not support the idea of a statewide guard placed across the commonwealth, protecting white people against uprising but also interfering with enslavers' claimed monopoly on power. With some reform, Gray argued, slavery could not only survive but expand.[17]

White Virginians grasped at least one of Gray's lessons: enslaved people's Christianity could be dangerous. It would be going too far to argue that the rebellion introduced this concept. But the clarity of what appeared to be Nat's words carried the message home. This was a surprisingly recent fear. Until the late eighteenth century, many white southerners seemed unconcerned with enslaved people's religion. That changed over the early nineteenth century when mass revivals converted more enslaved people, and northern evangelicals began critiquing southern slaveholders for failing to provide for enslaved people's spiritual education. With Denmark Vesey's purported rebellion, planters embraced the idea that they should control the spread of Christianity both to silence their northern critics and to determine what their enslaved people heard.

Nat's rebellion reinforced the fear of unrestrained conversion among enslaved people. "The case of Nat Turner warns us," the Richmond *Enquirer* wrote: "No black man ought to be permitted to turn a Preacher through the country." Virginia's governor, John Floyd, came to believe—against all evidence—that "every black preacher in the whole country east of the Blue Ridge was in on the secret, that the plans as published by those Northern presses were adopted and acted upon by them." Floyd particularly worried that Black preachers had distributed the abolitionist *Liberator* newspaper and David Walker's *Appeal*.[18]

On the ground, the Southampton rebellion prompted many local churches to debate the future of biracial worship. They looked to Nat's testimony about his beliefs as well as the testimony of Beck about the plotting at Raccoon Swamp Baptist. Many whites could not feel comfortable around Black congregants. Raccoon Swamp and Black Creek Baptist Churches banned Black people for weeks and skipped the Lord's Supper altogether in October and November 1831. But this could go on for only so long; white congregation leaders needed to affirm the utility of Christianity for saving Black people or else risk their own beliefs. By December 1831, Black Creek brought every Black member back into fellowship once the congregation had examined their faith and their claims of loyalty. In 1832, most of the churches in the region returned to a perhaps-grudging embrace of biracial congregations, possibly in hopes of sustaining their oversight of the religious education of enslaved people. At Raccoon Swamp, Beck's church, the congregation seemed to be faltering over 1832, falling to 42 white members and having virtually no communication with Black members. But by 1833, the church had returned to 141 members and by 1834 was baptizing large numbers of Black people.

In part Raccoon Swamp's trajectory may reflect not just a defense of biracial churches but also wariness about Beck's testimony, demonstrated in the county's negotiation with the free Black man she had testified against.[19] Some Black congregants, however, refused to return to biracial churches, like a free Black woman in North Carolina who was threatened by militia and decided, "I would not go to church there anymore."[20]

Methodist churches debated the issue particularly bitterly. In December 1831, the presiding elder of the Methodist Church in the region let the licenses of three enslaved preachers lapse, a step toward excluding all Black preachers from the pulpit. But seven white Methodists fought stridently against this ruling and in defense of their authority over their own congregations. Led by "an imperious sense of duty from which it would be cowardice to shrink," they protested that the Methodist conference "have made a test" of slavery "which we think is not recognized by our Discipline . . . How dare any man or set of men, stop or hinder one who is thus chosen of God to call Sinners to repentance?" Was it not "unjust and cruel" that the church "united with heartless Politicians and interested Slave holders in depriving them of their few Religious rights & priviledges? . . . Shall we, because a few desperadoes in Southampton have inhumanly butchered our fellow Citizens, spurn from our bosom those innocent but unfortunate blacks who have taken Shelter under our protection?"[21]

Still, change was under way. In the year after the rebellion, Virginia Methodists lost 934 Black members while gaining 2,225 whites. And the message changed, too. While white Virginia Methodist ministers had long preached in favor of slavery, they now sharpened their claims, defending slavery as part of God's plan. They critiqued northern antislavery ministers as heretics who interpreted the Bible instead of reading its plain text. They combined these sermons with injunctions to their white congregants to convert enslaved people and disarm slavery's northern critics. These sermons helped bolster the already-developing slaveholder ideology of paternalism, in which white southerners convinced themselves, and sometimes others, that they fashioned mutually dependent, morally virtuous relationships with enslaved people, relationships rooted in the principles of family hierarchy but also of family love. These sermons also helped fuel the regional divisions between northern and southern churches, as white southern ministers defended their plain-text reading of the Bible—especially its passages acknowledging slavery—as a cross-denominational regional dogma. But this line between pro-slavery reaction and plain-text readings can take us only so far: Nat, too, believed he understood the Bible's plain text and was wary of people who did not take the Bible's meaning at face value.[22]

Another lesson of the Nat rebellion was that free Black people were a danger to the state. This was a peculiar lesson since the evidence suggested the opposite. Although free Black people played only a marginal role in the rebellion, many white Virginians feared their presence, and many free Black people understandably feared for their own safety. The American Colonization Society arrived to allegedly solve both issues by raising money from white people to pay the passage to Liberia for free Black people. Many white Virginians donated to the ACS not because they opposed slavery but because they wanted to cleanse the land of Black people. This was not entirely new. Already, a few dozen free Black people had left Southampton for Liberia in 1824, 1825, and 1830. But the process accelerated after the rebellion. By early September 1831, weeks after Nat's uprising, fifty free Black people from Southampton arrived in Norfolk to prepare a ship for Liberia. By September 23, there were two hundred people ready to leave, perhaps one-sixth of the county's free Black population. At the end of November, they boarded the *James Perkins* in Norfolk and embarked on December 5 for Africa, arriving in Liberia a little more than a month later. Other groups left from Norfolk in May, July, November, and December 1832, including a total of perhaps three hundred Southampton people between September 1831 and December 1832. These were family pilgrimages both to Africa and away from a United

States that seemed uninhabitable: fourteen Whiteheads and sixteen Whitefields left, along with a "celebrated Black Doctor and Doctress," and at least six people named Artis.[23]

Some free Black people from the region also moved to the Midwest. Mrs. Colman Freeman, who later ended up in Canada, said that she had grown up free in North Carolina, not far from Southampton. She "came away from North Carolina in consequence of persecution," she later told a white abolitionist. Although her people had no prior knowledge of the rebellion, whites threatened them with pistols, so "I made up my mind not to remain in that country. We had to stay a while to sell our crop." She fled to Ohio since the "laws were all against the colored men" in the South. "They allowed us no schools nor learning." When she found prejudice in Ohio, she left for Canada.[24]

Prominent white Virginians wrestled with the lessons of the rebellion, and some took the uprising as a sign that they should remake the state into a white haven, a place for neither free Black people nor slavery. This was not so unthinkable as it might seem to us now. The political debates over slavery had been fiery in mid-Atlantic states; even in Maryland, where slavery survived, the growth of the free Black population raised questions about slavery's life span. The prominent white Virginian Jane Randolph, fearful for her safety and for the future of the commonwealth, asked her husband, Thomas Jefferson Randolph, if he would consider moving to Ohio, where slavery was illegal (and where Black people faced high hurdles for entry). Randolph did not move, but he did contemplate a different way to preserve his wife's happiness in Virginia. With some elite allies and with strong support from western Virginia legislators, he developed plans to follow the suppression of the rebellion with the slow extermination of slavery.[25]

In December 1831, Governor John Floyd called the legislature into special session to consider a plan for pacifying and eventually removing Black people. Drawing upon his condemnation of the rebels as religious fanatics, Floyd denounced Black preachers for "stirring up the spirit of revolt" and called for "the negro preachers to be silenced" before they destroyed "the public tranquility." He also recommended the legislature approve funds to remove free Black people from the state. For almost thirty years Virginia legislators had debated similar deportations as a way of helping preserve slavery. But Floyd had other motives. He did not say publicly what he wrote in his journal: state-funded colonization would be the "first step to emancipation." He wrote that he "will not rest until slavery is abolished in Virginia."[26]

In the session's early days, Patrick Henry's grandson introduced a petition from Quakers asking for an ultimate end to slavery by emancipating people born to enslaved mothers and then paying to deport them. In Spanish America, this path to gradual emancipation was called a free womb law, and the path it promised was indeed a slow one. The chairman of the committee that received the petition was William Henry Brodnax, who led militia just west of Cross Keys during the Southampton rebellion, whose brother prosecuted Nat, and who himself claimed ownership of twenty-six people. While some delegates wanted to bar any mention of the petition, Brodnax insisted on taking it under consideration. "Does any man doubt that Slavery is an evil?" Brodnax asked. The legislature had authority to contemplate "an entering wedge, towards ultimate emancipation." It may seem strange that the governor who dispatched the militia that put down the rebellion and a man who helped command that militia should consider emancipation, but perhaps they knew the cost of upholding slavery better than most. In the short run, they would protect white planters from enslaved people; in the long run, the only protection, they might have come to believe, was creating a state without either slavery or Black people.[27]

After pro-slavery legislators tried to end debate, Thomas Jefferson Randolph introduced a bill to end slavery in Virginia by freeing children born to enslaved women on or after July 4, 1840. Those children would be hired out until they had earned enough money to pay for their transportation out of state. The limits of the plan are obvious in retrospect. This was a plan to whiten Virginia, not a plan to weaken slavery in the United States. Enslavers would have had a vested interest in selling or moving enslaved people into states that continued to sustain slavery. Nothing required that any individual in Virginia in 1831 either be freed or see their offspring free unless their enslaver for some reason chose to remain in the commonwealth. For the other enslaved people, the law would have meant personal catastrophe as white enslavers sold or moved them to Mississippi or Texas and broke up family networks that existed in places like Cross Keys. And yet in the longer run the plan would have weakened slavery in the United States by removing one of the most politically powerful states from the rolls of slave states. Without slavery Virginia's politics would have remained pro-slavery but hewed closer to those of Maryland or Delaware or New Jersey, and even farther away from Mississippi and Alabama. Who can say what difference this might have made in the decades to come?[28]

NAT'S REBELLION AND the bitter 1820s fights over apportionment had opened up space for denouncing the institution of slavery. What ensued in the legislature was a fierce debate, one that revealed a long-standing, bitter, and potentially transformative conflict over the future of Virginia. Virginians submitted more than forty petitions signed by two thousand people to the state legislature, asking legislators to reduce the power of slavery. Fearful of more rebellions and of the growth of the Black population, these petitioners called for reducing the state's Black population by forced deportation. Those from the western part of the state also called for gradual abolition, while those from the east emphasized only the expulsion of free Black people.

White Virginians had by this point debated the future of slavery for generations. In the early republic, those debates turned on the question of whether Black people had natural rights, a reflection of the ideas circulating during the Revolution. But the debates of 1831–1832 were shaped by the 1829–1830 constitutional convention fights over apportionment and the rights of white people who owned few or no slaves. Western Virginia legislators once again debated the rights not of Black people but of white people who were starved of power and access to land by the political and economic power of elite eastern enslavers. As one historian wrote, "Under the Randolph proposal, the 'Day of Jubilee' in Virginia would be celebrated by whites who had rid themselves simultaneously of slavery and blacks." Although this argument does not appear particularly virtuous to modern ears, it was somewhat effective. In the Civil War this western alienation from eastern planters would be part of the impetus for the creation of a breakaway state in West Virginia.[29]

Eastern conservatives ardently defended their property rights in enslaved people. Rather than claiming slavery as virtuous, many acknowledged that slavery was problematic but suggested it would die naturally if left alone. But taking an enslaved person without the owners' consent would be a violation of planters' property rights, even if that freed person were a fetus not yet born, a child not yet conceived; planters' property rights, in their view, were perpetual. Brodnax, charting a middle position, opposed Randolph's plan but believed that colonization schemes could over time deport all free Black people and then many enslaved people if (and only if) the enslavers wished to sell them, and if (and only if) the full weight of the state was brought to bear to force free Black people to move. He wished for the "gradual diminution, or ultimate extermination of the black population of Virginia" more than an end to slavery.[30]

The House of Delegates voted first on a resolution that it was "inexpedient" to act on any scheme to end slavery. This resolution carried by 65–58, closing the debate on emancipation. This outcome likely misrepresents the opposition to emancipation. If the House had been apportioned according to the 1830 census, not the 1820 census as the constitutional convention required, it is likely that the margin of defeat for emancipation would have been only one vote. Western delegates largely backed Randolph's proposition. Then the legislature passed a preamble that declared slavery an evil and acknowledged the potential for future reform. The House passed funds for voluntary removal of free Black people, but the Senate let the measure die.[31]

Having reconfirmed the role of slavery in the commonwealth,

Virginia legislators made conditions harsher for both enslaved and free Black people. The legislators took aim at the lessons they learned from Nat's rebellion. They prohibited religious meetings of Black people and barred enslaved people, free Black people, and "mulattos" from licenses to preach. The law necessitated a more strictly hierarchical form of biracial Christianity, requiring enslavers to manage enslaved people's religious lives. Enslaved people could attend religious meetings only if white enslavers were with them. The legislature turned as well to free Black people, putting them under the oyer and terminer courts that enslaved people faced; this would have eliminated the delay and extra formality in the trials of Haithcock and the other free Black people who were charged in the Southampton rebellion and then tried by jury. Free Black people could also be deported and sold out of state if convicted of a crime punishable by law. Some of the lines that separated free Black people from enslaved people were being erased.[32]

The lessons spread beyond Virginia. In Alabama, Mississippi, and Louisiana, lawmakers passed laws against importing enslaved people into the state, as if the contagion were geographic, not structural. But whites evaded these laws even when they were on the books, and in time the laws were repealed. Many southern states instead expanded the duties of slave patrols, the formal mechanism for policing enslaved people's movements between plantations, aiming to prevent the creation of sizable, and thus more threatening, slave neighborhoods. Several states prohibited enslaved people from learning to read or write, a regulation already on the books in Virginia. Thus they attacked what they perceived as the social conditions of Nat's rebellion: his literacy, his faith, and his relationships with people beyond his home plantation.[33]

The Virginia legislature's unwillingness to act against slavery confirmed one aspect of Nat's revolt: his skepticism that rebellion would draw in earthly white allies. This may seem obvious in retrospect, but it marked a change from earlier North American rebellions. In the colonial Americas, enslaved rebels often hoped that their actions would draw the attention of a distant, potentially sympathetic monarch, perhaps one who had already ordered an end to slavery but whose rule was being disobeyed, at least according to the optimistic rumors that spread.[34]

From our perspective these rebels were both right and wrong. When enslaved people in 1823 Demerara interpreted limitations on whipping and work hours as a promise of royal emancipation, they indeed misread the facts. But they also created new meanings. Their revolt opened space in the British Empire for a discussion of slavery's ultimate fate. And then, six weeks after Nat's death, enslaved people in Jamaica also rebelled. They were inspired by a Baptist preacher named Daddy Sharpe, with his own proclamations of religiously inspired war and of thwarted royal emancipation. Robert Gardner, a plantation teamster in the inner circle of the revolt's organizers, testified, "I firmly believed that the negroes were free by order of the king and the Parliament."[35] In fact enslaved people might have heard about British frustration with Jamaican authorities for refusing to ban the whipping of enslaved women. Once again, this interpretation of British policy was incorrect, but that error helped change British policy. The Jamaica uprising and the brutality of the Baptist War inspired parliamentary inquiries that helped lead to the 1833 emancipation act. So these calls upon earthly sovereignty need not be accurate to be effective.[36]

But Nat did not look to a king—or to any earthly sovereign—for support. Instead, he looked to the celestial king, the Spirit. This view of God's sovereignty made it possible to say that conditions on earth were not as they should and must be and that they could change. Nat's motivation thus resembled these imperial rebellions, in their hopes for favor from above, but he located that power not on a throne on earth but on a throne in heaven.

Nat's turn to the heavens emerged from his faith but also from his recognition that enslaved rebels in the 1830s United States faced a problem of sovereignty. The Jamaican rebels needed to persuade a distant empire that was beholden to many interests, not just to planters.

But Nat's company had to change the minds of the sovereign at home, the State of Virginia, which was controlled by enslavers, or of the federal government, itself much more influenced by slaveholders than were European empires. Nat's pessimism was perhaps too sweeping; the revolt did open up space in that sovereign legislature but not enough to force the kinds of changes that were possible in the British Empire, and, therefore, in Jamaica. In the United States, that space would depend upon finding support from the broader sovereign—the whole population of white people, North and South—amid a destabilizing crisis; only then could enslaved rebellion transform the country. That seemed like a distant possibility in 1831. To find hope amid no hope, Nat therefore looked to the only counter-sovereignty he could discern, the power of God.

Conclusions

Although Nat's *Confessions* was not truly his, it has spoken to readers around the world across the nearly two centuries since his death. In Southampton County itself, however, it is hard to assess the effects of the rebellion. If white Southampton residents had doubts about slavery, they mostly kept those doubts to themselves. Their elected officials joined their Southside neighbors in resisting any limitations on the institution. The number of enslaved and free Black people of working age living in the county and in the Cross Keys neighborhood fluctuated in the two years after the rebellion, but by 1834 and 1835 it had stabilized to the point that a demographer could not see the effect of the rebellion on the population of either group. The white families who owned enslaved people largely kept on purchasing them. Nathaniel Francis had lost as much as any white person—seven white family members and seven enslaved people—but by 1833 he paid taxes on one more enslaved person than he had in 1831, in part because he inherited property from his dead brother and sister. In a sign of how quickly the world turned, in 1835, seeking an overseer, Nathaniel Francis hired none other than Etheldred T. Brantley, the white man baptized by Nat.[1]

So, too, did the town attempt to move on. In 1833 the town judges decided to destroy the courthouse where Nat was tried and to construct a new one on the same site. Half a century later, the town renamed itself, dropping Jerusalem and taking the name it still has today: Courtland. The town left almost no record of its reasons for the change, and most people have tied the renaming to the contemporaneous completion of the first railroad line through town, the Atlantic and Danville that connected the region to Norfolk. Recently a scholar speculated that the name change could be tied to the 1883 racial massacre in Danville, the town at the western end of the railroad line, a massacre that might have raised uneasy memories of Southside rebelliousness.[2]

Moving on was not possible for many Black people in Southampton. For individual Black families, the loss of a spouse, parent, child, neighbor, or friend must have left an aching gap, and surely this was true for Nat's family. But it is hard to pin his family down and impossible to know their precise response. No one matching the name of Nat's wife or child appeared in documents from the region for at least thirty-nine years following the rebellion. Notably this is true even of the estate documents for the Reese family, who had claimed ownership of Cherry and Riddick. Only in 1870 is there evidence of their survival. They appear in the census as "Cherrie" Turner, a sixty-five-year-old housekeeper, living with a Black family not far from Cross Keys. "Reddick" Turner was fifty, living with a woman his age and a small child, in Belfield in neighboring Greensville County, where Nat's father was rumored to have grown up. Neither claimed the ability to read; neither owned any land; Reddick Turner was a farm laborer.[3]

Over time, several local people have claimed lines of descent. Seventy years after the rebellion, someone told the local historian William Drewry that Nat's mother was named Nancy and his son Redic, the first mention of a child, but Drewry recorded no mention of his wife. In 1955, Lucy Mae Turner published a two-part essay in the *Negro History Bulletin* stating that she was Nat's granddaughter, and that her father, Gilbert Turner, was Nat's son, but she did not mention Reddick or Cherry. A Black man named Herbert Turner by the mid-twentieth century co-owned the land where the cave was located and claimed to be a descendant of Nat's but apparently did not state the line of descent. Most recently, the historian Vanessa Holden traced an enduring local claim back to Sidney Turner, a farmer and Black resident who bought land near Cabin Pond, where Nat's cave was located, a claim carried on by Sidney Turner's grandchildren. Turners, white and Black, were commonplace in lower Southampton County, making it even more difficult to discern lines of descent.[4]

In different form, stories of Nat circulated among Southampton's Black people, recorded later in folktales and local histories; many moved farther afield as well. Some of those were recorded a century later by agents of the New Deal Federal Writers' Project. Allen Crawford, interviewed in the 1930s, said he was born at Peter Edwards's plantation, where Nat was brought after his surrender. Crawford narrated the rebellion in precise, mostly accurate detail, though with an additional story of Nat escaping from capture. Farther away Nat became a folk hero. Formerly enslaved people told other interviewers that "old Nat" was a common reference to the idea that Black people "could always out-smart . . . white folks." A formerly enslaved woman from Richmond said in the 1930s that she was raised "near Oak Grove where Lincoln and Garfield and Nat Turner met and talked about slavery." Mysterious references like these show an affiliation in popular memory between Nat and the broader story of emancipation even if the precise nature of that association is hard to pin down.[5]

Beyond Southampton, Nat became an emblem of rebelliousness, even of victory, for many Black people and for some of their white allies. Dead, Nat became a safer icon than he was when living, a hero to be summoned up when needed, for proof that heroism was available close at hand.

His memory helped sustain a rebellious, bloody aspect of Black Christianity, one that did not shy from but sought armed conflict. This Christianity would move Black people to imagine their own exodus, not by flight, but by fight. The white abolitionist publisher William Lloyd Garrison saw this potential immediately, warning southern legislators—with a strong sense of irony—that they should ban Gray's book before Garrison's *Liberator* since Gray's pamphlet would "only serve to rouse up other leaders and cause other insurrections, by creating among the blacks admiration for the character of Nat, and a deep, undying sympathy for his cause." The Black minister

and militant abolitionist Henry Highland Garnet in 1843 told a narrative of continuous Black armed rebellion from Denmark Vesey to
Nat to the leaders of the uprisings on the *Amistad* and *Creole* ships.
Garnet urged the audience, "Let your motto be resistance!" A couple of years after Nat's hanging, a mob denounced a young Frederick Douglass as "another Nat Turner" for starting a Sunday school, a
threat that destroyed Douglass's "confidence in the power of southern
religion to make men wiser or better." While Douglass at times spoke
guardedly about Nat, he also compared him to the "Revolutionary fathers." And these connections were clear to some white allies, too. The
inspired white terrorist John Brown heard his own call from the Spirit
and would, with a few Black allies, launch his own holy war of rebellion in the 1850s, first in Bloody Kansas and then in Harpers Ferry,
Virginia. In prison, awaiting his own hanging, Brown compared his
struggle to Moses's efforts to "deliver Israel out of the hand of the Philistines" and his death to the fate "of prophets and apostles and Christians of former days."[6]

In the 1860s, enslaved people interpreted the Civil War as an
apocalyptic conflict by tying it to the struggles of Nat and other religiously inspired rebels. While some slaves doubted the efficacy of
the northern forces in 1861, many embraced the Civil War as a holy
war that might scourge the slave owners and drive evil from the land.
They hoped for antislavery policies from the U.S. Army, of course, but
some also prayed that the conflict would inaugurate God's kingdom.
In June 1861, Frederick Douglass told a crowd in Rochester, "In the
apocalyptic vision, John describes a war in heaven. You have only
to strip that vision of its gorgeous Oriental drapery, divest it of its
shining and celestial ornaments, clothe it in the simple and familiar
language of common sense, and you will have before you the eternal
conflict between right and wrong, good and evil, liberty and slavery,
truth and falsehood, the glorious light of love, and the appalling darkness of human selfishness and sin . . . Michael and his angels are still
contending against the infernal host of bad passions, and excitement
will last while the fight continues, and the fight will continue till one

or the other is subdued . . . Such is the struggle now going on in the United States. The slaveholders had rather reign in hell than serve in heaven." Even though Douglass likely stripped away the very parts of Revelation that most moved Nat, his speech and others like it gave the Civil War a "cosmic definition," the historian David Blight argues. In March 1863, Douglass, seeking to inspire Black men to volunteer for the first Black regiments in the Civil War U.S. Army, invoked the "glorious martyrs" of Black history, including Nat. Over the war years, white abolitionists Thomas Wentworth Higginson and Harriet Beecher Stowe used Nat to explain Black people's understanding of the stakes and meaning of the Civil War.[7]

Although it is impossible to pin down the exact moment when some specific stories began to circulate, Black people in the region turned Nat's rebellion into a harbinger of the Civil War. One legend stated that on the day of his hanging Nat's body was left on the gallows overnight. The next morning, the letter *W* appeared in blue under each of his feet, proclaiming that "there would be wars and rumors of war." By the later decades of the nineteenth century, some Black Virginians called the Civil War the "Second War" to differentiate it from the "first War" of Nat's rebellion, and some even dated time from the year of Nat's uprising.[8]

Perhaps these references and legends may help us interpret the prophetic stories that circulated among Black soldiers and their families during the Civil War. At Beaufort, South Carolina, formerly enslaved people gathered to celebrate Abraham Lincoln's signing of the Emancipation Proclamation on January 1, 1863. The night before, Colonel Thomas Wentworth Higginson did not expect a mass celebration. "I do not think there is a great visible eagerness for tomorrow's festival: it is not their way to be very jubilant over anything this side of the New Jerusalem," Higginson wrote. "They know also that those in this Department are nominally free already, and that the practical freedom has to be maintained, in any event, by military success." Higginson had written histories of Black rebels, including Nat, for *The Atlantic*. Now he led a regiment of Black men as white commander of the First South Carolina Volunteers, later renamed

the Thirty-Third U.S. Colored Infantry. Despite his modest expectations for the celebration, the next day a "multitude" gathered, "chiefly
colored women, with gay handkerchiefs on their heads." They waited
near the companies of Black volunteers who gathered in the "beautiful grove" of live oaks at Camp Saxton, now a National Park Service
site. A chaplain gave a prayer, and a white South Carolinian who had
emancipated some enslaved people read the proclamation. After the
flag was presented, two Black men spoke, Sergeant Prince Rivers and
Corporal Robert Sutton.[9] As the event closed, they sang the "John
Brown hymn," about a different Christian martyr who hoped to inaugurate a new godly kingdom on earth.[10]

Over the next years, Black people in Beaufort celebrated Emancipation Day on those same grounds in ceremonies they planned and
organized. In January 1864, more than four thousand people attended.
At the January 1865 celebration, the Black musicians of the 102nd Infantry led a "wagon drawn by eight white horses, . . . festooned with
evergreens, and draped with Union flag." The wagon carried "twelve
little girls and a colored woman representing the Goddess of Liberty."
After the close of the commanding officer's speech, "the Goddess of
Liberty struck up" the spiritual "In That New Jerusalem." Its words
could be the words of Nat:

> In that New Jerusalem
>   In that New Jerusalem,
> In that New, in that New Jerusalem,
>   We must fight for liberty
>   We must fight for liberty
> We must fight, we must fight
>   For liberty
> I am not afraid to die, etc.
> We shall wear a starry crown, etc.

The missionary teacher Elizabeth Hyde Botume called the song the
"Marseillaise of the slaves." She wrote that the "words are simple

enough," but when they were "chanted by 3,000 people," the "effect was electrical." The next year, on January 1, 1866, Botume attended the emancipation "jubilee on the race-course in Charleston," South Carolina. Only a year before, Charleston had been under the control of the Confederacy, and slavery endured. Now Charleston was home to an extraordinary Emancipation Day celebration. "It was estimated there were over ten thousand colored people around the speaker's stand . . . The streets of the city were filled with happy freed people. According to their spiritual, they had 'fought for liberty,' and this was their 'New Jerusalem,' of which they so often sang. Even the poorest, and those most scantily clothed, looked as if they already 'walked that golden street,' and felt 'that starry crown' upon their uncovered heads . . . These people were living their 'New Jerusalem.'"[11]

Those emancipated South Carolinians drew their understanding of this world and of the world to come from many histories, individual and collective, and it is important not to attribute too much to Nat. No single person had to teach enslaved people to rebel; no single person had to inspire them to connect the biblical stories of warfare and apocalypse to their own lives. The world did that work. Still, the people who carry ideas forward and refine them are important, sometimes more important than the people who coin the ideas in the first place.

Just as Nat drew upon eighteenth- and early nineteenth-century repertoires of rebellion developed by Black people like Moses Wilkinson and Gabriel and Denmark Vesey, so, too, did his example help transmit these same repertoires into the 1860s. History travels both back into the past and ahead to the future. Nat and the cause he represented helped to sustain a Black military tradition in a country where Black military service was generally illegal. Nat likely heard about the doings of neighbors in the War of 1812 when he was a boy and possibly of their ancestors in the Revolutionary War. Perhaps he heard about Black soldiers in Florida or in Haiti or in Cuba. Maybe he heard of rebellions launched across the Atlantic. The tradition did not have to be simple or unified to be useful.

So, too, did Nat take up a religious tradition—militaristic evangelical Christianity—and continue it forward. His prophecy resonated with his neighbors, presumably, because it was comprehensible within the world of early nineteenth-century Methodism. By his adulthood, that mode of Methodism was fading, and would fade even more by 1861. But Nat helped sustain the notion of the warlike prophet-priest for those emancipated South Carolinians of the 1860s. We need not make his actions their sole inspiration to make them a piece of the world they understood, a world that helped make their enlistment, and their bloodshed, understandable, too.

In the years after the Civil War, Black people frequently invoked Nat as an inspiration for their prophetic fights for freedom and equality. On August 7, 1867, the Colored Shiloh Regular Baptist Association convened near Richmond and heard applications from seventeen new churches for inclusion. When the association considered the case of Cool Spring Baptist Church in Southampton County, Elder Williams asked the Cool Spring delegates to rise, reminding the convention that this "church was located where Nat Turner first struck for freedom." The Southampton delegates "marched forward" with "much shaking of hands and general felicitation." To the white-owned *Richmond Dispatch*, this was a worrisome sign that Black Virginians retained their rebelliousness.[12]

Nat remained an icon of Black power. The U.S. veteran, politician, and historian George Washington Williams called Nat "Prophet" and compared him to Moses and John the Baptist. "The image of Nat. Turner is carved on the fleshly tablets of four million hearts," Williams wrote. The great historian and sociologist W. E. B. Du Bois wished to write a biography of Nat but was talked into writing one of John Brown instead; still, his book placed Brown's attack in the context of Nat's rebellion. In the now-famous July 1905 meeting of activists at Niagara Falls, Du Bois gave an honor roll of martyrs that included John Brown, William Lloyd Garrison, Charles Sumner, Wendell Phillips, Robert Gould Shaw, Nat, "and all the hallowed dead who died for freedom!"[13]

Nat's heroic reputation was not limited to the intellectual or political elite. An analysis of Black teachers' textbooks published between the 1890s and the 1920s suggested that Black teachers "across geographic locations" represented him "as a hero to their students" with "immense courage" and intelligence, a form of what one scholar called "race vindicationism" that coexisted with better-known representations of respectability and that was often balanced by acknowledgment of white advocates of liberty. In 1890, the Indianapolis *Freeman* asked readers to name the ten greatest Black Americans. Of the seven hundred respondents who submitted an entry, seventy-five named Nat. Tellingly, the *Freeman*'s list of the ten greatest Black people omitted Nat while including Frederick Douglass, Toussaint Louverture, Senator Blanche Bruce, Bishop D. A. Payne, George Washington Williams, T. Thomas Fortune, and four others (including the *Freeman*'s editor). Nat was admired, but often by people wary of acknowledging their admiration—an emblem of a heroic era, Du Bois claimed, but of an era that might (or might not) be past, an era of warriors, an epoch of prophets.[14]

Postscript: Anthony Kaye's Nat

At this point, Tony Kaye, had he lived to complete this book, might well have drawn upon the growing work on Nat's memory to make claims about the contested uses of Nat's words today. Nat directly inspired novelists and filmmakers and historians and activists, and continues to inspire them still. Tony's judgment of that shifting portrayal died with him, in large part.

What did not die was Tony's belief that there was something new to say about Nat. Tony studied Nat's rebellion for many years as an extension of his curiosity about the way rural neighborhoods formed building blocks for enslaved people's politics and imposed limits on those politics, issues he explored in his first book, *Joining Places*. Tony applied concepts of community formation and alliance making to the world of rural enslaved people to illustrate how they drew upon very local knowledge to judge whom to trust, whom to doubt; this process helped them build community with neighbors but also made it difficult for them to construct farther-flung alliances. Parts of this book show Tony's absorption in the neighborhood life of Nat and the other rebels, and of the problems they encountered when they left their neighborhood. Before the rebellion, Nat was known as a prophet by the people of his neighborhood, and his reputation rang loudly, but not necessarily widely. While Nat stood out within his neighborhood, he could not rely on this reputation once he crossed into other neighborhoods. This geographic limit raised questions about enslaved Southampton residents' view of the world and their place in it, and about Nat's prospects for success. That analysis shaped Tony's book *Joining Places* and formed one of his early approaches to the portrayal of Nat here.

Tony's always capacious curiosity led him over time to pursue

ever-widening geographic explorations, examining slavery, slave politics, and slave society up and down the Americas. He became fascinated
by the ways that Nat's rebellion looked like other early nineteenth-
century rebellions, especially those in Demerara and Jamaica. His
notes include hundreds of pages about those relationships, pages that I
tried to incorporate, and also pages that showed his mind at work in a
way I, with my own limitations, could not. Much of that comparative
spirit still inspires these claims, but some of the comparisons have disappeared, and all of them have been reduced. Still, in what remains, we
can see a Nat acting like other early nineteenth-century slave rebels in
his tactics, approaches, motivations, and obstacles. These comparisons
were important for Tony because they illuminated common aspects
of early nineteenth-century conditions of enslavement, what he and
other scholars called the second slavery, and also because they suggested methods and arguments that U.S. historians could utilize to pry
open assumptions within their field.

Placing Nat within those American currents helped Tony reconstruct Nat's role as a military leader. He understood well that many
modern scholars admired Nat's bold actions, but he was less certain
that they understood the military logic Nat operated within, in part
because scholars have turned away from military history since the
1970s. A slave rebellion was not simply a strike against oppressors,
or an act of resistance. It was the beginning of a war. Tony was heart-
ened by the turn toward military histories of slave rebellions that was
germinating during his lifetime, and he would have been delighted by
those that have been published since his death.

Nor, Tony thought, should Nat's place within Atlantic rebellions be
read seamlessly into the history of Atlantic revolutions. Tony admired
efforts to compare American rebellions, but he was skeptical of the
way scholars sometimes impose master narratives of revolution on top
of rebellions by enslaved people. These narratives of liberal revolutionary ideologies—ideologies of freedom and equality—placed enslaved
people's rebellions within Atlantic history by making them exemplars
of tendencies previously attributed to a predominantly white Atlan-

tic tradition. Instead of ignoring the relationship of rebellions to the liberal revolutions of the Age of Revolution, as historians once did, scholars now often make rebellions archetypes of these Atlantic revolutions, thus creators of a present epoch.

This reading, while plausible and well intentioned, can blur our sense of Nat within his own world. Tony believed that enslaved people had views of sovereignty that could not always be squared with liberal ideas. He was interested in monarchism among enslaved people, a monarchism rooted in both West African examples and an Atlantic history where empires, for all their horrors, might offer more avenues for escape than republics. He was interested as well in the ways enslaved people developed the concept of the sovereignty of the Christian God. Tony believed this vision of divine sovereignty animated a series of early nineteenth-century rebellions whose trajectories can be obscured if read into the stories of Atlantic revolutions that were propelled by very different notions of individual sovereignty.

The most significant misreading of Nat, however, lay in the discipline's commitment to secular visions of the world. Tony believed scholars rescued Nat into secular time for understandable reasons. To treat Nat as a religiously inspired leader was to risk making him a fanatic. Therefore scholars paid Nat the respect of making him respectable, driven by the recognizable politics of race pride, a quest for equality, and personal circumstance. Scholars genially turned Nat's religious language into a mechanism for conveying a real story, a set of clues to be unraveled for what they revealed about the experience of enslavement or even the weather.

But Tony sought to answer a different question: How do people make hope from no hope? How do radical movements survive periods of the most abject disappointment?

For Nat and for some of his followers, the reason for hope was not a liberal revolutionary American tradition or even a timeless Black nationalism but something more peculiar, Nat's religious beliefs. Tony asked how the evangelical world of the early nineteenth century and the presence of prophets created alternatives to standard political thinking that people like Nat could use to imagine entirely new worlds.

To Tony, perhaps particularly as he battled his own diagnoses, Nat had to be understood through the language left to us: a language that rejected secular readings of history and time. Nat's religion does not serve to communicate the real story; it is the real story. Nat has to be understood as a person who believed he was a prophet, who believed in the presence of types that blurred chronological distinctions, whose actions helped to bring about the fulfillment of the kingdom of God. Too often, Tony thought, historians reduced religion to an amalgam of things that scholars are more comfortable discussing: ideologies or material interests or intellectual ideas or communal organizations, rather than religion itself. Over his years with the manuscript, his initially rigid sense of religion evolved into the sustained engagement visible on these pages.

Late in this process, when Tony began to critique secular understandings of historical time and to read Nat into biblical history, he started to draw connections he had not previously seen and to ask questions that he believed had not been properly posed. Many of those questions turned not upon Nat's fanatical certainty but upon his unexpressed doubt. If the Spirit spoke to Nat, why did Nat wait to act?

Tony began to develop a vision of Nat that unloosed Nat from the narratives of the Age of Revolution, and thus propelled him into a biblical age and time. Tony had not, to my knowledge, fully worked out the limits of this view of history. Did he believe that the people around Nat shared this view? I believe so, but his notes are sketchy, and I have tried to respect what I do not know about his interpretations. I'm sure he would have been delighted by recent work that reinterprets the people who supported or watched Nat, but I cannot be sure exactly how their efforts would have changed his views. Nor can I be certain of Tony's own ideas about when (or if) these religious visions of time stopped shaping Black life in the nineteenth-century

South, and what role these religious views might play in the ways we think about history today.

Thus, in listening for Tony's voice, I have also tried to listen for his own doubts, knowing that he turned this manuscript over to me in a period of white-hot enthusiasm, not of cool calculation. I have tried to sustain his insights, honor his enthusiasms, and, at times, cull places where I suspect he would have wished to rein in his claims, if he had the time.

I have also had to make some decisions that Tony left undone or uncertain. Tony in his notes sometimes left paragraphs without clear citations or with citations I suspect were partial, as is not unusual when historians are writing raw drafts. To help readers and to acknowledge our collective debts, I have included numerous citations to works he read and admired, especially the terrific books by Patrick Breen and David Allmendinger that were published while Tony worked on his manuscript. Allmendinger's careful social history provided invaluable background, and its influence is evident throughout this manuscript, as it is in the notes, even if Tony arrived at some different conclusions. Like those two, Tony also drew on the work of Kenneth S. Greenberg, Thomas Parramore, Scot French, Daniel Crofts, Donald Mathews, Eric Sundquist, Henry Tragle, F. Roy Johnson, and William S. Drewry, among many others, as well as the work of numerous scholars of religion and Atlantic rebellions.

While Tony wrote, two other scholars worked on books that appeared after Tony's death. One of these, Vanessa Holden's *Surviving Southampton*, offered a perspective that I am certain Tony would have admired and that also differed significantly from Tony's goals and that I have incorporated into the text when appropriate. More challenging to incorporate is the vast work published by Christopher Tomlins, *In the Matter of Nat Turner: A Speculative History*. Tomlins and Tony corresponded prior to Tony's death, as Tomlins acknowledged, but I am not aware of what, if anything, Tony knew of Tomlins's arguments or vice versa. Therefore, I have primarily written without reference to Tomlins's work, except in cases where I am aware that Tomlins discovered errors of fact by prior scholars that Tony would not have wished to repeat. The overlap and divergence between the two books' arguments is one that will likely interest scholars, and perhaps one day I will write about this in my own voice.[1]

On issues of language, a few quick notes: Tony was attuned to changes in the way people use language but died before I could have learned his precise response to the return of the uppercase B in "Black" and to some of the changes in ways of referring to enslaved people. In keeping with my sense of general practice now, I used "Black" or "African American," and, mostly, though not exclusively, have tried to center the personhood of enslaved people and the active role of enslavers. At times, however, I continue to use "slave" and "planter" to avoid repetition or confusing sentence constructions.

Finally, a note about Nat's name. Tony sometimes referred to Nat as "Nat" and sometimes as "Nat Turner." Tony wrestled with Kenneth Greenberg's doubts about using a white enslaver's name to refer to Nat, when that name was rarely used to refer to him in life prior to his trials, and then mostly by white people. The arguments for and against using "Turner" as part of his name are serious: to not use it risks diminution or disrespect; to use it risks imposing an identity claim that the man himself might have rejected or even despised. After some internal debate, I have settled on using only the first name, Nat, in the text itself (though I have used the full name in the title) as a guard against any certainty about whether Nat thought of himself as Nat Turner prior to August 1831. Had Nat been freed by the white Turner family in his childhood, as his parents hoped, it seems quite likely he would have called himself Nat Turner, but whether he would have still thought of his name in that way after ten years claimed by other families is a question I don't believe we will ever be able to answer. I am more confident that Nat deserves the respect of a full name than I am of the specific name he would have preferred to use.[2]

In writing about a figure as elusive and mysterious as Nat, there is always a measure of uncertainty and a reliance on induction and deduction. To save the reader from tedium, I have not used qualifiers in every sentence, but readers should recognize that Tony was making well-informed, deeply considered guesses at times, guesses that I think are persuasive but that can never be factually proved.

SO, TOO, HAVE I at times had to surmise Tony's precise meaning in moments where his notes were sketchy. It is an unfortunate but unavoidable fact that I will never know when I judged correctly, when not. This is as it must be. Although Nat and his people believed Christianity a triumph over death, for those of us on this mortal plane, a death is not a triumph but a loss. We are left uncertain about where a life would have proceeded, had it continued. A life may have afterlives in memory and in the words and deeds that are left behind. Yet the mystery of the life that did not continue cannot ever be resolved.

This book is an act of multiple ventriloquisms. Tony, through his deep knowledge of history, hoped to explain the context of Nat's words, which themselves were ventriloquized through Thomas Gray. I, less successfully, tried to reconstruct the meaning of the words that Tony left behind. In the end, words do not explain themselves, no matter how much we might hope that they do. Nat cannot escape Thomas Gray. Tony could not escape the mysteries that envelop Nat's words. And I cannot escape the shroud that makes Tony's intentions at times unclear to me.

Yet words, even if their meanings are sometimes murky, still resonate, still prompt other words, other ideas. Tony dreamed of a comprehensive history of Nat, one that would incorporate every aspect of history, each of its wonderful methods, to make Nat more fully visible. My rendition of what Tony left behind cannot hope to accomplish that. But Tony also believed in history as a discipline, as a field where people produce knowledge socially, in conversation, where the work we do stands not as a monument to ourselves but as an inspiration (positive or negative) for the work of others. History is a field in which our survival is heard not in the ringing of our names but in the endurance of our ideas in other, better guises, in the future brilliant work to come that will outlast us and connect those in the future to those from the past along the shared experiences of our mortal human condition.

So, too, with this work. I did not carry all of Tony's words forward. I have left undone things he hoped to do and muddled points he would have clarified. I hope I have left enough traces that others can find their own resonances that they will bear with them in work on Nat and slave rebellions and slave religion and on the nature of history itself.

Notes

INTRODUCTION

1. *The Confessions of Nat Turner, the Leader of the Late Insurrection in Southampton, Va.* (Baltimore: Thomas R. Gray, 1831), 9–11, 18, docsouth.unc.edu/neh/turner /turner.html (hereafter cited as *Confessions*).
2. William Styron, *The Confessions of Nat Turner* (New York: Random House, 1967); John Henrik Clarke, ed., *William Styron's Nat Turner: Ten Black Writers Respond* (Boston: Beacon Press, 1968).
3. "Nat Turner, the Leader of a Violent Slave Uprising, Will Be Honored on a New Emancipation Statue in Richmond," *Richmond Times-Dispatch*, Sept. 21, 2017, www.richmond.com/news/virginia/government-politics/nat-turner-the -leader-of-a-violent-virginia-slave-uprising/article_ff963fe8-d438-5a59-858a -272120f2eb5a.html; "Should Nat Turner Be Included on a Planned Anti- slavery Monument?," *Fredericksburg (Va.) Free Lance Star*, fredericksburg.com /should-nat-turner-be-included-on-a-planned-anti-slavery-monument/poll _522449e6-91fa-52b9-ab9a-dd64039342c4.html; "An Emancipation Statue Debuts in Virginia Two Weeks After Robert E. Lee Was Removed," NPR, Sept. 22, 2021, www.npr.org/2021/09/22/1039333919/new-emancipation-statue -richmond-virginia-monument.
4. Richmond *Constitutional Whig*, Sept. 26, 1831, in *The Confessions of Nat Turner and Related Documents*, ed. Kenneth S. Greenberg (Boston: Bedford Books, 1996), 79–80.
5. Greenberg, *Confessions of Nat Turner*, 45–46.
6. *Confessions*, 4, 18, 21; Mary Kemp Davis, *Nat Turner Before the Bar of Judg- ment: Fictional Treatments of the Southampton Slave Insurrection* (Baton Rouge: Louisiana State University Press, 1999), 18–20; Rosamond C. Rodman, "O Jeru- salem, Jerusalem, Which Killest the Prophets," *Virginia Magazine of History and Biography* 131, no. 1 (2023): 9.
7. Wonderful scholars have utilized nearly secular definitions of prophecy when writing of Black religious leaders. Richard S. Newman states, "Prophetic lead- ership emphasizes a people's or a nation's destiny . . . Black prophetic leadership has critiqued American glorification in favor of a broader vision of national salvation." David Blight centers his reading of Frederick Douglass on Douglass's "deep grounding in the Bible, especially the Old Testament" and his repeated invocations of apocalyptic breaks in history and "the oldest and most powerful stories of the Hebrew prophets," in reading Douglass's message that "the American Jerusalem, its temples and its horrid system of slavery, had to be destroyed; the nation had to face exile or extinction and bloody retribution;

and only then could the people and the nation experience renewal, reinvention, and a possible new history . . . Jeremiah and Isaiah, as well as other prophets, were his guides; they gave him story, metaphor, resolve, and ancient wisdom in order to deliver his ferocious critique of slavery and his country before emancipation, and then his strained but hopeful narrative of its future after 1865." While deeply grounded in Douglass's "King James cadences," Blight's narrative presents a different kind of prophet from Nat, a religious thinker seeking wisdom and analogy, not a man certain that the Spirit had bestowed on him a new revelation. It is also intriguing that Douglass foresaw the improvement of the United States, Nat the end of the world. Richard S. Newman, *Freedom's Prophet: Bishop Richard Allen, the AME Church, and the Black Founding Fathers* (New York: New York University Press, 2008), 297–98; David W. Blight, *Frederick Douglass: Prophet of Freedom* (New York: Simon & Schuster, 2018), xvii–xviii, 228–29; *Merriam-Webster's*, s.v. "prophet," www.merriam-webster.com/dictionary/prophet.

8. Norman Cohn, *The Pursuit of the Millennium: Revolutionary Millenarians and Mystical Anarchists of the Middle Ages* (New York: Oxford University Press, 1957; rev. ed., 1970), 223–332; Roland Boer, *Political Grace: The Revolutionary Theology of John Calvin* (Louisville, Ky.: Westminster John Knox Press, 2009), 9–11, 15.

9. In his careful reading of Anne Hutchinson, Michael Ditmore argued that her confessions—imperfectly preserved by later generations—reflect a "complex, unified sensibility, the imaginative design of which can be construed only by an awareness of the order and significance of her scriptural allusions. Thus, I have assumed throughout that, although the confession was given on the spur of the moment, each Bible reference and the total interconnection of such references were products of a carefully considered, deeply felt amalgamation of spirituality and intellect, although tracing those connections requires some hunches and speculation." Ditmore lamented writers' "disregarding" of her "biblical pietistic character" as "condescension." Michael G. Ditmore, "A Prophetess in Her Own Country: An Exegesis of Anne Hutchinson's 'Immediate Revelation,'" *William and Mary Quarterly* 57, no. 2 (April 2000): 350, 353, 356, 376, 381–82, 385.

10. John Wesley, "Notes on St. Paul's First Epistle to the Corinthians XII:8," *John Wesley's Notes on the Bible*, Wesley Center Online, wesley.nnu.edu/john-wesley/john-wesleys-notes-on-the-bible/notes-on-st-pauls-first-epistle-to-the-corinthians/.

11. *Confessions*, 10; Ditmore, "Prophetess in Her Own Country," 381–82.

12. Christine Leigh Heyrman, *Southern Cross: The Beginnings of the Bible Belt* (New York: Alfred A. Knopf, 1997), esp. 51; Laurie F. Maffly-Kipp, *Setting Down the Sacred Past: African-American Race Histories* (Cambridge, Mass.: Belknap Press of Harvard University Press, 2010), 75–76.

13. Richard S. Newman writes, "Divine retribution of unrepentant American masters was biblically ordained." Newman, *Freedom's Prophet*, 116; Richard Allen, *The Life Experience and Gospel Labours of the Rt. Rev. Richard Allen* (Philadelphia: Martin & Boden, 1833), 45–46; Daniel Coker, "A Dialogue Between a Virginian and an African Minister," in *Pamphlets of Protest: An Anthology of Early African-American Protest Literature, 1790–1860*, ed. Richard Newman, Patrick Rael, and Philip Lapsansky (Abingdon, U.K.: Routledge, 2001), 60, 62; Isaiah 1:4, 26:21.

14. Peter P. Hinks, ed., *David Walker's Appeal to the Coloured Citizens of the World* (University Park, Pa.: Pennsylvania State University Press, 2000), 42, 49, 51, 69.

15. See, especially, Vincent Brown, *Tacky's Revolt: The Story of an Atlantic Slave War* (Cambridge, Mass.: Belknap Press of Harvard University Press, 2020); Emilia Viotti da Costa, *Crowns of Glory, Tears of Blood: The Demerara Slave Rebellion of 1823* (New York: Oxford University Press, 1994); Marjoleine Kars, *Blood on the River: A Chronicle of Mutiny and Freedom on the Wild Coast* (New York: New Press, 2020); Manuel Barcia Paz, *The Great African Slave Revolt of 1825: Cuba and the Fight for Freedom in Matanzas* (Baton Rouge: Louisiana State University Press, 2012); Ada Ferrer, *Freedom's Mirror: Cuba and Haiti in the Age of Revolution* (New York: Cambridge University Press, 2014); Tom Zoellner, *Island on Fire: The Revolt That Ended Slavery in the British Empire* (Cambridge, Mass.: Harvard University Press, 2020).

16. Henry Irving Tragle, ed., *The Southampton Slave Revolt of 1831: A Compilation of Source Material* (Amherst: University of Massachusetts Press, 1971), 270.

1. HOLY WARRIORS AGAINST THE NEW EGYPT

1. Patrick H. Breen, *The Land Shall Be Deluged in Blood: A New History of the Nat Turner Revolt* (New York: Oxford University Press, 2015), 128, 244n56; Tragle, *Southampton Slave Revolt*, 189–90; F. Roy Johnson, *The Nat Turner Story: The History of the South's Most Important Slave Revolt, with New Material Provided by Black Tradition and White Tradition* (Murfreesboro, N.C.: Johnson, 1970), 97.

2. Johnson, *Nat Turner Story*, 160.

3. *Norfolk Herald*, Nov. 4, 1831, quoted in Greenberg, *Confessions of Nat Turner*, 87.

4. Thomas C. Parramore, *Southampton County, Virginia* (Charlottesville: University Press of Virginia in association with the Southampton County Historical Society, 1978), 6, 29–30.

5. Parramore, *Southampton County*, 6, 29–30.

6. Johnson, *Nat Turner Story*, 15.

7. David F. Allmendinger, *Nat Turner and the Rising in Southampton County* (Baltimore: Johns Hopkins University Press, 2014), 26–28; Daniel W. Crofts, *Old Southampton: Politics and Society in a Virginia County, 1834–1869* (Charlottesville: University of Virginia Press, 1992), 5–6.

8. *Heads of Families at the First Census of the United States Taken in the Year 1790: Records of the State Enumerations of Virginia, 1782 to 1785* (Washington, D.C.: GPO, 1908), 9.

9. Charles F. Irons, *The Origins of Proslavery Christianity: White and Black Evangelicals in Colonial and Antebellum Virginia* (Chapel Hill: University of North Carolina Press, 2008), 41–50; Claudia Stokes, *The Altar at Home: Sentimental Literature and Nineteenth-Century American Religion* (Philadelphia: University of Pennsylvania Press, 2014), 27.

10. Don Higginbotham, "The Federalized Militia Debate: A Neglected Aspect of Second Amendment Scholarship," *William and Mary Quarterly* 55, no. 1 (Jan. 1998): 41–42.

11. Michael A. McDonnell, *The Politics of War: Race, Class, and Conflict in Revolutionary Virginia* (Chapel Hill: University of North Carolina Press, 2007), 40–43.

12. McDonnell, *Politics of War*, 85; Robert L. Scribner, ed., *Revolutionary Virginia: The Road to Independence; A Documentary Record*, with Brent Tarter, 7 vols. (Charlottesville: Virginia Bicentennial Commission, 1975), 3:378, 381.

13. McDonnell, *Politics of War*, 65.

14. Scribner, *Revolutionary Virginia*, 4:334.

15. Cassandra Pybus, "Jefferson's Faulty Math," *William and Mary Quarterly*, 3rd ser., 72 (2005): 243–64.

16. Cassandra Pybus, "Mary Perth, Harry Washington, and Moses Wilkinson," in *Revolutionary Founders: Rebels, Radicals, and Reformers in the Making of the Nation*, ed. Alfred F. Young, Gary B. Nash, and Raphael Ray (New York: Alfred A. Knopf, 2011), 157; McDonnell, *Politics of War*, 152–53.

17. Pybus, "Perth, Washington, and Wilkinson," 156–57; Cassandra Pybus, *Epic Journeys of Freedom: Runaway Slaves of the American Revolution and Their Global Quest for Liberty* (Boston: Beacon Press, 2006), 15; L. Henry Whelchel, "'My Chains Fell Off': Heart Religion and the African American Methodist Tradition," in *"Heart Religion" in the Methodist Tradition and Related Movements*, ed. Richard B. Steele (Lanham, Md.: Scarecrow Press, 2001), 104.

18. David Patrick Geggus, "Slavery, War, and Revolution in the Greater Caribbean, 1789–1815," in *A Turbulent Time: The French Revolution and the Greater Caribbean*, ed. David Barry Gaspar and David Patrick Geggus (Bloomington: University of Indiana Press, 1997), 7–11, 46–50; Steven Hahn, *A Nation Under Our Feet: Black Political Struggles in the Rural South from Slavery to the Great Migration* (Cambridge, Mass.: Harvard University Press, 2003); Edward B. Rugemer, *The Problem of Emancipation: The Caribbean Roots of the American Civil War* (Baton Rouge: Louisiana State University Press, 2008).

19. Alan Taylor, *The Civil War of 1812: American Citizens, British Subjects, Irish Rebels, and Indian Allies* (New York: Alfred A. Knopf, 2010); Graham Russell Hodges, *The Black Loyalist Directory: African Americans in Exile After the American Revolution* (New York: Garland, 1996); McDonnell, *Politics of War*, 145.

20. Pybus, *Epic Journeys of Freedom*, 14–15.

21. McDonnell, *Politics of War*, 343–44.

22. McDonnell, *Politics of War*, 400.

23. Thomas Ludwell quoted in Pybus, "Perth, Washington, and Wilkinson," 157–58.

24. Elizabeth A. Fenn, *Pox Americana: The Great Smallpox Epidemic of 1775–82* (New York: Hill and Wang, 2001), 58–60.

25. Fenn, *Pox Americana*, 60.

26. Pybus, "Perth, Washington, and Wilkinson," 159–60.

27. McDonnell, *Politics of War*, 250–51.

28. Pybus, "Perth, Washington, and Wilkinson," 160–61.

29. Ruma Chopra, *Unnatural Rebellion: Loyalists in New York City During the Revolution* (Charlottesville: University of Virginia Press, 2011), 144.

30. Pybus, *Epic Journeys of Freedom*, 33–34.

31. Chopra, *Unnatural Rebellion*, 136–87; Pybus, *Epic Journeys of Freedom*, 57–74; Pybus, "Perth, Washington, and Wilkinson," 160–62.

32. Parramore, *Southampton County*, 36–38; John Crump Parker, "Old South Quay in Southampton County: Its Location, Early Ownership, and History," *Virginia Magazine of History and Biography* 83, no. 2 (April 1985): 160–72.

33. Pybus, "Perth, Washington, and Wilkinson," 161–62.
34. Pybus, "Perth, Washington, and Wilkinson," 162.
35. Ruma Chopra, ed., *Choosing Sides: Loyalists in Early America* (Lanham, Md.: Rowman & Littlefield, 2013), 198.
36. Chopra, *Choosing Sides*, 48, 168.
37. Pybus, "Perth, Washington, and Wilkinson," 163; Grant Gordon, *From Slavery to Freedom: The Life of David George, Pioneer Black Baptist Minister* (Hantsport, Nova Scotia: Lancelot Press, 1992), 91.
38. Charles Bruce Ferguson, ed., *Clarkson's Mission to America, 1791–1792* (Halifax: Public Archives of Nova Scotia, 1971), 108; Zachary Macaulay Journal, March 24, 1796, Huntington Library, cited in Gordon, *From Slavery to Freedom*, 143.
39. Boston King, *Memoirs of the Life of Boston King, a Black Preacher* (1798), in *Unchained Voices: An Anthology of Black Authors in the English-Speaking World of the Eighteenth Century*, ed. Vincent Carretta (Lexington: University of Kentucky Press, 1996), 356.
40. Gordon, *From Slavery to Freedom*, 91.
41. James W. St.G. Walker, *The Black Loyalists: The Search for a Promised Land in Nova Scotia and Sierra Leone, 1783–1870* (Toronto: University of Toronto Press, 1993), 78.
42. John Marrant, "Journal," in *"Face Zion Forward": First Writers of the Black Atlantic, 1785–1798*, ed. Joanna Brooks and John Saillant (Boston: Northeastern University Press, 2002), 124.
43. Marrant resorted to the passive voice to elide Wilkinson's part in allowing him to speak to his congregation. "I was permitted to preach in the Arminian meeting (because there was no other in the place) to a very large congregation." Marrant, "Journal," in Brooks and Saillant, *"Face Zion Forward,"* 104. Someone gave Marrant permission, however, almost certainly Wilkinson.
44. Acts 3:22; Joanna Brooks, "John Marrant's *Journal*: Providence and Prophecy in the Eighteenth-Century Black Atlantic," *North Star: A Journal of African American Religious History* 3, no. 1 (Fall 1999): 3.
45. On the power of Exodus in late colonial and early national Black intellectual thought, see Maffly-Kipp, *Setting Down the Sacred Past*, 163.
46. Alan Gilbert, *Black Patriots and Loyalists: Fighting for Emancipation in the War for Independence* (Chicago: University of Chicago Press, 2012), 220.
47. Cassandra Pybus, "'One Militant Saint': The Much Traveled Life of Mary Perth," *Journal of Colonialism and Colonial History* 9, no. 3 (Winter 2008); Ferguson, *Clarkson's Mission to America*, 61.
48. Gilbert, *Black Patriots and Loyalists*, 221.
49. Pybus, "'One Militant Saint.'"
50. Pybus, *Epic Journeys of Freedom*, 183.
51. Cato Perkins and Isaac Anderson, Oct. 26, 1793, in *Our Children Free and Happy: Letters from Black Settlers in Africa in the 1790s*, ed. Christopher Fyfe (Edinburgh: Edinburgh University Press, 1991), 37.
52. Catherine Hall, *Macaulay and Son: Architects of Imperial Britain* (New Haven, Conn.: Yale University Press, 2012), 25.
53. Hall, *Macaulay and Son*, 26.

54. Viscountess Knutsford, ed., *Life and Letters of Zachary Macaulay* (London: Edward Arnold, 1900), 60–61, 145.
55. Pybus, *Epic Journeys of Freedom*, 186.
56. Gordon, *From Slavery to Freedom*, 147.
57. Perkins and Anderson, Oct. 26, 1793, in Fyfe, *Our Children Free and Happy*, 37.
58. Perkins and Anderson, Oct. 26, 1793, in Fyfe, *Our Children Free and Happy*, 38.
59. Pybus, *Epic Journeys of Freedom*, 188–90.
60. Knutsford, *Life and Letters of Macaulay*, 132.
61. Sundry Settlers, April 16, 1795, in Fyfe, *Our Children Free and Happy*, 45.
62. Fyfe, *Our Children Free and Happy*, 74n.
63. Gordon, *From Slavery to Freedom*, 143.
64. Gordon, *From Slavery to Freedom*, 147, 148.
65. Hall, *Macaulay and Son*, 32. Macaulay saw antinomianism at the foundation of all the Black Loyalists' churches—the Methodists as well as the Huntingdonians and Baptists—although he recorded his views on the Baptists at greatest length when he took the matter up with David George, whom he regarded most highly among all the settlers' preachers in Sierra Leone. Gordon, *From Slavery to Freedom*, 142–43, 147–50.
66. Pybus, *Epic Journeys of Freedom*, 179.
67. Luke Jordan and others, Nov. 19, 1794, in Fyfe, *Our Children Free and Happy*, 43–45.
68. Pybus, *Epic Journeys of Freedom*, 178–79.
69. Hall, *Macaulay and Son*, 30; Knutsford, *Life and Letters of Macaulay*, 84.
70. Ellen Gibson Wilson, *The Loyal Blacks* (New York: Capricorn Books, 1976), 343; Pybus, "'One Militant Saint'"; Pybus, *Epic Journeys of Freedom*, 186, 189; Hall, *Macaulay and Son*, 31.
71. Gordon, *From Slavery to Freedom*, 147.
72. Macaulay quoted in Wilson, *Loyal Blacks*, 352.
73. Pybus, *Epic Journeys of Freedom*, 182.
74. Pybus, *Epic Journeys of Freedom*, 185. On the exodus doctrine of these leaders of the breakaway community, see James Sidbury, "'African' Settlers in the Founding of Freetown," in *Slavery, Abolition, and the Transition to Colonialism in Sierra Leone*, ed. Paul E. Lovejoy and Suzanne Schwarz (Trenton: Africa World Press, 2015), 134–35.
75. Pybus, *Epic Journeys of Freedom*, 195.
76. The elected offices of hundredors and tithingmen were provided for in the original plan of government drawn up by Granville Sharp and adopted by Governor Thomas Clarkson. Pybus, *Epic Journeys of Freedom*, 109, 171.
77. Pybus, *Epic Journeys of Freedom*, 198.
78. Walker, *Black Loyalists*, 234.
79. Anderson's note concerned not an attack on the government's headquarters but the terms under which his men and their families would be permitted to leave the camp. Pybus, *Epic Journeys of Freedom*, 199–202.
80. J. David Hacker reaches some slightly different numbers from the census based on efforts of later scholars to include uncounted enslaved people in territories. J. David Hacker, "From '20. and Odd' to 10 Million: The Growth of the Slave Population in the United States," *Slavery and Abolition* 41, no. 4 (2020): 840–55; *A Cen-*

tury of Population Growth from the First Census of the United States to the Twelfth, 1790–1900 (Washington, D.C.: Government Printing Office, 1909), 132–34.

81. Laurent Dubois, *Avengers of the New World: The Story of the Haitian Revolution* (Cambridge, Mass.: Harvard University Press, 2004); Jeremy D. Popkin, *You Are All Free: The Haitian Revolution and the Abolition of Slavery* (New York: Cambridge University Press, 2010); Brandon R. Byrd, *The Black Republic: African Americans and the Fate of Haiti* (Philadelphia: University of Pennsylvania Press, 2020); Matthew J. Clavin, *Toussaint Louverture and the American Civil War: The Promise and Peril of a Second Haitian Revolution* (Philadelphia: University of Pennsylvania Press, 2010).

82. Douglas R. Egerton, *Gabriel's Rebellion: The Virginia Slave Conspiracies of 1800 & 1802* (Chapel Hill: University of North Carolina Press, 1993), esp. x; James Sidbury, *Ploughshares into Swords: Race, Rebellion, and Identity in Gabriel's Virginia, 1730–1810* (New York: Cambridge University Press, 1997); Parramore, *Southampton County*, 65; Peter P. Hinks, *To Awaken My Afflicted Brethren: David Walker and the Problem of Antebellum Slave Resistance* (University Park: Pennsylvania State University Press, 1997), 58.

83. Parramore, *Southampton County*, 65; Arthur Scherr, "Governor James Monroe and the Southampton Slave Resistance of 1799," *Historian* 61, no. 3 (Spring 1999): 557–58.

84. William Sidney Drewry, *The Southampton Insurrection* (Washington, D.C.: Neal, 1900), 121; Scherr, "Monroe and the Southampton Slave Resistance," 578.

85. Parramore, *Southampton County*, 67; Patrick H. Breen, "Nat Turner's Revolt: Rebellion and Response in Southampton County, Virginia" (PhD diss., University of Georgia, 2005), 21.

86. Alan Taylor, *The Internal Enemy: Slavery and War in Virginia, 1772–1832* (New York: W. W. Norton, 2013), 113–14.

87. Taylor, *Internal Enemy*, 200–201.
88. Taylor, *Internal Enemy*, 162, 271–72.
89. Taylor, *Internal Enemy*, 271–73, 288–89.
90. Taylor, *Internal Enemy*, 2.
91. Taylor, *Internal Enemy*, 200–205.
92. Taylor, *Internal Enemy*, 246–47.
93. Taylor, *Internal Enemy*, 207–8.
94. Taylor, *Internal Enemy*, 281.
95. Taylor, *Internal Enemy*, 209.
96. Taylor, *Internal Enemy*, 3–4, 176, 211.
97. Taylor, *Internal Enemy*, 5.

2. NAT, METHODIST

1. Kenneth S. Greenberg, "Name, Face, Body," in *Nat Turner: A Slave Rebellion in History and Memory*, ed. Kenneth S. Greenberg (New York: Oxford University Press, 2003), 3–23.
2. *Confessions*, 8–9.
3. 2 Samuel 7:4–17, 12:1–13; 1 Kings 1:38; 1 Chronicles 17. I have utilized the King

James Version of the Bible for biblical quotations unless I am quoting someone else referring to a biblical quote, in which case I have reproduced their words.

4. John 1:37–51; "John 1 Bible Commentary," *John Wesley's Explanatory Notes*, www.christianity.com/bible/commentary.php?com=wes&b=43&c=1.

5. John 1:37–51; "John 1 Bible Commentary," *John Wesley's Explanatory Notes*, www.christianity.com/bible/commentary.php?com=wes&b=43&c=1.

6. Johnson, *Nat Turner Story*, 15.

7. *Confessions*, 8.

8. *Confessions*, 7–8. Christine Heyrman emphasized the power of young testifiers in early national Methodism. Heyrman, *Southern Cross*, 77–116.

9. As Tragle notes, the efforts to correct this myth are nearly as old as Nat, and Thomas Wentworth Higginson tried to counter this misapprehension, rooted in Nat's role in a well-known immersion, the tendency to treat all southern evangelicalism as Baptist, and the even stronger impulse to turn nineteenth-century Methodism into something more akin to its contemporary, quieter form. For portrayals of Nat as Baptist, see Drewry, *Southampton Insurrection*, 26; Tragle, *Southampton Slave Revolt*, 331. On the role of gender and emotion in early Methodism, see especially Phyllis Mack, *Heart Religion in the British Enlightenment: Gender and Emotion in Early Methodism* (Cambridge, U.K.: Cambridge University Press, 2008); Stokes, *Altar at Home*, 27.

10. Johnson, *Nat Turner Story*, 32–33, Drewry, *Southampton Insurrection*, 27; Allmendinger, *Nat Turner and the Rising*, 31–35.

11. *Confessions*, 7, 9.

12. Allmendinger, *Nat Turner and the Rising*, 28–35.

13. Allmendinger, *Nat Turner and the Rising*, 41–43.

14. Allmendinger, *Nat Turner and the Rising*, 41–43.

15. *Confessions*, 8.

16. Allmendinger, *Nat Turner and the Rising*, 37.

17. Allmendinger, *Nat Turner and the Rising*, 37–39.

18. Allmendinger, *Nat Turner and the Rising*, 37–39.

19. Johnson, *Nat Turner Story*, 49.

20. Johnson, *Nat Turner Story*, 50; Drewry, *Southampton Insurrection*, 28.

21. Advertisement, Freedom on the Move database, fotm.link/Tym3urKVdsPhPxR2RJ94S.

22. Allmendinger, *Nat Turner and the Rising*, 37; *Confessions*, 46.

23. Greenberg, *Confessions of Nat Turner*, 46.

24. Jonathan M. Yeager, ed., *Early Evangelicalism: A Reader* (New York: Oxford University Press, 2013), 354–55.

25. Greenberg, *Confessions of Nat Turner*, 44.

26. Ann Taves, *Fits, Trances, and Visions: Experiencing Religion and Explaining Experience from Wesley to James* (Princeton, N.J.: Princeton University Press, 1999), 88, 90, 103.

27. Parramore, *Southampton County*, 32, 47, 62.

28. Parramore, *Southampton County*, 47, 62.

29. Taves, *Fits, Trances, and Visions*, 90, 103; Minton Thrift, *Memoir of the Rev. Jesse Lee with Extracts from His Journals* (New York: N. Bangs and T. Mason, 1823),

94–98; Robert Paine, *Life and Times of William McKendree, Bishop of the Methodist Episcopal Church* (Nashville: M. E. Church, South, 1874), 34–35.

30. Parramore, *Southampton County*, 50.
31. Parramore, *Southampton County*, 61–62.
32. Hinks, *To Awaken My Afflicted Brethren*, 56.
33. Greenberg, *Confessions of Nat Turner*, 45.
34. T. M. Luhrmann, *When God Talks Back: Understanding the American Evangelical Relationship with God* (New York: Vintage, 2012), 545–47.
35. Dee E. Andrews, *The Methodists and Revolutionary America, 1760–1800: The Shaping of an Evangelical Culture* (Princeton, N.J.: Princeton University Press, 2000), 93.
36. Andrews, *Methodists and Revolutionary America*, 76–77.
37. Zilpha Elaw, "Memoirs of the Life, Religious Experience, Ministerial Travels, and Labors of Mrs. Zilpha Elaw," in *Sisters of the Spirit: Three Black Women's Autobiographies of the Nineteenth Century*, ed. William L. Andrews (Bloomington: Indiana University Press, 1986), 71.
38. Elaw, "Memoirs," 60.
39. Drewry, *Southampton Insurrection*, 27.
40. *Confessions*, 8.
41. *Confessions*, 8–9.
42. The implicit instruction in social practices that took place in Methodist churches goes by different names among scholars of reflexive sociology including Pierre Bourdieu's "practical mastery" and Anthony Giddens's "reflexive monitoring." Pierre Bourdieu, *Outline of a Theory of Practice* (New York: Cambridge University Press, 1977), 87–88; Anthony Giddens, *The Constitution of Society* (Berkeley: University of California Press, 1986), xxiv, 4; Taves, *Fits, Trances, and Visions*, 10.
43. Luhrmann, *When God Talks Back*, 647.
44. Louis F. Benson, *The English Hymn* (New York: Hodder & Stoughton, 1915), 239, 249–50, 253, 284; Stith Mead, preface to *A General Selection of the Newest and Most Admired Hymns and Spiritual Songs Now in Use* (Richmond: Seaton Grantland, 1807).
45. Franz Hildebrandt, Oliver Beckerlegge, and James Dale, preface to *A Collection of Hymns for the Use of the People Called Methodists*, ed. Franz Hildebrandt and Glenn Beckerlegge, vol. 7 of *The Works of John Wesley* (Nashville: Abingdon Press, 1989), xi.
46. Hymn 495:13–15, in Hildebrandt and Beckerlegge, *Collection of Hymns*, 684.
47. Robin A. Leaver, "Hymnody and the Reality of God," *Hymn* 44, no. 3 (July 1993): 17, 19; Stokes, *Altar at Home*, 75–77.
48. Taves, *Fits, Trances, and Visions*, 84.
49. Stokes, *Altar at Home*, esp. 47–51.
50. Greenberg, *Confessions of Nat Turner*, 45. Perhaps Nat's experiments were with gunpowder and other activities that absorbed him, according to notes later attributed to him, or perhaps the word "experiments" in this context referred to Nat's religious testing, as the word was used by some other awakened Christians of the era.

278 NOTES TO PAGES 39-45

51. Johnson, *Nat Turner Story*, 14–15.
52. Bill. T. Arnold, *Genesis* (New York: Cambridge University Press, 2008), 301; Richard L. Bushman, *Joseph Smith and the Beginnings of Mormonism* (Urbana: University of Illinois Press, 1984), 65.
53. Russell E. Richey, *Methodism in the American Forest* (New York: Oxford University Press, 2015), 37–43, 107–15, esp. 107, 111, 113; Elaw, "Memoirs," 60.
54. Andrews, *Methodists and Revolutionary America*, 78–79, 292–93n30.
55. Andrews, *Methodists and Revolutionary America*, 83.
56. Finney quoted in Luhrmann, *When God Talks Back*, 510–11.
57. Elaw, "Memoirs," 56.
58. Andrews, *Methodists and Revolutionary America*, 77.
59. William Apess, "An Indian's Looking-Glass for the White Man," in *On Our Own Ground: The Complete Writings of William Apess, a Pequot*, ed. Barry O'Connell (Amherst: University of Massachusetts Press, 1992), 155, 158, 159, 161.
60. Michael P. Johnson, "Denmark Vesey's Church," *Journal of Southern History* 86, no. 4 (Nov. 2020): 805–48; Newman, *Freedom's Prophet*, esp. 191–94; Peter P. Hinks, ed., *David Walker's Appeal to the Coloured Citizens of the World* (State College: Pennsylvania State University, 2000), 20–21; Mia Bay, *The White Image in the Black Mind: African-American Ideas About White People, 1830–1925* (New York: Oxford University Press, 2000), 7–9, 13–74.
61. Tragle, *Southampton Slave Revolt*, 15.
62. Breen, *Land Shall Be Deluged in Blood*, 155.
63. Irons, *Origins of Proslavery Christianity*, 53.
64. Breen, *Land Shall Be Deluged in Blood*, 155–57; Parramore, *Southampton County*, 62.
65. Cynthia Lynn Lyerly, *Methodism and the Southern Mind, 1770–1810* (New York: Oxford University Press, 1998), 122.
66. David Hempton, *The Religion of the People: Methodism and Popular Religion, c. 1750–1900* (New York: Routledge, 1996), 80; *Works of John Wesley*, 11:71–79.
67. Hempton, *Religion of the People*, 78–82; Jason E. Vickers, *Wesley: A Guide for the Perplexed* (New York: T & T Clark, 2009), 26–27; Richard P. Heitzenrater, *The Elusive Mr. Wesley* (Nashville: Abingdon Press, 1984), 2:116–27.
68. James P. Byrd, *Sacred Scripture, Sacred War: The Bible and the American Revolution* (New York: Oxford University Press, 2013).
69. Eva Sheppard Wolf, *Race and Liberty in the New Nation* (Baton Rouge: Louisiana State University Press, 2006), 10, 89–91; Irons, *Origins of Proslavery Christianity*, 73–74.
70. Wolf, *Race and Liberty in the New Nation*, 92–93.
71. Wolf, *Race and Liberty in the New Nation*, 89–95.
72. Lyerly, *Methodism and the Southern Mind*, 5, 20–23. Garrettson's activities are placed in the Chesapeake. Russell E. Richey, *Early American Methodism* (Bloomington: Indiana University Press, 1991), 5–6, 25–27; William Henry Williams, *The Garden of American Methodism: The Delmarva Peninsula* (Wilmington, Del.: Scholarly Resources, 1984), 30–35.
73. Robert Drew Simpson, ed., *American Methodist Pioneer: The Life and Journal of the Rev. Freeborn Garrettson, 1752–1827; Social and Religious Life in the U.S.*

During the Revolutionary and Federal Periods (Rutland, Vt.: Academy Books, 1984), 48–49, 146–47, 189, 241–42.

74. Wolf, *Race and Liberty in the New Nation*, 91.
75. Frederick C. Gill, ed., *Selected Letters of John Wesley* (London: Epworth Press, 1956), 236–37.
76. Lyerly, *Methodism and the Southern Mind*, 55.
77. Wolf, *Race and Liberty in the New Nation*, 56, 89.
78. Irons, *Origins of Proslavery Christianity*, 75.
79. Andrews, *Methodists and Revolutionary America*, 127.
80. Andrews, *Methodists and Revolutionary America*, 127.
81. Lyerly, *Methodism and the Southern Mind*, 128–35.
82. Greenberg, *Confessions of Nat Turner*, 44–45.
83. Andrews, *Methodists and Revolutionary America*, 124.
84. Peter Joseph Albert, "The Protean Institution: The Geography, Economy, and Ideology of Slavery in Post-Revolutionary Virginia" (PhD diss., University of Virginia, 1976), 293, 291, graph 7.3; Theodore Stoddard Babcock, "Manumission in Virginia, 1782–1806" (master's thesis, University of Virginia, 1974), 21; Alison Goodyear Freehling, *Drift Toward Dissolution: The Virginia Slavery Debate of 1831–1832* (Baton Rouge: Louisiana State University Press, 1982), 24.
85. Wolf, *Race and Liberty in the New Nation*, 59–60, 77, 79–80, 83. Wolf identified the religious affiliation of sixty-two manumitters in eight counties in four different regions of Virginia between 1775 and 1806. More than one-half, thirty-three of sixty-two, were Methodists. Calculated from ibid., 239–41, appendix A: Religion of Manumitters in Deeds of Manumission Whose Religious Affiliation Could Be Identified.
86. A total of 365 slaves were manumitted by deed in Isle of Wight and 216 in Surry in 1782–1806. These counties had the first- and second-highest number of manumissions of sixteen counties in all six regions of Virginia. The two counties combined account for more than one-fourth (571 of 2,085, or 27 percent) of slaves manumitted by deed in all sixteen counties. Calculated from Wolf, *Race and Liberty in the New Nation*, 282. These figures do not include an additional unknown number of slaves manumitted by wills (either recorded or executed during these years). However, wills at least provided for the manumission of an additional one-third of the slaves manumitted by deed in the sixteen total counties. Nearly one out of five documents of manumission (183 of 963, or 19 percent) were wills (versus 780 of 963, or 81 percent, deeds), and the wills accounted for nearly one-fourth (672 of 2,757, or 24 percent) of all slaves manumitted during these years. Whereas nearly all deeds provided for immediate manumission, wills typically provided for manumission in the future. It is unknown how many of the manumissions provided for in wills were executed. Albert, "Protean Institution," 286, 287, table 7.4.
87. Albert, "Protean Institution," 306n26.
88. Donald G. Mathews, *Slavery and Methodism: A Chapter in American Morality, 1780–1845* (Princeton, N.J.: Princeton University Press, 1965), 19.
89. Albert, "Protean Institution," 189.
90. Mathews, *Slavery and Methodism*, 300–303.
91. Wolf, *Race and Liberty in the New Nation*, 73.

92. Albert, "Protean Institution," 276. For other Virginia examples of manumitters' influence on family members, see Wolf, *Race and Liberty in the New Nation*, 59.

93. Albert, "Protean Institution," 275.

94. Albert, "Protean Institution," 276.

95. Irons, *Origins of Proslavery Christianity*, 64–65.

96. Albert, "Protean Institution," 244–45.

97. Wolf, *Race and Liberty in the New Nation*, 125, 131.

98. Wolf, *Race and Liberty in the New Nation*, 135; John H. Russell, *The Free Negro in Virginia* (Baltimore: Johns Hopkins University Press, 1913), 156.

99. The 1819 amendment to the manumission law also raised the requirements for approval of a petition to remain in Virginia, which had to gain the unanimous support of country magistrates and the commonwealth attorney. Petitioners who prevailed were required to remain in their home county. Wolf, *Race and Liberty in the New Nation*, 134–35.

100. Greenberg, *Confessions of Nat Turner*, 44–45.

101. Allmendinger, *Nat Turner and the Rising*, 28–31.

102. Allmendinger, *Nat Turner and the Rising*, 28–31, 50–57.

103. Allmendinger, *Nat Turner and the Rising*, 31–36.

104. Allmendinger, *Nat Turner and the Rising*, 37, 44.

105. Allmendinger, *Nat Turner and the Rising*, 44–49.

106. Allmendinger, *Nat Turner and the Rising*, 49; Drewry, *Southampton Insurrection*, 28.

107. Allmendinger, *Nat Turner and the Rising*, 49–53.

108. Allmendinger, *Nat Turner and the Rising*, 50–57.

109. Greenberg, *Confessions of Nat Turner*, 45.

110. Wolf, *Race and Liberty in the New Nation*, 34.

111. On Nat's age and the death of Samuel Turner, see Allmendinger, *Nat Turner and the Rising*, 15.

112. Allmendinger, *Nat Turner and the Rising*, 62–63.

113. Allmendinger, *Nat Turner and the Rising*, 59–60, 128–35.

114. Sally Moore, who inherited Nat Turner with her husband, Thomas Moore, was the younger sister of Samuel Turner's first wife. Allmendinger, *Nat Turner and the Rising*, 14, 25–26, 62–63.

115. Crofts, *Old Southampton*, 81–89.

116. Johnson, *Nat Turner Story*, 21.

117. Johnson, *Nat Turner Story*, 14–15.

118. Allmendinger, *Nat Turner and the Rising*, 64–66.

119. Allmendinger, *Nat Turner and the Rising*, 64–66.

120. For a good overview of positions, see Breen, *Land Shall Be Deluged in Blood*, 194–95n9; Davis, *Nat Turner Before the Bar of Judgment*, 173, 175; Vanessa M. Holden, *Surviving Southampton: African American Women and Resistance in Nat Turner's Community* (Champaign: University of Illinois Press, 2021), 122–23.

121. Allmendinger, *Nat Turner and the Rising*, 70–72.

122. Greenberg, *Confessions of Nat Turner*, 46.

123. Irons, *Origins of Proslavery Christianity*, 105, 133.

124. William Spottswood White, *The African Preacher* (Philadelphia: Presbyterian Board of Publication, 1849), 7.

125. White, *African Preacher*, 9–14.
126. White, *African Preacher*, 22, 76, 80.
127. White, *African Preacher*, 19, 23, 47.
128. White, *African Preacher*, 43–44.
129. White, *African Preacher*, 55, 59, 16, 19, 24, 29, 81, 109.
130. White, *African Preacher*, 81.
131. The material in this paragraph is drawn from South Quay Baptist Church Minute Book, 1827–1899, 53–58, Manuscript Collections, Library of Virginia. For figures on offenses in Baptist church discipline in Southampton, Isle of Wight, and Sussex Counties, see Randolph Ferguson Scully, *Religion and the Making of Nat Turner's Virginia: Baptist Community and Conflict, 1740–1840* (Charlottesville: University of Virginia Press, 2008), 157–58, tables 8, 9. For the figures on charges of drunkenness in Virginia, North Carolina, South Carolina, and Georgia, see Sylvia R. Frey and Betty Wood, *Come Shouting to Zion: African American Protestantism in the American South and British Caribbean to 1830* (Chapel Hill: University of North Carolina Press, 1998), 189, 246n20.
132. White, *African Preacher*, 60–61.
133. George White, "A Brief Account of the Life, Experience, Travels, and Gospel Labours of George White, an African," in *Black Itinerants of the Gospel: The Narratives of John Jea and George White*, ed. Graham Russell Hodges (Madison, Wis.: Madison House, 1993), 6–7, 13, 53, 64–67, 71. White dated his conversion to 1791, but Hodges notes that the correct year was 1795.
134. Greenberg, *Confessions of Nat Turner*, 45.
135. Patrick D. Miller, *They Cried to the Lord: The Form and Theology of Biblical Prayer* (Minneapolis: Fortress Press, 1994), 21–22.
136. Psalms 35:1–3, 13–14.

3. NAT, FEARFUL PROPHET

1. The verse that Nat prayed on was from Matthew (6:33), though the King James Version refers to the "kingdom of God" not of "heaven." Greenberg, *Confessions of Nat Turner*, 45–46. On hearing God, see Leigh Eric Schmidt, *Hearing Things: Religion, Illusion, and the American Enlightenment* (Cambridge, Mass.: Harvard University Press, 2000).
2. Greenberg, *Confessions of Nat Turner*, 45–46.
3. Susan Juster, *Doomsayers: Anglo-American Prophecy in the Age of Revolution* (Philadelphia: University of Pennsylvania Press, 2010), 3–4.
4. Paul E. Johnson and Sean Wilentz, *The Kingdom of Matthias* (New York: Oxford University Press, 1994), 6.
5. Erich Auerbach, *Scenes from the Drama of European Literature* (New York: Meridian Books, 1959), 28–49.
6. Paul quoted from the Greek in Auerbach, *Scenes from the Drama of European Literature*, 49.
7. Augustine quoted in Auerbach, *Scenes from the Drama of European Literature*, 41.
8. Wesley, "Notes on St. Paul's First Epistle to the Corinthians XII:8."
9. John Winthrop quoted from his address on the *Arbella* in Theophus Harold Smith, *Conjuring Culture: Biblical Formations of Black America* (New York: Ox-

ford University Press, 1994), 102; Sacvan Bercovitch, "Typology in Puritan New England: The Williams-Cotton Controversy Reassessed," *American Quarterly* 19, no. 2 (1967): 175–76; Reiner Smolinski, "Israel Redivivus: The Eschatological Limits of Puritan Typology in New England," *New England Quarterly* 63, no. 3 (1990): 361, quotations from 390; Abram C. Van Engen, *City on a Hill: A History of American Exceptionalism* (New Haven, Conn.: Yale University Press, 2020).

10. Bercovitch, "Typology in Puritan New England," 168, 174–77, 182; Mason I. Lowance, "Typology and the New England Way: Cotton Mather and the Exegesis of Biblical Types," *Early American Literature* 4, no. 1 (1969): 15–16.

11. Lowance, "Typology and the New England Way," 15–37; Smolinski, "Israel Redivivus," 374–80, 388–89.

12. Werner Sollors, *Beyond Ethnicity: Consent and Descent in American Culture* (New York: Oxford University Press, 1986), 43–47.

13. Esau McCaulley, *Reading While Black: African American Biblical Interpretation as an Exercise in Hope* (Downers Grove, Ill.: InterVarsity Press, 2020), 138–63; Albert J. Raboteau, *Slave Religion: The "Invisible Institution" in the American South* (New York: Oxford University Press, 1980); Milton C. Sernett, *Black Religion and American Evangelicalism: White Protestants, Plantation Missions, and the Flowering of Negro Christianity, 1787–1865* (Metuchen, N.J.: Scarecrow Press, 1975).

14. Hinks, *Walker's Appeal*, 37.

15. Hinks, *Walker's Appeal*, 42, 51, 69.

16. Bushman, *Joseph Smith*, 39–42.

17. Johnson and Wilentz, *Kingdom of Matthias*, 37–38.

18. Elaw, "Memoirs," 72.

19. Elaw, "Memoirs," 66–67, 81–82, 125.

20. Elaw, "Memoirs," 90.

21. Elaw, "Memoirs," 89, 135.

22. Jarena Lee, "The Life and Religious Experience of Jarena Lee," in Andrews, *Sisters of the Spirit*, 34, 37.

23. Lee, "Life and Religious Experience," 35.

24. John Marrant, "A Funeral Sermon Preached by the Desire of the Deceased, John Lock," in Brooks and Saillant, *"Face Zion Forward,"* 168; John Saillant, "'Wipe Away All Tears from Their Eyes': John Marrant's Theology in the Black Atlantic, 1785–1808," *Journal of Millennial Studies* 1, no. 2 (Winter 1999).

25. Greenberg, *Confessions of Nat Turner*, 46; Allmendinger, *Nat Turner and the Rising*, 15.

26. Greenberg, *Confessions of Nat Turner*, 46; Allmendinger, *Nat Turner and the Rising*, 15.

27. Jeremiah 1:5; Jack R. Lundbom, *The Hebrew Prophets: An Introduction* (Minneapolis: Fortress Press, 2010), 9.

28. Greenberg, *Confessions of Nat Turner*, 46.

29. The Black prophetic tradition literature is vast and includes Cornel West, *Black Prophetic Fire* (Boston: Beacon Press, 2014); Andre E. Johnson, *No Future in This Country: The Prophetic Pessimism of Bishop Henry McNeal Turner* (Jackson: University Press of Mississippi, 2020); Newman, *Freedom's Prophet*; Blight, *Frederick Douglass*.

30. Greenberg, *Confessions of Nat Turner*, 46.

31. Allmendinger, *Nat Turner and the Rising*, 62; Greenberg, "Name, Face, Body," 14.

32. Allmendinger, *Nat Turner and the Rising*, 64–66.

33. Allmendinger, *Nat Turner and the Rising*, 62–63, 68–70, 73–75.

34. Stephanie M. H. Camp, *Closer to Freedom: Enslaved Women and Everyday Resistance in the Plantation South* (Chapel Hill: University of North Carolina Press, 2004).

35. Camp, *Closer to Freedom*.

36. Johnson, *Nat Turner Story*, 60–61.

37. *Confessions*, 9.

38. Matthew 16:23; Craig A. Evans, *Matthew* (New York: Cambridge University Press, 2012), 354; Warren Carter, *Matthew and the Margins: A Sociopolitical and Religious Reading* (Maryknoll, N.Y.: Orbis Books, 2000), 403–5.

39. Greenberg, *Confessions of Nat Turner*, 46; Luke 12:47–48.

40. Jean McMahon Humez, ed., *Gifts of Power: The Writings of Rebecca Jackson, Black Visionary, Shaker Eldress* (Amherst: University of Massachusetts Press, 1981), 84. For another instance of Jackson's belief that God was punishing her for disobedience, see ibid., 110–11.

41. Elaw, "Memoirs," 77–78.

42. Elaw, "Memoirs," 87–88.

43. Irons, *Origins of Proslavery Christianity*.

44. Breen, *Land Shall Be Deluged in Blood*, 20–21; Lunsford Lane, *Narrative of Lunsford Lane, Formerly of Raleigh, N.C., Embracing an Account of His Early Life, the Redemption by Purchase of Himself and Family from Slavery, and His Banishment from the Place of His Birth for the Crime of Wearing a Colored Skin* (Boston: J. G. Torrey, 1842), 21, docsouth.unc.edu/neh/lanelunsford/lane.html.

45. Allen, *Life Experience and Gospel Labours*, 80, 84.

46. *Confessions*, 9.

47. *Confessions*, 10. Quotations appear in the text as they appear in the original without correction of errors or irregularities in spelling, punctuation, or usage.

48. Exodus 14:31–15:25; Sarah Lebhar Hall, *Conquering Character: The Characterization of Joshua in Joshua 1–11* (New York: T & T Clark, 2010), 117–18; Thomas B. Dozeman, *Joshua 1–12: A New Translation with Introduction and Commentary* (New Haven, Conn.: Yale University Press, 2015), 1–2.

49. Marrant, "Funeral Sermon," 168.

50. Elaw, "Memoirs," 83, 241n18, citing Genesis 37:1–5; 2 Timothy 4:16; Matthew 3:57.

51. John Moulton, ed., *The Journal and Major Essays of John Woolman* (New York: Oxford University Press, 1971), 219.

52. Exodus 15:25; 16:35–17:4.

53. Elaw, "Memoirs," 56–57.

54. Elaw, "Memoirs," 55–56, 135.

55. Elaw, "Memoirs," 77.

56. Elaw, "Memoirs," 55.

57. *Confessions*, 10.

58. We know that Gray had learned about these spirits weeks before meeting Nat; Allmendinger, *Nat Turner and the Rising*, 18; Greenberg, *Confessions of Nat Turner*, 46. Wayne Durrill suggests that these 1825 visions might have been a conflation of 1827–1828 climactic events: the September 1827 visibility of the aurora borealis

in the Norfolk area, the sunspots visible between 1824 and 1827 in parts of Virginia and the East Coast; and the earthquake of March 9, 1828, that could have produced a sound like thunder. Durrill, "Nat Turner and Signs of the Apocalypse," in *Varieties of Southern Religious History: Essays in Honor of Donald G. Matthews,* ed. Regina D. Sullivan (Columbia: University of South Carolina Press, 2015), 78–80. Durrill's labors to find exact climactic counterparts to the vision are deeply honorable pieces of historical research, yet they also preclude the possibility that Nat actually saw visions, not simply interpreted things seen and felt by many.

59. Revelation 4:1–5. See also Revelation 8:5, 16:18.

60. Revelation 14:19–20. See also Revelation 16:4. Mead, *Hymns and Spiritual Songs,* 44.

61. Luke 3:5.

62. John Henry Jowett, *The Whole Armour of God* (New York: Fleming H. Revell, 1916), 163–64.

63. Byrd, *Sacred Scripture, Sacred War,* esp. 170, table 8.1, appendix.

64. Miles Ogborn, *Global Lives: Britain and the World, 1550–1800* (New York: Cambridge University Press, 2008), timeline facing 1.

65. Byrd, *Sacred Scripture, Sacred War,* 5, 73–76, 79–80, 92–93; George William Pilcher, *Samuel Davies: Apostle of Dissent in Colonial Virginia* (Knoxville: University of Tennessee Press, 1971), 86, 88–89, 93.

66. Byrd, *Sacred Scripture, Sacred War,* 45–47.

67. Greenberg, *Confessions of Nat Turner,* 47–48.

68. Byrd, *Sacred Scripture, Sacred War,* 152.

69. Revelation 19:11, 15, 16, 19; Byrd, *Sacred Scripture, Sacred War,* 156–60.

70. Samuel Davies, "The Mediatorial Kingdom and Glories of Jesus Christ, a Sermon on John XVIII," quoted in Byrd, *Sacred Scripture, Sacred War,* 230–31n37.

71. Revelation 12:1–9; Greenberg, *Confessions of Nat Turner,* 46, 47–48.

72. Jeffrey Williams, *Religion and Violence in Early Methodism: Taking the Kingdom by Force* (Bloomington: Indiana University Press, 2010); Mead, *Hymns and Spiritual Songs,* 48; Richard Allen, *A Collection of Hymns and Spiritual Songs: From Various Authors* (Philadelphia: T. L. Plowman, 1801), xxv, 21, 94–95.

73. Lyerly, *Methodism and the Southern Mind,* 40; Williams, *Religion and Violence in Early Methodism,* 71; Andrews, *Methodists and Revolutionary America,* 118, 216–17; Dennis Alonzo Watters, *First American Itinerant of Methodism, William Watters* (Cincinnati: Curts & Jennings, 1898), 154–55; Heyrman, *Southern Cross,* 227–38, 241–45.

74. White, "Brief Account," 6, 13, 53, 63.

75. Lee, "Life and Religious Experience," 34.

76. Elaw, "Memoirs," 76, 79, 81.

77. Williams, *Religion and Violence in Early Methodism,* 1–2, 72, 134–43; Allen, *Collection of Hymns and Spiritual Songs,* xxv, 21, 95–96, 121–23.

78. Allen, *Collection of Hymns and Spiritual Songs,* 40, 49, 111–13.

79. Hinks, *Walker's Appeal,* 5, 14, 22, 49.

80. On Vesey and Zechariah 14:2–3, see below.

81. Zechariah 14:1–2, quoted in *Denmark Vesey: The Slave Conspiracy of 1822,* ed. Robert S. Starobin (Englewood Cliffs, N.J.: Prentice-Hall, 1970), 99–100. Michael P. Johnson has cast a skeptical eye on the conspiracy record, especially

the coerced testimony of charged rebels, and rightly guards against taking the testimony at face value. Nevertheless, there remains utility in reading the testimony for evidence of enslaved and free Black people's social and religious worlds. Therefore, I acknowledge the questions Johnson raises but do not discard the testimony. Johnson cast doubts on Vesey's relationship to the AME church in Charleston and emphasized his relationship to Presbyterians in "Denmark Vesey's Church." More generally, see Douglas Egerton, *He Shall Go Out Free: The Lives of Denmark Vesey* (Madison, Wis.: Madison House, 1999; rev. ed., Lanham, Md.: Rowman & Littlefield, 2004); Johnson, "Denmark Vesey and His Co-conspirators," *William and Mary Quarterly* 58, no. 4 (2001): 915–76; Robert L. Paquette, "From Rebellion to Revisionism: The Continuing Debate About the Denmark Vesey Affair," *Journal of the Historical Society* 4, no. 3 (2004): 291–334.

82. Hinks, *To Awaken My Afflicted Brethren*, 44.
83. Hinks, *To Awaken My Afflicted Brethren*, 22–62.
84. Catherine Brekus, *Strangers and Pilgrims: Female Preaching in America, 1740–1845* (Chapel Hill: University of North Carolina Press, 1998), 186, 190–91; Andrews, introduction to *Sisters of the Spirit*, 4–5; Elaw, "Memoirs," 86.
85. Lundbom, *Hebrew Prophets*, 124–27.
86. Amos 7:15, quoted in Lundbom, *Hebrew Prophets*, 11, 16.
87. Moses questioned God eight times in all. Carol L. Meyers, *Exodus* (New York: Cambridge University Press, 2005), 55; Exodus 3:12.
88. Exodus 5:1–5, 22.
89. Ferrer, *Freedom's Mirror*.
90. Elaw, "Memoirs," 86–87.
91. Da Costa, *Crowns of Glory, Tears of Blood*.
92. Arnold, *Genesis*, 153, 157–60.
93. Genesis 12:1–2; Arnold, *Genesis*, 130–31, 130n14. See John A. Emerton, "The Origin of the Promises to the Patriarchs in the Older Sources of the Book of Genesis," *Vetus Testamentum* 32 (1982): 14–32; Paul R. Williamson, *Abraham, Israel, and the Nations: The Patriarchal Development in Genesis* (Sheffield, U.K.: Sheffield Academic Press, 2000).
94. Genesis 17:8; Arnold, *Genesis*, 141.
95. Arnold, *Genesis*, 151–52; Genesis 15:1–6.
96. Genesis 15:1; Arnold, *Genesis*, 155–56.
97. Exodus 6:3.
98. Lee, "Life and Religious Experience," 12.
99. William G. Dever, *Who Were the Early Israelites, and Where Did They Come From?* (Grand Rapids, Mich.: William B. Eerdmans, 2003), 15–21.
100. Dozeman, *Joshua 1–12*, 329–30.
101. Leviticus 25:9–10.
102. Leviticus 25:41–42.
103. Jeremiah 15:15–18; 17:18.
104. Simon Sebag Montefiore, *Jerusalem: The Biography* (New York: Alfred A. Knopf, 2011), 95; J. Maxwell Miller and John H. Hayes, *A History of Ancient Israel and Judah* (Philadelphia: Westminster Press, 1986), 342–44, 351–53.
105. Ezekiel 22:1–2, 7–8.
106. Ezekiel 22:3, 11.

107. Ezekiel 22:27.
108. Isaiah 1:22, 24. Smelting, of course, entails fire. Walter Brueggemann, *Isaiah* (Louisville, Ky.: Westminster John Knox Press, 1998), 1–39, 22.
109. Ezekiel 15:6; Jeremiah 34:2, 22; Keith W. Carley, *The Book of the Prophet Ezekiel* (New York: Cambridge University Press, 1974), 92–93.
110. Ezekiel 14:21. Jeremiah 14:12, 16; 15:2–4; 18:11, 21; 21:6–8; 32:36; 34:17; 38:2–3; Carley, *Book of the Prophet Ezekiel*, 81–83.
111. Jeremiah 4:19. Vengeance was a theme in Jeremiah's laments (18:23).
112. Jeremiah 10:19.
113. Deuteronomy 32:41, 42; Richard D. Nelson, *Deuteronomy: A Commentary* (Louisville, Ky.: Westminster John Knox Press, 2002), 377–78.
114. Hinks, *Walker's Appeal*, 14.
115. Hinks, *Walker's Appeal*, 23–24.
116. Hinks, *Walker's Appeal*, 30.

4. NAT, WARRIOR

1. Matthew 24; Mark 13:24–31; Luke 21:1–38; Revelation 8:6–9, 21; 15:3–4; 16:1–4; Exodus 7–11, 15:3; cited in P. W. L. Walker, *Jesus and the Holy City: New Testament Perspectives on Jerusalem* (Grand Rapids: W. B. Eerdmans, 1996), 239–40.
2. *Confessions*, 10–11.
3. Allmendinger, *Nat Turner and the Rising*, 20, 68–70, 237.
4. Richmond *Constitutional Whig*, Sept. 26, 1831, quoted in Greenberg, *Confessions of Nat Turner*, 79.
5. Richmond *Constitutional Whig*, Sept. 26, 1831, quoted in Greenberg, *Confessions of Nat Turner*, 78–79.
6. *Norfolk Herald*, Nov. 4, 1831, quoted in Greenberg, *Confessions of Nat Turner*, 87.
7. Elaine H. Pagels, *Revelations: Visions, Prophecy, and Politics in the Book of Revelation* (New York: Viking, 2012), 1.
8. On the theme of war in Revelation, see Pagels, *Revelations*, 4–7, 50–53.
9. Pagels, *Revelations*, esp. 16–17, 69; Eugene V. Gallagher, "Millennialism, Scripture, and Tradition," in *The Oxford Handbook of Millennialism*, ed. Catherine Wessinger (New York: Oxford University Press, 2011), 141.
10. Craig R. Koester, *Revelation: A New Translation with Introduction and Commentary* (New Haven, Conn.: Yale University Press, 2014), 264, 363, 367, citing Ezekiel 3:27, 4:1–14; Isaiah 1:10; Jeremiah 2:4; Revelation 2:7.
11. Mead, *Hymns and Spiritual Songs*, 13.
12. Allen, *Collection of Hymns and Spiritual Songs*, 51.
13. John J. Collins, *The Apocalyptic Imagination: An Introduction to Jewish Apocalyptic Literature* (New York: Crossroad, 1984), 273–74; Pagels, *Revelations*, 16–17; Revelation 1:12–17.
14. Ezekiel 1:5–10; Revelation 4:6–8, 10–11, 5:8–10, 14:1–3, 15:2–4.
15. Revelation 12:11, 16:4–6.
16. Revelation 8:7, 16:3, 17:5–6, 19:13.
17. Allen, *Collection of Hymns and Spiritual Songs*, Hymn 7, 52, 60, 92, 95; Mead, *Hymns and Spiritual Songs*, 12.
18. Koester, *Revelation*, 356–57, 474.

19. *Elizabeth, a Colored Minister of the Gospel Born in Slavery* (Philadelphia: Tract Association of Friends, 1889), 3–5, docsouth.unc.edu/neh/eliza2/menu.html; Revelation 4:1, 7:9, 10:1; Koester, *Revelation*, 359.

20. On the cycles in John's visions, see Koester, *Revelation*, esp. 30, 36, 39, 40–42, 71–72, 75, 116, 161.

21. On John's sparse interpretations of his visions, in contrast to Daniel, see Judith Kovacs and Christopher Rowland, *Revelation: The Apocalypse to Jesus Christ* (Malden, Mass.: Blackwell, 2004), 8.

22. Revelation 2:7.

23. Kovacs and Rowland, *Revelation*, 4–5, 11–12; Pagels, *Revelations*, 74.

24. Revelation 22:6.

25. Revelation 17:11–14.

26. Revelation 11:15.

27. Abraham J. Herschel, *The Prophets* (New York: Jewish Publication Society, 1962), 1, chaps. 2–8.

28. Revelation 21:12, 24–26; 22:2; Koester, *Revelation*, 419.

29. Revelation 22:3–5.

30. Revelation 22:4.

31. Revelation 21:9.

32. Revelation 21:3; *A General Collection of Hymns and Spiritual Songs, for Camp Meetings and Revivals*, 3rd ed. (Derby, England: G. Wilkins, 1816), 65–66.

33. Pagels, *Revelations*, 77–79.

34. Greenberg, *Confessions of Nat Turner*, 47.

35. Matthew 5:48.

36. 2 Corinthians 7:1.

37. E. Brooks Holifield, *Theology in America: Christian Thought from the Age of the Puritans to the Civil War* (New Haven, Conn.: Yale University Press, 2003), 269–70; Lee, "Life and Religious Experience," 27, 29, 33–34; Sojourner Truth quoted in Margaret Washington, *Sojourner Truth's America* (Champaign: University of Illinois Press, 2009), 73–78, 85.

38. Humez, *Gifts of Power*, 21–22, 88n30.

39. Greenberg, *Confessions of Nat Turner*, 47.

40. Matthew 28:19–20; Walker, *Jesus and the Holy City*, 30–31, 40.

41. Revelation 21:3; Koester, *Revelation*, 797–98n21.

42. Deuteronomy 20:1.

43. Joshua 1:5.

44. Jeremiah 1:8, 18–19.

45. Elaw, "Memoirs," 128; Margaret Washington, ed., *Narrative of Sojourner Truth* (New York: Vintage Books, 1993), 93–97; Washington, *Sojourner Truth's America*, 73–78, 85, 165–67.

46. Elijah H. Burritt, *Atlas Designed to Illustrate the Geography of the Heavens* (1832; repr., New York: Francis J. Huntington and Mason Brothers, 1850); *Confessions*, 10.

47. Luke 24:15–16, 36–37, 39, 50.

48. Revelation 1:12–14, 20; Koester, *Revelation*, 245–46, 250.

49. Greenberg, *Confessions of Nat Turner*, 47. Durrill ties this to the occasional phenomenon of "blood rain" caused at times by the presence of red dust. Durrill, "Nat Turner and Signs of the Apocalypse," 81.

50. Revelation 6:12–13, 8:7–9; Mead, *Hymns and Spiritual Songs*, 35, 39; Richard Allen's hymn "See! How the Nations Rage Together" is reprinted in ibid., 5–6, and in Allen, *Collection of Hymns and Spiritual Songs*, 104; Jon Michael Spencer, *Black Hymnody: A Hymnological History of the African-American Church* (Knoxville: University of Tennessee Press, 1992), 5–6. Durrill ties the figures to the aurora borealis sightings. Durrill, "Nat Turner and Signs of the Apocalypse," 81.

51. Richmond *Constitutional Whig*, Sept. 26, 1831, quoted in Greenberg, *Confessions of Nat Turner*, 78–79.

52. Durrill, "Nat Turner and Signs of the Apocalypse"; Donald G. Mathews, *Religion in the Old South* (Chicago: University of Chicago Press, 1977), 223, 231; Johnson, *Nat Turner Story*, 64.

53. Richmond *Constitutional Whig*, Sept. 26, 1831, quoted in Greenberg, *Confessions of Nat Turner*, 78–79.

54. James Stevens Curl, *Egyptomania: The Egyptian Revival, a Recurring Theme in the History of Taste* (New York: Manchester University Press, 1994); Richard G. Carrott, *Egyptian Revival, 1808–1858* (Berkeley: University of California Press, 1978); John A. Wilson, *Signs and Wonders upon Pharaoh: A History of American Egyptology* (Chicago: University of Chicago Press, 1964), chaps. 1–2. On Joseph Smith and hieroglyphics, see John L. Brooke, *The Refiner's Fire: The Making of Mormon Cosmology, 1644–1844* (New York: Cambridge University Press, 1994), 218, 228.

55. Greenberg, *Confessions of Nat Turner*, 79.

56. Adela Yarbro Collins, *Cosmology and Eschatology in Jewish and Christian Apocalypticism* (Boston: Brill, 1996), 78–80, 114–15, 130–34.

57. Collins, *Cosmology and Eschatology*, 83–85, 105–8, 114–15, 118–19.

58. Revelation 6:4.

59. Revelation 7:4–8.

60. Revelation 14:3. The protective seal in Revelation recalls the protective mark God placed on Cain and the sign put on the foreheads of the faithful in Ezekiel before six men executed God's judgment to destroy the idolatrous in Jerusalem. Koester, *Revelation*, 416, citing Genesis 4:15, Ezekiel 9:4.

61. Paul Keith Conkin, *American Originals: Homemade Varieties of Christianity* (Chapel Hill: University of North Carolina Press, 1997), 118; David L. Rowe, *God's Strange Work: William Miller and the End of the World* (Grand Rapids: William B. Eerdmans, 2008), 66–69, 72–81, 83–87, 95–97; Crawford Gribben, *Evangelical Millennialism in the Trans-Atlantic World, 1500–2000* (Basingstoke: Palgrave Macmillan, 2011), 75, 80.

62. Revelation 6:10.

63. Revelation 6:11.

64. Collins, *Cosmology and Eschatology*, 64–65.

65. Greenberg, *Confessions of Nat Turner*, 47. Seeing figures on the leaves as a sign of Judgment Day, Nat took heed of a sign Jesus held up in the parable of the fig tree. "Look . . . at all the trees," Jesus told the apostles, "as soon as they come out in leaf, you see for yourselves and know that summer is near." Just as trees mark the change of seasons, so from the signs Jesus describes in the apocalyptic discourse, the apostles "know that the kingdom of God is near." Luke 21:29–31.

66. Revelation 16:14, 20:8.

67. *Confessions,* 11.

68. Sharla M. Fett, *Working Cures: Healing, Health, and Power on Southern Slave Plantations* (Chapel Hill: University of North Carolina Press, 2002); Carter, *Matthew and the Margins,* 378; E. Brooks Holifield, *Health and Medicine in the Methodist Tradition: Journey Toward Wholeness* (New York: Crossroad, 1986); Humez, *Gifts of Power,* 89–91; Lundbom, *Hebrew Prophets,* 24–25; Miller, *They Cried to the Lord,* 89; Mircea Eliade, *Shamanism: Archaic Techniques of Ecstasy* (Princeton, N.J.: Princeton University Press, 1964), chaps. 10–11.

69. Elaw, "Memoirs," 100–101.

70. In 1772, an early quarterly conference of American Methodists prohibited the society's ministers from performing baptisms. Russell E. Richey, *The Methodist Conference in America: A History* (Nashville: Kingswood Books, 1996), 23.

71. Johnson, *Nat Turner Story,* 65.

72. Breen, *Land Shall Be Deluged in Blood,* 22–23; Delbert Burkett, *An Introduction to the New Testament and the Origins of Christianity* (New York: Cambridge University Press, 2002), 66–67; Allmendinger, *Nat Turner and the Rising,* 19.

73. *Confessions,* 11.

74. Luke 4:24; Jeremiah 38:4–6; Ernest W. Nicholson, *The Book of the Prophet Jeremiah* (New York: Cambridge University Press, 1975), 26–52, 112–13.

75. Allmendinger, *Nat Turner and the Rising,* 20.

76. Allmendinger, *Nat Turner and the Rising,* 73–75, 77–78.

77. Drewry, *Southampton Insurrection,* 28.

78. Allmendinger, *Nat Turner and the Rising,* 73–75, 77–78.

79. Kenneth Greenberg has suggested Turner maneuvered the revolt to avoid the farm where his wife lived. See "Introduction: Text and Context," in Greenberg, *Confessions of Nat Turner,* 11–12. Richmond *Constitutional Whig,* Sept. 26, 1831, in ibid., 81; David F. Allmendinger Jr., "Construction of *The Confessions,*" in ibid., 31–34. See also Richmond *Enquirer,* Sept. 2, 1831, in Tragle, *Southampton Slave Revolt,* 58; Allmendinger, *Nat Turner and the Rising,* 92–93.

80. Allmendinger, *Nat Turner and the Rising,* 73–75, 77–78; Drewry, *Southampton Insurrection,* 28. A local story claimed that Nat skipped Giles Reese's house deliberately during his attacks and that Giles Reese asked Nat on the gallows why this was so. Allegedly, Nat replied that Giles was "too powerful a man to begin with, and besides we were afraid of your two fierce bulldogs. But we were going to return to you after we had collected a sufficient force." While Reese likely rented a property adjoining the first two sites attacked, he was to the north, beyond Cabin Pond, while the company moved south toward sites of special interest to Nat's collaborators, so it might not have been strategically logical to divert to attack Reese anyway. Drewry, *Southampton Insurrection,* 36; Allmendinger, *Nat Turner and the Rising,* 78, 92.

81. Arnold, *Genesis,* 67; Revelation 12:9, 20:2. Durrill ties the loud noise to the "several large meteors that plunged to earth in the American South from July through October 1828, some of which created the appearance of a serpent in the sky." Durrill points to evidence that Huntsville, Alabama, residents thought they saw a "blazing serpent" on the evening of August 31, 1828. Durrill, "Nat Turner and Signs of the Apocalypse," 82.

82. Revelation 12:7–9, 20:2–3.

83. Revelation 12:10.
84. Greenberg, *Confessions of Nat Turner*, 47–48.
85. Matthew 20:16.
86. Arnold, *Genesis*, 153, 156.
87. Revelation 4:1; William Burkitt, *Expository Notes with Practical Observations on the New Testament of Our Lord and Saviour Jesus Christ* (New York: Dunning and Hyer, 1796), 1116; Koester, *Revelation*, 359n4.
88. Mark 10:28–31.
89. Matthew 20:1–16; Evans, *Matthew*, 350.
90. Greenberg, *Confessions of Nat Turner*, 48.
91. Allmendinger, *Nat Turner and the Rising*, 80–83; Drewry, *Southampton Insurrection*, 27; Greenberg, "Name, Face, Body," 6, 252n8.
92. Freehling, *Drift Toward Dissolution*, 45, 54, 77, 78; Wolf, *Race and Liberty in the New Nation*, xi, 186–87; Irons, *Origins of Proslavery Christianity*, 148.
93. Freehling, *Drift Toward Dissolution*, 45, 54, 77, 78; Wolf, *Race and Liberty in the New Nation*, xi, 190; Irons, *Origins of Proslavery Christianity*, 148.
94. Freehling, *Drift Toward Dissolution*, 45, 54, 77, 78; Wolf, *Race and Liberty in the New Nation*, xi, 190; Irons, *Origins of Proslavery Christianity*, 148.
95. Drewry, *Southampton Insurrection*, 116; Sidbury, *Ploughshares into Swords*, 139; James Sidbury, "'Reading, Revelation, and Rebellion': The Textual Communities of Gabriel, Denmark Vesey, and Nat Turner," in Greenberg, *Nat Turner*, 119–33.
96. Walker, *Jesus and the Holy City*, 3, 58.
97. Walker, *Jesus and the Holy City*, 3, 34; Luke 19:41–47; Mark 11:15–17.
98. Luke 19:41; *Elizabeth, a Colored Minister*, 13; David Lenz Tiede, *Prophecy and History in Luke-Acts* (Philadelphia: Fortress, 1980).
99. 1 Corinthians 15:55; Allen, *Collection of Hymns and Spiritual Songs*, 11, hymn 4. This hymn, "O God my heart with love inflame," also appeared in a number of hymnals, from *Hymns and Spiritual Songs, for the Use of Christians* (Baltimore: Warner & Hanna, 1803), 153–54; John J. Harrod, *The New and Most Complete Collection of Camp, Social, and Prayer Meeting Hymns and Spiritual Songs Now in Use* (Baltimore: J. J. Harrod, 1830), 161–62; www.hymnary.org/text/o_god _my_heart_with_love_inflame.
100. Matthew 26:37–39; Luke 22:42.
101. Hinks, *To Awaken My Suffering Brethren*, 136–37; John B. Duff and Peter M. Mitchell, *The Nat Turner Rebellion: The Historical Event and the Modern Controversy* (New York: Harper & Row, 1971), 5; Freehling, *Drift Toward Dissolution*, 82; Irons, *Origins of Proslavery Christianity*, 142.
102. Durrill, "Nat Turner and Signs of the Apocalypse," 81–82, 85.
103. Allmendinger, *Nat Turner and the Rising*, 93–96.
104. Isaiah 13:9–11; Micah 3:6; Durrill, "Nat Turner and Signs of the Apocalypse," 83–84.
105. Mark 13:24; Matthew 24:29–30.
106. Revelation 6:12–13.
107. I base this on my reading of historical newspaper coverage of the 1811 eclipse and the absence of coverage of subsequent ones, as well as the NASA historical chart of solar eclipses. "Five Millennium Catalog of Solar Eclipses: 1801 to 1900 (1801 CE to 1900 CE)," eclipse.gsfc.nasa.gov/SEcat5/SE1801-1900.html; *Alexandria*

Daily Gazette, Commercial & Political, Sept. 18, 1811, 3; Aug. 1, 1821, 2; Richmond *Enquirer*, Sept. 24, 1811, 3; Aug. 14, 1821, 4; Oct. 12, 1821, 3; Durrill, "Nat Turner and Signs of the Apocalypse," 83.

108. Louis P. Masur, *1831, Year of Eclipse* (New York: Hill and Wang, 2001), 3–5.
109. Breen, *Land Shall Be Deluged in Blood*, 19.
110. Revelation 8:12; Koester, *Revelation*, 450n8.
111. Humez, *Gifts of Power*, 88.
112. Revelation 5:3.
113. Revelation 6:1–12; Koester, *Revelation*, 393–95n6.
114. Revelation 22:10.
115. Greenberg, *Confessions of Nat Turner*, 48.

5. ALARM IN THE NEIGHBORHOOD

1. Richmond *Constitutional Whig*, Sept. 26, 1831, in Greenberg, *Confessions of Nat Turner*, 81. Allmendinger persuasively attributes this dispatch to Gray in "Construction of *The Confessions*," 31–34.
2. Anthony E. Kaye, "Neighborhoods and Nat Turner: The Making of a Slave Rebel and the Unmaking of a Slave Rebellion," *Journal of the Early Republic* 27, no. 4 (2006): 711; Allan Kulikoff, *Tobacco and Slaves: The Development of Southern Cultures in the Chesapeake, 1680–1800* (Chapel Hill: University of North Carolina Press, 1986), 92–96, 141–48, maps 2, 8; Parramore, *Southampton County*, 76–77.
3. Allmendinger, *Nat Turner and the Rising*, 87–96.
4. 2 Samuel 20:8–9.
5. Greenberg, *Confessions of Nat Turner*, 47–48; Patrick H. Breen, "A Prophet in His Own Land: Support for Nat Turner and His Rebellion Within Southampton's Black Community," in Greenberg, *Nat Turner*, 111–13; Parramore, *Southampton County*, 78–79, 85, 247n42; Thomas C. Parramore, "Covenant in Jerusalem," in Greenberg, *Nat Turner*, 63.
6. Greenberg, *Confessions of Nat Turner*, 54, 100–101; Scot French, *The Rebellious Slave: Nat Turner in American Memory* (New York: Houghton Mifflin, 2004), 41, 60–64.
7. Richmond *Constitutional Whig*, Sept. 26, 1831, in Greenberg, *Confessions of Nat Turner*, 60; Allmendinger, *Nat Turner and the Rising*, 96.
8. Durrill, "Nat Turner and Signs of the Apocalypse," 85; Thomas Wentworth Higginson, "The Story of Denmark Vesey," *Atlantic Monthly*, June 1861, www .theatlantic.com/magazine/archive/1861/06/denmark-vesey/396239.
9. *Confessions*, 11.
10. Parramore, *Southampton County*, 75; Allmendinger, *Nat Turner and the Rising*, 97; "This Day in Virginia History: 1831 Observations on Solar Phenomena," *Republican Standard*, Aug. 20, 2017, therepublicanstandard.com/history/day -virginia-history-1831-observations-solar-phenomena/susan-constant/2017/08; Durrill, "Nat Turner and Signs of the Apocalypse," 87–88.
11. *Confessions*, 11.
12. Tragle, *Southampton Slave Revolt*, 51–52.
13. Drewry, *Southampton Insurrection*, 114.
14. Johnson, *Nat Turner Story*, 85.

15. Mitch Kachun, "Antebellum African Americans, Public Commemoration, and the Haitian Revolution: A Problem of Historical Mythmaking," *Journal of the Early American Republic* 26, no. 2 (Summer 2006): 249–73.

16. Allmendinger, *Nat Turner and the Rising*, 98.

17. Greenberg, *Confessions of Nat Turner*, 48–49; Allmendinger, "Construction of The Confessions," 28; Parramore, *Southampton County*, 79, 85.

18. *Confessions*, 12; Allmendinger, *Nat Turner and the Rising*, 98.

19. Allmendinger, *Nat Turner and the Rising*, 99–100.

20. *Confessions*, 11.

21. *Confessions*, 12.

22. Allmendinger, *Nat Turner and the Rising*, 166–68; Drewry, *Southampton Insurrection*, 75; Johnson, *Nat Turner Story*, 90.

23. *Confessions*, 12.

24. Judges 8:21.

25. *Confessions*, 12–13.

26. *Confessions*, 12.

27. Allmendinger, *Nat Turner and the Rising*, 169; *Confessions*, 12.

28. On laws of war in U.S. history, see John Fabian Witt, *Lincoln's Code: The Laws of War in American History* (New York: Free Press, 2012).

29. Drewry, *Southampton Insurrection*, 114.

30. Judges 5:31.

31. Deuteronomy 9:1–4; Joshua 12:24.

32. Philip Jenkins, *Laying Down the Sword: Why We Can't Ignore the Bible's Violent Verses* (New York: HarperOne, 2011).

33. Joshua 8:1–23.

34. Da Costa, *Crowns of Glory, Tears of Blood*, 7–8, 125–30, 158.

35. Deuteronomy 7:1, 2; Philip D. Stern, *The Biblical* Herem: *A Window on Israel's Religious Experience* (Atlanta: Scholars Press, 1991), 89.

36. Dozeman, *Joshua 1–12*, 54, 56, 246, 352, 424, 456; Norman K. Gottwald, *All the Kingdoms of the Earth: Israelite Prophecy and International Relations in the Ancient Near East* (New York: Harper & Row, 1964), 299.

37. Stern, *Biblical* Herem, 89, 95–96.

38. Joshua 6:2–20.

39. Joshua 6:16–17.

40. Joshua 6:21; Dozeman, *Joshua 1–12*, 305.

41. Dozeman, *Joshua 1–12*, 424.

42. Joshua 10:28–30.

43. Joshua 10:31–39.

44. Dozeman, *Joshua 1–12*, 54, 58–59, 306n5, 312n6, 456. On *herem* as a sacrifice to Yahweh in Deuteronomy, see Stern, *Biblical* Herem, 1, 16, 106–7.

45. Joshua 5:13–15.

46. Joshua 6:17, comparing King James Version and New Revised Standard Version.

47. 1 Samuel 15:3, 8–9, 11, 23, 26, 32–33.

48. Ezekiel 9:1–8; Isaiah 6:11–13, 9:18–20.

49. "The Court Releases Its Explanation of the Causes of the Plot," in Starobin, *Denmark Vesey*, 99–100. Joshua 6:21 is correctly quoted by the court but misidentified as Joshua 4:21 in ibid.

50. Egerton, *He Shall Go Out Free*, 112–15.
51. Exodus 21:16; "The Confession of Mr. Enslows Boy John," in Starobin, *Denmark Vesey*, 65–66.
52. "Confession of Mr. Enslows Boy John," 65.
53. "Confession of Bacchus, the Slave of Mr. Hammet," in Starobin, *Denmark Vesey*, 62.
54. Hinks, *Walker's Appeal*, 4, 15, 23, 39, 51, 72.
55. Hinks, *Walker's Appeal*, 41–42, 45, 69.
56. Elaw, "Memoirs," 81, 103, quoting Joshua 1:5. See also ibid., 115–16.
57. Judges 8:17, 22–23.
58. *Confessions*, 11.
59. *Confessions*, 11.
60. Breen, *Land Shall Be Deluged in Blood*, 40; Drewry, *Southampton Insurrection*, 37.
61. *Confessions*, 12–13.
62. Joshua 8:10–18.
63. Allmendinger, *Nat Turner and the Rising*, 169–70; Breen, *Land Shall Be Deluged in Blood*, 43.
64. Allmendinger, *Nat Turner and the Rising*, 105.
65. *Confessions*, 12; Parramore, *Southampton County*, 83; Parramore, "Covenant in Jerusalem," 60; Allmendinger, *Nat Turner and the Rising*, 105, 169–70.
66. Allmendinger, *Nat Turner and the Rising*, 106–7.
67. *Confessions*, 12; Allmendinger, *Nat Turner and the Rising*, 170–71.
68. Deuteronomy 32:25; Nelson, *Deuteronomy*, 373–74.
69. Dozeman, *Joshua 1–12*, 328, 456; Hall, *Conquering Character*, 179–80; Joshua 5:13.
70. Ezekiel 14:21; Jeremiah 15:3.
71. Isaiah 1:20; Brueggemann, *Isaiah*, 1–39, 20.
72. 2 Samuel 23:10; Zechariah 9:13.
73. Hannah Geffert, "Local Involvement in the Raid on Harpers Ferry," in *The Legacy of John Brown*, ed. Peggy A. Russo and Paul Finkelman (Athens: Ohio University Press, 2005), 41n53.
74. *Confessions*, 13.
75. Allmendinger, *Nat Turner and the Rising*, 171–72.
76. *Confessions*, 13.
77. *Confessions*, 13.
78. Allmendinger, *Nat Turner and the Rising*, 172–73.
79. Allmendinger, *Nat Turner and the Rising*, 120–22.
80. Allmendinger, *Nat Turner and the Rising*, 173–75.
81. *Confessions*, 13; Johnson, *Nat Turner Story*, 65, 99.
82. Breen, *Land Shall Be Deluged in Blood*, 47, 48; Holden, *Surviving Southampton*, 36.
83. *Confessions*, 12–13. Allmendinger, *Nat Turner and the Rising*, 173–74, notes that Nat's account is the only one to survive of this killing.
84. The strongest critiques of Styron's liberties and interpretations are collected in Clarke, *William Styron's Nat Turner*.
85. Allmendinger, *Nat Turner and the Rising*, 173–75; Breen, *Land Shall Be Deluged in Blood*, 48–49, 77, 90–91.
86. Allmendinger, *Nat Turner and the Rising*, 174–75.
87. 1 Samuel 14:6.
88. Allmendinger, *Nat Turner and the Rising*, 174–75.

89. Allmendinger, *Nat Turner and the Rising*, 174–75.

90. Allmendinger, *Nat Turner and the Rising*, 109.

91. *Confessions*, 13.

92. Allmendinger, *Nat Turner and the Rising*, 176–77.

93. Breen, *Land Shall Be Deluged in Blood*, 51, 58–60; Allmendinger, *Nat Turner and the Rising*, 176–77.

94. Tony wrote about this idea at length in Anthony E. Kaye, *Joining Places: Slave Neighborhoods in the Old South* (Chapel Hill: University of North Carolina Press, 2007).

95. *Confessions*, 13.

96. Allmendinger, *Nat Turner and the Rising*, 102–4, 114–15, 176–77.

97. Allmendinger, *Nat Turner and the Rising*, 110.

98. Allmendinger, *Nat Turner and the Rising*, 110; Holden, *Surviving Southampton*, 27.

99. This is one reason why the historian David Allmendinger reads the *Confessions* as based in Nat's point of view, even if not necessarily always his exact words. Allmendinger, *Nat Turner and the Rising*, 179–80.

100. Allmendinger, *Nat Turner and the Rising*, 179–81; Parramore, *Southampton County*, 85.

101. Holden, *Surviving Southampton*, 27–28.

102. Allmendinger, *Nat Turner and the Rising*, 179–81.

103. *Confessions*, 14; Allmendinger, *Nat Turner and the Rising*, 111.

104. *Confessions*, 14; Breen, *Land Shall Be Deluged in Blood*, 61; Allmendinger, *Nat Turner and the Rising*, 181.

105. Allmendinger, *Nat Turner and the Rising*, 126–29.

106. *Confessions*, 20; Allmendinger, *Nat Turner and the Rising*, 181–82.

107. Holden, *Surviving Southampton*, 36.

108. Allmendinger, *Nat Turner and the Rising*, 128–35.

109. In fact the "thirty" numbered "thirty and seven" according to 2 Samuel. 2 Samuel 23:9, 23, 39.

110. *Confessions*, 14; Allmendinger, *Nat Turner and the Rising*, 182–84.

111. Allmendinger, *Nat Turner and the Rising*, 182–84.

112. Johnson, *Nat Turner Story*, 108.

113. 1 Kings 20:25; Allmendinger, *Nat Turner and the Rising*, 136.

114. Allmendinger, *Nat Turner and the Rising*, 140.

115. *Confessions*, 14.

116. *Confessions*, 18–20; Allmendinger, *Nat Turner and the Rising*, 185–86; Parramore, *Southampton County*, 90.

117. *Confessions*, 18–20; Allmendinger, *Nat Turner and the Rising*, 185–86; Parramore, *Southampton County*, 90.

118. Allmendinger, *Nat Turner and the Rising*, 139–46, 187–89.

119. Greenberg, *Confessions of Nat Turner*, 17–18; Allmendinger, *Nat Turner and the Rising*, 164–65.

120. Ezekiel 18:14–17, chaps. 40–48.

121. Deuteronomy 20:11, 14, 15, 18.

122. Joshua 9:6, 23, 27.

123. *Confessions*, 14; Allmendinger, *Nat Turner and the Rising*, 139–46, 187–89; Holden, *Surviving Southampton*, 36.

124. Allmendinger, *Nat Turner and the Rising*, 149–53, 187–89.
125. *Confessions*, 14; Parramore, "Covenant in Jerusalem," 63; Allmendinger, *Nat Turner and the Rising*, 156.
126. *Confessions*, 14.
127. Isaiah 7:11–14.
128. Allmendinger, *Nat Turner and the Rising*, 189–90.

6. PARKER'S GATE

1. Allmendinger, *Nat Turner and the Rising*, 154–56; *Confessions*, 14–15.
2. *Confessions*, 14–15.
3. Judges 6:14–16.
4. Allmendinger, *Nat Turner and the Rising*, 191–94.
5. *Confessions*, 15.
6. *Confessions*, 15.
7. Allmendinger is particularly good at describing the town and its approaches. Allmendinger, *Nat Turner and the Rising*, 157.
8. Allmendinger, *Nat Turner and the Rising*, 162–64.
9. Allmendinger, *Nat Turner and the Rising*, 157–64.
10. Allmendinger, *Nat Turner and the Rising*, 157–62.
11. Kamau Brathwaite's studies of the Baptist War stand out among excellent accounts by Mary Reckord Turner, B. W. Higman, and Michael Craton in its analysis of the way the landscape, and specifically the watershed, "were to dictate the shape and ultimately the fate of the enterprise." "The Slave Rebellion in the Great River Valley of St. James—1831/32," *Jamaican Historical Review* 13 (1982): 11–30, quotation on p. 12.
12. Judges 1:8; Joshua 5:13–14.
13. 2 Kings 19:32–35. See also Isaiah 37:33–36.
14. Isaiah 6:1–8; Zechariah 1:1, 13:1; Micah 1:1–3.
15. Revelation 21:2, 9.
16. Luke 13:33.
17. Acts 21:13; Marrant, "Funeral Sermon," 165.
18. *Confessions*, 15; Allmendinger, *Nat Turner and the Rising*, 154–56.
19. *Confessions*, 15.
20. Allmendinger, *Nat Turner and the Rising*, 192; Breen, *Land Shall Be Deluged in Blood*, 89–91; Breen, "Prophet in His Own Land," 118; Greenberg, *Confessions of Nat Turner*, 51–52. The forces who attacked the rebels at Parker's gate might have included citizens as well as local militia. They are variously identified in primary and secondary sources as a "white patrol" and "local militia, or citizens of the county," initially under the command of Captain Aubin Middleton of the county militia, later in the day under Alexander P. Peete, whom Gray refers to parenthetically as "Captain Alexander P. Peete." Parramore, "Covenant in Jerusalem," 27; Richmond *Enquirer*, Sept. 27, 1831, in Tragle, *Southampton Slave Revolt*, 100.
21. Allmendinger, *Nat Turner and the Rising*, 183, 192; Breen, *Land Shall Be Deluged in Blood*, 89–91.
22. Allmendinger, *Nat Turner and the Rising*, 192.
23. *Confessions*, 15; Judges 20:18; 1 Samuel 15:3, 30:8; Deuteronomy 20:1–3.

24. Revelation 20:9; Judges 6:11, 7:20–22.
25. *Confessions*, 15.
26. Allmendinger, *Nat Turner and the Rising*, 191–93.
27. Allmendinger, *Nat Turner and the Rising*, 191–93.
28. *Confessions*, 15.
29. Allmendinger, *Nat Turner and the Rising*, 194.
30. *Confessions*, 16; 2 Samuel 5:23; Judges 8:10–12.
31. *Confessions*, 16.
32. 1 Samuel 14:15; Joshua 10:13; Judges 1:19.
33. *Confessions*, 16.
34. Allmendinger, *Nat Turner and the Rising*, 194–95.
35. Allmendinger, *Nat Turner and the Rising*, 195; Breen, *Land Shall Be Deluged in Blood*, 68–69.
36. Testimony of Sam, Trial of Ben, Nov. 21, 1831, Southampton Quarter Court, "Trial Record," in Tragle, *Southampton Slave Revolt*.
37. French, *Rebellious Slave*, 38; Breen, *Land Shall Be Deluged in Blood*, 128, 244n56; Johnson, *Nat Turner Story*, 97, 160.
38. Parramore, *Southampton County*, 86, 95–96.
39. Holden, *Surviving Southampton*, 46–47; Judges 4:10.
40. Parramore, *Southampton County*, 85–89, 97–99.
41. Allmendinger, *Nat Turner and the Rising*, 195–96; Parramore, *Southampton County*, 97.
42. Breen, *Land Shall Be Deluged in Blood*, 69; Allmendinger, *Nat Turner and the Rising*, 195–96.
43. *Confessions*, 16; Judges 7:2–7.
44. Breen, *Land Shall Be Deluged in Blood*, 70; Allmendinger, *Nat Turner and the Rising*, 196–97; Judges 7:20.
45. Breen, *Land Shall Be Deluged in Blood*, 70; Allmendinger, *Nat Turner and the Rising*, 196–97.
46. Allmendinger, *Nat Turner and the Rising*, 196–97; Breen, *Land Shall Be Deluged in Blood*, 70–72.
47. Breen, *Land Shall Be Deluged in Blood*, 131–32; Parramore, *Southampton County*, 86, 95–96.
48. Parramore, *Southampton County*, 94–96.
49. French, *Rebellious Slave*, 39.
50. Breen is especially clear in portraying the limited support of Black people for Nat over the course of the day. Holden, likewise, captures women's divided responses, from active participation to cautious support to outright opposition. Breen, *Land Shall Be Deluged in Blood*; Holden, *Surviving Southampton*.
51. Breen, *Land Shall Be Deluged in Blood*, 89–91; Allmendinger, *Nat Turner and the Rising*, 200.
52. Breen, *Land Shall Be Deluged in Blood*, 76–77, 90–91.
53. Allmendinger, *Nat Turner and the Rising*, 197.
54. Breen, *Land Shall Be Deluged in Blood*, 71; Allmendinger, *Nat Turner and the Rising*, 197.
55. *Confessions*, 17.
56. *Confessions*, 17.

57. *Confessions*, 17; 1 Samuel 13:5–7, 14:23.
58. *Confessions*, 17; 1 Thessalonians 5:17–18.
59. *Confessions*, 16–17; Allmendinger, *Nat Turner and the Rising*, 196–98.
60. *Confessions*, 17; Allmendinger, *Nat Turner and the Rising*, 196–98.

7. VENGEANCE

1. Allmendinger, *Nat Turner and the Rising*, 200–202.
2. Allmendinger, *Nat Turner and the Rising*, 199, 223; Richmond *Constitutional Whig*, Sept. 3, 1831, in Greenberg, *Confessions of Nat Turner*, 52–53, 73; *Norfolk American Beacon*, Aug. 29, 1831; Richmond *Enquirer*, Sept. 2, 1831; "Trial Record," Sept. 3, 1831, all in Tragle, *Southampton Slave Revolt*, 49–50, 58–59, 191–93.
3. Parramore, *Southampton County*, 69–71, 94–96.
4. Breen, *Land Shall Be Deluged in Blood*, 9, 91–93; Allmendinger, *Nat Turner and the Rising*, 200; Parramore, *Southampton County*, 69; Drewry, *Southampton Insurrection*, 85.
5. Breen, *Land Shall Be Deluged in Blood*, 9.
6. Parramore, *Southampton County*, 97–99.
7. Tony developed this argument further in Kaye, *Joining Places*.
8. Henry Kamen, *Empire: How Spain Became a World Power* (New York: HarperCollins, 2003), 139–40, 167–70, 326–29, 449–53, 464–66, esp. 169; Thomas H. Naylor and Charles W. Polzer, *The Presidio and Militia on the Northern Frontier of New Spain, 1570–1700* (Tucson: University of Arizona Press, 1986), 21.
9. Entries, Feb. 1 and 4, 1802, in *Lady Nugent's Journal of Her Residence in Jamaica from 1801 to 1805*, ed. Philip Wright (Mona: University of the West Indies Press, 2002), 54–56; Jerome Handler, "Freedmen and Slaves in the Barbados Militia," *Journal of Caribbean History* 19 (May 1984): 2–4; Natalie A. Zacek, *Settler Society in the English Leeward Islands, 1670–1776* (Cambridge, U.K.: Cambridge University Press, 2010), 46–53; Lowell J. Ragatz, *The Fall of the Planter Class in the British Caribbean, 1673–1833: A Social and Economic History* (New York: Century, 1928), 31; Karl S. Watson, *The Civilised Island Barbados: A Social History, 1750–1816* (Barbados: Caribbean Graphic Production, 1979), 8; Kamau Brathwaite, *Development of a Creole Society in Jamaica, 1770–1820* (Oxford: Clarendon Press, 1971), 26n3; Janet Schaw, *Journal of a Lady of Quality: Being the Narrative of a Journey from Scotland to the West Indies, North Carolina, and Portugal, in the Years 1774 to 1776*, ed. Evangeline Walker Andrews (New Haven, Conn.: Yale University Press, 1923), 109; Kamen, *Empire*, 139–40, 167–70, 326–29, 449–53, 464–66, esp. 169.
10. McDonnell, *Politics of War*, 329–30.
11. Taylor, *Internal Enemy*, 271–73; Sally E. Hadden, *Slave Patrols: Law and Violence in Virginia and the Carolinas* (Cambridge, Mass.: Harvard University Press, 2011), 74–75, 163.
12. John C. Cheveley, "The Demerara Rising of 1823," typescript, 14–15, Council of World Mission Archives, Yale Divinity School Library.
13. Breen, "Prophet in His Own Land," 118; Greenberg, *Confessions of Nat Turner*, 51–52; Parramore, "Covenant in Jerusalem," 27; Richmond *Enquirer*, Sept. 27, 1831, in Tragle, *Southampton Slave Revolt*, 100; Stephen B. Oates, *The Fires of Jubilee: Nat Turner's Fierce Rebellion* (New York: Harper and Row, 1975), 85.

14. The eight families are the Bradshaws, Carrs, Corbitts, Daughtreys, Hollands, Johnsons, Parkers, and Vaughans. Pay Roll of a Company of Militia Command of Captain Joseph L. Holland, Insurrection Records, RG 48, Library of Virginia, Richmond.

15. The maiden names of soldiers' wives appear in Jordan R. Dodd et al., *Early American Marriages: Virginia to 1850* (Bountiful, Utah: Precision Indexing, 1990), online in the database of Virginia Marriages, 1740–1850, in Birth, Marriage, and Death Records, ancestry.com, searched on June 6, 2008.

16. Pay Roll of a Company of Militia Command of Captain Joseph L. Holland.

17. Virginia Land Tax Records, microfilm reel 309, Southampton County Land Tax Books, entry for John Vick (of Jordan), Book B, 1822, p. 19; 1831, p. 26. For the two other households receiving land from the estate of Jordan Vick, see entry for Polly Vick & Ann, Book B, 1822, p. 19; entry for Lewis Vick, Book B, p. 19; entry for Pegga Vick, Book B, 1831, p. 26; entry for Mills W. Vick, Book B, 1831, p. 26; entries for Matthew Vick, Book B, 1823, p. 20; 1824, p. 21; entry for John Vick of Joel, ibid., Book B, 1820, p. 17, all at Library of Virginia.

18. Data tabulated by Tony Kaye from work in Virginia Land Tax Records, microfilm reel 309, Southampton County Land Tax Books, Library of Virginia.

19. Entry for John Vick of Joel, ibid., Book B, 1820, p. 17, Library of Virginia.

20. Tera Hunter, *Bound in Wedlock: Slave and Free Black Marriage in the Nineteenth Century* (Cambridge, Mass.: Belknap Press of Harvard University Press, 2017).

21. The eight families making up one-third of the congregation were the Barneses, Dardens, Daughtreys, Edwardses, Gardners, Hollands, Lawrences, and Vaughans. List of Members, South Quay Baptist Church Minute Book, 1775–1827, 1–8, Manuscript Collections, Library of Virginia. For a thoughtful discussion of Baptist churches in Isle of Wight, Southampton, and vicinity, see Scully, *Religion and the Making of Nat Turner's Virginia*. South Quay Baptist was located in Nottoway Parish, north of the Nottoway River in Southampton County. Crofts, *Old Southampton*, 91, map 4.

22. "The Baptist Church Covenant," South Quay Baptist Church Minute Book, 3, Library of Virginia.

23. Brathwaite, "Slave Rebellion in the Great River Valley," 15–16, 23; Mary Reckord, "The Jamaica Slave Rebellion of 1831," *Past and Present* 40 (1968): 124; Michael Craton, *Testing the Chains: Resistance to Slavery in the British West Indies* (Ithaca, N.Y.: Cornell University Press, 1982), 300–301; Theodore Foulks, *Eighteen Months in Jamaica; with Recollections of the Late Rebellion* (London: Whittaker, Treacher, and Arnott, 1833), 61–62; Cheveley, "Demerara Rising of 1823," 14–15. For a review of different aims in large slave revolts, see David P. Geggus, "The Causation of Slave Rebellions," in *Haitian Revolutionary Studies* (Bloomington: Indiana University Press, 2002), 64–67.

24. Allmendinger, *Nat Turner and the Rising*, 201.

25. Allmendinger, *Nat Turner and the Rising*, 295–96.

26. Allmendinger, *Nat Turner and the Rising*, 210.

27. Breen, *Land Shall Be Deluged in Blood*, 78–79; Johnson, *Nat Turner Story*, 200.

28. Breen, *Land Shall Be Deluged in Blood*, 89–91; Richmond *Constitutional Whig*, Sept. 3, 1831, in Greenberg, *Confessions of Nat Turner*, 72–73.

29. Johnson, *Nat Turner Story*, 133; Allmendinger, *Nat Turner and the Rising*, 203.

30. Parramore, *Southampton County*, 99.
31. Benjamin Drew, *A North-Side View of Slavery. The Refugee; or, The Narratives of Fugitive Slaves in Canada, Related by Themselves, with an Account of the History and Condition of the Colored Population of Upper Canada* (Boston: John P. Jewett, 1856), 332–33.
32. Johnson, *Nat Turner Story*, 136.
33. Breen, *Land Shall Be Deluged in Blood*, 94.
34. Breen, *Land Shall Be Deluged in Blood*, 94; Greenberg, *Confessions of Nat Turner*, 16–17; Johnson, *Nat Turner Story*, 136; Parramore, *Southampton County*, 101.
35. Thomas Wentworth Higginson and local whites both circulated claims of large numbers of mass killings during the nineteenth century, and until recently those estimates—and follow-up work by the historian John Wesley Cromwell in 1920—shaped the literature. While Greenberg gives a wide range of 24 to 120 Black people killed without trial, Patrick Breen suggests the answer is closer to 36, and David Allmendinger closer to two dozen. John Wesley Cromwell, "The Aftermath of Nat Turner's Insurrection," *Journal of Negro History* (April 1920): 212–34; Drewry, *Southampton Insurrection*, 85; Greenberg, *Confessions of Nat Turner*, 16–17; Breen, *Land Shall Be Deluged in Blood*, 92; Allmendinger, *Nat Turner and the Rising*, 205–9.
36. *Richmond Compiler*, Aug. 24, 1831, and Richmond *Constitutional Whig*, Aug. 29, 1831, both in Greenberg, *Confessions of Nat Turner*, 60, 62; Breen, *Land Shall Be Deluged in Blood*, 95; Allmendinger, *Nat Turner and the Rising*, 208–9.
37. Drewry, *Southampton Insurrection*, 85; Breen, *Land Shall Be Deluged in Blood*, 93–94, 101.
38. Allmendinger, *Nat Turner and the Rising*, 201; Breen, *Land Shall Be Deluged in Blood*, 10, 63, 80; Richmond *Constitutional Whig*, Sept. 3, 1831, in Greenberg, *Confessions of Nat Turner*, 52–53, 73; *Norfolk American Beacon*, Aug. 29, 1831; Richmond *Enquirer*, Sept. 2, 1831; "Trial Record," Sept. 3, 1831, all in Tragle, *Southampton Slave Revolt*, 49–50, 58–59, 191–93.
39. Breen, *Land Shall Be Deluged in Blood*, 95–101.
40. Allmendinger, *Nat Turner and the Rising*, 203–4; Richmond *Constitutional Whig*, Sept. 3, 1831, in Greenberg, *Confessions of Nat Turner*, 72–73.
41. Breen, *Land Shall Be Deluged in Blood*, 105; Allmendinger, *Nat Turner and the Rising*, 210–12.
42. Richmond *Enquirer*, Aug. 26, 1831; Diary of Governor John Floyd, Aug. 26, 29, 1831, both in Tragle, *Southampton Slave Revolt*, 46, 252, 254; Parramore, *Southampton County*, 71.
43. Hinks, *To Awaken My Afflicted Brethren*, 165–66.
44. *Richmond Compiler*, Aug. 24, 1831; *Norfolk American Beacon*, Aug. 26, 1831; Richmond *Enquirer*, Aug. 30, 1831, all in Tragle, *Southampton Slave Revolt*, 36–38, 40–42, 43. For discussions of the extent of the rebellion in terms of "neighborhood," see *Petersburg Intelligencer*, Aug. 26, 1831, and *Lynchburg Virginian*, Sept. 8, 1831, both in Tragle, *Southampton Slave Revolt*, 38, 73. On attempts to craft an official narrative assuaging fears of a widespread rebellion, including the role of John Hampden Pleasants and Thomas R. Gray, see French, *Rebellious Slave*, chap. 2.
45. Richmond *Constitutional Whig*, Aug. 29, 1831, Sept. 3, 1831, in Tragle,

Southampton Slave Revolt, 33–47; Richmond *Enquirer*, Aug. 30, 1831, Sept. 27, 1831, Nov. 15, 1831, in Tragle, *Southampton Slave Revolt*, 51, 54–55, 70, 99–100, 139.

46. Richmond *Constitutional Whig*, Sept. 3, 1831, in Greenberg, *Confessions of Nat Turner*, 52–53, 73; *Norfolk American Beacon*, Aug. 29, 1831; Richmond *Enquirer*, Sept. 2, 1831; "Trial Record," Sept. 3, 1831, all in Tragle, *Southampton Slave Revolt*, 49–50, 58–59, 191–93.

47. See, for example, the struggle of state elites to impose their vision of the law over local people in Laura F. Edwards, *The People and Their Peace: Legal Culture and the Transformation of Inequality in the Post-Revolutionary South* (Chapel Hill: University of North Carolina Press, 2009).

48. Allmendinger, *Nat Turner and the Rising*, 201–2, 216–17.

49. Allmendinger, *Nat Turner and the Rising*, 223.

50. Allmendinger, *Nat Turner and the Rising*, 224.

51. Allmendinger, *Nat Turner and the Rising*, 225, 228–29.

52. Breen, *Land Shall Be Deluged in Blood*, 80; Johnson, "Denmark Vesey and His Co-conspirators," 915–76; Justin Behrend, "Rebellious Talk and Conspiratorial Plots: The Making of a Slave Insurrection in Civil War Natchez," *Journal of Southern History* 77, no. 1 (2011): 17–52.

53. Allmendinger, *Nat Turner and the Rising*, 225–26. For the portrayal of women in the evidence, see especially Holden, *Surviving Southampton*.

54. Breen, *Land Shall Be Deluged in Blood*, 108–11.

55. Breen, *Land Shall Be Deluged in Blood*, 129–31; Allmendinger, *Nat Turner and the Rising*, 295–96.

56. Breen, *Land Shall Be Deluged in Blood*, 122; Allmendinger, *Nat Turner and the Rising*, 230–32.

57. Breen, *Land Shall Be Deluged in Blood*, 112–13; Allmendinger, *Nat Turner and the Rising*, 228–32.

58. Breen, *Land Shall Be Deluged in Blood*, 126–27; Allmendinger, *Nat Turner and the Rising*, 241.

59. Greenberg, *Confessions of Nat Turner*, 100; Peter H. Wood, "Nat Turner: The Unknown Slave as Visionary Leader," in *Black Leaders of the Nineteenth Century*, ed. Leon Litwack and August Meier (Urbana: University of Illinois Press, 1988), 34–36; French, *Rebellious Slave*, 37–41.

60. Greenberg, *Confessions of Nat Turner*, 100; Wood, "Nat Turner," 34–36; French, *Rebellious Slave*, 37–41.

61. Greenberg, *Confessions of Nat Turner*, 54, 100–101; French, *Rebellious Slave*, 41, 60–64; *Confessions*, 18–19.

62. Parramore, *Southampton County*, 105–6; Allmendinger, *Nat Turner and the Rising*, 231–34, 291.

8. THE BOOK OF NAT

1. Richmond *Enquirer*, Oct. 4, 1831, Nov. 15, 1831; Samuel Warner, *Authentic and Impartial Narrative of the Tragical Scene Which Was Witnessed in Southampton County*, all in Tragle, *Southampton Slave Revolt*, 116–18, 139–40, 296–98.

2. Greenberg, *Confessions of Nat Turner*, 53.

3. Tony wrote about the suspicion of strangers from outside the neighborhood in *Joining Places*. See also Dylan C. Penningroth, *Claims of Kinfolk: African American Property and Community in the Nineteenth-Century South* (Chapel Hill: University of North Carolina Press, 2003). For shining examples of the work on slave resistance, see Stephanie Camp, *Closer to Freedom*, a work that influenced Tony greatly, and recent work including Marisa Fuentes, *Dispossessed Lives: Enslaved Women, Violence, and the Archive* (Philadelphia: University of Pennsylvania Press, 2016); Jessica Marie Johnson, *Wicked Flesh: Black Women, Intimacy, and Freedom in the Atlantic World* (Philadelphia: University of Pennsylvania Press, 2020); Holden, *Surviving Southampton*; Jennifer L. Morgan, *Reckoning with Slavery: Gender, Kinship, and Capitalism in the Early Black Atlantic* (Durham, N.C.: Duke University Press, 2021).

4. Greenberg, *Confessions of Nat Turner*, 53; Parramore, *Southampton County*, 108; Matthew 26:21, 27:3; Mark 14:18.

5. Allmendinger, *Nat Turner and the Rising*, 241.

6. Drewry reported a story that Nat "meditated surrender" and knocked on the door of one of the Francis family, hoping to turn himself in to a fellow Methodist, and also later went to Jerusalem to surrender but then turned around. While possible, there is no other evidence for this. Drewry, *Southampton Insurrection*, 90.

7. Matthew 4:1–4; Deuteronomy 8:1–3.

8. Matthew 4:5–7; Deuteronomy 6:16.

9. Matthew 4:6–10; Deuteronomy 6:13.

10. Matthew 4:11. With some variations in wording and order, Luke 4 presents a similar narrative.

11. Matthew 17:1–8.

12. 1 Kings 19:10–14.

13. 1 Kings 19:15–20; 2 Kings 2:1.

14. 1 Samuel 22:2; 2 Samuel 23:13; 1 Chronicles 11:15–23.

15. Psalm 57:1–6.

16. Psalm 142:1–7.

17. Hebrews 11:1, 13, 33–40.

18. *Confessions*, 17.

19. Allmendinger, *Nat Turner and the Rising*, 4, 241.

20. Allmendinger, *Nat Turner and the Rising*, 4–5, 241.

21. *Confessions*, 17.

22. Victoria Dawson, "Nat Turner's Bible Gave the Enslaved Rebel the Resolve to Rise Up," *Smithsonian*, Sept. 13, 2016, www.smithsonianmag.com/smithsonian -institution/nat-turners-bible-inspiration-enslaved-rebel-rise-up-180960416.

23. 1 Kings 18:1–16.

24. Allmendinger, *Nat Turner and the Rising*, 5–6; Breen, *Land Shall Be Deluged in Blood*, 143–44.

25. Holden, *Surviving Southampton*, 1–2; Charles L. Perdue, Thomas E. Barden, and Robert K. Phillips, eds., *Weevils in the Wheat: Interviews with Virginia Ex-slaves* (Charlottesville: University of Virginia Press, 1976), 74–76.

26. *Norfolk Herald*, Nov. 4, 1831, quoted in Greenberg, *Confessions of Nat Turner*, 86–87; Allmendinger, *Nat Turner and the Rising*, 5–6.

27. *Norfolk Herald*, Nov. 4, 1831, quoted in Greenberg, *Confessions of Nat Turner*, 86–87; Allmendinger, *Nat Turner and the Rising*, 5–6.

28. Allmendinger, *Nat Turner and the Rising*, 6; Breen, *Land Shall Be Deluged in Blood*, 143–44.

29. Allmendinger, *Nat Turner and the Rising*, 6, 242–43.

30. Allmendinger, *Nat Turner and the Rising*, 7; Parramore, *Southampton County*, 109–10.

31. Ecclesiastes 4:14.

32. Psalms 68:6; 146:7–8.

33. Revelation 2:10–11.

34. Allmendinger, *Nat Turner and the Rising*, 218–19; Richmond *Constitutional Whig*, Sept. 26, 1831, and "To the Public," both in Greenberg, *Confessions of Nat Turner*, 81, 40, 42; Parramore, *Southampton County*, 105–7; Allmendinger, "Construction of *The Confessions*," 24; "Summation of Trials," in Tragle, *Southampton Slave Revolt*, 230–31, 233–34, 243.

35. Allmendinger, *Nat Turner and the Rising*, 215–16, 220–21.

36. Richmond *Constitutional Whig*, Sept. 26, 1831, and "To the Public," both in Greenberg, *Confessions of Nat Turner*, 81, 40, 42; Parramore, *Southampton County*, 105–7; "Summation of Trials," in Tragle, *Southampton Slave Revolt*, 230–31, 233–34, 243.

37. Greenberg, *Confessions of Nat Turner*, 78–79; Allmendinger, *Nat Turner and the Rising*, 235–37, 241.

38. Tragle, *Southampton Slave Revolt*, 99–101; Allmendinger, *Nat Turner and the Rising*, 216, 229, 232, 238–39.

39. Allmendinger, *Nat Turner and the Rising*, 232.

40. *Confessions*, 3.

41. *Confessions*, 3, 18; Allmendinger, *Nat Turner and the Rising*, 244–45.

42. Allmendinger, *Nat Turner and the Rising*, 253–56; *Confessions*, 21.

43. Christopher Tomlins, *In the Matter of Nat Turner* (Princeton, N.J.: Princeton University Press, 2020), examines this question in detail.

44. *Confessions*, 4, 7; Greenberg, *Confessions of Nat Turner*, 7, 40, 44, 46–48, 51–53; Allmendinger, "Construction of *The Confessions*," 32. Tomlins is especially intriguing in the distinct ways to read the printed book and its text in Tomlins, *In the Matter of Nat Turner*.

45. Allmendinger, *Nat Turner and the Rising*, 22.

46. Allmendinger, *Nat Turner and the Rising*, 246–51.

47. Breen, *Land Shall Be Deluged in Blood*, 145. Breen raises a distinct and important question about the religiosity of Nat's followers, a much thornier issue than the question of Nat's own clearly demonstrated faith. Breen states, "The slaves of Southampton did not follow Nat Turner because they believed he was a prophet. While Turner never disowned his religious vision, his rebellion was not limited to disciples. In fact, it may not have included any disciples. Slaves and free blacks joined his rebellion because they wanted to fight against slavery." It is possible that Breen's sharp dichotomy is correct, but it is not clear why Breen assumes that they didn't find Nat's prophecy itself proof of the efficacy of the fight. Breen, "Prophet in His Own Land," 118.

David Allmendinger likewise thinks that Gray's discussion of "fanaticism" reflected the period's emphasis on broader, rather than personal, explanations for rebellion. While a chronicler in the "sentimental" 1850s might have looked to Nat's separation from his wife, Gray "settled for an easier, stock explanation of motives." Allmendinger, *Nat Turner and the Rising*, 67.

Religious motivations do not preclude other motivations; at the same time, we should be wary of assuming that the existence of other motivations proves that religious motivations were unimportant. It remains curious that historians can treat religious motivations as a cover for true motivations, despite the numerous examples, past and present, that prove human beings can be motivated by religious beliefs, including those inaccessible to scholars.

48. Greenberg, *Confessions of Nat Turner*, 10.
49. *Confessions*, 18.
50. *Confessions*, 18–19.
51. *Confessions*, 11–12.
52. *Confessions*, 10.

9. LEGACIES

1. Allmendinger, *Nat Turner and the Rising*, 232, 253.
2. Allmendinger, *Nat Turner and the Rising*, 223, 229, 231, 233, 253.
3. Allmendinger, *Nat Turner and the Rising*, 253; *Confessions*, 22.
4. Allmendinger, *Nat Turner and the Rising*, 254; Greenberg, *Confessions of Nat Turner*, 100; Breen, *Land Shall Be Deluged in Blood*, 150.
5. Allmendinger, *Nat Turner and the Rising*, 254–55.
6. *Confessions*, 22; Allmendinger, *Nat Turner and the Rising*, 254–56.
7. John 18:1–5; Matthew 26:53–54.
8. John 18:36–37, 19:11; Luke 23:28–30.
9. Allmendinger, *Nat Turner and the Rising*, 256–57.
10. Allmendinger, *Nat Turner and the Rising*, 275, 279; Parramore, *Southampton County*, 119–20.
11. *Norfolk Herald*, Nov. 14, 1831, in Tragle, *Southampton Slave Revolt*, 140, and Greenberg, *Confessions of Nat Turner*, 87–88; Breen, *Land Shall Be Deluged in Blood*, 151–52; Allmendinger, *Nat Turner and the Rising*, 258; Johnson, *Nat Turner Story*, 181.
12. John 19:2, 17, 26–28, 30; Luke 23:36, 43; Mark 15:34; Matthew 27:46.
13. Daina Ramey Berry, *The Price for Their Pound of Flesh: The Value of the Enslaved, from Womb to Grave, in the Building of a Nation* (Boston: Beacon Press, 2017), 101–16; Justin Fornal, "Inside the Quest to Return Nat Turner's Skull to His Family," *National Geographic*, Oct. 7, 2016, www.nationalgeographic.com /history/article/nat-turner-skull-slave-rebellion-uprising. Berry's book and the *National Geographic* story on the skull were not available to Tony as he wrote his drafts. Greenberg, "Name, Face, Body," 20–21; Dawson, "Nat Turner's Bible Gave the Enslaved Rebel the Resolve to Rise Up."
14. Berry, *Price for Their Pound of Flesh*, 101–16; Fornal, "Inside the Quest to Return Nat Turner's Skull to His Family"; Breen, *Land Shall Be Deluged in Blood*, 151; Greenberg, "Name, Face, Body," 20–21; Drewry, *Southampton Insurrection*, 102; French, *Rebellious Slave*, 280–81; Allmendinger, *Nat Turner and the Rising*, 258.

15. On the value that whites assigned to dead Black bodies, see Berry, *Price for Their Pound of Flesh*, 101–16.
16. *Confessions*, 3; Allmendinger, *Nat Turner and the Rising*, 256–57.
17. *Confessions*, 3; Allmendinger, *Nat Turner and the Rising*, 256–57.
18. Irons, *Origins of Proslavery Christianity*, 144; Greenberg, *Confessions of Nat Turner*, 19–20; Hinks, *To Awaken My Afflicted Brethren*, 152–53.
19. Irons, *Origins of Proslavery Christianity*, 151–54; Breen, *Land Shall Be Deluged in Blood*, 157–58; French, *Rebellious Slave*, 60–63.
20. Drew, *North-Side View of Slavery*, 332.
21. Reginald F. Hildebrand, "'An Imperious Sense of Duty': Documents Illustrating an Episode in the Methodist Reaction to the Nat Turner Revolt," *Methodist History* 19 (1980–81): 155–57, 162.
22. Irons, *Origins of Proslavery Christianity*, 156, 169.
23. Parramore, *Southampton County*, 72, 114–16; Greenberg, *Confessions of Nat Turner*, 19–20; Irons, *Origins of Proslavery Christianity*, 150; Anthony E. Kaye, "Nat Turner Rebellion," in *The International Encyclopedia of Revolution and Protest*, ed. Immanuel Ness (Malden, Mass.: Wiley-Blackwell, 2009), doi:10.1002/9781405198073.wbierp1069.
24. Drew, *North-Side View of Slavery*, 332–33.
25. Freehling, *Drift Toward Dissolution*, 134; Masur, *1831*, 50–53.
26. Freehling, *Drift Toward Dissolution*, 122–23; Tragle, *Southampton Slave Revolt*, 433; Masur, *1831*, 50–51.
27. Freehling, *Drift Toward Dissolution*, 122–26.
28. Freehling, *Drift Toward Dissolution*, 129, 140–42; Masur, *1831*, 50–53.
29. Freehling, *Drift Toward Dissolution*, 146–48; Wolf, *Race and Liberty in the New Nation*, 198–206; Greenberg, *Confessions of Nat Turner*, 21.
30. Freehling, *Drift Toward Dissolution*, xii–xiii, 116, 142, 155; Wolf, *Race and Liberty in the New Nation*, 217; French, *Rebellious Slave*, 58–60.
31. Freehling, *Drift Toward Dissolution*, 162, 164, 182; French, *Rebellious Slave*, 58–60.
32. Freehling, *Drift Toward Dissolution*, 189–93; Irons, *Origins of Proslavery Christianity*, 155; Greenberg, *Confessions of Nat Turner*, 19–20; Masur, *1831*, 62.
33. Kaye, "Nat Turner Rebellion."
34. Geggus, "Slavery, War, and Revolution in the Greater Caribbean," 7–11, 46–50. For other discussions of rumors of emancipation in North American contexts, see Hahn, *Nation Under Our Feet*; Rugemer, *Problem of Emancipation*.
35. "[Confession of] Robert Gardner," Feb. 11, 1832, *Report of the House Assembly*, Parliamentary Papers, 561, in *Irish University Press Series of British Parliamentary Papers: Correspondence and Papers Relating to Slavery and the Abolition of the Slave Trade, 1831–1834* (Shannon: Irish University Press, 1969), 80:226; B. W. Higman, *Plantation Jamaica, 1750–1850: Capital and Control in a Colonial Economy* (Kingston, Jamaica: University of the West Indies Press, 2005), 264, 270–71; Zoellner, *Island on Fire*.
36. S. G. Checkland, *The Gladstones: A Family Biography, 1764–1851* (Cambridge, U.K.: Cambridge University Press, 1971), 185–87; Reckord, "Jamaica Slave Rebellion of 1831," 109; Sidbury, "'African' Settlers in the Founding of Freetown," 140.

CONCLUSIONS

1. Allmendinger, *Nat Turner and the Rising*, 259–60.
2. Rodman, "O Jerusalem, Jerusalem," 2–29.
3. Allmendinger, *Nat Turner and the Rising*, 64–66, 261.
4. Davis, *Nat Turner Before the Bar of Judgment*, 175; Tragle, *Southampton Slave Revolt*, 13; Allmendinger, *Nat Turner and the Rising*, 64–66; Breen, *Land Shall Be Deluged in Blood*, 18, 194–95n9; Holden, *Surviving Southampton*, 122–23; French, *Rebellious Slave*, 205.
5. Holden, *Surviving Southampton*, 1–2; French, *Rebellious Slave*, 205–6; Interview of Jennie Butler, *Federal Writers' Project: Slave Narrative Project*, vol. 2, *Arkansas, Part 1*, Abbott–Byrd, November–December, 1936, 342, Manuscript / Mixed Material, www.loc.gov/item/mesn021/; Perdue, Barden, and Phillips, *Weevils in the Wheat*, 74–76.
6. Parramore, *Southampton County*, 113; Zoe Trodd, "John Brown's Spirit: The Abolitionist Aesthetic of Emancipatory Martyrdom in Early Antilynching Protest Literature," *Journal of American Studies* 49 (2015): 309–10; Frederick Douglass, *My Bondage and My Freedom* (New York: Miller, Orton & Mulligan, 1855), 200; Blight, *Frederick Douglass*, xvii, 198; Henry Highland Garnet, *Walker's Appeal with a Brief Sketch of His Life by Henry Highland Garnet and Also Garnet's Address to the Slaves of the United States of America* (New York: J. H. Tobitt, 1848), 96.
7. French, *Rebellious Slave*, 133; Blight, *Frederick Douglass*, xvii–xviii, 344–45.
8. Johnson, *Nat Turner Story*, 180–81.
9. Thomas Wentworth Higginson, "Leaves from an Officer's Journal," *Atlantic Monthly*, Dec. 1864, www.theatlantic.com/magazine/archive/1864/12/leaves-from-an-officer.
10. Dr. Seth Rogers to Hannah Mitchell Rogers, Jan. 1, 1863, quoted in Matthew Pinsker, "Emancipation Among Black Troops in South Carolina," Nov. 6, 2012, House Divided Project, Dickinson College, housedivided.dickinson.edu/sites/emancipation/2012/11/06/emancipation-among-black-troops-in-south-carolina/.
11. Quoted from Hahn, *Nation Under Our Feet*, 113–14; Elizabeth Hyde Botume, *First Days Amongst the Contrabands* (Boston: Lee and Shepard, 1893), 76, 204.
12. Hildebrand, "'Imperious Sense of Duty,'" 155–74; Crofts, *Old Southampton*, 243; Greenberg, *Confessions of Nat Turner*, 25.
13. French, *Rebellious Slave*, 150–51, 180–81.
14. French, *Rebellious Slave*, 155–56; Jarvis R. Givens, "'He Was, Undoubtedly, a Wonderful Character': Black Teachers' Representations of Nat Turner During Jim Crow," *Souls* 18, no. 2–4 (April–Dec. 2016): 218–19, 223; Maffly-Kipp, *Setting Down the Sacred Past*, 213.

POSTSCRIPT: ANTHONY KAYE'S NAT

1. Tomlins, *In the Matter of Nat Turner*, 226.
2. For the best discussion of the complexity of the name, see Greenberg, "Name, Face, Body," 3–14.

Acknowledgments

Tony left no draft of acknowledgments. It is impossible for me to reconstruct all the people who helped him and whom he would have wished to thank. Tony was a generous person, grateful for the critique, praise, and support he received. There are so many people he spoke highly of—none more so than Barbara J. Fields, his graduate adviser—and I wish I could name here all the people he admired and appreciated.

For myself, I have in other published books thanked people who support and encourage and critique me and will leave their contributions aside. A few people aided me and Tony a great deal in the overwhelming task of bringing this manuscript to completion. Several people who loved and admired Tony agreed to read the manuscript and provided exceptional feedback. Adam Rothman brought his usual humor and insight. Kate Masur provided extraordinarily detailed comments on big-picture ideas and the word choices that sometimes clouded my communication of Tony's big ideas. William Sturkey pressed me to engage more intimately with Nat's feelings and urged me to stand strong on the issue of declining to call Nat by his enslaver's name. Amy Greenberg offered needed encouragement. My friend Abram Van Engen didn't know Tony but gave careful readings of the religious history sections that saved me from butchering Tony's understanding and causing confusion. Luke Harlow pressed me to follow Tony's lead in taking religious beliefs seriously, even literally, in understanding motivations. Tony's old friend Michael West encouraged me to tie Tony's work here to Tony's broader project of asking how people found political hope in times of seeming no hope. I have held to those words in my revisions, in the necessity of finding hope where there seems to be no hope at all.

Navigating the publication of a book primarily by a deceased author is a challenging task. I and Tony's family are deeply grateful that Alex Star at Farrar, Straus and Giroux took on the task joyfully and with patience, humor, and understanding. Along the way, Ian Van Wye and others played crucial roles in bringing the book to light.

I hope the dedication captures the people Tony talked to the most, and the people I am sure he would have dedicated the book to, had he left those instructions. I also want to thank some of them. Tony's mom, Ellen Kaye, has been a constant source of encouragement and understanding. Tony's brother Chip sent me a startlingly apropos music discovery while I labored through the book's late stages, and that album (by the Philadelphia band Nat Turner Rebellion) boosted my spirits in the final days. For multiple reasons, the book would not exist without the consistent support and patience of Tony's wife, Melissa. It has been a joy to speak about the book in front of her and to send her drafts and updates, and it will be a bigger joy to see the book in her hands and in the hands of their children. Learning in the last stages that the book's proceeds will help support their younger child's celebration filled me with awe and gratitude that I could help Tony fulfill a role he would so deeply have wished to carry out in person.

For myself, I want to thank Tony for the personal and professional gift of asking me to take this on. On a human level, what more gratifying way to live the presence of a lamented friend than to strive to uphold his legacy so that his loved ones can see it come to fruition? I am honored and humbled.

But Tony left more than a legacy; he left work. In reading his work and in reading the work of so many wonderful historians mentioned in the notes, I have once again been awed by the difficult, lucky, and honorable life we historians get to live, while we can. Tony's excitement for the hard toil of history, and his joy in the often unglamorous work others had done, have been a final gift from a friend, a reminder of why we do what we do. I hope I have managed to convey his joy, his curiosity, and his intellect and have allowed others to share in that gift, the joy of trying the impossible task of understanding life, while we are here to be puzzled and inspired and awed by it.

Index

A NOTE ABOUT THE AUTHORS

Anthony E. Kaye (1962–2017) taught history at Pennsylvania State University and was the vice president of scholarly programs at the National Humanities Center. An influential scholar of Atlantic slavery and American history, he served as an associate editor of *The Journal of the Civil War Era*. His final book, *Nat Turner, Black Prophet,* was completed with the assistance of Gregory P. Downs.

Gregory P. Downs is a professor of history at the University of California, Davis. He is the author of *After Appomattox* as well as other scholarly books, and his writing has appeared in *The Atlantic* and *The Washington Post*. He received a master's in fine arts from the Iowa Writers' Workshop and is also the author of *Spit Baths*, which won the Flannery O'Connor Award for Short Fiction.